Clinicians want—and need—more than theory to guide the[m in the]ir work contending with grief of all kinds. They also seek effective, how-to information to assist those [contending with grief of all kinds,] whether prompted by death or non-death loss. Nowhere else in the literature can professionals find such a wealth of interventions that help the mourner identify, express, and transform their responses to loss, reaffirm meaning, revamp life narratives, and develop healthy continued connection to lost loved ones. This book is a must have; it's a veritable gold mine for all who treat the bereaved, from the newest students to the most seasoned therapists.

—**Therese A. Rando, PhD, BCETS, BCBT**, *author of* Treatment of Complicated Mourning *and co-author of* Treating Traumatic Bereavement: A Practitioner's Guide

Robert Neimeyer brings us a third outstanding collection in his excellent series on grief counseling and therapy. It features fifty-nine accessible chapters by authors from around the world; addresses diverse challenges in learning how to live meaningfully not only with bereavement but also with non-death-related losses; and concentrates on concrete techniques (illustrated by real-life examples) for supporting others in meeting those challenges. It is filled with innovative methods for practitioners, understanding for advanced students; and wisdom for both.

—**Thomas Attig, PhD**, *author of* How We Grieve: Relearning the World

At last! A text that deals with death-related grief as well as that resulting from non-death loss. It offers a broad range of methods for helping persons negotiating both normative and traumatic life transitions. Along with dozens of creative contributors, Bob Neimeyer brings together in this volume his vast clinical experience, artistic talent and novel educational methods to enrich the field and the lives of those it serves.

—**J. Shep Jeffreys, EdD, FT**, *Department of Psychiatry and Behavioral Science, Johns Hopkins School of Medicine and author of* Helping Grieving People: When Tears Are Not Enough

This volume continues Robert Neimeyer's quest to bring creative insights and interventions to clinicians working with loss and bereavement. The international cast of contributors provides a rich trove of practical tools together with case reports to anchor the learning experience. Whether you are a newcomer to the field or a highly experienced practitioner, this book will broaden and deepen your perspective. My recommendation—Go for it!

—**Simon Shimshon Rubin, PhD**, *director of the International Laboratory for the Study of Loss, Bereavement, and Human Resilience and author of* Working with Loss and Bereavement

This highly anticipated volume brims with therapeutic exercises for people coping with death and non-death losses, providing expert guidance on how, when, and for whom they might be engaged. These versatile techniques to address shattering life events will be essential tools in every clinician's toolkit.

—**Donna Schuurman, PhD**, *Director of Advocacy and Training, Dougy Center*

Like the two volumes that precede it, *New Techniques of Grief Therapy* is an indispensable resource that provides practical, road-tested techniques that are firmly grounded in theory. Each technique is clearly described and, notably, is illustrated by case examples. Whether a student, a clinician, or researcher, the reader will find a treasure trove of new and useful tools to help them serve those who are grieving both death and non-death losses. This volume does much to broaden our responses to the grieving person and to serve them more creatively and effectively.

—**Christopher Hall**, *Chief Executive Officer, Australian Centre for Grief and Bereavement*

New Techniques of Grief Therapy

New Techniques of Grief Therapy: Bereavement and Beyond expands on the mission of the previous two *Techniques* books, featuring innovative approaches to address the needs of those whose lives have been shadowed by loss—whether through bereavement, serious illness, the rupture of a relationship, or other complex or intangible losses, such as of an identity-defining career.

The book starts with several framing chapters by prominent theorists that provide a big-picture orientation to grief work and follows with a generous toolkit of creative therapeutic techniques described in concrete detail and anchored in illustrative case studies to convey their use in actual practice. *New Techniques of Grief Therapy* is an indispensable resource for professionals working in hospice, hospital, palliative care, and elder care settings; clinicians in broader health-care and mental health–care practices; executive coaches; and students in the field of grief therapy.

Robert A. Neimeyer, PhD, is Professor Emeritus of Psychology at the University of Memphis and Director of the Portland Institute for Loss and Transition, which provides online and onsite training in grief therapy for an international and interdisciplinary community of professionals. Neimeyer has published over 30 books, including *Techniques of Grief Therapy: Assessment and Intervention* and *Grief and the Expressive Arts: Practices for Creating Meaning*, the latter with Barbara Thompson. He serves as editor of the journal *Death Studies*. The author of over 500 articles and book chapters and a frequent workshop presenter, he is currently working to advance a more adequate theory of grieving as a meaning-making process. Neimeyer served as president of the Association for Death Education and Counseling (ADEC) and chair of the International Work Group for Death, Dying, and Bereavement. In recognition of his scholarly contributions, he has been granted the Eminent Faculty Award by the University of Memphis, made a fellow of the Clinical Psychology Division of the American Psychological Association, and given Lifetime Achievement Awards by both the Association for Death Education and Counseling and the International Network on Personal Meaning.

The Series in Death, Dying, and Bereavement

Volumes published in the Series in Death, Dying and Bereavement are representative of the multidisciplinary nature of the intersecting fields of death studies, suicidology, end-of-life care, and grief counseling. The series meets the needs of clinicians, researchers, paraprofessionals, pastoral counselors, and educators by providing cutting edge research, theory, and best practices on the most important topics in these fields—for today and for tomorrow.

Series Editors: Robert A. Neimeyer, PhD, Portland Institute for Loss and Transition, Oregon, USA and Darcy L. Harris, PhD, Western University Canada, Ontario, Canada

The Crafting of Grief
Constructing Aesthetic Responses to Loss
Lorraine Hedtke and John Winslade

Sibling Loss Across the Lifespan
Research, Practice, and Personal Stories
Edited by Brenda J. Marshall and Howard R. Winokuer

Understanding Child and Adolescent Grief
Supporting Loss and Facilitating Growth
Edited by Carrie Arnold

Chronic Sorrow
A Living Loss, 2nd Edition
Susan Roos

Continuing Bonds in Bereavement
New Directions for Research and Practice
Edited by Dennis Klass and Edith Steffen

Prescriptive Memories in Grief and Loss
The Art of Dreamscaping
Edited by Nancy Gershman and Barbara E. Thompson

Loss, Grief, and Attachment in Life Transitions
A Clinician's Guide to Secure Base Counseling
Jakob van Wielink, Leo Wilhelm, and Denise van Geelen-Merks

Non-Death Loss and Grief
Context and Clinical Implications
Edited by Darcy L. Harris

Superhero Grief
The Transformative Power of Loss
Edited by Jill A. Harrington and Robert A. Neimeyer

New Techniques of Grief Therapy
Bereavement and Beyond
Edited by Robert A. Neimeyer

For more information about this series, please visit www.routledge.com/Series-in-Death-Dying-and-Bereavement/book-series/SE0620.

New Techniques of Grief Therapy

Bereavement and Beyond

Edited by Robert A. Neimeyer

Routledge
Taylor & Francis Group

NEW YORK AND LONDON

First published 2022
by Routledge
605 Third Avenue, New York, NY 10158

and by Routledge
2 Park Square, Milton Park, Abingdon, Oxon, OX14 4RN

Routledge is an imprint of the Taylor & Francis Group, an informa business

Library of Congress Cataloging-in-Publication Data
Names: Neimeyer, Robert A., 1954– editor.
Title: New techniques of grief therapy : bereavement and beyond / edited by Robert A. Neimeyer.
Description: New York : Routledge, 2021. | Includes bibliographical references and index.
Identifiers: LCCN 2021001884 (print) | LCCN 2021001885 (ebook) | ISBN 9780815352020 (hardback) | ISBN 9780815352037 (paperback) | ISBN 9781351069120 (ebook)
Subjects: LCSH: Grief therapy. | Bereavement.
Classification: LCC RC455.4.L67 N49 2021 (print) | LCC RC455.4.L67 (ebook) | DDC 616.89/14—dc23
LC record available at https://lccn.loc.gov/2021001884
LC ebook record available at https://lccn.loc.gov/2021001885

ISBN: 978-0-8153-5202-0 (hbk)
ISBN: 978-0-8153-5203-7 (pbk)
ISBN: 978-1-351-06912-0 (ebk)

DOI: 10.4324/9781351069120

Typeset in Minion
by Apex CoVantage, LLC

Cover art: *Journey to the Center* by Lisa Jennings. Published here with permission.

Contents

Preface

We are wired for attachment in a world of impermanence. This succinct statement captures a truth at the heart of the human condition, one that Buddhism in particular, among other wisdom traditions, fully recognizes. That is to say that in the end, every person, every place, every project, every possession and every position that we hold dear will fade away—if only when we do—at least in an earthly sense. If living well implies investing ourselves in our lives with others, it also implies cultivating the grace of relinquishing the concrete expression of our attachments to our worlds and reconstructing them in more sustainable terms as we move forward through an unending series of life transitions.

New Techniques of Grief Therapy: Bereavement and Beyond is premised on this understanding. Life is by nature transitory and transitional, confronting us nearly continually with both the foreclosure of previous connections that conferred meaning on our existence and the opening up of new potential connections with people and projects that can revive this meaning as we live into a changed future. But nearly inevitably, the cyclical loss of such investments ushers in grief, as we are prompted to review, reaffirm or reconstruct the world of meaning anchored in each at the point that it concretely passes away. Building the personal and social resources to embrace these changes is of course a central goal of loss-oriented counseling and grief therapy, whatever the disciplinary, institutional or societal context in which it is conducted. The goal of this volume, like its predecessors, is to enrich the fund of creative ideas, resources and practices that can add substance and novelty to this work.

ORGANIZATION OF THE BOOK

The 59 brief chapters that follow are divided into 14 parts, each of which focuses on a shared objective, which finds expression in the several chapters that comprise it. Part I, *Framing the Work*, situates many of the techniques that follow in both the spontaneous flow of responsive and improvisational individual therapy and the structured organization of planned group interventions and considers culturally coherent perspectives on finding meaning in loss. Other chapters in this section reflect on the ethical complexities of end-of-life decisions, the ambiguity and importance of non-death losses and the prospect of post-loss growth. Part II, *Evaluating Grief*, presents four new measures for assessing personal and social complications in grief and bereavement, as a function of associated symptomatology; the impact of sometimes traumatic loss on survivors' worlds of meaning; mourners' previous relations to the deceased and the responses of other people to the griever's attempt to make sense of the loss. Part III, *Moving Through Bereavement*, outlines several creative procedures for identifying and processing people's distinctive grieving styles, fostering more self-awareness of how they traverse the landscape of loss and how they might envision doing so in a more centered and mindful fashion.

Part IV, *Articulating Ambiguous Loss*, directly engages the unique challenges of voicing and validating more abstract, subtle and pervasive losses associated with the death of a pet as well as a vast domain of unwelcome life transitions that lack the clarity and recognition of bereavement. Part V, *Practicing Self-Care*, offers a first-of-its-kind internet compendium of evidence-informed practices, video case studies and psychoeducation concerning loss in the lives of adults and children. It further includes chapters for both clients and therapists to assist both in discriminating grief from depression and attending resourcefully to the needs implicit in both experiences, as well as using yoga, dance and movement as means of self-healing. Part VI, *Fostering Compassion*, extends readers' capacities for empathic engagement with themselves and others through the cultivation of morally responsive practices for the living and dead, including specific coaching in drafting condolence letters to bereaved people.

In Part VII, *Working with Emotion*, contributors help therapists find the delicate balance between supporting clients in pain and challenging them to engage it differently, practice creative dialogues with their externalized suffering and use a variety of metaphoric procedures for recognizing and addressing their reluctance to relinquish a distressing but familiar feeling to embrace vulnerability and possible transformation. Part VIII, *Utilizing Imagery*, draws on both literal photographic images and those conjured through drawing or fantasy to explore the emotional and relational aftermath of loss. Part IX, *Revising Personal Meaning*, presents and illustrates both simple and more substantial procedures for fostering client reflection, repositioning, reconstruction of self and reconsolidation of memory in the crucible of therapeutic conversation and identity composition.

Part X, *Reaffirming Attachment*, opens with a comprehensive conceptualization of the Transition Cycle, integrating the essential phases of attachment, loss and meaning reconstruction that underpin our lives, and goes on to offer numerous practical tools for honoring the difficulties posed by grief, surmounting them and constructing new connections with the deceased and others. Part XI, *Dialoguing with the Deceased*, deepens this theme of reorganizing attachments through a creative variety of guided imaginal conversations. Part XII, *Validating Lives*, presents concrete methods for articulating and dignifying the lives of patients in terminal care settings and bereavement, ranging from biographical interviewing to symbolic affirmation of the deceased in the context of grief therapy. Part XIII, *Re-storying Loss*, comprises a sampling of theatrical, narrative and expressive procedures that foster deeper recognition of clients' own needs and values, whether in the private medium of journaling, therapeutic processing with the counselor or, in some cases, in the collective context of community. Finally, Part XIV, *Facilitating Support*, offers reflective resources for fostering deeper, more compassionate connections with loved ones with whom we are negotiating a hard transition, be they older family members entering assisted care, loved ones facing death or intimate others grieving the same loss. Taken together, the volume complements its predecessors, greatly augmenting the fund of tools and techniques made available to grief therapists.

ACKNOWLEDGEMENTS

In closing, I want to express my gratitude to the scores of colleagues worldwide who have contributed their enthusiasm and effort to this project, particularly the front-line workers in the fields of psychotherapy, counseling, coaching and the expressive arts, who are often given little opportunity to share the intelligent and inspired practices that inform their work with clients. No less than the recognized theorists and researchers whose contributions also fill the volume, they have helped make grief therapy the vital contributor to the healing arts that this volume illustrates. I am proud to call many members of all of these groups my friends.

I also would like to thank Anna Moore, my acquisition editor at Routledge, whose unflagging efforts to champion this volume and its predecessors have helped make this "series within a series" a reality. And finally, I want to extend my sincere gratitude to the many clients whose willingness to share their stories, their pain and their hope in these pages offers inspiration to those of us who work alongside them to reaffirm or recover meaningful lives in the wake of loss. In many respects, they are our greatest teachers.

Robert A. Neimeyer, PhD
Portland, OR, USA

How to Use This Book

Given the scope of the present volume, readers might well engage its diverse content in different ways, depending on their personal and professional contexts of work. I will therefore offer a few suggestions for three potential audiences in particular: (a) clinicians and coaches, (b) researchers and (c) educators.

Clinicians and coaches, broadly construed to include psychologists, counselors, therapists, social workers, chaplains, life coaches and others who work with loss and transition in different settings, can consider the volume as a source of conceptual orientation to the work of grief therapy as well as instruction in several dozen practical methods to add power and novelty to the counseling process. Beginning with Part I, readers will encounter several chapters that help situate specific techniques in such contexts as grief therapy for a complicated bereavement; a systematic protocol of meaning-oriented group work; culturally sensitive interventions; medical assistance in dying; ambiguous, non-death related loss and posttraumatic growth. The assessment resources (in Part II) further extend the clinical utility of the book by making accessible highly relevant scales and questionnaires (with scoring keys) to aid practitioners in identifying a client's individual and social vulnerabilities, as well as to document the efficacy of therapeutic interventions. Drawing on a great range of experiential, verbal, expressive, cognitive and body-oriented approaches, the dozens of technique chapters that constitute the core of the book (Parts III through XIV) then invite browsing for clinical instruction and inspiration, while also being organized into clusters of chapters that facilitate targeted searches for specific guidance in pursuing particular therapeutic issues and goals.

Researchers can find in the material of Part I a helpful introduction to evidence-informed models of grief and post-loss growth, extending broader surveys of the literature offered in previous volumes (Neimeyer, 2012, 2016; Neimeyer, Harris, Winokuer, & Thornton, 2021). Part II is likely to have particular value for this readership, conveniently including as it does a psychometrically informed presentation of new measures that can help operationalize specific psychosocial challenges encountered by the bereaved, while also providing valid and reliable means to evaluate the efficacy of targeted interventions. The remaining chapters, viewed from the standpoint of psychotherapy research, represent something of a handbook or manual of therapeutic procedures that invite further study, research that could be greatly advanced by the clarity with which they are conveyed. Thus, theoretically, technically and psychometrically, the contents of the present volume, like its predecessors, should help sharpen the scientific agenda of the field as well as fostering more creative practice.

Finally, **educators** are likely to find the present volume, along with its two predecessors, to be attractive as texts for advanced undergraduate and especially graduate classes in bereavement and grief therapy. Beyond the useful introduction to meaning-based practices provided in Part I, the remaining sections of the book offer detailed instruction in concrete methods of intervention, greatly alleviating the anxieties of students struggling to close the gap between theory and practice. Moreover, the structure of the book invites *experiential learning* through the assignment of readings of relevance to the students' own history of losses, as well as those of their clients. For example, the 14 parts of the book are amenable to incorporation as weekly readings in a syllabus that scaffolds a typical semester: Part I in Weeks 1 and 2, Part III in Week 2, Part IV in Week 3, etc., occasionally combining shorter parts and perhaps distributing the measurement scales of Part II across weeks with similar content to facilitate student self-assessment. As many of the chapters present techniques that are easily done as group exercises or individual homework, students can be encouraged to actually try out one of the methods of their choice from most units by considering their application to a death-related or non-death loss of their own. A brief reflective paper on the student's experience in doing so—with appropriate safeguards regarding personal disclosure—can greatly deepen their lived understanding of a given concept, process or technique before they attempt to implement it in field settings and can make for lively and often moving class discussions. The references in the bibliography of each chapter also point students toward additional resources that could help scaffold a class paper or project. Indeed, this structure has already led to adoption of earlier *Techniques* volumes as texts in a number of graduate curricula in psychology, counseling and social work, as well as programs of pastoral training and continuing professional education in grief therapy.

In summary, I hope the structure and content of *New Techniques of Grief Therapy: Bereavement and Beyond* address the needs of different stakeholders engaged in the fields of grief therapy and research and promote greater cross-fertilization and integration of pedagogy, science and practice.

Robert A. Neimeyer, PhD

References

Neimeyer, R. A. (Ed.). (2012). *Techniques of grief therapy: Creative practices for counseling the bereaved.* New York: Routledge.

Neimeyer, R. A. (Ed.). (2016). *Techniques of grief therapy: Assessment and intervention.* New York: Routledge.

Neimeyer, R. A., Harris, D., Winokuer, H., & Thornton, G. (Eds.). (2021). *Grief and bereavement in contemporary society: Bridging research and practice.* New York: Routledge.

Series Foreword

It is with great anticipation that we have awaited the release of this third volume of the *Techniques* series. This edition continues the tradition of offering a wonderfully diverse collection of ideas and helpful prompts by many highly qualified and experienced therapists who work with grieving individuals across many different types of losses and in a multitude of contexts. New foundational material expands upon our understanding of grief, including topics such as meaning making, continuing bonds, non-death loss and grief, cultural sensitivity, medical assistance in dying and the potential for posttraumatic growth after significant losses occur. Another section explores new measures that have been developed for research in the field that may also be useful in clinical applications, providing an opportunity for therapists to better understand their clients' processes—and for clients to better understand their own experiences as well.

Perhaps what underpins all of the *Techniques* books, and which is captured eloquently in this edition, is the awareness that grief is a universal experience that manifests itself in our clients in myriad ways. Many of the techniques described here seem simple, but that doesn't preclude how profound they may be when introduced within the therapeutic relationship. We are reminded that there is no defined roadmap for the grieving process. There is no single approach in grief therapy that will be helpful with every client; however, it is highly likely that therapists will land upon a chapter, a description or a technique that will help inspire and expand their "toolkit" and deepen their practice. Whether this collection of writings is read from cover to cover or in a piecemeal fashion, the ideas and useful approaches shared here enrich all of us who do this work. There is no doubt that the reader will find a wealth of knowledge and wisdom, practical suggestions and a deep appreciation for the many ways that we live—and grieve—our losses.

Darcy Harris, Ph.D., FT
Series Co-Editor

Contributors

Anita Bakker, De School voor Transitie, Leusden, the Netherlands; info@anitabakker.com

Benjamin W. Bellet, MS, Department of Psychology, Harvard University, Boston, MA; x01735@gmail.com

Paul A. Boelen, PhD, Utrecht University, Utrecht, the Netherlands; P.A.Boelen@uu.nl

Allan Botkin, PsyD, Director of the Center for Grief and Traumatic Loss, LLC, Chicago, IL; DrAL53@aol.com

Jamison S. Bottomley, PhD, Medical University of South Carolina, SC; bottomle@musc.edu

Laurie A. Burke, PhD, Burke Psychological, Portland, OR; laburke@burkepsychological.com

Sara Gody Jackson Bybee, College of Nursing, University of Utah, Salt Lake City, UT; sara.bybee.lcsw@gmail.com

Lawrence G. Calhoun, PhD, University of North Carolina Charlotte, Charlotte, NC; lcalhnjr@uncc.edu

Judy H. F. Chew, PhD, University of Calgary, Wellness Centre, Calgary, Alberta, Canada; chew@ucalgary.ca

Harvey Max Chochinov MD, PhD, Distinguished Professor of Psychiatry, University of Manitoba, Winnipeg, Canada; hchochinov@cancercare.mb.ca

Lisa L. Clark, PhD, St. Jude Children's Research Hospital, Memphis, TN; Lisa.Clark@stjude.org

Claudia Coenen, CGC, MTP, Private practice, Hudson, NY; claudia@thekarunaproject.com

Elizabeth Coplan, BA, Grief Dialogues, Seattle, WA, ecoplan@coplan.com

Shelly Cory, MA, Canadian Virtual Hospice; shelly@virtualhospice.ca

Rhonda Davis, MDiv, MSW, LCSW, Hospice of Davidson County, North Carolina; rhondainsight@gmail.com

Kenneth J. Doka, PhD, College of New Rochelle, New Rochelle, NY; kndok@aol.com

Gilbert Fan, DProf, Department of Psychosocial Oncology, National Cancer Center, Singapore; mssgfan@nccs.com.sg

Riet Fiddelaers-Jaspers, PhD, Expertisecentrum Omgaan met Verlies, Heeze, The Netherlands; riet@rietfiddelaers.nl

Denise van Geelen-Merks, Tiel, The Netherlands; info@denisevangeelen.nl

Darcy Harris, PhD, FT, King's University College at Western University, London, Ontario, Canada; darcy.harris@uwo.ca

Cynthia Louise Harrison, MSW, RSW, Private practice, London, ON, Canada; thialouise@gmail.com

Elizabeth Sheppard Hewitt, MSW, Eastern Health, St. John's, Newfoundland, Canada; Elizabeth.SheppardHe@easternhealth.ca

An Hooghe, PhD, MFT, Verbinding in Verlies [Connection in Loss], Boutersem, Belgium, and Context, University Hospital Leuven, Leuven, Belgium; an.hooghe@verbindinginverlies.be

Erica D. Huber, BS, Portland, OR; artist.erica@gmail.com

John R. Jordan, PhD, Private practice, Pawtucket, RI; Jjordan50@gmail.com

Agnieszka Konopka, PhD, Private practice, The Hague, The Netherlands; agnieszkakonopka@yahoo.com

Sherman A. Lee, PhD, Department of Psychology, Christopher Newport University, Newport News, VA; sherman.lee@cnu.edu

Geok Ling Lee, PhD, University of Singapore, Singapore; swklgl@nus.edu.sg

Wendy G. Lichtenthal, PhD, Memorial Sloan Kettering Cancer Center & Weill Cornell Medical College, New York; lichtenw@mskcc.org

Christopher J. MacKinnon, PhD, McGill University, Montreal, Quebec, Canada; christopher.mackinnon@mcgill.ca

Joshua Magariel, LCSW, Seasons Hospice & Palliative Care, Chicago, IL; joshua.magariel@gmail.com

Katarzyna Małecka, PhD, Department of English Studies, University of Social Sciences, Łódź, Poland; kmalecka@san.edu.pl

Melissa Masterson, MA, Department of Psychology, Fordham University, Bronx, NY; Mmasterson1@fordham.edu

Evgenia (Jane) Milman, PhD, Department of Psychology, St. Edwards University, Austin, Texas; evgenia.milman@mail.mcgill.ca

Lori Montross-Thomas, PhD, Department of Family Medicine and Public Health, University of California San Diego, La Jolla, CA; lpmontross@ucsd.edu

Nancy J. Moules, PhD, Faculty of Nursing, University of Calgary, Calgary, Alberta, Canada; njmoules@gmail.com

Robert A. Neimeyer, PhD, Director, Portland Institute for Loss and Transition, Portland, OR; neimeyer@portlandinstitute.org

Fred Nelson, MSW, Canadian Virtual Hospice; fnelson@mymts.net

Carolyn Ng, PsyD, Portland Institute for Loss and Transition, Singapore; carolyn@portlandinstitute.org

Joanne Ng, BS, Children's Cancer Foundation, Singapore, joanne.ng@ccf.org.sg

Aliza A. Panjwani, MA, Department of Psychology, City University of New York, New York, NY; Apanjwani@gradcenter.cuny.edu

Cindy S. Perkiss, LCSW, Wyndmoor, PA; CPerkiss@aol.com

Alyssa Rheingold, PhD, Director of Clinical Operations, National Crime Victims Research and Treatment Center, Department of Psychiatry and Behavioral Sciences, Medical University of South Carolina, HYPERLINK "mailto:rheingaa@musc.edu" rheingaa@musc.edu

Peter Rober, PhD, Context, Katolijke Universiteit, Leuven, Belgium; peter.rober@kuleuven.be

Kathleen Rogers, MFA (Creative Writing), Art Department, University of Memphis, Memphis, TN; thebluestgreen@gmail.com

Edward K. Rynearson, MD, University of Washington, Separation and Loss Service, Virginia Mason Medical Center, Seattle, WA; edward@rynearson.com

Diana C. Sands, PhD, Bereaved by Suicide Centre for Intense Grief, Australia; dianasands@karridale.org

Antonio Sausys, Fairfax, CA; antonio@yogaforgriefrelief.com

Jessica Sawyer, BS, Counseling, Educational Psychology and Research, University of Memphis, Memphis TN; jessie-sawyer@hotmail.com

Rickie Simpson, PhD, APRN-CNS, Department of Nursing, Stratford University, Woodbridge, Virginia/Private practice; rickie.simpson@verizon.net

Geert Smid, PhD, Utrecht University, Utrecht, The Netherlands; g.smid@centrum45.nl

Erica G. Srinivasan, PhD, University of Wisconsin-La Crosse, La Crosse, WI; esrinivasan@uwlax.edu

Kerry-Lyn Stanton-Downes, Post Grad Psychotherpist, UKCP and MBACP.

Edith Maria Steffen, PhD, Roehampton University, London, UK; Edith.Steffen@roehampton.ac.uk

Leigh Stephens, MSW, ALS Society of Quebec, Montreal, Quebec, Canada; Lstephens73@gmail.com

Nele Stinckens, PhD, Naiade Center for Psychotherapy, Leuven, Belgium; nele.stinckens@naiade-therapie.be

Dina Szynkarsky, MSW, McGill University Health Center, Montreal, Quebec, Canada; dina.szynkarsky@muhc.mcgill.ca

Janie Taylor, BA, Department of Psychology, University of Memphis, Memphis, TN; taylor.janie22@gmail.com

Richard G. Tedeschi, PhD, University of North Carolina Charlotte, Charlotte, NC; rtedesch@uncc.edu

Jessica Thomas, PhD, Marriage, Couple and Family Therapy, Graduate School of Education and Counseling at Lewis and Clark College, Portland, OR; jessicathomas@lclark.edu

Nils Van Uffelen, MS, Executive Career Coaching, Ramsel, Belgium; nilsvanuffelen@gmail.com

Deborah Ummel, PhD, Université de Sherbrooke, Sherbrooke, Quebec, Canada; deborah.ummel@usherbrooke.ca

César Valdez, LMSW, Partners in Healing Psychotherapy Training Affiliates, Ann Arbor, MI; cesvaldez@gmail.com

Florence Vinit, PhD, Université du Québec à Montréal, Montreal, Quebec, Canada; vinit.florence@uqam.ca

Doris Chambers Vaughans, PhD, LPC, NCC, Tuscaloosa Center for Cognitive Therapy, Tuscaloosa, AL; dorisvaughans@yahoo.com

Andrea Warnick, RN, MA, Registered psychotherapist, Andrea Warnick Consulting, Toronto, Ontario, Canada; aw@andreawarnick.com

Leo Wilhelm, De School voor Transitie, The Hague, The Netherlands; info@troostcoach.nl

R. Jane Williams, MDiv, PhD, Moravian Theological Seminary, Bethlehem, PA; williamsrj@moravian.edu

Joah L. Williams, PhD, University of Missouri-Kansas City, Kansas City, MO; williamsjoah@umkc.edu

Andria Wilson, MS, Department of Psychology, University of Memphis, Memphis, TN; andriawilson@yahoo.com

Jakob van Wielink, De School voor Transitie, Leusden, The Netherlands; jakob@deschoolvoortransitie.nl

Part I
Framing the Work

Reconstructing the Continuing Bond

A Process Analysis of Grief Therapy[1]

Robert A. Neimeyer and An Hooghe

Twenty-five years since publication of the pioneering work on mourners' continuing bonds to the deceased (Klass, Silverman, & Nickman, 1996), contemporary bereavement theorists and practitioners have clearly embraced its relevance for grief therapy (Neimeyer, 2015b). But just how does attention to the relationship between the client and the deceased help direct the subtle give-and-take of the counseling process as it unfolds in the intimate crucible of therapeutic dialogue? Our intent in the present chapter is to address this question by closely examining an actual session of grief therapy conducted along meaning reconstruction lines (Neimeyer, 2001, 2015a). We will begin by sketching a few of the cardinal themes of this perspective before introducing the detailed case study that will scaffold the chapter.

LOSS AND THE RECONSTRUCTION OF MEANING

Viewed through a constructivist lens, a central process in grieving is the attempt to reaffirm or reconstruct a world of meaning that has been challenged by loss (Neimeyer, 2006a). This does not imply that all experiences of bereavement entail a search for meaning, however, as we need not search for that which was not lost in the first place. Thus, when an important figure in our lives dies what we deem to be an "appropriate" death, one that fits comfortably enough into the narrative we hold of how life is or should be, it may pose minimal challenges to the practical patterns, relational scaffolding and world assumptions that undergird our existence. But when that death is sudden, horrific, premature or violent, or deprives us of a central figure on whom our sense of identity and security depends, we may be launched into an agonizing search for meaning in the loss and in our lives in its aftermath. The result, when we are unable to find meaning in what has befallen us, can be a grief that is perturbing, preoccupying and prolonged, and perhaps even life-threatening (Prigerson et al., 2009).

To date, a great deal of evidence converges to support the outlines of this meaning reconstruction model (Neimeyer, 2019). For example, inability to make sense of the loss has been associated with intense grief symptomatology in families anticipating the death of a loved one in palliative care (Burke et al., 2015), bereaved young adults (Holland, Currier, & Neimeyer, 2006), parents who have lost children (Keesee, Currier, & Neimeyer, 2008; Lichtenthal, Currier, Neimeyer, & Keesee, 2010) and older widows and widowers, for whom it prospectively predicts difficult adjustment a full 18 to 48 months after the death (R. A. Coleman & Neimeyer, 2010). Moreover, a struggle to find meaning in loss has proven to be a potent mediator of the impact of suicide, homicide and fatal accident, where it accounts for nearly

DOI: 10.4324/9781351069120-2

all the difference between these forms of violent death and death from natural causes (Currier, Holland, & Neimeyer, 2006; Rozalski, Holland, & Neimeyer, 2016). Conversely, the ability to find meaning in the loss prospectively predicts well-being and positive emotions over a period of four years (R. A. Coleman & Neimeyer, 2010) and moderates the impact of highly "central" or life-defining death events, substantially nullifying their deleterious impact (Bellet, Neimeyer, & Berman, 2016).

In light of the growing evidence base for the role of meaning making in bereavement, adaptation in its wake has been theorized to entail two forms of narrative activity (Neimeyer, 2019; Neimeyer & Thompson, 2014). The first of these is the need to *process the event story of the death itself* and its implications for our lives in its aftermath. Making sense of the event story is particularly important when the loss is horrific and tragic, calling for a trauma-informed approach to integrating the narrative of the dying (Perlman, Wortman, Feuer, Farber, & Rando, 2014; Rynearson & Salloum, 2021). The second involves an effort to *access the back story of the relationship to the deceased*, in order to resolve unfinished business and restore a measure of attachment security. Because this typically requires experientially vivid engagement with memories and images of the deceased, therapeutic work to reorganize the continuing bond requires an attachment-informed approach to grief therapy (Kosminsky & Jordan, 2016; Rubin, Malkinson, & Witztum, 2011). Either or both of these forms of narrative processing may be called for in a given case, giving rise to a great range of creative therapeutic techniques (Neimeyer, 2012b, 2016; Thompson & Neimeyer, 2014).

THE PRESENT CASE

Inge and Erik were a Flemish couple in their 40s living in Belgium with their two children, ages 4 and 7, when they sought relationship therapy at Context, the Center for Marital and Family Therapy at the University Hospital in Leuven. Both confessed to An Hooghe, their therapist, that they had grown apart over the ten years of their relationship, a pattern linked to Inge's intense engagement in her work as an international business consultant. Across eight sessions of earnest efforts in couple's therapy, both spouses stated that they had increased their mutual understanding, felt closer, made behavioral changes in their lives to permit more time together and recommitted to their relationship. But in the course of exploring significant family relationships with each partner, Inge reported to An that she had lost her mother when she was 17 years old, a disclosure that was accompanied by an immense wave of sadness and tears. Of course, Erik knew this, but he had never met her mother, and Inge rarely spoke of her. Over the course of the sessions, all noticed that Inge's grief for her mother remained a very sad and vulnerable place for her, one that continued to take her breath away tearfully each time the conversation of therapy touched on it. As the marital therapy came to a successful conclusion, Inge approached An with a request for additional individual sessions to work on her prolonged and preoccupying grief, feeling that it would be too difficult to do so with her husband present. Both partners readily consented to the plan, with the intention to then bring them back together and share the story once Inge herself had found words for a grief so deep and pervasive that it seemed to elude expression.

In the ten sessions of grief therapy that followed, Inge remained very "stuck" in her grief, nearly unable to access memories of her childhood or of her time with her mother. Witnessing this striking disconnection from her own history and Inge's visible suffering with each mention of her mother's death over 20 years before, An noted that "it was as if everything were put away in a very secure place, which made it possible for her to function in her job and daily life." Working very slowly and with great caution, the two gradually began to access some memories of Inge's mother and, as she became better able to "hold" them, invited Erik back in to share the story. It was at this point that Robert Neimeyer (Bob) visited

Belgium to offer some days of professional training in grief therapy, opening the prospect of Inge having a single session of therapy with him to supplement An's efforts, in view of Inge's near-native proficiency in English. After discussing this possibility as a couple, Inge and Erik accepted the offer, choosing to have Inge meet with Bob individually but on camera, while Erik watched the session alongside An and 15 other therapists in another room, to relieve each of the partners of the immediate impulse to take care of or "rescue" the other. This then was the arrangement as Bob welcomed Inge and Erik, intentionally limiting the background provided him (learning only that she struggled with her grief following the death of her mother) so as to allow Inge to present the problem to him in her own terms, unconstrained by previous case conceptualization. By mutual agreement, Inge, Bob, Erik, An and the reflecting team of other therapists would then meet in a circle immediately afterward to share respectful questions about the therapy process before returning the couple to An's care for additional processing of its implications. The text that follows represents a verbatim transcription of the filmed interview, interspersed with Bob's first-person reflections on the work, which centered strongly on re-accessing and reorganizing Inge's continuing bond with her mother. The chapter then concludes with a summary of the subsequent couple's session, offering a window on the consultation's impact.

The Loss of Balance

THERAPIST (T; *SPEAKING INITIALLY IN DUTCH*): Inge, *dank je wel nog eens* [Thank you once again]. I'm eager to learn something of your experience, and I wonder if we might begin with just asking you what kind of hopes or expectations you might have about this hour, about how it might be useful for you?

INGE (I): Uhm, I don't have a lot of expectations, and I'm not sure what to expect, but one thing that would help me is to find other ways of thinking about, uhm, thinking about [long silence] your *place* in the world among people, when there's a change in configuration, like when you lose someone, how you come back into your *balance*.

T: Yeah, yeah, because the loss of another throws us *off balance* [gestures with arms and torso like a tightrope walker], and we find ourselves having a hard time finding our footing in the world again, in the sense of a solid *place*. And the loss that you've had, I understand, is the loss of your mother? [Client nods, and immediately struggles with tears.] And just with the mention of her name, the feeling rises in you. [Client begins to cry.] Yeah [gently]. So what is that feeling [gesturing with hand at the level of his torso, like a rising fountain], if you were to describe it in words that were even partially adequate to the experience. . . . What would we call that, the feeling that comes now?

I: Uhm (sigh) . . . Being *overwhelmed*. [T: Overwhelmed, yeah.] [Pause] And in a way reliving it a bit [crying].

T: Reliving it a bit. Reliving the experience of her dying?

I: [Nods yes, tearfully.]

T: So the overwhelming feeling is one of . . . ?

I: Yeah. Just, uhm, the loss, the loss of balance, loss of the whole way that you thought your universe was functioning. And to have that go, disappear and be changed, and feel that's out of your control.

In response to my invitation to articulate her expectations about how this hour might be helpful to her—a bid to foster client "agency" in co-constructing the therapy (Coleman & Neimeyer, 2014)—Inge pauses and then, in a slightly self-distancing, second-person voice, seeks a way to make sense of her "place" in the world in the wake of loss, to recover a sense of "balance." Hearing these vocally emphasized *quality terms* that begin to shape an implicit metaphor of her existential position (Neimeyer, 2009), I echo the significant phrasing, lightly "performing" the image to give it more embodied presence in the room. A simple mention of her loss evokes strong emotion and tears as we seek a preliminary verbal handle for the feeling and spontaneously elaborate Inge's position in a universe that loses balance and coherence in light of her mother's death.

The Center of the Universe

T: Yeah. It's a deeply, deeply unwelcome change in the structure of the world, and you're left trying to relearn that world and relearn yourself because both are changed in this experience. . . . What position did your mother have in this world, in this universe of your childhood and young adulthood?

I: I was 17 when she died. [T: 17.] And she'd been ill on and off for a long time. But when she died, it was still a surprise because we didn't talk a lot of those things, and she was very much a pillar figure in our house. She was a very dominant person, but not in a bad way. But she was called "Mrs. Thatcher" in her workplace [T: Ah, Mrs. Thatcher, the Iron . . .] The Iron Lady! [smiling and slightly laughing]. And she was, not in a bad way, but she got her way in everything, had control over everything, she *governed* everything. In a way, she knew exactly what she wanted, what to do . . . when to do that.

T: The structures were there, and she was the one who kind of helped build them and keep them in good order.

I: Right. And she did that for us children, but she did that for other relatives, for my father. There wasn't a big balance there, so she was very much a governing person in every sense of the word.

T: So in a way she was almost like a center of gravity or something for this solar system of the family, right? [Client nods.] And it's almost like, how does the solar system reorganize when the sun is extinguished, right?

I: Right [long pause, crying silently].

Our exploration of her mother's "governing" position in the family leads Inge to offer an affectionate characterization of her as "Mrs. Thatcher," the United Kingdom's forceful Prime Minister during the 1980s, whose unbending political will inspired the moniker used by her admirers. With my suggestion of a modest extension of Inge's metaphor of her imbalanced universe following her mother's death, she moves into several moments of wordless weeping, leading ultimately to my gentle intervention.

Introducing the Loved One

T: I wonder if you would be comfortable doing something with me just a moment, and that is, I would invite you just to close your eyes with me for just a second [closing eyes as client follows]. And allow us to concentrate our breathing . . . just to allow our lungs to fill and empty . . . fill and empty [speaking slowly and opening eyes to follow client's nonverbal behavior], in a natural rhythm. Just feeling maybe with each breath just a little release of the overwhelming feeling, recognizing that it's always accessible . . . and that that feeling probably has something to tell us . . . and teach us about this woman who was your mother and still is your mother, in an important sense. [Client opens eyes.] And as we sit here speaking to each other, and as we kind of invite her to join us for that conversation in the ways we can, our goal is mutually to learn something about who you are, what you need, but also about who she is and what she would need, in seeing her daughter now, carrying this grief. [Client nods, silently.] So I wonder, would you be willing or be able to introduce her a little more, this Iron Lady [client laughs] who is the governor and the center of this kind of universe. What was her name?

I: Yvette. [T: Yvette.] Uhm, she worked always very hard, and she herself was an accident. At the time when she was born that was a big deal. [T: Ah.] But she had felt and we felt as children that she felt as an unwanted person for a large part of her life. [T: Wow.] And so that was something. She read a lot of books about it. She never talked to us about it, but we could sense that she had that feeling in respect of her own parents.

T: And a real effort, it seems, across a period of years to make sense of that? Or to say, "Who am I and where do I fit in?"

I: Yes, and to get appreciation from her parents, which never really was to her satisfaction, and that was very frustrating. And I think that's probably why she worked so hard. [T: Ah.] Because it was something she felt she needed to make up for. And so she was a kind of person who would make all her own vegetables in the garden; she made all of our clothes [T: Wow.] She worked as a teacher; she did a lot of things. Even the evening before she would go to the hospital, she would wash all her clothes, and she made sure all the food was in place, and the laundry was done. She did it by hand, even if she was meant to be in the hospital the next day. So she was this kind of indestructible force [smiling].

In the presence of Inge's strongly dysregulating and isolating grief, I begin with a nearly meditative moment of mindful breathing, matching her respiration and gradually slowing it in synchrony with my own. As her strong emotion softens in response and she spontaneously re-engages me, I invite Inge to "introduce her loved one," to appreciatively conjure her mother for me to re-access a seemingly broken bond (Hedtke, 2012). What emerges is a proud but incipient narrative of her mother's relentless work ethic, rooted, Inge surmises, in her being an unplanned and unwanted child and her lifelong effort to compensate for that.

A Quest for Connection

T: Yeah, almost an indestructible force. And how strange that must have been for her as well for you to witness this force having to contend with the force of illness. [Client: Yeah.] A cancer of some sort?

I: Yes, for years. And there were times, all through my high school period, she was ill on and off. And there were times when I was young and I would go to the hospital to visit her, and I *liked* those times because she would sit still and not work. And I could talk to her! [laughs with therapist] And she would talk to me, and so we had that special time together. So there were times when her illness was not a *threat* in that way. . . .

T: Was almost a *friend* in that way?

I: Yes. It was something that was there.

T: And it opened a space for a special kind of mother-daughter conversation that with all of her busyness would otherwise be hard to find.

I: Right. And there were other times or times when she got really ill, and she asked me to read to her. She had a book that was by Siegel, Bernie Siegel. She read a lot of books about self-healing with thoughts about positive thinking. And she was in a lot of pain; in the end, she was in a lot of pain because the cancer had spread. And we read to her, and it was books in English [laughs]. And she would say, "Is it okay for you to read so long to me in English?" [T: Wow.] And so we would sit with her, sometimes reading. . .

T: So part of your remarkable English language competence was really born in the crucible of that connection with her and reading to her?

I: Probably.

T: Wow, so you were giving that to her as a kind of *gift*. But she also kind of gave that to *you* as kind of gift, that you bring forward to *me*, even.

I: [Smiling tearfully] She was an English teacher [tenderly].

T: Ahh. She was an *English* teacher [nodding].

I: So that's why they called her Mrs. Thatcher [smiling]. English teacher with an iron hand! [Both laugh.]

T: How perfect that is! I'm sorry to say I'm not Ronald Reagan. I can't exactly be the counterpart in the story of relationships across the sea! But it's a fascinating thing to meet her in this way. If you could picture her to convey what she looked like physically, what would I see in a picture of her?

Echoing but qualifying Inge's description of her mother as an "almost" indestructible force, I subtly open the door to the event story of her dying, having already begun accessing the back story of her personhood. What emerges is surprising: the periods of her mother's illness were more friendly than threatening, slowing her mother's otherwise intense activity to permit a special sort of mother-daughter bond. Significantly, this involved long exchanges in English as Inge read to her mother during her treatment, consolidating Inge's language competence at the same moment it consolidated the relationship. It is a short inferential step to formulate this as a legacy gift from her mother, as well as a reciprocal gift given to an ailing parent by a loving child. Connecting these dots to our own exchange in this same language completes the circle and continues the work of invoking Mother's presence as a third participant in the therapeutic triad (Rynearson, 2012).

Inviting Mom's Presence

I: I have pictures of her with me, so I can show them!

T: Yes, if you're willing to show her.

I: So I have a picture of her [shows a framed black-and-white photo].

T: Ah, yeah [enthusiastically].

I: She looks a bit Thatcher-like! [Both laugh.]

T: Now in this picture, right, where we see this sort of expression, almost like a slight smile, and the eyebrows are a little arched; what do you see in this expression?

I: Uhm, her strength, I think [T: Yeah] because she was already fighting at this point; she was already ill. This photo is taken not long before, six months or so.

T: You wouldn't know that, would you? [Client begins to lay the photo flat on the small table between them as the therapist gently takes the frame and lifts it to standing.] Could we place her here because we're certainly inviting her to be with us in the conversation today [client assists in situating the framed picture] and, yeah, to maybe just lend us her sense of presence, lend *you* her sense of presence, as you do this difficult work of addressing the relationship and the pain that comes with her physical dying? [Client weeps, and therapist gently hands her a tissue.]

I: Thank you [wipes nose and eyes].

Making a literal "place" in the shared space of therapy for her mother, we position her as a potential support figure in Inge's therapy. Deeply moved, she accepts this positioning as she acknowledges her grief.

A Frozen Grief

T: Yeah . . . What do you sense now that you need in the aftermath of her dying, all those years ago? There's something now about this, of course, that touches you so deeply. But what would help there, with that?

I: [Pause.] I have been wondering that for a long time too. Uhm, because it still feels like a very short time ago, to me at least. And it doesn't feel to me like the feeling changes between now and five years ago or ten years ago. It stays too, uhm, *open.*

T: It stays too open. And when you say, "It doesn't feel like it changes, to me at least," is there a feeling that it *has* changed for others, even for others who knew her, or who know and love you, that somehow their grief or feeling about her dying has evolved in a different way?

I: Mainly I'm thinking in terms how it normally *should* be. [T: Aha.] You think that these things will pass a little bit, but I think my brother and sister, as far as I can tell, don't have the same feeling, I think, but I'm not sure they would share it with me. I'm not sure. I was wondering; it should be, it should be something I should be able to talk about now without being overwhelmed.

T: "*Should*" . . . Who would say this *should*? Is this an expectation voiced by people or just present in the culture in some way or. . . ?

I: Yeah, I think [pause]. Or maybe it's something that I would expect from *myself*, to think I should be able to move past.

T: So like, almost a part of you [raising right hand to represent that part] is saying, "Inge, you need to be able to move past this, you need to be able to speak of her without the tears." But there's another part [raising left hand] that is very tender and very hurt, very sad [client weeps, but maintains strong eye contact], that feels that the structure of the universe lost its balance, has shifted somehow. And *you* feel off balance.

I: It's *stayed* out of balance. [T: Stayed out of balance.] And I kind of assumed [pauses, weeping] that I would regain the balance, in some way, over time.

T: Yeah, that time would *heal* the wounds. [C: Yeah.] We kind of have a cultural prescription about that, don't we? And it doesn't seem like that's happened for you.

In response to my attempt to discern the need implicit in Inge's grief, she immediately notes its "open," unchanging character as the years of her bereavement turn to decades. Probing gently for a possible contextual or familial discourse underpinning her expectation of her course of grieving, Inge suggests that her siblings are less haunted by the loss and hints that she "should" be moving past it herself. I frame this compassionately as an inner dialogue in two voices, both to validate her own possible double positioning regarding her grieving and to foster greater self-compassion rather than self-criticism.

The Loss of Safety in the Family

I: No. And the feeling I had had when she died was one that [long pause] . . . We didn't talk about this very much at home, and so I think each of us had our own emotion and just took that and lived with it the best we could. So there wasn't a lot of conversation. I think the feeling that I had was that there was no. . . *safe place* anymore. There was no *protection* [T: No safe place.] because she had been kind of the pillar of our family.

T: The protector, the supporter, the structure of the family, and now it's like the pillar of the family has collapsed.

I: Right, and there was nothing that ever really substituted for that. So we just each stayed on the ground, each individually finding our way back.

T: So she was not only the pillar but also like the *floor* or *foundation* of the family, and each of you found your way of standing on that in relation to each other. [C nods.] But with the collapse of that floor, each of you was kind of lost in your own world. [C: Right.] I see. [Pause] And you said something about finding your way back. Have you as a family—this is a brother, a sister, a father too?

I: A father, too, who also died in the meantime.

As we continue to explore the meaning of this loss for Inge and its implications for her life now, Inge underscores in vivid metaphor the collapse of the secure base once provided by her attachment to her mother and the resulting fragmentation of the family in the aftermath of her death.

A Silent Story

T: And did the three of you find your way back to connect again [C shakes head no] or. . . ?

I: Not really. [T: Not really.] I think we get along—we see each other; we took care of my father when he passed. But we never talk about the experience. And we never shared that.

T: So there's a lot that's unsaid. A lot of silent stories that live within you and that have no audience in the world.

I: Right [nodding repeatedly].

T: Have you been able to seek out and find others who can hear the stories that your family could not? About your mom, about her illness, about her dying, about life since that time?

I: I haven't, really. I spoke to some friends about it, to my husband a little bit but. . .

T: What kind of responses do you get?

I: What I expect . . . listening, people listening. But it's such an overwhelming . . . I think because it's such an overwhelming feeling, I'm trying not to let it loose [gestures outward with her hands].

T: Ah, I see. So partly to not to overwhelm them, you kind of hold it in? Or not to overwhelm yourself?

I: Not to overwhelm myself. And putting me and them in a position . . . It would be awkward; I wouldn't know how to get out of it.

T: Yeah, yeah, yeah. How are you feeling now, in just this moment with me? You clearly experience and express in your tears, your face and your words some of this emotion.

I: I think now it's okay, I'm not overwhelmed anymore, at this moment. Because I'm trying to describe it, uhm, as opposed to experience it. I'm trying to do my best to not sit in it. So I guess it's a little better.

Although the narration of loss naturally occurs on every level from the intimately individual (Neimeyer, Klass, & Dennis, 2014), in Inge's case, her grief has become a silent story, one that finds no audience in the world of others (Neimeyer, 2006b). In large part, this arises from a kind of self-censorship whose purpose is to avoid arousing overwhelming feelings in oneself or another, as is often observed in families going through a mutually devastating loss (Hooghe, Neimeyer, & Rober, 2012). However, in this case, experiential avoidance of the core pain of grief seems only to have prolonged vulnerability to it, estranging Inge from family members, from herself and, in some sense, from her mother. What seems called for, then, is a safe and supportive exploration of this grief in the crucible of a trusting relationship, in a way that takes into account its substantially wordless nature.

Analogical Listening

T: Yeah. Let me ask you this and see of this makes sense to you, to see if it's worth doing, but with no attempt to press this. How would it be if we were to almost accept that invitation to try to describe it, some of how you carry this grief about your mom, without having you be swallowed up in that? If we were to do a kind of inner scan and visualization of how you carry the grief [gesturing with a slow wave over his torso, with eyes closed], allow it to speak to you from a place close to but not within it [gesturing to suggest this proximity to an inner shape]. Would that be a welcome thing to be able to give it words but not to be overwhelmed [making a wave-like gesture washing toward client] by those words?

I: Yeah. I don't know if I would be able to do it, but I would like to try it.

T: Would you?

I: I think it would help because it's just what I experience, not intentionally, but that's what I'm experiencing right now. I'm trying to make this useful, to describe it to you, as opposed to just being overwhelmed. I think when I'm talking to a friend, I'm just more overwhelmed, but now I really want to try and explain it, and so I think that is a better way.

T: Right. So here's my invitation, a little bit like we did a few minutes ago, just kind of to allow ourselves [slowing voice and closing his eyes] to close our eyes and enter this place of quiet breathing, just kind of allowing our chest to rise and fall in a naturally deep rhythm [opening eyes to track client's nonverbal signals], emptying fully and filling fully. As we just try to clear a space, a space between and around us, to invite this feeling to come [pause] in a way that gives it perhaps form and voice. Kind of a respectful invitation to a visitor, without having the visitor move in permanently. And what I would invite, if this feels okay to you, with your eyes closed, is to just do a kind of scan [gestures with hand slowly raising and lowering in front of his torso] through your body, allowing your awareness to maybe turn in and down [gesturing with his hand to suggest this movement] and into the space of your body, your torso or wherever it might be drawn, as you just ask yourself the question: "Where in me do I carry this grief for my mother now?" [pause] And just wait for it to speak, and you might gesture toward it [touches chest lightly with fingers] to show the place where you feel its presence.

I: [Sighs, wipes her eyes and places hand on her belly while weeping softly.]

T: Yeah. Kind of in your abdomen, almost, a deep place within your body, right? Just kind of retaining the privacy of closed eyes [closes his own, with hand on his abdomen, as client then does the same], just ask yourself in this place [speaking very slowly], this physical location that holds the grief: If the grief had a form or a shape, what might it be?

I: [Pause] Something like a blotch, something very changeable and expandable [gestures in and out with fingers].

T: A blotch. Changeable and expandable [mimicking and enlarging client's gesture]. And with your fingers, you kind of make the shape of expansion and contraction?

I: Right.

T: Does that have a color to it, as you just attend to it? [Closes eyes, as client then does the same. Pause] If it had a color, what might the color or colors be?

I: Something reddish and purplish.

T: Reddish and purplish. [Pause] Kind of a constant color or changing color?

I: Changing.

T: Changing. Describe that change for me. What would it be looking like, changing from and to?

I: Like waves.

T: Waves. Like waves in the sea or. . . [making wave-like gestures with his hand]?

I: That rise up and that calm down again.

T: Ah. Rising up and calming down. That's that kind of expansion and contraction [making these gestures with his hand]. Is that a good word for it?

I: Yeah.

T: Yeah [closing eyes, as client then does same]. Is there a feeling associated with that image, that rising up and calming down? A bodily feeling or an emotional feeling?

I: A tightness, a muscle tightness.

T: A muscle tightness, like in your abdomen? [C: Right.] Right, yeah. I wonder if you can focus your attention in those abdominal muscles now. And just tighten them almost like you're doing sit-ups or something, like an exercise. Can you feel the tightening?

I: Yes.

T: As you do, does that shape or image or color change in any way?

I: [Pause] It is a little more stable [laughs].

T: More stable, less fluctuation.

I: Yeah.

T: And if you just release that muscle tension . . . with me for a moment and maybe just take a deep abdominal, diaphragmatic kind of breath, what happens with the image then?

I: [Pause] It becomes a little more, how to say that, less of a [smiling, making smoothing motions with her hands] . . . more calmer, laid out, like it's lying down.

T: Ooh, like it's lying down [smiling].

I: Like instead of the waves, it's more. . .

T: Less a tumultuous [C: Right.] raising up and falling but more of a calming. Calmer waters?

I: Right [pause].

Responding to my invitation to cultivate an unhurried, internal awareness through the breath-focused procedures of analogical listening (Neimeyer, 2012a), Inge quickly feels and visualizes where she holds the pain—in a reddish-purple blotch (almost like a bruise) sensed in her abdomen. As we explore its sensory qualities of a wave-like expansion and contraction, Inge accepts my encouragement to consciously exaggerate the latter tension and finds (perhaps surprisingly) greater "stability" in doing so. Releasing the tension at my invitation, she then notices a "calming" or "lying down" of the feeling, suggesting that she has some control over her terms of engagement with it, making further exploration of her relation to the abdominally held grief sufficiently safe to be feasible.

An Internal Dialogue

T: That's interesting [whispered]. Just placing your attention near but not in that kind of watery expansive place, not drowning in it, but just sort of standing on the shore, I wonder if you would be willing to listen to it? Listening to anything that has to tell you. If it had a voice, how would it speak? What would its vocal quality be like? [Client sighs.] Do that again [blowing softly out, as client does the same]. How do you imagine it would speak, with what kind of voice?

I: I can't imagine it having a voice.

T: How would it communicate what it has to tell us or teach us?

I: [Pause] I see it more as something that is not something communicative, but more something that is there to deal with and *carry*.

T: To deal with and carry.

I: Rather than it being communicative or. . .

T: Uh huh, uh huh. . . . So I wonder if, from that place [that] is near but not in it, I wonder if you can just try some words like these and see if they feel true to you? And if not, change them to make them so. Something like "I'm willing to carry you." [Long pause] How would you need to change those words to make them fit for you? [Client begins to cry.] What's the feeling that comes to you with that?

I [WEEPING]: I was going to say, "I'm having a hard time carrying you."

T: I'm having a hard time carrying you.

I: [Nods yes.]

T: I'm having a hard time carrying you. Then use those words: "I'm having a hard time carrying you." Tell her or it or him what it is that is hard about that. [Long pause.] What would you say about the difficulty carrying that dark, expansive and contractive, sometimes tranquil and sometimes more turbulent space?

I: [Long pause.] I guess it's difficult to carry because I sometimes feel like it's too overwhelming; it's too much and that it swallows me. And it feels like it's something I have to stay ahead of.

As we search for a way to dialogue with the image, we learn that it is less "communicative" than it is something to "carry," though at great emotional cost. Even with repeated efforts to establish a safe nearness to the feeling to explore the relationship to it, Inge is easily swallowed by the sea of grief and seems at risk of drowning in it. What seems required, then, is a degree of separation that would make exposure to the feeling possible, but at greater distance.

Externalizing the Felt Sense

T: Something you have to stay ahead of? What if you could speak those words directly to the kind of feeling? And I wonder if we were to offer that image a place here with us, but a place a little bit outside you, would that be okay? [T places a third empty chair facing C, forming a triangle.] So if we offer a kind of comfortable chair here where it can repose so it doesn't have to be lodged in your abdomen in this moment, I wonder if you can just return to those words, speak them to this sensed feeling, right? [Gesturing with both hands toward the empty chair.] "Sometimes it's overwhelming to carry you." What would you say to it about that?

I: Sometimes it's overwhelming to carry you [weeping]. And it seems like it is never getting easier. It seems that it should get easier over time. Or that I should get better. It feels that I always have to be on my toes to not let it swallow me.

T: Say this and see if it feels like it fits: "It's like I have to be vigilant or guard myself in some way." What's the "staying on my toes" feeling? What would you say about that?

I: It's also this feeling that I lost my place and universe a little bit. And so I have no safe position from within to carry you.

T: So you have no safe position?

I: No position of strength.

T: No position of strength to carry you.

I: And I have to do my best all the time.

T: Yeah, yeah. What would that position of strength look like if it had a physical shape or structure?

I: [Pause.] Something very upright, like a rectangle, something very square.

Speaking to the now-externalized feeling, Inge voices the essence of her struggle: deprived of the secure base provided by her mother, she has "no safe position from within to carry [her grief]." Turning her inner gaze from the visualized pain to the strength needed to carry it, she sketches briefly what it would look like: upright and rectangular. The geometry of her language and gesture suggests the next move.

Standing Up to the Feeling

T: Shall we stand? Let's stand up and see how that is. [T and C stand up as C chuckles.] So here we are, kind of rectangular [standing almost at attention, like a soldier]. So how does it feel relating to this same image [gesturing downward, toward chair]? Is it still a quiet form, or is it more turbulent? What is it?

I: It's turbulent.

T: It's turbulent?

I: Yeah.

T: How does it feel to just regard it [gesturing toward it] from this position of standing up [lifting hands to body] to it? Is there a difference between that and the kind of sitting with it? [As T speaks the word "sitting," he slowly sits down again, and client follows.]

I: No, it feels the same. Whatever shape it has or whatever shape I have, it can overpower anything. [T: I see.] So that's why I try to contain it in a *box* [C forms box with hands at level of her abdomen] [T: Oh, contain it in a box.] to make sure it doesn't get out of certain boundaries.

T: Oh, I see. That's the kind of almost abdominal tightness [forms tight box with hands] that's the boxing up of this? [C: Yeah.] [Pause] And if it kind of leaks out of the box or spills over [gesturing to suggest these actions], then it feels more overwhelming?

I: [Nods yes.]

Inner strength, it seems, is not enough; soon enough, the grief leaks out or over the embodied box that contains it. Something more is needed.

Consulting With Mom

T: Who or what might help you carry that sense, that feeling?

I: I thought a lot about that, and I don't know. [Pause] I don't know [crying].

T: I wonder, if you were to meet your mother's eyes in this moment of clear pain, what might she have to tell you about how pain can be carried, from a position of strength? [Turns photo toward client and gazes at Mother.] What message would she have for us about that?

I: I remember she would read me from those books that she kept reading about thinking positive.

T: The Bernie Siegel kinds of books. [C: Right.] So what kind of model or message might she have for you?

I: She was a strong person; she would say that I should shut up and move on.

T: Shut up and move on?

I: Yeah, she would have just said that: "Deal with it."

T: And she was able to somehow do that even in the midst of her cancer? [Client nods.] Were there times that it was even too hard for her?

I: I think there were times that were hard for her, but she showed those very rarely.

T: She had that kind of strength to contain the turbulence, the pain, in her own way [C: Yeah, yeah.] . . . not wanting you to see that. [Long pause as client gazes at Mother.] What difference does it make, if any, to invite her into this conversation about the pain, about the grief? To have this very inner grief, right, this kind of reddish, purplish, swimming, elastic kind of form [gesturing to suggest the wavy, expanding and contracting shape at level of his abdomen] and then to bring Mom's kind of structure and centering and strength [making a vertical, upright gesture at abdominal level, melding to a circle and then to two closed fists, in synchrony with each description] to bear on that?

I: [crying] It's hard because she *caused* it.

T: Because she caused it? I see. . . . So how does it make that hard, that she caused it by dying?

I: [Nods.] So sometimes thinking about her is good and gives strength, but sometimes thinking about her causes the feeling to be more overwhelming. So thinking about her is not a *safe place*.

T: It's not a safe place, I see. . . . So sometimes you need a little distance from her just as you need the distance from this feeling?

I: Yeah. I used to spend—I told someone who was surprised about that—up until about a year or two ago, I spoke with her almost daily. Not explicitly, not in spoken words, but in thoughts.

T: In your mind? Did you ever write those down? Like in a letter to her, or. . . ?

I: No.

T: Did you ever sense her speaking back to you and kind of making it into a dialogue rather than a monologue?

I: Sometimes, when things would happen . . . for example, today is her birthday [smiling].

T: Today is her birthday?

I: Today is her birthday! [T: Ahh (warmly).] And so I felt this was a very odd setting. And my second son was born on her birthday too. I remember I had a conversation with her at the time: "I don't want him to be born on Friday the 13th or on Sunday, because there was no doctor in the hospital, and so he was born on her birthday three days later. So there are ways—and these are probably in my mind—there are ways in which I sometimes feel like there is some part of a conversation.

T: Yeah, yeah. And when you feel that conversation like really including her and that she's responsive to it, what does that do to the kind of reddish, purplish. . . ?

I: It calms it; it's a nice feeling because it's a presence, I guess it's more [that] I feel her presence rather than her absence.

T: You feel her presence rather than her absence.

I: [Nods yes.] And sometimes when I think about it, I only feel her absence.

T: Yeah, so I'm wondering, would it feel right to offer your mom this chair [pulling the chair in a little closer] instead of the grief? [Client: Right.] We can allow the grief to go wherever it needs to go, whether it's back into you or to just take a place in the hall for now. [Client smiles and chuckles: Right.] As we kind of invite your mother's presence there in that chair, I don't know if we should sing her "Happy Birthday" or not. . .

I: [laughing] Probably not!

T: Probably not, but we could wish her that in some way. [Looking at Mother's photo, which he has placed in the chair] . . . She looks like she's amused in this picture now to me, with that little smile.

I: [smiling and gazing at the photo]: Right . . . yeah.

As we consider what would help Inge carry her grief, we turn naturally toward her original secure base: her mother, visibly present in the room in the form of her picture. However, initial barriers must be acknowledged and overcome—Mom's stern gruffness and, more significantly, perhaps, the fusion of memories of Mom with painful images of her dying. Seeking a way to soften, even a little playfully, into the relationship and to begin to differentiate between the mother Inge still needs and the grief over her death, I shift grief out of the chair and invite Mom to occupy it. Inge's expectant gaze suggests that more steps toward renewing the bond are now feasible.

Renegotiating Attachment

T: You know one of the hard things about grief, I think, is that in some ways we're having to negotiate a change between losing what we had [reaching out with both hands toward the photo, as client returns gaze to it] and then attempting to have what we have we've lost [pulling hands inward, toward abdomen, as if taking the photo into himself, as client follows the gesture with her eyes] but without the material presence of the other to anchor and structure that. [Client nods.] Almost like we have to find a way to take that secure base and structure [gesturing to suggest the upright structure] and find a place for it inside us [drawing the gesture in, covering his heart].

I: Yes . . . [spoken softly and evocatively].

T: So we can carry some of what we need with us. [Leans in, as if moving forward.] [Client: Yeah.] And sometimes hearing the voice of the other or inviting that voice is a part of that. It's like the echoes of the conversation remain accessible, right? Do you ever sense that yourself?

I: Yeah, yeah.

T: What would you hear her saying to you at those times?

I: Umm, for example, there are times that I hear her say things, when I'm traveling in foreign cities, and I would say, "Look, Mom, where I am now," especially when I was younger and on my first trips for work, and I could hear her say, "Wow that's great!" [T: Ahh!] "Like you're doing all this traveling and all of these things that I never got a chance to do." [T: Ahh. . .] So those are conversations that were nice to have.

T: She would be sort of cheering you on and really celebrating your living large.

I: Yeah, that's encouraging.

T: Encouraging. Like your moving out into a bigger world was not an abandonment of her. She was, in a way, going right along with you and commenting on the experiences too.

I: [smiling] Right. Sometimes I do feel that, like when we are decorating our Christmas tree and I use all the old ornaments [shaping her hand into an ornament with a hook], and I show my kids, and I see her, and I put the music on that we had, too; I put on those old records that she used to put on. And she made us decorate the tree together, even when we were older and didn't want to do that together. And now I'm doing this with my kids, and then I sense that she would probably be looking on in some way.

T: Sure, sure. That's a lovely image. I mean, I have the sense of your being a *link* [holds up right hand] between her [reaching higher up] and these kids [reaching down, as if to the next generation], even to a point where they're being a little reluctant now; they're getting a little *big* for this [voice suggesting a joking tone]. But it's part of the family culture [voice slowing, becoming serious], and you're transmitting in some way something precious and unique, probably stories of her with the little ornaments that you're hanging in the tree [forming hands and fingers into ornaments with hooks and attaching them to a "tree" before him]. You're hanging a memory or connection.

I begin by sketching, in experience-near language and gestures, a brief rationale for our work: grieving is partly a matter of importing a portable secure base, derived from our ongoing relationship to the deceased, into our ongoing lives at a heartfelt level. Inge strongly resonates to this and produces two vivid examples, in the form of her proud inner conversations with Mom as she began living large in the world, fulfilling mother's dreams, and the sweet commemoration of Mother, her music and her stories during the holidays. Each ornament hung with her children on the tree is a link to Mom, as Inge is herself a link in a transgenerational story.

Holding the Feeling

I: Yeah. So there are things that *most* of the time, I should say, when I'm thinking of her, it makes me positive. It's more the feeling that comes when I don't invite it to. [Wipes eye.]

T: Ah, yeah, yeah [glancing up thoughtfully and shaking head slowly]. So sometimes those feelings will come uninvited. And of course, even if they're born of love, they carry strong feelings of loss. And I wonder if at those times it would be possible to find ways to invite Mom's presence alongside them, almost to help you *carry* them, you know [extends open hands, as if carrying something]. [Client nods.] When you describe this kind of box [makes box shape with hands at the level of his abdomen] that you kind of contain the feelings in, what did you say it is made of?

I: I don't know, something metal or very strong.

T: Like iron?

I: Yeah!

T: And what did you call her?

I: Oh! The Iron Lady!

T: The Iron Lady. Maybe she's in a very good position to help you with this. Maybe she specializes in some of the strength that you now need as you carry this feeling and share it with others who are willing to stand in it, for even a short time. It needn't be something you're alone with.

I: Yeah. [Nods.]

As she begins rewriting the terms of attachment to Mom, Inge confesses a problem: the invited memories may bring joy, but the uninvited ones can still bring pain. I then weave back to the metaphor of finding help carrying the grief and associate it to the container Inge and I co-constructed earlier: it, like Mom, is strong as iron. Completing this surprising connection, Inge brightens, and I feel a rush of emotion and admiration for Inge and the deep reconstruction of relation she is opening to after decades of impasse.

Re-engaging With Mom

T: [spoken emotionally] And that can be a loving gift that you allow your mother to give you, still, right? [Pause while client cries and nods, choked with emotion.] Do you have any mementos of her that you keep close to you?

I: I have a lot of things; I have her jewelry; I have her diaries that I have not read. I started to read, but I thought they were too personal and not meant for her children [laughs], so after reading a little bit. . .

T: [jokingly] Maybe some stories that we're not ready to hear! [Both laugh.]

I: So I have a lot of things of her. I put her *engagement ring* on [pointing to it proudly]. I never put it on, but I thought today. . .

T: Can I see? [Inge begins to take the ring off.)] No, leave it on. . . . It's quite beautiful [leaning in, touching it appreciatively].

I: So today I put it on because I thought. . .

T: Yeah, it's a large diamond, right? And is it surrounded by other stones, or is that a beautiful setting?

I: I think it's just a setting. And I never carried it. It's just in a box in my bathroom.

T: An *engagement* ring. And you *are* still engaged with her, aren't you? You're engaging with her right now.

I: Right.

T: [spoken with emotion] And this is a kind of present she gave you. [Pause, as client cries softly and nods.] The *present* of *presence*. And she *is* here with us, in a way. In this moment and this action. [Long pause, as client nods, gazes at the ring and exhales audibly.] Maybe this spontaneous action on your part, right [handing client a tissue to replace the one she has used], bringing this ring and wearing it as you have—it's almost like an intuitive recognition that this is what you need a little more of. It's not her *absence* but her *presence*, invited in this concrete way. And you bring her here to be with me [looking and gesturing to Mother's photo in the chair]; you invite others to hear the story. You kind of listen and look for opportunities to speak something of the beauty and the sadness of her life to those who are willing to hear the story. And there *are* some others [client nods, looking at therapist intently], if we seek them out carefully.

In deep and substantially shared emotion, Inge and I discover in her impromptu decision to wear her mother's engagement ring for the first time on this, her birthday, a remarkable linking object that helps cement their "re-engagement" with one another, after decades of disconnection. This "present of presence," given originally by mother to daughter and reciprocated by Inge's proudly wearing the ring to her session with me, now fully invokes Mom's presence in our therapy and, more importantly, in Inge's ongoing life. Reorienting in my remarks to this broader social world—with Erik in particular, watching with An and others in another room—I suggest that she has already taken strong steps toward the reopening of her mother's story to appreciative others, hinting at a social as well as personal reconstruction of the meaning of their shared lives in a way that calls forward Mother's presence.

Closing Reflections

T: [continuing emotionally] As we come into our final minutes of this session, Inge, I just want to acknowledge that I'm touched by your story. I'm touched by the love that you carry beyond the grave, giving it a place in you as you carry it with you through a life that continues to be touched by her absence but also by her strength. [Client nods.] And it feels like an offering to her that you don't only reserve only for her birthday. But in some important way, she's with you year-round. [Client cries and smiles.] [Pause] And I wonder if you have any thoughts or questions or concerns for me in these last minutes of our session, to anything we have spoken about, or where you would like to go with this?

I: I think I have realized through hearing this that I have tried to keep *her* in a box and keep the *feeling* very much in a box. But for me [spoken slowly, reflectively], I would feel better not putting it in a box but having her help me through it.

T: (summarizing, emotion in voice) "Maybe I would feel better not putting her in a box but having her help me through it." I don't think anyone could say it any better than that [both teary].

I: 'Cause I saw it as a negative thing, and maybe it's not a negative thing.

T: Maybe it's not a negative thing, right? Maybe that kind of silent sea can also become something other than just a threatening space, like it could become something *not* negative?

I: Yeah [nodding]. And I have had this feeling when she died, because I was so close to her, I think, that I was somewhat *uninvited* after her life.

T: That you were *uninvited* after her life?

I: [weeping] That there was something there that I knew I had to do my best to still be. . .

T: Like *she* was requiring that of you, or. . . ?

I: No, that she had been a *safe* place, and with her gone, I would have to fend for myself and prove my own worth without a safe place. . .

T: Just as she did.

I: Right.

T: Just as she did. To work hard to prove your worth? [Client nods yes.] But you also phrase that in the past tense, almost with an implication that maybe it doesn't have to *stay* that way? Maybe there's a *different* way to find security or. . . ?

I: [nodding] I realized, when I was younger, I thought I would just feel better once I had worked hard and earned a spot. And then I realized because I turned 40 this year, and I thought this feeling hasn't really changed, so it's not about getting better at things because I could get better and better in many things, but the feeling is not going to change.

T: Maybe this is a lesson of her life? [Client nods repeatedly.] And so what would be [spoken slowly] needed then, rather than more hard work? Is there a second message of her life that would give us a hint about that? Another way?

I: [long pause] I don't know.

T: There *seemed* to be something, right, that you glimpsed, in that idea of not just having to grimly carry it yourself in this contained fashion but having her help you with it. [Client nods.] It seemed almost as if that would be a shared weight to carry. I was just trying to imagine ways of inviting her in. Maybe this [gesturing to suggest the ring], the ring of *engagement*, is a way of inviting her in. But maybe there are other ways too?

I: Right [nodding], right.

Summarizing the key themes of the session and validating Inge's impressive if incipient reconstruction of her relationship with her mother, I invite her thoughts on where she is now. She responds with the articulation of new awareness: she has struggled for decades to box up both her grief and her mother, creating a prolonged, complicated grief that has changed minimally in 23 years. Her solution to this grief and the loss of the "safe place" her mother provided was, by identification with Mom, unremitting hard work to "prove" herself and earn a place in the world. Now, however, she realizes that no amount of success can achieve this, and she glimpses the radical possibility that inviting her mother's greater presence in her life might help restore the strength and safety she requires. In our closing minutes, we add further fuel to this bright flame of possibility.

Future Steps

T: What would be some? I guess you're inviting her in, in this conversation, right, with me. [Client: Yes.] This is one step. Would there be another step in the same direction?

I: [pause] That's hard to say. Because it's been such a long time, and the world where I am in now is very different.

T: Yeah. The world has changed, and you're still trying to learn it. But it seems like you're also still trying to find a world that is safe for your *mother*, right?

I: Yes.

T: How would it be to keep your mother's stories *alive*, in this world? And who might join you sometimes, in that? Just like at the Christmas tree. But not having to wait for *Kerstfeest* [Christmas] to do it, right?

I: Yeah [laughs]. My family, my children. It's hard with them because I feel I have to do my best.

T: Sure. But maybe the definition of what is the *best* can be [gesturing fluidly with hands] flexible, and not quite so. . . [gesturing to form the box], you know?

I: Yeah.

T: [looking up and nodding slowly] I had an idea . . . that your mom kept a journal; she obviously wrote about things that were personal and important and emotional to her. And my guess is that *you* are personal and important and emotional for her. And I wonder if in the way that you might have the conversations with Mom and maybe can even imagine writing a letter to Mom, if you could imagine *her* writing a letter back to *you*, right? [Picking up pad and pen.] What would she say? And did she call you Inge?

I: Yes.

T: And so if you would write a "Dear Mom" letter, what would the "Dear Inge" letter look like? [Pause] It might be something to experiment with, to almost give her your pen [extending pen toward client] and your hand [pantomiming writing]. Because I take it you *do* hold her inside of you [gestures toward heart] some ways. She's with you in a lot of ways [gesturing to suggest engagement ring]. And maybe she could have some voice. [Client: Yeah, yeah.] That could be her birthday gift. [Client, nodding repeatedly: Yeah, yeah.] A birthday letter to Inge. Now are you currently seeing a therapist?

I: I saw An; I'm seeing An, so yes.

T: Yeah, you're seeing An. So I wonder if we were to—if I were [to] help to share this crazy idea with An about a kind of correspondence with Mom, just as something to try out to invite her in a bit more, would that be of interest to you?

I: Yeah.

T: You think you could do that?

I: Yeah [nodding repeatedly].

T: So what I'll do, I'll look for a couple of moments to talk with An and just share this and brainstorm with her, and then maybe you and she could just try it out and see how it is for you, with no obligation to continue with it.

I: Yeah. That's a nice idea, yeah.

T: It's a nice idea. Well, you're a nice daughter. [Client laughs softly, moved.] And I think you are giving her the gift of your love *still*, on this birthday. [Client maintains strong eye contact through tears, as therapist leans in and shakes her hand firmly.] Thank you so much.

The session concludes with tears not of grief, but of hope, with the prospect that Mom's stories might find broader circulation in the world and that a daughter's outreach to a mother she still needs might be imaginatively reciprocated with the assistance of her therapist. A handshake concludes a session that honors not only the day of her mother's birth but also a day that symbolizes the rebirth of their relationship in continuing love.

THERAPEUTIC POSTSCRIPT

Viewing the live session by video feed in another room, An later noted that "Erik [and I] cried most of the session, being grateful to witness this from a distance and to hear many of Inge's stories about her mother, which, as he said afterward, he had never heard before. After the session he said he hoped this would stimulate more stories for them to share [about her mother and her grief], because this felt like something very connecting in an open and authentic way." Indeed, this hope was richly fulfilled in the days following the session, as documented in An's summary of their next marital therapy appointment a few days later, written immediately on its conclusion by drawing on notes that she, Inge and Erik decided to take in the session. Forwarded to Bob "as a gift coming from a feeling of gratitude," it read:

I just had a session with Inge and Erik, and of course we looked back on the session last week. This is what they told me:

About the Grief That Moved from a Box to an Externalized but Reachable Place

Inge was very surprised at having a "different feeling" toward her mother since the session. Working with TWO chairs, one for her grief and overwhelming sadness and one for her mother, was amazingly important to her, as she could now, for the first time in her grief process (!!), separate these two externalized "others." Importantly, she could now see and think about her mother in a way that was not only about an intense grief ("because that one was in the other chair"). Since Wednesday she has been able to connect with the memories of her mother, think about her, and recall all kinds of memories, without the grief interfering with them. She now was able to access a wide recollection of childhood memories with her mother in many situations (when they were at home during the weekends, when mom was working or preparing dinner, when they went for a trip with the family). She realized that she had captured her mother in a box of sadness for years, so that she could not reach her mother anymore without the overwhelming sadness.

Working with the two chairs has really helped her to separate the two, combined with your saying that "We need the dead person to help us in our grief, and be able to connect with them again."

About Her Realization of the Importance of Mothers

Another thing happening in the days following the session was her new understanding of the enormous importance of mothers for their children. Inge and Erik have 2 kids, and she has now started to think about her own importance as a mother to them and what she wants to be for them. This really touched me a lot, as this, too, was something she was struggling with, to find her significance as a mother to her kids. Wow!!

About the Gift for Her Mother

We made the connection that these new/old memories of her mother are also a gift for her deceased mother as well (what mothers would like NOT to be remembered because all their memories evoke is pain and sadness?!!). As mothers (or parents) we want to be remembered by our kids with a smile on their faces:-) You can guess I was very emotionally touched by this!!

About Erik's Presence

Erik added that he was very thankful to join her and witness this session from another room. He stressed the fact that it was very important that he got the opportunity not to be next to her but instead to watch this session from a place in which he was not drawn to help or comfort her. Now he was able to listen more carefully to what his wife told you. Inge agreed: if Erik would have been in the same room, she would attune with him, taking care of him, or being afraid to burden him, and being burdened by him. Being there on her own, with Bob, gave her "at least some sense of control."

Now that he witnessed this session, he felt he had the possibility or space to ask questions about her mother during this weekend, like "What did you do with your mother during the weekends when you were a kid?"

About the Importance of the Reflecting Team

They both stressed the importance of the opportunity they had to hear us reflect on this session. For them this created an opportunity to go over the session again and look at it from a more outside perspective, "making it more normal and objective in some way, being less 'abnormal.'"

Bob, for me this has been a very important training in grief therapy, in which (to note only one of many impacts) I am now very motivated to work with chairs to externalize feelings and the deceased. Thank you, Bob!! And as an immediate "proof": the next session, after Inge and Erik, I worked with several chairs . . . It was fascinating!!!—*Warmly, An*

CONCLUSION

The advent of contemporary scholarship concerning the continuing bond, amply documented in the present volume, has made clinical as well as conceptual contributions to many approaches to grief therapy. In this chapter, we have explored this contribution in the context of a model of grieving as meaning reconstruction (Neimeyer, 2019), which helps the client identify, symbolize, articulate and renegotiate a world of passionate meanings that have been challenged by loss. Although this orientation to grief work can be, and indeed has been, expressed in a structured treatment protocol incorporating specific modules and techniques (Neimeyer & Alves, 2016; see also Chapter 2), we have emphasized here the high degree of tailoring and improvisation of interventions characteristic of responsive psychotherapy of any kind, which are particularly close to the heart of constructivist practice (Neimeyer, 2009; Neimeyer & Mahoney, 1995). In this view, the conversation of therapy unfolds as a collaborative co-construction, as the therapist "leads from one step behind" to deepen and direct the client's engagement with implicit questions, significant emotion and experiential impasses that arise in the course of grieving. The result commonly is the generation of a series of "innovative moments" (IMs) in the process of therapy, in which client and therapist alike discover fresh meaning in the form of novel reflections, actions and emerging reconceptualization of the "dominant narrative" of the client's prolonged and intense mourning (Alves, Mendes, Gonçalves, & Neimeyer, 2012). Indeed, close process analysis of sessions of master therapists working in constructivist, existential and person-centered therapies with bereaved clients clearly documents the link between the sustained cultivation of IMs in grief therapy and improved outcome over the course of treatment (Piazza-Bonin, Neimeyer, Alves, Smigelsky, & Crunk, 2016; Piazza-Bonin, Neimeyer, Alves, & Smigelsky, 2016). As illustrated in the work with Inge, when the therapist is sufficiently attuned to the growing edge of the client's meaning making, the outcome can be a rapid reconstruction of how the client holds her grief and, equally important, how she holds the relationship to the deceased.

Given the prominence of cognitive behavioral formulations in contemporary psychotherapy, it could be tempting to construe such meaning reconstruction in highly cognitive terms, viewing therapy as a process of testing and revising the client's misinterpretations or dysfunctional beliefs in the context of bereavement (Malkinson, 2007). But without denying the utility of this perspective, we find the approach to grief work exemplified in this and other cases (Neimeyer, 2004, 2008) to bear greater similarity to emotion-focused (Greenberg, 2010), coherence-oriented (Ecker, 2012) and narrative therapies (Hedtke & Winslade, 2016), all of which share a constructivist or social constructionist epistemology. Like these kindred models, meaning reconstruction encourages the client to "follow the affect trail" to identify the client's implicit *need* and *readiness* to address it in each conversational turn of therapy. Therapeutic conversation itself is understood as a nuanced engagement with meaning only partially conveyed in explicit language and at least equally resident in the language of gesture, expression and embodiment on the part of both participants. Less evident in a typescript than in a video recording, even spoken language is taken as a multidimensional resource, conveying meaning in the prosodic rhythms and emphases of speech and in poetic and metaphoric exchanges as much as in denotative descriptions or directions (Mair, 2014; Neimeyer, 2009). Like two jazz musicians or improvisational actors, therapist and client each respond to the "offer" of the other in a way that moves therapy artfully in directions that neither could have predicted.

Finally, although our focus on a session of individual therapy risks suggesting that we view therapy, and indeed grieving itself, as a highly individualized psychological process, in fact we strongly believe that *all grief therapy is family therapy in absentia* (Hooghe & Neimeyer, 2012). This proposition holds at two levels. Most obviously, just as a continuing bonds perspective implies, grief therapy is inherently about the *relationship* between the living and the dead, so therapy sessions like the one with Inge conjure and utilize the presence of the deceased as a key component in treatment. But equally important, work done in even the most private of therapies carries active implications for the client's field of significant others, changing conversations, realigning relationships and inviting integration of the event story of the loss or the back story of the bond with the deceased into the family's shared narrative. In Inge's case, this was deliberately orchestrated in collaboration with her and her husband, Erik, who viewed the session from another room, thereby offering the couple both a desired buffer and bridge at the same moment. The subsequent processing of the experience in couples therapy and in their family life completed the circle and stimulated the ongoing performance of change initiated in the individual consultation. Therapists fostering reconstruction of meaning with a given client therefore require attunement to relevant family, social and cultural discourses that both support and constrain these efforts and that are subtly or substantially altered by them in turn.

In summary, grief therapy informed by a conceptualization of the continuing bond consists of far more than bereavement support for troubling feelings in the wake of loss—although it is that too. More fundamentally, such therapy seeks to surmount complications entailed in pervasive and prolonged grieving by helping mourners with (a) processing the sometimes tragic story of the death while also (b) accessing the back story of their relationship to the deceased, resolving issues in it and often restoring a measure of attachment security that was shattered by loss. We hope the illustration of this process in the re-engagement of Inge with her mother helps demystify this dimension of grief therapy for those colleagues who join us in this work, whatever their theoretical orientation.

Note

1. An abbreviated version of this chapter appeared in Klass, D., & Steffen, E. (Eds.). (2018). *Continuing bonds in bereavement: New directions for research and practice*. New York: Routledge. Included here with permission.

References

Alves, D., Mendes, I., Gonçalves, M., & Neimeyer, R. A. (2012). Innovative moments in grief therapy: Reconstructing meaning following perinatal death. *Death Studies, 36*, 785–818.

Bellet, B. W., Neimeyer, R. A., & Berman, J. S. (2016). Event centrality and bereavement symptomatology: The moderating role of meaning made. *Omega*. doi:10.1177/0030222816679659

Burke, L. A., Clark, K. A., Ali, K. S., Gibson, B. W., Smigelsky, M. A., & Neimeyer, R. A. (2015). Risk factors for anticipatory grief in family members of terminally ill veterans receiving palliative care services. *Journal of Social Work in End-of-Life and Palliative Care, 11*, 244–266. doi:10.1080/1552 4256.2015.1110071

Coleman, R. A., & Neimeyer, R. A. (2010). Measuring meaning: Searching for and making sense of spousal loss in later life. *Death Studies, 34*, 804–834.

Coleman, R. A., & Neimeyer, R. A. (2014). Assessment of subjective client agency in psychotherapy: A review. *Journal of Constructivist Psychology, 28*, 1–23.

Currier, J. M., Holland, J. M., & Neimeyer, R. A. (2006). Sense making, grief and the experience of violent loss: Toward a mediational model. *Death Studies, 30*, 403–428.

Ecker, B. (2012). Overt statements for deep work in grief therapy. In R. A. Neimeyer (Ed.), *Techniques of grief therapy: Creative practices for counseling the bereaved* (pp. 152–154). New York: Routledge.

Greenberg, L. S. (2010). *Emotion focused psychotherapy.* Washington, DC: American Psychological Association.

Hedtke, L. (2012). Introducing the deceased. In R. A. Neimeyer (Ed.), *Techniques of grief therapy: Creative practices for counseling the bereaved* (pp. 253–255). New York: Routledge.

Hedtke, L., & Winslade, J. (2016). *The crafting of grief.* New York: Routledge.

Holland, J. M., Currier, J. M., & Neimeyer, R. A. (2006). Meaning reconstruction in the first two years of bereavement: The role of sense-making and benefit-finding. *Omega, 53*, 173–191.

Hooghe, A., & Neimeyer, R. A. (2012). Family resilience in the wake of loss: A meaning-oriented contribution In D. Becvar (Ed.), *Handbook of family resilience.* New York: Springer.

Hooghe, A., Neimeyer, R. A., & Rober, P. (2012). "Cycling around an emotional core of sadness": Emotion regulation in a couple after the loss of a child. *Qualitative Health Research, 22*, 1220–1231.

Keesee, N. J., Currier, J. M., & Neimeyer, R. A. (2008). Predictors of grief following the death of one's child: The contribution of finding meaning. *Journal of Clinical Psychology, 64*, 1145–1163.

Klass, D., Silverman, P. R., & Nickman, S. (1996). *Continuing bonds: New understandings of grief.* Washington, DC: Taylor & Francis.

Kosminsky, P., & Jordan, J. R. (2016). *Attachment-informed grief therapy.* New York: Routledge.

Lichtenthal, W. G., Currier, J. M., Neimeyer, R. A., & Keesee, N. J. (2010). Sense and significance: A mixed methods examination of meaning-making following the loss of one's child. *Journal of Clinical Psychology, 66*, 791–812.

Mair, M. (2014). *Another way of knowing: The poettry of psychological inquiry.* London: Raven Books.

Malkinson, R. (2007). *Cognitive grief therapy.* New York: Norton.

Neimeyer, R. A. (Ed.). (2001). *Meaning reconstruction and the experience of loss.* Washington, DC: American Psychological Association.

Neimeyer, R. A. (2004). *Constructivist psychotherapy. Series 1: Systems of psychotherapy* [VHS video/DVD]. Washington, DC: American Psychological Association.

Neimeyer, R. A. (2006a). *Lessons of loss* (2nd ed.). New York: Routledge.

Neimeyer, R. A. (2006b). Widowhood, grief and the quest for meaning: A narrative perspective on resilience. In D. Carr, R. M. Nesse, & C. B. Wortman (Eds.), *Spousal bereavement in late life* (pp. 227–252). New York: Springer.

Neimeyer, R. A. (2008). *Constructivist psychotherapy over time* [DVD]. Washington, DC: American Psychological Association.

Neimeyer, R. A. (2009). *Constructivist psychotherapy.* London and New York: Routledge.

Neimeyer, R. A. (2012a). Analogical listening. In R. A. Neimeyer (Ed.), *Techniques of grief therapy: Creative pracices for counseling the bereaved* (pp. 55–58). New York: Routledge.

Neimeyer, R. A. (Ed.). (2012b). *Techniques of grief therapy: Creative practices for counseling the bereaved.* New York: Routledge.

Neimeyer, R. A. (2015a). Meaning in bereavement. In R. E. Anderson (Ed.), *World suffering and quality of life.* New York: Springer.

Neimeyer, R. A. (2015b). Treating complicated bereavement: The development of grief therapy. In J. Stillion & T. Attig (Eds.), *Death, dying and bereavement: Contemporary perspectives, institutions and practices* (pp. 307–320). New York: Springer.

Neimeyer, R. A. (Ed.). (2016). *Techniques of grief therapy: Assessment and intervention.* New York: Routledge.

Neimeyer, R. A. (2019). Meaning reconstruction in bereavement: Development of a research program. *Death Studies, 43*, 79–91. doi:10.1080/07481187.2018.1456620

Neimeyer, R. A., & Alves, D. (2016). Seeking meaning in loss: An online narrative constructivist intervention for complicated grief. *Grief Matters: The Australian Journal of Grief & Bereavment, 19*, 68–73.

Neimeyer, R. A., Klass, D., & Dennis, M. R. (2014). A social constructionist account of grief: Loss and the narration of meaning. *Death Studies* (38), 485–498.

Neimeyer, R. A., & Mahoney, M. J. (1995). *Constructivism in psychotherapy.* Washington, DC: American Psychological Association.

Neimeyer, R. A., & Thompson, B. E. (2014). Meaning making and the art of grief therapy. In B. E. Thompson & R. A. Neimeyer (Eds.), *Grief and the expressive arts: Practices for creating meaning* (pp. 3–13). New York: Routledge.

Perlman, L. A., Wortman, C. B., Feuer, C. A., Farber, C. H., & Rando, T. (2014). *Treating traumatic bereavement: A practitioner's guide.* New York: Guilford Press.

Piazza-Bonin, E., Neimeyer, R. A., Alves, D., & Smigelsky, M. A. (2016). Innovative moments in humanistic therapy II: Analysis of change across the course of three cases of grief therapy. *Journal of Constructivist Psychology*, 1–20. doi:10.1080/10720537.2015.1118713

Piazza-Bonin, E., Neimeyer, R. A., Alves, D., Smigelsky, M. A., & Crunk, E. (2016). Innovative moments in humanistic therapy I: Process and outcome of eminent psychotherapists working with bereaved clients. *Journal of Constructivist Psychology*, 1–29. doi:10.1080/10720537.2015.1118712

Prigerson, H. G., Horowitz, M. J., Jacobs, S. C., Parkes, C. M., Aslan, M., Goodkin, K., Raphael, B., . . . Maciejewski, P. K. (2009). Prolonged grief disorder: Psychometric validation of criteria proposed for DSM-V and ICD-11. *PLoS Medicine*, 6(8), 1–12.

Rozalski, V., Holland, J. M., & Neimeyer, R. A. (2016). Circumstances of death and complicated grief: Indirect associations through meaning made of loss. *Journal of Loss and Trauma.* doi:10.1080/15325024.2016.1161426

Rubin, S. S., Malkinson, R., & Witztum, E. (2011). *Working with the bereaved.* New York: Routledge.

Rynearson, E. K. (2012). Invoking an alliance with the deceased after violent death. In R. A. Neimeyer (Ed.), *Techniques of grief therapy* (pp. 91–94). New York: Routledge.

Rynearson, E. K., & Salloum, A. (2021). Restorative retelling: Revisiting the narrative of violent death. In R. A. Neimeyer, D. Harris, H. Winokuer, & G. Thornton (Eds.), *Grief and bereavement in contemporary society: Bridging research and practice* (pp. 177–188). New York: Routledge.

Thompson, B. E., & Neimeyer, R. A. (Eds.). (2014). *Grief and the expressive arts: Practices for creating meaning.* New York: Routledge.

2

The Meaning in Loss Group
Principles, Processes and Procedures

Robert A. Neimeyer, Evgenia (Jane) Milman
and Edith Maria Steffen

One notable feature of contemporary research in thanatology is the predominance of research in bereavement, eclipsing all other categories of studies in leading journals in the field (Wittkowski, Doka, Neimeyer, & Vallerga, 2015). In significant part, this burgeoning attention to grief and its treatment has been driven by the resurgence of time-honored theoretical perspectives in the field, such as attachment theory (Kosminsky & Jordan, 2016; Shaver & Fraley, 2008), alongside the emergence of new models of adaptation to loss that are generating their own evidence base and clinical implications (Neimeyer, 2015). In this chapter, we draw on one such perspective on grieving as a process of meaning reconstruction (Neimeyer, 2019) in outlining a novel Meaning in Loss Group intervention for mourners struggling with complicated bereavement, illustrating its core principles, processes and procedures with vignettes derived from its application in three quite different contexts. We begin with a brief research review to ground this effort and proceed to offer of a flexible manual of the group to provide guidance to fellow clinicians and researchers interested in implementing it in their own settings.

MEANING RECONSTRUCTION AND THE EXPERIENCE OF LOSS

As one major contribution to the "new look" in bereavement studies, a narrative constructivist approach posits that *a central process in grieving entails an attempt to reaffirm or reconstruct a world of meaning that has been challenged by loss* (Neimeyer, 2006, 2001). According to this view, we as human beings are inveterate constructors of meaning, who attempt to punctuate the endless flow of events into meaningful sequences and recurrent themes that allow us some measure of understanding, anticipation and control over our experiential worlds (Kelly, 1955). When life is going smoothly, this organization of experience proceeds implicitly, largely outside the purview of explicit awareness, forming a tacit backdrop for our conscious perceptions, intentions and actions (Polanyi, 1958). In such circumstances, life simply "makes sense," as we play our part in a social world populated by significant people and discourses on which we necessarily draw to construct a self-narrative that is uniquely our own and, with it, a sense of our evolving identity (Neimeyer, 2004; Neimeyer, Klass, & Dennis, 2014).

But in the context of traumatic life events of all kinds, and the death of significant people in our lives especially, this taken-for-granted meaning of our assumptive worlds can be profoundly tested and sometimes shattered (Janoff-Bulman & Berger, 2000). As a result,

DOI: 10.4324/9781351069120-3

survivors can be catapulted into a landscape made strange by loss, as well as into a painfully pressing search for meaning in its wake. A great deal of evidence has accrued over the last decade to support this meaning-making model, as research on diverse samples of bereaved young adults, parents and elders, who lose loved ones to both natural and violent death, has demonstrated that those who struggle to find significance in the experience are prone to intense, complicated and prolonged grief responses (Neimeyer, 2019). In contrast, those who are able to integrate the loss into their meaning systems show concomitant reductions in complicated grief symptomatology (Holland, Currier, Coleman, & Neimeyer, 2010) as well as the emergence of positive emotional states a year and a half to a full four years later (Coleman & Neimeyer, 2010). Finally, meaning making appears to mediate between such risk factors as violent death bereavement (Currier, Holland, & Neimeyer, 2006; Rozalski, Holland, & Neimeyer, 2016) or spiritual crisis in loss (Lichtenthal, Burke, & Neimeyer, 2011) on the one hand and the intensity of complicated grief symptoms on the other, as well as to moderate the impact of "high centrality" loss events on bereavement adaptation (Bellet, Neimeyer, & Berman, 2017).

In keeping with this evidence base, a growing range of meaning-oriented narrative interventions has been proposed, generating a great variety of psychotherapeutic and expressive arts methods (Neimeyer, 2012b, 2012e, 2021; Thompson & Neimeyer, 2014). Moreover, several therapies drawing on such methods are beginning to be assessed using both open and randomized trial methodologies, with encouraging results (Lichtenthal & Cruess, 2010; MacKinnon et al., 2012; Neimeyer & Young-Eisendrath, 2015; Saindon et al., 2014).

A MEANING IN LOSS GROUP INTERVENTION

Our present attempt to extend these promising developments outlines a Meaning in Loss Group (MLG) intervention, which we have been developing and refining in a multi-site collaboration in Canada, the United Kingdom and the United States. Here we will orient readers to a few of the principles that frame the group and then describe its format and procedures, illustrating each of the weekly modules by drawing on case vignettes arising from our use of the group in all three nations. Throughout, we will note variations in modules to enhance their relevance in different settings or with different populations and will offer process observations and recommendations for colleagues interested in implementing it in part or in full in their own contexts.

PRINCIPLES

Situated within a narrative constructivist theoretical frame (Neimeyer, 2009), the MLG shares core principles exemplified by other therapies animated by this perspective. These include a respect for clients as inveterate makers of meaning and a view of therapy as a process for enhancing clients' "connoisseurship" of their experience: that is, for helping them name and claim the nuances of their own responses to life circumstances, allowing them to make more informed choices moving forward. In the present context, this implies that therapy should assist participants in enhancing their "emotional literacy" regarding their grief, drawing on a broad range of procedures for exploring, articulating and renegotiating the implicit meanings that have been challenged and changed by the loss. Beyond this, the MLG embodies a number of other principles, summarized here:

- *The therapist operates more as a "guide on the side" than as a "sage on the stage."* That is, therapy is less psychoeducational than exploratory, with group leaders introducing methods of client self-discovery and empowerment and offering support for their use, in contrast to adopting an expert stance as teachers of an approved set of coping skills, Socratic critics of members' dysfunctional thoughts or authorities in correct or incorrect ways to grieve a loss (Neimeyer, 2009).

- *Therapists are process directive more than content directive.* As a corollary of the first principle, group leaders introduce tools and topics for group exploration and discussion, leaving it to members to address their relevance in the context of their unique losses.

- *All change arises in moments of experiential intensity; everything else is merely commentary.* That is, modules are designed to promote emotionally vivid engagement with the "event story" of the death, as well as the "back story" of the relationship to the bereaved (Neimeyer & Thompson, 2014). More "cognitive" reflections on this experience can play a role in consolidating change, but less in stimulating it.

- *As a form of experiential learning, therapy is anchored in concrete experience, promotes personal reflection, engages clients with new ideas and possibilities and prompts active experimentation with a changed world.* It is this iterative process of feeling, reflecting, reconceptualizing and acting (Kolb, 1984) that reconstructs a world of meaning that has been challenged by loss.

- *New meaning arises between people, as well as within them.* In the crucible of group therapy, poignant and often lively dialogue with other bereaved persons promotes the voicing and validation of personal experience, as well as opportunities to approach the loss differently. Another way of phrasing this is that mourning and meaning are *situated, interpretive and communicative activities* or forms of social construction, rather than merely emotional or cognitive processes situated within individuals (Neimeyer et al., 2014).

THERAPISTS

Before presenting the content of the modules that comprise the MLG, a word about the leadership of the groups is required. To date, all implementations of the protocol have been conducted by doctoral-level psychotherapists in the fields of clinical or counseling psychology or graduate-level trainees or interns in these disciplines under the supervision of experienced doctoral-level mentors. Alternative credentials in other therapeutic professions such as social work, psychiatry, pastoral care or advanced practice nursing could certainly be equally suitable. However, especially when applied to complicated cases of bereavement as defined by various risk factors associated with the mourner, the circumstances of the death or the relationship to the deceased (Neimeyer & Burke, 2017), ensuring adequate professional training in working with bereavement and with groups is essential; the MLG is not designed for use in bereavement support contexts by volunteers or entry-level therapists unless they are closely supported and supervised. This said, some of the modules that follow may be used electively in a support group context as noted.[1]

A further recommendation is to engage a team of two co-therapists in running each group, although an experienced therapist can run a successful group alone. However, working with a colleague permits a division of responsibilities in conducting different activities within a single group session, allows one therapist to focus on group management while the other attends to member signals of engagement or emotion and carries practical advantages in implementing the distinctive dyadic format within the context of the larger group, as noted later. It is also an optimal structure for mentoring and modeling in training contexts, where a more experienced colleague can be paired with a developing therapist for implementing and supervising the group.

GROUP FORMAT

In the process of implementing the MLG, we have found that the optimal arrangement for the MLG is a series of two-hour sessions, held at the same day and time across 12 successive weeks. Care should be taken to avoid major religious and secular holidays, and pre-screening interviews (see later in this chapter) should confirm the workability of the schedule with prospective members to minimize absences. The MLG adopts a closed-group structure, meaning that participation each week is expected (with allowances for unforeseen events and illness), with a consistent membership from the first session to the last. Because modules (and group cohesion) build across sessions, care should be taken not to add new members once a group is underway. However, some variations in this format can prove workable (e.g., a 90-minute session in the case of smaller groups or even offering the MLG in a series of 4- to 6-hour weekend workshops, for a total of 24 hours).

A distinctive feature of the MLG is the frequent use of dyadic interactions within the larger plenary group structure, as noted in the description of modules to follow. This entails breaking the group of 6 to 12 members into pairs at a designated point in the session for one-on-one sharing on an assigned topic (e.g., introducing the loved one, sharing one's chapters of life or timeline or reading imaginal correspondence with the deceased). These exchanges are usually brief (15 to 30 minutes in total), during which the therapists circulate through the group, pausing to listen in briefly, sometimes offering support or making recommendations, or come to address a question or concern in response to a raised hand. Following the dyadic interaction, the pairs are reconvened in a larger group circle to process observations of the individual members, with the proviso that while self-disclosure is always welcome, members do a check-in with one another before sharing an observation about their partners. Often, this subsequent plenary session will then carry through the remainder of the session, though in some cases, it is held within a certain time frame to conserve time for a further topic or activity. Care is taken to organize different pairings of partners in each session so as to discourage subgrouping and promote broader group cohesion across sessions.

The dyadic format offers several advantages over a more typical plenary-only group format. These include:

- *Encouraging fuller engagement* on the part of all group members, with each having equal "talk time" in the pairing and sharing period.
- *Constraining group dominance* by more talkative, extraverted or high-need group members.
- *Participation of therapists in the dyads* to give extra time or support to especially high-need participants, as well as to even out a group having an odd number of members.
- *Provision of greater safety and intimacy* in the dyadic work, especially at the outset of the group, when speaking of intimate issues with a whole group of strangers can be daunting for many.
- *Multiplication of the time available*, through the opportunity for all group members to speak simultaneously, in effect adding another hour or more of conversational time (e.g., considering the seven to ten minutes available to each member of a ten-member group) without stretching the actual time block assigned for the session.
- *Priming of plenary group processing* with a rich variety of individual and relational observations garnered from the dyadic activity.
- *Promoting experiential intensity* by offering the necessary interpersonal intimacy, safety and individual speaking time required for adequate experiential processing. The dyadic format also fosters experiential intensity by compensating for the didactic atmosphere that can sometimes develop in the context of a strictly plenary group format.

In addition, subdividing the larger group of eight to ten into two smaller groups of four or five can be effective for group processes that encourage the sharing of personal writing (such as the Hello Again Letter or Virtual Dream Stories), with each being facilitated by one of two co-therapists. As with the dyadic format, this structure encourages participation on the part of more reticent members while offering greater diversity of responses, often easing members' transition into greater subsequent whole group sharing.

Content of the Modules

In both its online (Neimeyer & Alves, 2017) and group-therapy implementation, the Meaning in Loss intervention is organized according to a meaning reconstruction rationale, which views bereaved people as facing two narrative challenges posed by the death of a significant person in their lives (Neimeyer & Thompson, 2014). The first of these is to *process the "event story" of the death itself*, in order to make sense of it and its implications for their lives as survivors. The second is to *access the "back story" of the life shared with the loved one*, in order to restore or reconstruct a measure of attachment security and resolve any unfinished business with the deceased. Importantly, these are not viewed or engaged as merely "cognitive" processes but, in keeping with a constructivist epistemology, carry profound emotional and behavioral implications. As a reflective, emotion-focused, narrative intervention, the MLG has as its overarching goal the integration of the loss into the larger story of the survivor's life, in a way that informs rather than invalidates the client's intentions and actions going forward.

Contexts of the Present Groups

As part of our ongoing feasibility trial of the MLG, we intentionally have experimented with variations of the setting and structure of the group across trial implementations. Here we will briefly describe these variations, noting differences in group leadership, member composition, session format and institutional setting across each. Further vignettes from the three settings will then be offered in subsequent sections to illustrate the presentation of techniques in each module as well as features of group management and process, drawing on detailed session notes as well as recordings of sessions of therapy and supervision.

Montreal, Canada

This group was conducted by an advanced doctoral student in counseling psychology (JM), who had already completed a master's degree in this same program. Supervision took place on a weekly basis via videoconferencing with a PhD-level clinical psychologist with 40 years of experience (RAN). The group was offered at a Jewish community service organization that provides a range of outpatient mental health services to the general public in a large urban setting. (Clients need not be Jewish to qualify for care.) Prospective members of the group were pre-screened for appropriateness (see later in this chapter), yielding eight participants, seven women and one man, ranging in age from 23 to 59 years old. All participants had lost close relationships to death, including parents, a spouse, a child and a sibling. The deaths occurred from a variety of natural causes (e.g., cancer, cardiac arrest) and violent causes (e.g., fatal accident, suicide). The group met for 90 minutes in the evening for 12 weeks, with occasional hiatuses (e.g., to accommodate major Jewish holidays).

Memphis, USA

This group was conducted by a highly experienced PhD psychologist (RAN), in collaboration with two pastors in the context of a bereavement support group offered in a large Episcopal congregation. In keeping with the practice of bereavement support in that community, no pre-screening of participants took place, though most had attended one or both of the educational talks offered by the psychologist on "Grief and the Quest for Meaning" approximately two months before the group was launched. The three co-therapists met to allocate responsibilities before each session and briefly processed each group afterward. To accommodate the time constraints required by the church on the length of both individual sessions and the program as a whole, participants met weekly for a single hour, and using an abbreviated protocol of seven sessions. The 11 group members were considerably diverse in the character of their losses, with 3 bringing ambiguous, non-death losses (Harris, 2020) (e.g., of a marriage or career), and 1 bringing concerns about mortality more generally (i.e., personal death anxiety and fear of the impact of his ultimate death on his children, though he had no particular medical risk or suicide ideation). Literal bereavement was similarly diverse, ranging from the normative death of a partner in later life to quite traumatic losses, as in the stillbirth of one participant's grandchild, followed by the suicide of the child's mother (the participant's daughter) a few months later and, finally, the suicide of the surviving son-in-law two months after that. Similarly, another participant had lost not one, but two of his young adult children to suicide.

London, UK

This group was led by a PsyD counseling psychologist (EMS) with over ten years' clinical experience and a PhD clinical psychologist with eight years' clinical experience. The work was supervised via weekly-to-biweekly videoconferencing by RAN with the support of JM. The group ran in the research clinic at the Centre for Research in Social and Psychological Transformation (CREST) at the University of Roehampton, London, UK. The London iteration of the MLG was specifically designated for nonviolent losses and incorporated a greater continuing bonds focus throughout. Group members were recruited via the University's counseling service and two local bereavement services, Cruse Richmond and Kingston Bereavement Service. Following pre-screening, eight participants who had lost someone through natural causes such as cancer or cardiac arrest were recruited: six women and two men, ranging in age from late 20s to 80s. Participants had experienced a variety of losses: three had lost a parent, three had lost a partner, one had lost two grandparents and one had lost a child. The group ran one evening a week for 12 consecutive weeks. Each session was two hours in duration with a 15-minute tea-and-biscuit break in the middle to enable participants to make informal contact with each other, facilitating group cohesion.

Pre-Screening Session

Optimally, we recommend that therapists arrange a 30- to 60-minute individual screening session for prospective group members to evaluate their appropriateness for group work (their ability to work adequately with others as suggested by discussion of previous experiences in workplace or therapy groups and the screener's observations), their level of distress (not so high as to be likely to dominate the group process or pose a risk to self or others requiring closer individual monitoring) and their goals and expectations for the group (broadly compatible with the therapy to be offered). In addition to requesting a brief description of the interviewee's life circumstances and loss experience, the clinician describes the general structure and objectives of the group, offers admission to the group or recommends other services (such as individual or family therapy or psychiatric consultation) and addresses questions raised by the prospective participant. When admitted to the group, interviewees benefit from having begun to develop an alliance with the therapist, just as the therapist begins the group with greater foreknowledge of the members' circumstances, struggles and strengths. When pre-screening is infeasible, there exists a risk of greater heterogeneity in membership, high levels of need, and other factors that can prove challenging, especially for less-experienced group facilitators.

In the Memphis church-based "grief support" group, the unanticipated presence of several members presenting non-bereavement-related losses (of long-term marriages, personal concerns about mortality and dismissal from a lifelong career) required impromptu reframing of interventions in several modules, as noted later. It also called for adroit management of dyadic work to pair these participants initially with one another to promote a greater level of identification with the partner than might have been the case otherwise (e.g., if one client grieving divorce were paired with another struggling with the overdose of an adult son). Likewise, inability to screen for very high levels of emotional press on the part of some members necessitated skillful direction of the group process, as well as special accommodation of the needs of two group members (who were often paired with group leaders in the dyadic work to give them more attention). Although these efforts were largely successful, prudent screening could have led to the selection of members having greater commonality and ability to benefit from the group with fewer challenges.

Thorough assessment of whether a prospective participant is appropriate for the group therapy format not only serves the purpose of identifying those who are best suited for individual therapy, but also allows MLG facilitators to anticipate potentially disruptive interpersonal dynamics as well as to prepare future group members to work with other grieving individuals. In the Montreal iteration of the MLG, JM began by probing interviewees' experiences in diverse group settings (e.g., "When you find yourself in a group—at work, among friends or close family members—what are the challenges you encounter, and how do you benefit from being in a group?"). JM then followed with open-ended questions assessing interviewees' perceptions of how they contribute to group contexts. For example, prospective interviewees were asked: "What roles do you find yourself taking on when you are in a group? An example might be the caretaker, the expert, the voice of reason, the fly on the wall or the center of attention. Keep in mind that your role may change depending on the group you are in—you might be the caretaker among close family members but a fly on the wall at work. What role do you see yourself playing in this grief group?" In one case, an interviewee expressed that she planned to be the "grief expert" in the group. This was addressed in the pre-screening session first by validating the interviewee's positive intentions and the usefulness of the insights she has gained into the grief process. JM then highlighted the importance of not offering simple solutions to complex lived struggles and emphasized the varied and contrasting truths of every grieving individual. Following pre-screening, RAN and JM explored various means of minimizing the disruptive potential of this individual's self-proclaimed "expert" status. This included pairing her strategically in dyads either with the therapist or with other assertive group members as well as emphasizing active listening rather than advice giving as a norm at the onset of the group.

In the Montreal iteration of the MLG, the pre-screening session also explored interviewees' tolerance for diverse presentations of grief. In one case, an interviewee expressed disdain for anyone "capable of getting rid" of the deceased's belongings. Further probing revealed that this disdain developed in response to the interviewee receiving repeated instructions to "move on" by "cleaning out" her husband's closet. It can be challenging for the bereft to encounter presentations of grief that contrast their own, particularly if they have been exposed to judgments about the "right" and the "wrong" ways to grieve.

We will now provide a session-by-session discussion of the MLG, illustrating each with vignettes from groups conducted in the feasibility trial. As we do so, we will offer lessons learned and tips for implementing or extending various techniques in future iterations of the program.

Phase 1: Reopening the Story

Session 1: Introduction. Therapists meet members at the door of the group room to welcome them to the session, encouraging them to choose a chair from those drawn into a circle in a space lit by warm natural or incandescent light. Following an orientation to group rules and norms (e.g., confidentiality, turn taking), therapists describe the focus and structure of the group and invite members to give a brief summary of the losses they have sustained in a whole-group format to invite sharing and support among participants. Group leaders then facilitate a discussion of the members' concerns, hopes and goals for the therapy. The session concludes by inviting each to bring to the next session a special object that symbolizes the deceased (e.g., a cherished belonging of the loved one, a photo or something that symbolically reminds them of that person). For losses that are nonfinite, members may bring an object that represents what they have lost (e.g., a wedding band no longer worn, a musical instrument from a prior career in performance).

In the introductory session, we recommend that facilitators offer group members specific guidelines regarding the brief summary of loss they are invited to share. In the Montreal iteration of the MLG, JM instructed members to "describe the first day of either learning about or being present for the death of your loved one." She then reassured the group that "we will return to your stories of loss in just a couple of sessions and explore them in their entirety, making sure that we give these stories the time and attention they deserve." In addition to helping facilitators manage the time limits of the group, offering these explicit narrative parameters can relieve participants' anticipatory anxiety about capturing the entirety of their loss as they first introduce it to a group of near strangers. Crucially, specifying the focus of the loss story can also help contain group members whose narratives may be unstructured and emotionally overwhelming both for the individual sharing and for the remaining group members, many of whom may never have encountered numerous and diverse grief narratives prior to the first session of the MLG.

The discussion of group members' hopes, goals and concerns for therapy need not take on a routine or banal quality. To the contrary, this is one of the first opportunities for the facilitator to build group cohesion by highlighting similar sentiments among the group. It is also a forum for the facilitators to share their own hopes, goals and concerns as a means of building alliances and preempting problematic group processes that may have been flagged in the pre-screening session. For example, in the Montreal iteration of the MLG, JM shared her hope that the group would be a safe space that respected diverse presentations of grief; this prompted a discussion among group members about tolerating differences in each other's experiences. Accordingly, by sharing hopes, concerns and goals for the group, JM fostered a non-punitive and non-didactic discussion targeting potentially disruptive interpersonal dynamics signaled during pre-screening.

Session 2: Introducing Your Loved One. In keeping with a narrative conception of relational bonds (Hedtke & Winslade, 2016), therapists encourage group members to not merely share who had died but also who had lived. Forming the members into dyads, they invite each member of the pair to offer a "thick description" of who the loved one was as a person, as a member of the family and especially in relation to the client, using the significant objects they had brought as a "linking object" to the deceased in a way that helps them describe and validate their special qualities, signature strengths and particular moments in their lives that revealed who they were as people. To assist in this, partners are given a handout of possible interview questions, such as "Who was ___ to you? What did having ___ in your life mean to you?" "Are there particular stories that ___ would want us to know about her life?" and "What might ___ say he appreciated about you and how you might deal with the challenges you are facing now?" However, members are encouraged to innovate on these questions in directions that interest them or as they follow the leads provided by the story of who the deceased was. This dyadic phase, allowing as much as 15 minutes or more per partner, is followed by whole-group processing, beginning with each group member introducing the *partner's* description of their deceased loved one to the group. Witnessing a fellow group member introduce the loved one to the group promotes both a sense of empathic mirroring and a "self-distancing" perspective to help members modulate their own emotions and see the relationship in clearer terms (Kross & Ayduk, 2010). In the case of ambiguous losses, the leaders invite descriptions of spouses at a happier point in the relationship, before the divorce or of the self that preceded the loss of career or health, etc.

As mentioned earlier, the London iteration of the group had a stronger continuing bonds emphasis throughout, and the "Introducing Your Loved One" (Hedtke, 2012) activity fit particularly well with this focus. Within a group context, this activity encourages not only the narrative reconstruction of the bond between individual members and their deceased loved ones, but also the sharing of this bond with others, giving the deceased a new place among the living. A potentially narrow unitary relationship between the bereaved and the deceased is thus extended into a more complex network of relationships and meanings involving past, present and future. This process of "re-membering" (Hedtke, 2018) can take different forms, and the group context lends itself well to the integration of ritual, a shared act or practice of embodied meaning. In the London group, therapists therefore reserved some time at the end of Session 2 to introduce the idea of a "group legacy project" and to invite participants to consider different suggestions, contribute their own ideas and reflect on the alternatives between this session and the next. Among the ideas put forward were the creation of loss boxes (Krawchuk, 2016), a memory board to pin photos or cards with significant messages on or a table on which meaningful mementos of the loved ones could be placed. Group members expressed preference for such a "legacy table." A small table was placed at one end of the group room, and members were invited to bring in meaningful objects that could remain on the table during the session. The first items that were placed there were some of the objects that participants had brought in when introducing their loved ones. For example, one participant brought a bottle of perfume that had belonged to her mother and seemed to capture her mother's glamorous nature. The sensory quality of the beautifully shaped bottle and its scent bestowed a new bodily reality on the deceased, now accessible to everyone in the room. Another participant brought a small teddy bear, which had been a gift from her mother on her wedding day, one of two teddy bears incorporated into her wedding bouquet to represent the grandparents who could not be there, thus signifying a multi-generational continuing bond. One participant who had lost his wife brought in a small giraffe that had been on her desk and said that by having it there, it meant to him "She's here!" Another participant, who had lost her father, brought in a small toy deer, a rare gift from her father, which he had given to her to show how proud he was of her. She told us, "Putting it on the table so that everyone can see—this is really meaningful to me."

Phase 2: Processing the Event Story of the Loss

Session 3: Loss Timeline. As a way of scaffolding the group members' overall life trajectories and tracing their personal loss histories, therapists coach them to construct a *loss timeline* (Dunton, 2012) that includes significant points of personal transition, noting their emotional and practical response to each and segmenting these into *chapters of their lives* with distinct titles (Neimeyer, 2014). Alternatively, they are encouraged to construct this "table of contents" of their life story without the actual depiction of a timeline, though the addition of colors using oil pastel crayons and drawings or symbols of events can enrich the timeline exercise for many. Acknowledging previous losses that punctuated the members' life stories and placing them in chronological order allows participants to recognize the role of these events in giving shape to their self-narrative, revealing previous means of coping and biographical and relational sources of resilience. Likewise, breaking into dyads and combing through the timelines respectfully and with curiosity often allows them to recognize recurrent themes (e.g., of challenge and survival, self-sacrifice or the resurgence of hope) and to connect their experiences across time to relevant family, cultural or spiritual expectations and resources. Participants then return to the plenary group format after approximately half an hour (15 minutes for each partner) and report their most significant insights and observations.

Interest was high in the Memphis group when the timeline was presented, as members used oil pastel crayons and large format art paper to depict the ups and downs of their lives in a variety of roller-coaster, map and game-board motifs. While most participants wrote in words to mark and define both welcome changes (first love, giving birth to a child) and unwelcome ones (being made redundant, loss of a relationship, death of a family member), others conveyed these in symbols, usually anchored by significant dates or ages. Discussion was animated when this individual activity bridged to dyadic sharing and then back to the group, with pairs using one another's timelines to introduce their partner more fully to the group as a whole. Processing then continued on a whole-group level, as therapists asked questions to tease out major shared or distinctive themes, to prompt members to consider the role of loss in punctuating the stories of their lives and to imagine what the next chapter might look like were the story to move in a more hopeful direction. As nearly all members had encountered many similar disappointments, joys and struggles, whatever the loss they presented in the first session of the group, this session helped deepen their mutual identification with one another and build group cohesion. The group concluded with leaders encouraging members to commit to some concrete "action step" they could take before the next session to nudge their lifelines in a wished-for direction.

Session 4: Meaning Reconstruction Interview. Therapists welcome clients back and briefly review their experiences in attempting action steps in the intervening week, validating successes and troubleshooting impediments. Having sketched the landscape of loss in their lives in the previous session, group members are now in a position to delve into the stories of their losses more fully, drawing on the general structure of the Meaning Reconstruction Interview (Neimeyer, 2006). This flexible framework suggests a sequence of *Entry, Experiencing, Explanation* and *Elaboration* questions, with several examples of each that can be adapted to the client's needs. Breaking members again into pairs, therapists encourage clients to recall details of the loss, how they responded at that time and how this feeling has evolved since (Entry); deepen into visualization of critical scenes and their associated embodied emotions (Exploration); progress to inquiries into the sense they made about the loss when it occurred and any philosophic or spiritual beliefs that helped them do so (Explanation) and conclude with questions about the longer-term import or lessons the loss carried for their lives or sense of self (Elaboration).

Importantly, in longer-group formats or when the smaller number of members permits it, therapists implement special procedures for retelling the narrative of the death to promote greater emotion regulation and sense making in the face of a traumatic loss experience (Neimeyer, 2012c). Drawing on protocols developed by Rynearson and his colleagues, this involves encouraging dyads to slowly review the more difficult details of the dying narrative as therapists support them in achieving greater mastery over the experience without relying on avoidance coping (Rynearson & Salloum, 2021). In this case, Experiencing and Explanation questions are prioritized, whereas these are touched on more lightly when losses are more normative, when less time is available per participant or when a single therapist is present to offer support. This suggests the value of allotting additional group or individual sessions to this procedure when the MLG focus explicitly targets more traumatic forms of bereavement.

The session concludes with directed journaling homework, which encourages further reflective writing around specific prompts to help the client consolidate sense making and benefit finding regarding the experience (Lichtenthal & Neimeyer, 2012).

In the Montreal iteration of the MLG, the return to the plenary format during the Meaning Reconstruction Interview (MRI) session offered an opportunity for JM to foster group-level meaning making and, by extension, to build group cohesion. The Explanation and Elaboration components of the MRI were particularly relevant for this task because they encouraged group members to articulate their emerging sense of how grief had shaped their experience of the world, their lives, their identities and the future; other group members then reinforced, challenged or built on these tentative attempts at meaning making. JM guided this process by inviting group members to expand on verbal and nonverbal micro-expressions using comments such as "Michael, when Alice mentioned her lost sense of innocence after her daughter's death, you sighed—can you share with us what was happening for you?" or "Alice, it looked like it really touched you when Michael said that since his wife died, he really notices 'those little moments' of affection with his children—can you share what it was like for you to hear that?" By encouraging elaboration of group members' less formulated, emotion-laden micro-reactions, JM guided the group toward a more immediate and experiential engagement with the meaning-making process. In the absence of such process-level guidance, group members tended to hold back visceral moments of meaning making in favor of presenting intellectualized, cognitively focused responses to one another.

Phase 3: Exploring Sources of Meaning

Session 5: Models of Grief. Having drawn forth a good deal of emotionally significant material in the previous two sessions and the journaling that followed, Session 5 provides an opportunity for clients to sift through the memories, emotions and themes that have emerged and to gain further perspective on them in light of various contemporary models of grief. To facilitate this, therapists briefly describe the *Dual-Process Model* of coping, with its depiction of oscillating attention to the loss and restored living (Stroebe & Schut, 2010); the *Two-Track Model* of bereavement, with its emphasis on both biopsychosocial symptoms of grief and the pre- and post-mortem relationship with the deceased (Rubin, Malkinson, & Witztum, 2011) and the *Shattered Assumptions Model*, with its description of the fracturing of implicit beliefs in justice, predictability and control resulting from a tragic loss (Janoff-Bulman & Berger, 2000). In each case, therapists join with clients in considering the applicability of the concepts to their own experience of loss in order to give them greater intelligibility and to consider what one of the models implies about what most requires therapeutic attention in their case (e.g., reaching out to caring others to rebuild a shattered sense of trust, behavioral activities that help them confront avoided experiences or practice of meditation or exercise to regulate dysregulated emotion). Clients discuss these action steps with one another in dyads and commit to performing at least one in the next week. The session concludes with assigning the task of writing a *Hello Again Letter*, as discussed later, taking care to collaborate with the client in constructing conditions of safety and usually privacy in engaging this emotionally evocative assignment.

Despite its focus on describing various models of grief, this session is not intended to take on a didactic quality. Accordingly, in the Montreal iteration of the MLG, JM encouraged experiential engagement with each model of grief by tentatively drawing on group members' personal experiences to introduce the grief models. For example, rather than presenting a detailed description of the Dual-Process Model and then asking participants to offer relevant examples, JM began the discussion by noting, "Jen, a few sessions ago, you expressed feeling emotionally exhausted staying home alone and thinking about your brother's death all day long. Then, Michael, you mentioned feeling equally exhausted when you tried to distract yourself from thinking about your daughter's death by keeping extra busy with work and friends. That discussion reminded me of how grief has been described in terms of movement between times when you're focused on the loss, like you were describing, Jen, and times when you're focused on re-engaging with life, like you were describing, Michael. The idea is that staying only in one orientation can be exhausting, so it's helpful to focus on alternating between them. Does that feel like it fits what you both have experienced?" In this way, participants first encountered each model in the context of their lived realities, rather than as a didactic lesson.

During this session, for the first time in the course of the MLG, group members are given a between-session exercise to complete: the Hello Again Letter. Anxiety-based avoidance can be anticipated whenever group members are asked to engage in a new experience that challenges them to explore their grief. In sharing this anxiety with one another, members can sometimes reinforce each other's avoidance of such experiences. For this reason, in the Montreal iteration of the MLG, all between-session exercises were introduced at the end of the session with a concise description. At this point, questions and clarifications were welcomed; however, in order to steer the group away from anxious rumination and avoidance, JM did not encourage participants to discuss how they felt about the prospect of carrying out the exercise. Instead, in the following session, she explored the process of completing the exercise. In the absence of anticipatory anxiety, this post-hoc reflection prompted meaning making and built group cohesion.

Phase 4: Accessing the Back Story of the Relationship with the Deceased

Session 6: Hello Again Letter. Phase 4 marks a shift from focusing predominantly on the event story of the death to concentrating on the back story of the relationship to the deceased, not only in life but also beyond the loved one's death. In keeping with a contemporary continuing bonds model of bereavement (Klass & Steffan, 2017), the goal of this phase is to provide resources for helping the bereaved reconstruct, rather than relinquish, their attachment to the deceased, affirming it in a form that is sustainable in the person's physical absence. Session 6 builds on the preliminary work in Session 2 involving introducing the loved one by reviewing clients' writing of an unsent letter to the bereaved, the goal of which is to say "hello again" rather than a final "goodbye" (White, 1989). Many clients need no further encouragement than to write as if to the deceased, to speak to the heart of their relationship, how it is for them now and what they hope or plan for going forward, sometimes spontaneously addressing lingering concerns or regrets and seeking or extending forgiveness as well as affirming love. However, when they are uncertain how to begin, therapists can offer any of several "conversation starters" in the form of incomplete sentences, such as *My most treasured memory of you is . . ., The one question I have wanted to ask you is . . .* or *I want to keep you in my life by . . .* (Neimeyer, 2012a). Having completed this letter between Sessions 5 and 6, clients pair up and read the letter aloud to their partners (unless they request that their partners read it to them), in order to witness, validate and explore the passionate feelings and meanings it conveys. Dyadic conversations continue, discussing the emotions and insights that arose for each pair in both the writing and the reading. After further processing the content and process of this writing in the plenary group format, therapists suggest that clients write back letters to themselves on behalf of the loved one as between-session homework, in a way that addresses the feelings, questions and needs that their own letters implicitly or explicitly contained. For those dealing with nonfinite losses, writing to an earlier version of a partner or the self can substitute for a letter to the deceased, with equal effect.

In the London MLG, the group split in two small groups with one facilitator each in this session. One participant, Eva, spoke about the distant relationship she had had with her father. She explained that he had been in a helping profession and had helped a lot of people, had been very proactive and had wanted to make his own life more meaningful but that this had not been easy for those around him. Incorporating the optional underlined prompts distributed by the facilitators, Eva read out her letter:

"*What I have always wanted to tell you is* that you always meant a lot to me and that I looked up to you when you turned difficult situations or circumstances for yourself and others around. *What you never understood was* that I was growing up with a lot of internal and external problems, which you could not have been able to change to a greater extent." She paused, saying, "He had no idea of what it was like for me. It was very difficult. He couldn't have known what it was like for me growing up." She then continued:

"*What I want you to know about me is* that I am happy we managed to find a way to find each other, although it took a long time. *What I now realize is* that those difficult times we had were just a phase, however long it was, and it was very long, or it felt very long to me anyway. But there was always a possibility for growth and appreciation of one another. *The one question I have wanted to ask is* how it was when your own father was sent to a concentration camp during the war, and you were growing up without him and also when your brother died during the war. *I want to keep you in my life by* . . . [pausing as her eyes filled with tears] by remembering all the good things we had together, doing sports, travelling abroad or just having supper, a family supper, at Christmas dinner—that was very special to me." Eva paused briefly, and then continued, "Because you lived through such turbulent times and I also experienced a very unstable political situation myself, I am glad that we survived it all and had time to repair. Now I am only grateful for all we had, which was very positive." This led to a conversation in the small group about the value of opening up and sharing but also about the difficulty of doing this, both in the group and in the relationships with the loved ones. Another group member, who had been particularly quiet in previous sessions, spoke about how hard it was for her to open up. There was a sense of compassion, including self-compassion, and also hope for opening up and sharing more in the future. At the end of the activity, Eva contemplated the idea of continuing her letter to her father and telling him more about what life had been like for her during the times when there was so much distance between them.

Session 7: Response Letter from the Loved One. Having drafted a letter as if from the loved one as a between-session assignment, group members speak about the usually vividly emotional experience of doing so and read the letter to their partners in Session 7. Alternatively or additionally, partners also may read the letter to its author with expressiveness but not melodrama, which can deepen the sense of the letter speaking to the author with a voice outside the self. Again, dyadic observations are consolidated and extended in the subsequent plenary processing. For many clients, this restoration of a symbolic dialogue with the deceased (or other imaginal correspondent) introduces further letter writing, helping install their voices as a kind of "portable secure base" that remains accessible despite their physical absence. Accordingly, members can be encouraged to continue this exchange, to explore forgiveness or to petition the advice of the correspondent regarding practical steps that they might now take to restore their lives. To further consolidate this continuing bond, the client is assigned the life imprint exercise as homework prior to the next session.

The challenge in working with complicated grief often lies not only in facilitating meaning making about the loss, but also in facilitating meaning making about re-engagement in life. In the context of the Dual-Process Model, complicated grievers can be described as cultivating the loss orientation at the expense of the restoration orientation. In and of itself, the Response Letter is a loss-oriented meaning-making activity. However, MLG facilitators are encouraged to use the continuing bond fostered by the Response Letter as a means of guiding group members toward re-engagement in life. An example of this from the Montreal iteration of the MLG is presented in the exchange that follows, in which a group member, Jen, is reading a portion of the Response Letter written by her dyad partner, Karen, to the group:

JEN: [Reading letter] "I used to tell you: 'You need the right tools to live your life well'—and you really listened! You always made sure our family had the tools we needed for our lives. Remember how you'd drive Annie [couple's child] to that math tutor who lived in the middle of nowhere? It was exhausting, and we had no money for it, and Annie didn't want to go because she thought the math tutor had bad breath. [Group giggles.] But you made sure Annie went every week. And now, she's in medical school. I always said, 'All those lives she's gonna save as a doctor—if those people only knew that they're alive because you made sure to take Annie to a math tutor with bad breath!' [Group giggles.] Well, I wish I was there to do that for you now: to give you the tools you need to get through this." [Jen stops reading. There's a pause as the group takes in what was read.]

KAREN: I don't know, it just seems like: are we supposed to "get through this"? What does that say to the people we care about? "I loved you and all, but now that you're gone, I'll get through it." No! Now that my husband is gone, I'm going to suffer because I loved him.

JEN: I see what you're saying: if you're not suffering, then that diminishes your relationship with Jack [Karen's husband]. [Karen nods.]

JM: Hmmm . . . at the same time, listening to your letter, Karen, it sounds like Jack believed in having the necessary "tools" for life. I wonder if your relationship with him can be kept strong not just through your suffering but through your use of what he taught you about life tools.

JEN: Yeah. Exactly. I think what Jack used to say to Karen was really wise, and we should all listen to it. I was thinking how my daughter would always do everything 100%. Even the little things, like throwing a Halloween party for her little brother. She would just go all out, setting up a haunted house and everything. So maybe that's a tool my daughter gave me: do everything 100%. Maybe I should throw an all-out Halloween party the way she used to. I mean, it would still be painful, 'cause I'd rather she was here to do it. But at least I'd be using the "tool" she gave me and kind of keeping her essence in my life.

KAREN: Jack would get a kick out of what you just said, Jen. He loved being "Yoda" by giving advice to everyone. He'd love Jen praising his wisdom. [Karen and group laugh.]

As exemplified in this exchange, grieving group members often perceive engagement with life as a threat to their connection with the deceased. JM built on Karen's Response Letter to reframe engagement in life as a means of honoring and maintaining the continuing bond with her husband. After this exchange, JM continued tentatively exploring "tools" Karen could use to simultaneously restore her life and reaffirm the significance of her relationship with Jack. This discussion was also adapted for other group members, drawing on their respective Response Letters.

Session 8: The Life Imprint. In keeping with a postmodern conception of self, the meaning reconstruction approach presumes that our personalities are constructed as a pastiche or residue of innumerable relationships with others, especially those who play intimate roles in our lives. Accordingly, the life imprint encourages bereaved clients to trace the impact of the deceased on their personal identities, at levels ranging from their gestures and mannerisms through their choice of vocations and avocations to their most abiding characteristics and values (Neimeyer, 2012b). Reviewing these multiple imprints in the dyadic phase, with a partner who encourages elaboration on these embodied or enacted legacies in the form of memories and stories, conveys the deep sense in which the deceased have a continued existence in and through the clients' own lives. Although this is typically deeply affirming of cherished bonds, occasionally imprints are ambivalent or even negative, in which case therapists, in the closing plenary phase, collaborate with group members in discovering ways to relinquish or release them in a ritual of reinvention. The session can end with a plan to perform an activity that honors the imprint of the loved one, often by engaging in meaningful actions such as visiting a special, but previously avoided, location (Papa, 2016) or performing a dedicated act of kindness that honors the loved one or acts on his or her values (Cacciatore, 2012).

Session 9: Further Connections. In this session, clients report on their self-observations following the work on the back story of their relationship to the deceased over the last few weeks. Therapists engage clients in discussions of additional possible expressions of "continuing bonds" to their loved ones (Klass, Silverman, & Nickman, 1996; Klass & Steffen, 2018), as in dreams, experiences of their tangible or intangible presence in clients' daily lives and for many of the bereaved, a sense of spiritual connection that implies the prospect of reconnection in an afterlife. Leading from one step behind, therapists follow client cues in such discussions, taking care to respect their personal and cultural beliefs and practices. This session also serves as a kind of "expansion joint," permitting further attention to the correspondence or life imprint methods for clients who choose to explore them further.

Participants in the London group had been given a handout on "sense of presence" experiences, which was partly based on previous research by EMS (e.g., Steffen & Coyle, 2011), in the session before, and people started the group by sharing a range of such experiences in the group. One group member talked about having felt a touch or the close presence of his deceased wife, particularly in church. This led to a discussion on beliefs about an afterlife. With the diversity of views in the room, this could have been a difficult session, but people talked with openness and sensitivity about these issues, showing a great deal of respect for each other's points of view. The discussion moved back and forth, with one person sharing experiences followed by a joint wondering about how to make sense of this, which involved drawing on traditional faith views, alternative spiritual views and different scientific perspectives. The tolerance of different possibilities and the acceptance of ultimately not knowing became points of convergence in the group. This appeared increasingly to allow room for people's very personal meanings, rooted in stories about the deceased and promoting continuing bonds. For example, one group member talked about how the smell of burnt toast was associated with her grandfather and how she had learned as a child that this smell signaled the presence of her grandfather, a tradition she was now continuing with her own children, leading to a "Hello, Grandpa!" whenever such a smell came into awareness. Others in the group then started to share richly symbolic stories from their own families, similar to what Gudmundsdottir and Chesla (2006) have called "habits and practices of healing." It seemed that having had a thorough discussion of different explanatory positions earlier, it was now possible to somewhat let go of the need to explain and simply to allow the felt meanings of such experiences to stand without having to justify them.

Following the break, the group engaged in a visualization exercise, "Envisioning Connection Through Guided Imagery" (Armstrong, 2012). This led to some powerful experiences of presence and connection for many group members. A particularly meaningful experience of communication was narrated by one participant. Tanya, who had lost her mother, had visualized walking on the beach when she saw her mother approach. She asked her, "Are you okay?" and as if to answer her question, her mother's cat came running to her (Tanya). When making sense of this experience, Tanya concluded that her mother must be okay because she had always loved this cat, and it had been in their conversations that her mother would see the cat again in the afterlife. As she kept considering the meanings of this event, another layer of meaning unfolded for her, as she thought about how the cat had also been a symbolic representation of her mother's aunt, and Tanya wondered whether there was a message for her to contact that aunt, as she was quite old and frail, and Tanya had not heard from her in a while. Tanya commented on what a revelation this was for her, and this led again to a wondering about where such an important message could be coming from—a higher power or an inner source of wisdom—and people seemed to lean toward the conclusion that ultimately it did not matter whether it was "real" but only that it was "true."

Phase 5: Consolidation

Session 10: Virtual Dream Stories. To promote integration of the work of therapy by foster-ing an imaginative, "self-distancing" perspective (Kross & Ayduk, 2010), Session 10 engages clients in writing a brief "make believe" story about themes of loss in session, and therapists allow them eight to ten minutes to do so (Neimeyer & Young-Eisendrath, 2014). Termed a *virtual dream* because of its draw toward a fairy tale or magical realist fictional style, the method involves priming clients with two elements each of *setting* (e.g., a traumatic loss, an empty house), *figure with voice* (e.g., a crying child, a talking animal) and potentially *sym-bolic objects* or features (e.g., a mountain, a sunrise), which they are encouraged to include in any form they like into the narrative (Neimeyer, Torres, & Smith, 2011). The short time available for the writing tends to circumvent the interruption of a self-critical or editorial voice, and the resulting story is typically emotionally powerful and, at this point in therapy, hopeful, whether the plot of the story literally or figuratively recapitulates the plots or themes of clients' personal loss stories. After reading aloud and discussing the resulting narrative in dyads, therapists can use any of several additional techniques to extend the method in heal-ing directions in the subsequent plenary phase (e.g., facilitating imaginal dialogues between pairs of elements or prompting clients to retell the story from the perspective of one of the elements to de-center the narration and discover in it new possible meanings). Other alterna-tives prompt clients to consider what the story reveals about what they themselves need so that they can plan practical steps to meet these needs in the coming week (Neimeyer, 2012d).

In the London group, participants were asked to write a story using the following elements: an empty house, a storm, a voice in the wind, a mysterious stranger, the deep roots of a tree, a torn picture. This is what Julia, a young woman who had lost her grandparents, who were her closest relations and main caregivers during her childhood, wrote:

A Memory of Raging Wind

> *It was like the voice in the wind. Heathcliff was it or Rebecca? It must have been Heath-cliff who was the voice across the stormy moor, "Wuthering Heights." We both disliked it, the characters so unlikeable and proud. I remember now, it was De Maurier you liked, Rebecca, the film. The unfamiliar call of a roaming voice from a mysterious stranger and I was afraid, trembling as if this were not my house but an empty one. Some winter tale of specters in haunted stately homes abandoned. Gnarled trees lashing the window in the dark as the wind howls. Rain so violent I could have been a pitching ship in a raging gale rather than sitting at home. The power out, my surroundings unfamiliar to me. Then again, the voice rising to me up through the streams of air through the leaves, peering out into the garden where in sunnier childhood days we picnicked with bears and made green our dresses with grass stains. Muddy pools gathered around the deep roots of the old oak tree, the tree that had stood for hundreds of years before this house now family ever came by to admire it. There in the mud lay the remains of the summer house blasted apart by the storm. The summer house was really nothing more than a shed. There was your picture torn apart from impact with branches. The new neighbours stood among the wreckage enquiring if I was okay. I wasn't but I breathed not a word and returned myself to the comfort of a many-blanketed bed.*

Julia had previously shared that she had been unable to return to the house where her deceased grandparents had lived, a house that was her absolute place of safety. The house she had envisaged in her story was a different house: namely, the house she had grown up in, not the house she had been afraid to visit. In the next session, Julia told us that she was planning to return to her grandparents' house for the first time since their deaths. She said that she felt ready to do this now and that the group had helped her prepare for this important visit.

Session 11: Ritual Planning. As therapy moves toward termination, therapists coach group members to plan a *ritual of remembrance* that honors their loved ones or a *ritual of renewal* that symbolizes the new possibilities they wish to embrace in the future (Doka, 2012). For example, clients may pursue a legacy project such as launching or contributing to a charitable cause that reflects the core values of the deceased or plan a holiday ceremony as a family that acknowledges the deceased but also recommits the family members as a unit to their shared future in its new form. Some symbolic steps in these directions can be taken immediately, whereas others inherently represent longer-term projects to be nurtured over time. Members then develop these ideas in dyads and report back to the plenary group before adjourning. As an alternative or complementary activity, the group may decide on a collective ritual that honors their loved ones and the work of the group itself in the closing session.

The conclusion of the MLG can feel like a daunting prospect as group members who are already grieving the deceased begin grieving the end of the group. Accordingly, it is vital to leave space in this pre-termination session for normalizing, validating and exploring group members' anticipatory grief regarding the ending of therapy. In fact, in the Montreal iteration of the MLG, this discussion led to group members planning informal monthly meetings in coffee shops and at each other's homes as a means of honoring the "sacred" time the group had created to attend to the loss and re-engage in life. However, we decided that the therapist should not attend these meetings in order to differentiate them from group therapy, thereby preserving professional boundaries. Nevertheless, following such meetings, group members opted to pass cards and emails on to the facilitator, checking in and expressing their gratitude for the group therapy experience.

Session 12: Ritual Reporting and Termination. In the final session, clients perform together or report on their success and next steps with their rituals of remembrance and renewal and review turning points in their therapeutic journey toward greater hope and meaning. Therapists help orchestrate this enactment or discussion and affirm the work of the group with a simple exercise of their choice (e.g., asking each member to state one thing that she or he carried away from the MLG experience and sharing their own feelings about the shared passage).

The London group decided to share food that was meaningful with regard to their deceased loved ones as the ending ritual. The group began with a review of turning points, which sparked a good deal of mtua affirmation. People were then asked to show the food they had brought and explain its meanings, following which members engaged in an extended break to enjoy the food that everyone had brought and commemorate the deceased loved ones in this communal ritual. Some members had brought their deceased loved ones' favorite foods: for example, particular chocolates that one group member's deceased wife liked and a type of breakfast biscuit that one person's deceased mother always enjoyed. One member had made her deceased partner's favorite rice pudding—the first time she had made this since her partner's death. In addition, one group member brought a CD with music that her deceased grandfather had recorded, which was the music he typically played at family gatherings. Group members tried each other's foods, listened to the music and chatted. There was a sense of community rounding off the 12-week group program. Participants expressed later how much they had liked it that they had created this occasion. The group closed by sitting together in the group room again for one last time, sharing feelings about the meal and the ending of the group and wishing each other well until their three-month follow-up review meeting.

Additional Sessions. As many of the cases we have seen in our groups involve complicated grief responses (Neimeyer, 2016a) and/or quite tragic losses, such as the death of a child, early widowhood or sudden, violent death through suicide, overdose or fatal accident, allowance is made on an as-needed basis for an additional two sessions to provide further support and consolidation of therapeutic gains. Finally, in both research and clinical contexts, we encourage follow-up evaluations of clients at three and six months post-therapy to assess durability or continuation of progress over time or, alternatively, the need for referral to additional individual therapy when clients continue to struggle with their grief. In some settings, a "reunion" session is also possible approximately four to six weeks after termination, giving members a relatively unstructured opportunity to share developments in their lives and, in many cases, renew bonds.

CONCLUSION

Our ongoing experience in testing the feasibility of the MLG in three quite different contexts and in three different countries has laid the groundwork for a controlled trial of this novel intervention, drawing on validated instruments for assessing both meaning making and mourning across the course of treatment (Neimeyer, 2016a). Preliminary data from these small-scale uncontrolled trials are encouraging, suggesting that participants experience a reduction in complicated grief and other forms of suffering, as well as improvement in their ability to find sense and significance in life-altering stories of loss. We are therefore optimistic that a meaning-oriented therapy that draws on contemporary models, methods and measures will make a distinctive contribution to the treatment of those persons who suffer painful, protracted and preoccupying reactions to tragic loss and hope that others will join us in investigating the clinical utility of this novel approach to group work with the bereaved.

Note

1. For information on training and supervision in the protocol, contact the first author at neimeyer@portlandinstitute.org.

References

Armstrong, C. (2012). Envisioning connection through guided imagery. In R. A. Neimeyer (Ed.), *Techniques of grief therapy: Creative practices for counselling the bereaved* (pp. 256–258). New York: Routledge.

Bellet, B. W., Neimeyer, R. A., & Berman, J. S. (2017). Event centrality and bereavement symptomatology: The moderating role of meaning made. *Omega*. doi:10.1177/0030222816679659

Cacciatore, J. (2012). The kindness project. In R. A. Neimeyer (Ed.), *Techniques of grief therapy: creative practices for counseling the bereaved* (pp. 329–331). New York: Routledge.

Coleman, R. A., & Neimeyer, R. A. (2010). Measuring meaning: Searching for and making sense of spousal loss in later life. *Death Studies, 34*, 804–834.

Currier, J. M., Holland, J. M., & Neimeyer, R. A. (2006). Sense making, grief and the experience of violent loss: Toward a mediational model. *Death Studies, 30*, 403–428.

Doka, K. (2012). Therapeutic ritual. In R. A. Neimeyer (Ed.), *Techniques of grief therapy: Creative practices for counseling the bereaved* (pp. 341–343). New York: Routledge.

Dunton, A. J. (2012). Loss timelines. In R. A. Neimeyer (Ed.), *Techniques of grief therapy* (pp. 184–186). New York: Routledge.

Gudmundsdottir, M., & Chesla, C. A. (2006). Building a new world: Habits and practices of healing following the death of a child. *Journal of Family Nursing, 12*, 143–164.

Harris, D. (Ed.). (2020). *Non-death loss and grief: Context and clinical implications.* New York: Routledge.

Hedtke, L. (2012). Introducing the deceased. In R. A. Neimeyer (Ed.), *Techniques of grief therapy: Creative practices for counseling the bereaved* (pp. 253–255). New York: Routledge.

Hedtke, L. (2018). Remembering relations across the years and the miles. In D. Klass & E. M. Steffen (Eds.), *Continuing bonds in bereavement: New directions for research and practice.* New York: Routledge.

Hedtke, L., & Winslade, J. (2016). *The crafting of grief.* New York: Routledge.

Holland, J. M., Currier, J. M., Coleman, R. A., & Neimeyer, R. A. (2010). The integration of stressful life experiences scale (ISLES): Development and initial validation of a new measure. *International Journal of Stress Management, 17*, 325–352.

Janoff-Bulman, R., & Berger, A. R. (2000). The other side of trauma. In J. H. Harvey & E. D. Miller (Eds.), *Loss and trauma*. Philadelphia: Brunner Mazel.

Kelly, G. A. (1955). *The psychology of personal constructs*. New York: Norton.

Klass, D., Silverman, P. R., & Nickman, S. (Eds.). (1996). *Continuing bonds: New understandings of grief*. Bristol: Taylor & Francis.

Klass, D., & Steffen, E. M. (Eds.). (2017). *Continuing bonds in bereavement*. New York: Routledge.

Klass, D., & Steffen, E. M. (Eds.). (2018). *Continuing bonds in bereavement: New directions for research and practice*. New York: Routledge.

Kolb, D. A. (1984). *Experiential learning*. Englewood Cliffs, NJ: Prentice Hall.

Kosminsky, P., & Jordan, J. R. (2016). *Attachment informed grief therapy*. New York: Routledge.

Krawchuk, L. (2016). Loss boxes. In R. A. Neimeyer (Ed.), *Techniques of grief therapy: Assessment and intervention* (pp. 170–172). New York: Routledge.

Kross, E., & Ayduk, O. (2010). Making meaning out of negative experiences by self-distancing. *Current Directions in Psychological Science, 20*, 187–191. doi:10.1177/0963721411408883

Lichtenthal, W. G., Burke, L. A., & Neimeyer, R. A. (2011). Religious coping and meaning-making following the loss of a loved one. *Counseling and Spirituality, 30*, 113–136.

Lichtenthal, W. G., & Cruess, D. G. (2010). Effects of directed written disclosure on grief and distress symptoms among bereaved individuals. *Death Studies, 34*, 475–499.

Lichtenthal, W. G., & Neimeyer, R. A. (2012). Directed journaling to facilitate meaning making. In R. A. Neimeyer (Ed.), *Techniques of grief therapy* (pp. 161–164). New York: Routledge.

MacKinnon, C. J., Smith, N. G., Henry, M., Milman, E., Berish, M., Farrace, A., . . . Cohen, S. R. (2012). Meaning-based group counseling for bereavement: Results of a pilot study. *Journal of Palliative Care, 28*, 207.

Neimeyer, R. A. (Ed.). (2001). *Meaning reconstruction and the experience of loss*. Washington, DC: American Psychological Association.

Neimeyer, R. A. (2004). Fostering posttraumatic growth: A narrative contribution. *Psychological Inquiry, 15*, 53–59.

Neimeyer, R. A. (2006). *Lessons of loss* (2nd ed.). New York: Routledge.

Neimeyer, R. A. (2009). *Constructivist psychotherapy*. London and New York: Routledge.

Neimeyer, R. A. (2012a). Correspondence with the deceased. In R. A. Neimeyer (Ed.), *Techniques of grief therapy* (pp. 259–261). New York: Routledge.

Neimeyer, R. A. (2012b). The life imprint. In R. A. Neimeyer (Ed.), *Techniques of grief therapy: Creative practices for counseling the bereaved* (pp. 274–276). New York: Routledge.

Neimeyer, R. A. (2012c). Retelling the narrative of the death. In R. A. Neimeyer (Ed.), *Techniques of grief therapy* (pp. 86–90). New York: Routledge.

Neimeyer, R. A. (2012d). Virtual dream stories. In R. A. Neimeyer (Ed.), *Techniques of grief therapy: Creative practices for counseling the bereaved* (pp. 187–189). New York: Routledge.

Neimeyer, R. A. (Ed.). (2012e). *Techniques of grief therapy: Creative practices for counseling the bereaved*. New York: Routledge.

Neimeyer, R. A. (2014). Chapters of our lives. In B. E. Thompson & R. A. Neimeyer (Eds.), *Grief and the expressive arts: Practices for creating meaning*. New York: Routledge.

Neimeyer, R. A. (2015). Treating complicated bereavement: The development of grief therapy. In J. Stillion & T. Attig (Eds.), *Death, dying and bereavement: Contemporary perspectives, institutions and practices* (pp. 307–320). New York: Springer.

Neimeyer, R. A. (2016a). Complicated grief: Assessment and intervention. In J. Cook, S. Gold, & C. Dalenberg (Eds.), *APA handbook of trauma psychology*. Washington, DC: American Psychological Association.

Neimeyer, R. A. (Ed.). (2016b). *Techniques of grief therapy: Assessment and intervention*. New York: Routledge.

Neimeyer, R. A. (2019). Meaning reconstruction in bereavement: Development of a research program. *Death Studies, 43*, 79–91. doi:10.1080/07481187.2018.1456620

Neimeyer, R. A. (Ed.). (2021). *New techniques of grief therapy: Bereavement and beyond*. New York: Routledge.

Neimeyer, R. A., & Burke, L. A. (2017). What makes grief complicated? Risk factors for complicated grief. In K. Doka & A. Tucci (Eds.), *Living with grief: When grief is complicated* (pp. 73–93). Washington, DC: Hospice Foundation of America.

Neimeyer, R. A., Klass, D., & Dennis, M. R. (2014). A social constructionist account of grief: Loss and the narration of meaning. *Death Studies* (38), 485–498.

Neimeyer, R. A., & Thompson, B. E. (2014). Meaning making and the art of grief therapy. In B. E. Thompson & R. A. Neimeyer (Eds.), *Grief and the expressive arts: Practices for creating meaning* (pp. 3–13). New York: Routledge.

Neimeyer, R. A., Torres, C., & Smith, D. C. (2011). The virtual dream: Rewriting stories of loss and grief. *Death Studies, 35,* 646–672.

Neimeyer, R. A., & Young-Eisendrath, P. (2014). Virtual dream stories. In B. E. Thompson & R. A. Neimeyer (Eds.), *Grief and the expressive arts: Practices for creating meaning* (pp. 62–65). New York: Routledge.

Neimeyer, R. A., & Young-Eisendrath, P. (2015). Assessing a Buddhist treatment for bereavement and loss: The Mustard Seed Project. *Death Studies, 39.*

Papa, A. (2016). Contextual behavioral activation. In R. A. Neimeyer (Ed.), *Techniques of grief therapy: Assessment and intervention.* New York: Routledge.

Polanyi, M. (1958). *Personal knowledge.* Chicago: University of Chicago Press.

Rozalski, V., Holland, J. M., & Neimeyer, R. A. (2016). Circumstances of death and complicated grief: Indirect associations through meaning made of loss. *Journal of Loss and Trauma.* doi:10.1080/15 325024.2016.1161426

Rubin, S. S., Malkinson, R., & Witztum, E. (2011). *Working with the bereaved.* New York: Routledge.

Rynearson, E. K., & Salloum, A. (2021). Restorative retelling: Revisiting the narrative of violent death. In R. A. Neimeyer, D. Harris, H. Winokuer, & G. Thornton (Eds.), *Grief and bereavement in contemporary society: Bridging research and practice* (pp. 177–188). New York: Routledge.

Saindon, C., Rheingold, A., Baddeley, J., Wallace, M., Brown, C., & Rynearson, E. K. (2014). Restorative retelling for violent loss: An open clinical trial. *Death Studies, 38,* 251–258.

Shaver, P. R., & Fraley, R. C. (2008). Attachment, loss and grief: Bowlby's views and current controversies. In J. Cassidy & P. R. Shaver (Eds.), *Handbook of attachment: Theory, research and clinical applications* (2nd ed.). New York: Guilford Press.

Steffen, E., & Coyle, A. (2011). Sense of presence experiences and meaning-making in bereavement: A qualitative analysis. *Death Studies, 35,* 579–609.

Stroebe, M., & Schut, H. (2010). The Dual Process Model of coping with bereavement: A decade on. *Omega, 61,* 273–289.

Thompson, B. E., & Neimeyer, R. A. (Eds.). (2014). *Grief and the expressive arts: Practices for creating meaning.* New York: Routledge.

White, M. (1989). Saying hullo again. In M. White (Ed.), *Selected papers.* Adelaide, Australia: Dulwich Center Publications.

Wittkowski, J., Doka, K., Neimeyer, R. A., & Vallerga, M. (2015). Publication trends in thanatology: An analysis of leading journals. *Death Studies,* 1–10. doi:10.1080/07481187.2014.1000054

Culturally Sensitive Approaches to Finding Meaning in Traumatic Bereavement

Geert E. Smid and Paul A. Boelen

After the word of prohibition follows the word of judgment: "Thou shalt surely die." What it means to die, Adam of course cannot conceive; but if one assumes that these words were said to him, there is nothing to prevent his having a notion of the terrible. . . . The terrible becomes in this instance merely dread, for Adam has not understood what was said, and here again we have only the ambiguity of dread. The infinite possibility of being able (awakened by the prohibiting) draws closer for the fact that this possibility indicates a possibility as its consequence.

Thus, innocence is brought to its last extremity. It is in dread in relation to the prohibition and the punishment. It is not guilty and yet it is in dread, as though it were lost.

Further than this psychology cannot go, but so far it can reach, and moreover it can verify this point again and again in its observation of human life.

(Kierkegaard, 1844/1957, The concept of dread, pp. 40–41)

Traumatic events such as disasters, accidents, war or criminal violence are often accompanied by the loss of loved ones. Traumatic grief following the loss of loved ones due to violent circumstances may occur in people surviving cultural conflicts as well as profession-related risks. Traumatic grief can be conceptualized as a combination of traumatic distress and separation distress following an unnatural, violent loss. In terms of conditions distinguished in the DSM-5, traumatic grief reflects a combination of symptoms of posttraumatic stress disorder (PTSD) and persistent complex bereavement disorder (PCBD) (Boelen & Smid, 2017). PCBD is a condition similar to prolonged grief disorder (PGD) adopted in the ICD-11. Mourning behaviors and ways of dealing with bereavement comprise important aspects of an individual's cultural identity and profoundly affect the way the bereaved survivor finds meaning following traumatic loss. Finding meaning encompasses the bereaved individual's evaluation of the loss of the loved person and its implications for the future—a cognitive, emotional and spiritual process aimed at strengthening the individual's ability to live with the loss within his or her cultural context.

The aim of the current chapter is to describe culturally sensitive approaches to finding meaning following traumatic bereavement. First, we will describe how the therapist explores the context of meaning. This includes exploring cultural ways of dealing with bereavement and grief and listening to the story of the loss. In the second part of this chapter, we will illustrate how different modes of symbolic interaction with the deceased person may aid

DOI: 10.4324/9781351069120-4

in finding meaning in a culturally sensitive way. Selected interventions are presented, along with case vignettes of refugees as well as a military veteran illustrating their use.

EXPLORING MEANING

Exploring Cultural Ways of Dealing With Bereavement and Grief

The notions of historical trauma, loss and grief refer to the enduring, intergenerational effects of cultural oppression in the lives of immigrant, minority and indigenous peoples and communities (Kirmayer, Gone, & Moses, 2014). Specifically, persons from these backgrounds may experience *cultural incongruity* in case of dissimilarity between beliefs, expectations and practices in the culture of origin and the dominant culture (Bhugra & Becker, 2005). Consistent with this notion, disaster-exposed persons of immigrant cultural backgrounds who lost a loved one endorsed increased and more persistent stress-responsive distress than natives (Smid, Drogendijk, Knipscheer, Boelen, & Kleber, 2018).

Rituals provide powerful and affirming experiences for bereaved individuals in mediating the transition of the individual from one social status to another, affirming the importance of the deceased person, channeling emotions and offering vehicles for continuity and social cohesion of the social community (e.g., Romanoff & Terenzio, 1998). The loss of loved ones under traumatic circumstances often coincides with the impossibility of performing culturally appropriate rituals. This is illustrated in the following case vignette.

Jack, now 25 years old, from Liberia, was referred for treatment of PTSD and depression. When he was 14, his house was attacked by the rebels. His beloved grandmother was burned in the house while lying paralyzed on her bed. Jack wasn't at home; at that time, he was forced to be a child soldier. His mother, brothers and sisters are missing and most likely deceased. (His father left the family when Jack was a small child.) Jack has recurrent nightmares in which his grandmother appears with a suitcase in her hand, staring at him. Jack's interpretation is that she accuses him of her death because he wasn't there to protect her. He thinks her soul cannot find rest because there has been no burial ritual. He wants to accept her death but doesn't know how.

To enable a clinical estimation of the effects of rituals that could not be performed, therapists may conduct an assessment of cultural ways of dealing with bereavement and grief (Smid, Groen, de la Rie, Kooper, & Boelen, 2018). To this aim, cultural traditions related to death, bereavement and mourning, as well as coping and help-seeking activities related to the loss of loved ones, need to be explored.

Exploring cultural traditions related to death, bereavement and mourning. A key function of death-related rituals is to provide structured ways to mourn and express grief. Rituals may include time frames for immediate mourning, and actions to be completed at specific points in time thereafter, such as a wake or yearly commemorations, prescribe how to handle and dispose of the body of the deceased and when and in what way it is appropriate for people to talk about the deceased (Cacciatore & DeFrain, 2015). Encounters with the deceased that may occur in dreams or when bereaved persons see, feel, smell or talk to the deceased may have cultural explanations. Following such encounters, the person may experience exhortation and feel the urge to perform rituals (Eisenbruch, 1990; Hinton, Peou, Joshi, Nickerson, & Simon, 2013). Many rituals allow the bereaved to settle accounts or convey apologies or gratitude to the deceased. Mourning rituals are often *piacular* (Durkheim, 1995), i.e., not performing them creates guilt. While some rituals may be thought of as having implications for the afterlife (Hinton et al., 2013), performing prescribed rituals may be more generally necessary for proper role fulfillment or just doing things right (Staal, 1979). Within several religions, the mode of death (e.g., suicide) is thought of as having implications for the afterlife

(Cacciatore & DeFrain, 2015). Exploring these implications may be helpful to support adaptive coping.

Exploring help-seeking and coping activities related to the loss of loved ones. Many bereaved individuals engage in practices related to spiritual, religious or moral traditions to cope with the loss of a loved one, including prayer and meditation. In addition, they may participate in worships or religious gatherings or speak with other people in their religious group and with religious or spiritual leaders. These activities may be helpful in coping with the loss, especially in dealing with guilt. Survivor guilt frequently occurs among traumatically bereaved survivors, notably refugees (Eisenbruch, 1990). Concepts of guilt may be linked to broader cultural concepts of fairness and fate that may involve the afterlife. For example, the Buddhist concept of *karma* consists of the consequences of the good and evil deeds committed in all one's previous existences; suffering, therefore, is the karmic consequence of one's past sins, and one can only hope for a better existence in the next rebirth by performing numerous acts of merit (Boehnlein, 1987). Other kinds of help may have been suggested by family, friends or others. For clinicians, it is essential to explore these as well as other kinds of help the client or patient thinks would be most useful at this time to deal with the loss of loved ones.

Examples of questions that may be used to map cultural ways of dealing with bereavement and grief include:

- *If someone from your family, friends or others in your community die, how would people usually arrange the funeral?*
- *Are there other rituals after people have passed away?*
- *Is there a prescribed period of mourning or expressing grief?*
- *When and how do people talk about the deceased?*
- *When bereaved people have dreams or other types of encounters with the deceased, what may this mean?*
- *What do your family, friends and others in your community believe happens after death?*
- *Do you engage in spiritual or religious practices to help you cope with the loss of a loved one?*

The therapist uses gentle Socratic questioning to further explore the associated beliefs, values, traditions, and meanings.

The Story of the Loss

Important components of psychotherapy for disturbed grief include exposure to memories of the loss and the deceased person, facing the reality and irreversibility of the loss and confronting the associated pain (Boelen & Smid, 2017). Listening to the patient's narration of the story of the loss, the therapist explores other contextual and psychological determinants of meaning: i.e., the specific events and circumstances comprising the story of the loss. Besides cultural, spiritual, religious and moral traditions and the closeness of the relationship, the therapist learns about several other factors that may influence the patient's appraisal of the traumatic loss of the loved one, such as concomitant loss of resources, judicial procedures, availability of social support, previous trauma or loss experiences and history of mental health problems. Discerning these factors, the therapist may offer practical advice and emotional support in addition to specific grief-focused interventions and tailored psychoeducation. Several elements of psychoeducation following traumatic loss are discussed next.

Traumatic losses may present individuals with information that violates previously held positive beliefs about the self, life and the future. Such losses can also confirm negative beliefs or *schemas* (Beck, 2008) that are part of the personal meaning assignment system. For instance, early losses and other adverse developmental experiences may foster negative attitudes and biases about the self (Beck, 2008); the meaning of these events may be transformed into a durable attitude (e.g., helplessness, pervasive fear, anger or guilt), which may be activated by the traumatic loss and increase its negative meaning. Also, the attachment style of the individual and the nature of the attachment relation may shape the grief reaction (Maccallum & Bryant, 2013).

Negative cognitions and assumptions can be addressed in psychotherapy. There, the aim is not to "dispute" and "alter" negative cognitions about these broad themes but, instead, to explore ways to maintain a positive view of self, life and the future, incorporating the painful loss. Self-blame and negative views of responses of the social environment may lead to feelings of guilt and anger. Self-blame may be especially prominent if the death is felt as a failure of caregiving, such as following the death of a child. Therapists should not simply try to challenge the self-blame but rather help the bereaved individual to assimilate the inability to prevent the death into a favorable view of self (Boelen, Van den Hout, & Van den Bout, 2006; Neimeyer, 2006).

Interpretations of one's own grief reactions may be important. Bereaved individuals may interpret their emotional reactions—including intense despair, negative thoughts and vivid images associated with the loss—as intolerable, unbearable or signs of impending insanity or loss of control. Such negative appraisals may contribute to persistent separation and traumatic distress directly, by intensifying distress, and indirectly, by fueling tendencies to minimize confrontation with loss-related stimuli.

Direct exposure to horrific details of the traumatic loss of a loved one increases the risk of traumatic grief. This is so because such losses radically invalidate core assumptions about safety, trust and controllability, posing a greater challenge for the bereaved to maintain a positive view of the world and other people. Indeed, violent deaths are more likely to generate distressing intrusive memories than nonviolent deaths (Boelen, de Keijser, & Smid, 2015). Culturally sensitive care means that therapists try to appreciate and understand the nature and complexities of their patient's lived experiences—including the atrocities the individual may have been exposed to if he or she fled a country at war.

Ambiguity—i.e., a lack of information, such as with missing persons (ambiguous loss)—may also be associated with increased distress. Because the situation of ambiguous loss cannot be resolved, the individual's sense of mastery may be impaired (Boss, 2006). Ambiguous loss can lead to disenfranchised grief—a grief that is not acknowledged by people in the social context, particularly when it is part of a number of traumatic and loss events experienced in the context of war. Western bereavement rituals, based on a model of "letting go," are likely ineffective and inauthentic for non-Western people confronted with ambiguous loss.

Continuous searching for the deceased may lead to strong perceptual priming and a high likelihood of finding *matching triggers*: i.e., trauma and grief reminders that may reactivate memories of the traumatic loss and/or the deceased. In addition, *new stressful life events* may be perceived as more stressful. Stressful life events may include interpersonal tensions within bereaved families that may also be common after ambiguous loss (Boss, 2006). *Stress sensitization* refers to an increased susceptibility to the effects of new stressful events following exposure to extreme traumatic events. A contextual stress sensitization model (Smid et al., 2018) specifies processes contributing to enhanced stress sensitivity in three different dimensions: cognitive, interpersonal and neurobiological. The *cognitive* dimension includes enhanced responses to trauma-related memories, enhanced perception of threat and reinforced negative interpretations of events. The *interpersonal* dimension includes increased distrust, irritability, detachment or estrangement and identity disruption. The *neurobiological* dimension includes different neurobiological systems that may show increased responses due to previous excessive stress reactions. The impairments that result from stress-responsive distress may cause loss of resources through contextual mechanisms (for example, job loss after a conflict at work in a trauma survivor with increased irritability), leading to persistence or increases in distress over time. Matching triggers, new stressful life events and stress sensitization can, at least partially, account for the frequently fluctuating nature of persistent grief reactions over time.

FINDING MEANING

Culture is represented in the form of intersubjective perceptions: i.e., beliefs and values that members of a culture perceive to be widespread in their group (Chi-Yue, Michele, Toshio, Garriy, & Ching, 2010). Reconstructing the cultural intersubjective reality may be particularly helpful in dealing with a sense of injustice and guilt, which may maintain grief as well as PTSD symptoms (e.g., Tay et al., 2017). This may be achieved by encouraging the client or patient to engage in different ways of symbolic interaction with the deceased person.

Symbolic interactions with the deceased can find expression in writing assignments, imaginal conversations and culturally appropriate rituals. These interventions are part of evidence-based treatments for PTSD and prolonged grief. Specifically, brief eclectic psychotherapy for PTSD (BEPP), an evidence-based treatment for PTSD (Gersons, Meewisse, & Nijdam, 2015), and complicated grief treatment (CGT), a manualized treatment with proven effectiveness across several randomized controlled trials that has been implemented in different cultural settings (Shear et al., 2014; Shear, Reynolds, III, & Simon, 2016) comprise these interventions.

Writing Assignments

Writing assignments are useful tools to enable patients to evaluate meanings (Neimeyer, 2012) and to help bereaved individuals confront painful aspects of the loss at their own pace. An ongoing farewell letter is a letter to the deceased in which the patient writes what he has always wanted to say to the deceased and what he misses most, expressing his longing for the deceased. In people who have difficulty allowing feelings of sadness, it may promote emotional processing and finding meaning.

Writing an angry letter may be especially helpful to patients struggling with a sense of injustice who have difficulty dealing with feelings of anger. A letter can be written to a perpetrator of murder, negligent bystanders, the government or another agency that is held responsible, in which uncensored anger, including insults and diatribes, can be expressed. The letter is not sent. Sometimes, burning the angry letter is integrated into a ritual.

Mustaph is a 36-year-old refugee from Iraq who fled with his family to The Netherlands. Two years later, he received a telephone call in which he learned that his younger brother died in an attack on his parental home by the Islamic State. It was unclear whether the other relatives were still alive. Mustaph developed nightmares about this attack. He felt guilty and yearned for his brother. He was often angry with his wife and children. Mustaph felt strong anger toward the terrorists. A letter was written during the next session. Because Mustaph was illiterate, he dictated to the interpreter, and the therapist wrote. The letter started with revenge fantasies. As the therapist normalized his anger, he felt free to express his aggressive thoughts in the letter. Afterward, he felt able to hand over the judgment of the perpetrators to Allah. Mustaph also wrote a letter to his brother, saying that he felt sure he was now in a good place.

Imaginal Conversations

The therapist may guide an imaginal conversation with the person who died, in which the patient talks to the deceased person and also answers (Jordan, 2012). This technique may mitigate feelings of guilt and may foster disclosure of things that still need to be expressed toward the lost person ("unfinished business"). As a continuation of the previous vignette on Mustaph, the use of imaginal conversations is illustrated next.

Mustaph felt still very guilty, also because he had not been able to bury his brother. Therefore, it was decided to perform an imaginary conversation in which Mustaph would ask his brother for forgiveness and answer on behalf of his brother. His brother forgave him and hoped that Mustaph would find his parents so that he could take care of them. This conversation felt for Mustaph like saying goodbye.

In the case of Jack, an imaginal conversation has been used in a similar way.

In the course of therapy, Jack engages in an imaginal conversation with Grandmother. Grandmother is sitting on an empty chair and forgives Jack. She tells him that he may continue his life. Jack also imagines that he is a judge at the international court, where he sends the rebels to jail. Jack now realizes that he wants to live again.

The role of the therapist in the imaginal conversation is to encourage the bereaved individual to articulate meaningful questions, thoughts and feelings toward the lost person and to validate emotions that may arise during the conversation.

Farewell Ritual

Farewell rituals have been used traditionally in funerals when the body of the deceased is not present. The farewell ritual symbolizes a revised attachment bond with the deceased: the memory of the deceased may still be cherished, but the deceased is no longer symbolically kept alive (Van der Hart & Boelen, 2003). Rituals can be a bridge to the patient's culture or spirituality. They may symbolize continuity as well as transition and serve as reconciliation as well as affirmation (Doka, 2012).

The patient designs a farewell ritual that he finds appropriate. Examples of farewell rituals include visiting a special place, creating a symbol of remembrance, performing a culturally appropriate ritual, renouncing things related to the traumatic circumstances of the death and burning the angry letter. The therapist is not present at the ritual. The ritual also implies a departure from the therapist and a reunion with loved ones; therefore, the patient is encouraged to share the farewell ritual with a partner or a close friend.

David is a 55-year-old Dutch military veteran, married and the father of two children. During his first mission abroad (he was 17 years old), he had lost one of his closest comrades on site due to an accident. He first came into treatment 33 years later. He suffered from intrusive memories of his deployment experiences, his sleep was disrupted, and he couldn't stand loud noises. His wife reported sudden outbursts of anger. David obsessively kept himself busy and drank too much alcohol. David frequently experienced moments of intense grief over the loss of his comrade but could not bear the emotions that came along with this. David hadn't visited his comrade's grave. Therapy focused on being able to visit the graveyard and tolerating the associated emotions. When visiting his comrade's grave for the first time in 35 years, he felt overwhelmed with sadness. He wrote a letter to his comrade, in which he expressed his feelings of helplessness and sadness. In the final phase of treatment, David decided to arrange a small ceremony at his comrade's grave as a farewell ritual. His plan was to gather some close others at the cemetery and read his letter out loud. Then he would place a small keepsake at the grave. As the end of therapy approached, he felt as if the loss of his comrade had become part of his life. There were hardly any moments of agitation anymore. His wife confirmed this and was glad that she had a deeper understanding of what he had been through.

Writing assignments may be integrated with the ritual, as illustrated in the case of David and in the following case.

George, now 37 years old, from Liberia, had lived in The Netherlands since 2001. At the age of 13, his younger sister was killed. When he was 19, his parents were murdered by the rebels. George was forced to witness their murder. He was captured by the rebels and then forced to be a child soldier. George did not know what happened to the bodies of his parents. George had recurrent nightmares and flashbacks, in which he relived the murders of his parents. When he tried to fall asleep at night, intrusive memories of the murders kept him awake for hours. He had difficulties accepting the death of his parents and had strong feelings of guilt. He found his life meaningless without them. In the days surrounding the anniversary of his parents' death, he experienced acute physical pain. George was afraid of losing control and experienced a lot of anxiety about expressing his grief. Explaining the influence of avoidance on symptom maintenance helped him engage in the treatment. George talked about his safe and happy early childhood years and his warm relationship with his parents. With gradual exposure, he talked in detail about the day his parents were murdered and how he was taken by the rebels afterward. In between sessions, he had a hard time and got support from a friend as well as his religion. The therapist encouraged George to write letters to his parents about how he was doing and how he felt about them. At first this was very difficult for him, but eventually, he told that the writing of these letters had given him inner peace. George expressed more of his feelings and told about his struggle to find meaning in their death. He contemplated what his parents would have said about his current life and what advice they would have given him. This contributed to integrating the memory of his parents in a helpful manner. George started planning to visit the places he had lived with his parents and the place where they had died. He wanted to talk to people in that area and see if he could find out what had happened to his parents' bodies. He wanted to give them a proper burial. As a closing ritual of the therapy, he made plans to go to a church there and leave the letters to his parents behind.

Conclusion

For the bereaved survivor, the traumatic loss of loved ones evokes intense emotions as well as the uncertainties inherent in trauma, loss, fate and mortality that are now connected to the deceased person(s). Many cultural conceptions of death and the afterlife aim at filling the void arising from existential uncertainties. The Danish philosopher Kierkegaard, whose importance to psychology has been equated with that of Freud, explains in his book on the concept of fear (Kierkegaard, 1957) how the unknown, something that people do not understand but that nevertheless evokes many possibilities, is the source of our fear. It is linked to guilt, prohibition and punishment. Nowadays, fear of the unknown and intolerance of uncertainty are still key concepts in explaining the development of psychopathology, including disordered grief (Boelen, Reijntjes, & Smid, 2016). Therefore, a crucial therapeutic goal in grief therapy is to assist the patient in finding helpful meanings that promote emotional processing and grief resolution. Finding meaning refers to, as noted, a cognitive, emotional and spiritual process aimed at strengthening the individual's ability to live with the loss within his or her cultural context. In culturally diverse patients with symptoms of PTSD and PCBD/PGD following traumatic bereavement, exposure-based treatments may therefore be complemented with interventions aimed at finding meaning that include various modes of symbolic interaction with the deceased person.

Acknowledgement

The authors wish to thank Anouk van Berlo, Jannetta Bos, Annemiek de Heus and Marthe Hoofwijk for drafting the case descriptions.

References

Beck, A. T. (2008). The evolution of the cognitive model of depression and its neurobiological correlates. *American Journal of Psychiatry, 165*, 969–977.

Bhugra, D., & Becker, M. A. (2005). Migration, cultural bereavement and cultural identity. *World Psychiatry, 4*, 18–24.

Boehnlein, J. K. (1987). Clinical relevance of grief and mourning among Cambodian refugees. *Social Science & Medicine, 25*, 765–772.

Boelen, P. A., de Keijser, J., & Smid, G. E. (2015). Cognitive-behavioral variables mediate the impact of violent loss on post-loss psychopathology. *Psychological Trauma: Theory, Research, Practice, and Policy, 7*, 382–390.

Boelen, P. A., Reijntjes, A., & Smid, G. (2016). Concurrent and prospective associations of intolerance of uncertainty with symptoms of prolonged grief, posttraumatic stress, and depression after bereavement. *Journal of Anxiety Disorders, 41*, 65–72.

Boelen, P. A., & Smid, G. E. (2017). Disturbed grief: Prolonged grief disorder and persistent complex bereavement disorder. *BMJ: British Medical Journal, 357*, j2016. doi:10.1136/bmj.j2016

Boelen, P. A., Van den Hout, M. A., & Van den Bout, J. (2006). A cognitive-behavioral conceptualization of complicated grief. *Clinical Psychology: Science and Practice, 13*, 109–128.

Boss, P. (2006). *Loss, trauma, and resilience: Therapeutic work with ambiguous loss.* New York: Norton.

Cacciatore, J., & DeFrain, J. (2015). *The world of bereavement: Cultural perspectives on death in families. International and cultural psychology.* Cham, Heidelberg: Springer International Publishing.

Chi-Yue, C., Michele, J. G., Toshio, Y., Garriy, S., & Ching, W. (2010). Intersubjective culture: The role of intersubjective perceptions in cross-cultural research. *Perspectives on Psychological Science, 5*, 482–493. doi:10.1177/1745691610375562

Doka, K. J. (2012). Therapeutic ritual. In R. A. Neimeyer (Ed.), *Techniques of grief therapy: Creative practices for counseling the bereaved* (1st ed., pp. 341–343). New York: Routledge.

Durkheim, E. (1995). *The elementary forms of religious life: The totemic system in Australia (translation K. Fields).* New York: Free Press.

Eisenbruch, M. (1990). The cultural bereavement interview: A new clinical research approach for refugees. *Psychiatric Clinics of North America, 13*, 715–735.

Gersons, B. P. R., Meewisse, M. L., & Nijdam, M. J. (2015). Brief eclectic psychotherapy for PTSD. In U. Schnyder & M. Cloitre (Eds.), *Evidence based treatments for trauma-related psychological disorders* (pp. 255–276). Cham, Heidelberg: Springer.

Hart, O. van der, & Boelen, P. A. (2003). Therapeutische afscheidsrituelen in de behandeling van problematische rouw: een integratie [Therapeutic leave taking rituals in the treatment of problematic grief: An integration]. In O. van der Hart (Ed.), *Afscheidsrituelen – Achterblijven en verder gaan* (3rd ed., pp. 221–236). Lisse: Swets & Zeitlinger.

Hinton, D., Peou, S., Joshi, S., Nickerson, A., & Simon, N. (2013). Normal grief and complicated bereavement among traumatized Cambodian refugees: Cultural context and the central role of dreams of the dead. *Culture, Medicine & Psychiatry, 37*, 427–464. Article.

Jordan, J. R. (2012). Guided imaginal conversations with the deceased. In R. A. Neimeyer (Ed.), *Techniques of grief therapy: Creative practices for counseling the bereaved* (1st ed., pp. 262–265). New York: Routledge.

Kierkegaard, S. (1957). *The concept of dread: Translated with introduction and notes by Walter Lowrie* (2nd ed.). Princeton, NJ: Princeton University Press.

Kirmayer, L. J., Gone, J. P., & Moses, J. (2014). Rethinking historical trauma. *Transcultural Psychiatry, 51*, 299–319. doi:10.1177/1363461514536358

Maccallum, F., & Bryant, R. A. (2013). A cognitive attachment model of prolonged grief: Integrating attachments, memory, and identity. *Clinical Psychology Review, 33*, 713–727.

Neimeyer, R. A. (2006). Complicated grief and the reconstruction of meaning: Conceptual and empirical contributions to a cognitive-constructivist model. *Clinical Psychology: Science and Practice, 13*, 141–145.

Neimeyer, R. A. (2012). Correspondence with the deceased. In R. A. Neimeyer (Ed.), *Techniques of grief therapy: Creative practices for counseling the bereaved* (1st ed., pp. 259–261). New York: Routledge.

Romanoff, B. D., & Terenzio, M. (1998). Rituals and the grieving process. *Death Studies, 22*, 697–711. doi:10.1080/074811898201227

Shear, K. M. M., Wang, Y. P., Skritskaya, N. P., Duan, N. P., Mauro, C. M., & Ghesquiere, A. P. (2014). Treatment of complicated grief in elderly persons: A randomized clinical trial. *JAMA Psychiatry, 71*, 1287–1295. doi:10.1001/jamapsychiatry.2014.1242

Shear, M. K., Reynolds, C. F., III, & Simon, N. M. (2016). Optimizing treatment of complicated grief: A randomized clinical trial. *JAMA Psychiatry, 73*, 685–694. doi:10.1001/jamapsychiatry.2016.0892

Smid, G. E., Drogendijk, A. N., Knipscheer, J. W., Boelen, P. A., & Kleber, R. J. (2018). Loss of loved ones or home due to a disaster: Effects over time on distress in immigrant ethnic minorities. *Transcultural Psychiatry*.

Smid, G. E., Groen, S., de la Rie, S. M., Kooper, S., & Boelen, P. A. (2018). Towards cultural assessment of grief and grief-related psychopathology. *Psychiatric Services*, *69*(10), 1050–1052. doi:10.1176/appi.ps.201700422

Staal, F. (1979). The meaninglessness of ritual. *Numen*, *26*, 2–22. doi:10.2307/3269623

Tay, A. K., Rees, S., Steel, Z., Liddell, B., Nickerson, A., Tam, N. et al. (2017). The role of grief symptoms and a sense of injustice in the pathways to post-traumatic stress symptoms in post-conflict Timor-Leste. *Epidemiology and Psychiatric Sciences*, *26*, 403–413. doi:10.1017/S2045796016000317

4
Suffering a Death Wish
The Psychology of Medical Assistance in Dying

Christopher J. MacKinnon, Deborah Ummel,
Florence Vinit and Erica Srinivasan

INTRODUCTION

In December 2015, Quebec was the first Canadian province to legalize a form of euthanasia termed "medical assistance in dying" (MAiD). MAiD stipulates strict criteria for individuals with life-threatening illness to end their lives under a physician's supervision. MAiD was made available across the Dominion in 2016 by ruling of the Supreme Court of Canada.

Literature to date has largely been centered, among many foci, on clinical practice guidelines, observational studies, establishing criteria and procedures for MAiD and identifying factors that contribute to the request for MAiD, as well as detailing the pertinent ethical and moral priorities surrounding the right to end one's own life (Oczkowski et al., 2017). However, the various discourses surrounding MAiD may neglect a deeper treatment of the underlying psychological processes embedded within the request to die. To this end, a constructivist lens (Neimeyer, 2009) is adopted in an attempt to discern some of the deeper meanings found in the request for hastened death (HD).

This chapter begins by briefly outlining the structure and framework of MAiD in the Canadian context, followed by a constructivist-informed view of MAiD[1] illustrating some of the potential underlying psychological facets in the wish to die. Offered in conclusion are numerous clinical implications.

CANADA'S APPROACH TO ASSISTED DYING

Prior to June 2016, it was a criminal act in Canada for a physician or health-care team to assist patients in ending their lives. At present, under certain criteria, it is legally permissible for a form of euthanasia to be practiced.[2] The criteria for the act are as follows: The person must be 18 years of age or older, capable of making decisions and suffering from an illness or disability that is advanced and incurable. Furthermore, the illness or disability must be causing intolerable psychological and physical suffering that cannot be alleviated. MAiD is performed under the supervision of a physician, who administers the prescription necessary to cause death. The final decision rests with two evaluating physicians, who must confirm the patient's eligibility and have the authority to decline the request. While no physician can be compelled to perform MAiD, Canadian law requires that every public institution offer this option.

DOI: 10.4324/9781351069120-5

THE PSYCHOLOGICAL FACETS OF MAID

Worldwide, some countries have a longstanding history of and familiarity with patients requesting HD. In 2001, the Royal Dutch Medical Association declared that suffering due to existential distress, meaninglessness or loss of dignity was part of the medical domain. This, in effect, broadened the definition of suffering as it related to requests for physician-assisted death to include psychological and psychiatric phenomena (Koopman & Boer, 2016).

Both The Netherlands and Belgium subsequently legalized euthanasia and have in the past few years permitted broad and increased access for patients reporting unbearable suffering. These countries are reporting upward trends in overall numbers of requests for physician-assisted death of approximately 15% each year since 2007 (Boer & Lic, 2017). Consequently, people with various mental health conditions, including personality disorders, depression, autism, anorexia and prolonged grief have died by euthanasia in these two countries (Kim, De Vries, & Peteet, 2016). These authors also reported that while it was generally expected that access to euthanasia would decrease overall suicide rates, The Netherlands has reported a unique upward trend in suicide compared to several European countries.

What seems to be true in both Europe and North America is that most requests for MAiD have some relevant psychological dimensions. Prior research suggests that many people requesting aid in dying reported concurrent emotional distress, including loss of meaning, existential distress and grief, as well as anxiety related to anticipated future suffering and loss of control (Breitbart et al., 2008; Mystakidou et al., 2005). A study of family members of those who died an assisted death in Oregon discussed anticipated future suffering and loss of control, noting that patients took comfort in the fact that they could have a sense of control in the dying process (Srinivasan, 2018). A commonality among many studies is the association between depression and desire for HD (Wilson et al., 2016). Social factors, including loss of identity or role, isolation and the desire to avoid being a burden to others, can also contribute to the motivation for a hastened death (Pearlman et al., 2004; Rodríguez-Prat, Balaguer, Booth, & Monforte-Royo, 2017). Finally, approximately 20 years of data concerning Oregon's Death With Dignity Act have been collected, highlighting major end-of-life concerns including various psychological aspects (e.g., loss of autonomy, decreased ability to engage in activities that make life enjoyable, loss of dignity, loss of control over bodily functions and being a burden on others) (Oregon Health Authority, Public Health Division, 2018).

ASSESSING THE MEANINGS OF MAID

Seeking to end one's life remains one of the most complex and arguably least understood of all human behaviors (Stillion & McDowell, 1996). For instance, suicide can mean many things to people, including reuniting with a loved one in the afterlife, a means to exact revenge on another or a way out of an untenable situation (Sands, Jordan, & Neimeyer, 2011). Similarly, the circumstances surrounding the desire and decision for MAiD are equally multifaceted and worthy of considered attention.

A constructivist approach is often applied to circumstances that demand in-depth reflection and tolerance for ambiguity. It is largely concerned with the subjective meanings individuals attribute to their lives and how these adopted scripts promote difficulties that may be re-authored into productive approaches to complex life dilemmas through psychotherapeutic intervention (Neimeyer, 2009). Constructivists work with individuals who are in a crisis of meaning, perhaps unable to make sense of a seemingly incomprehensible event.

Meaning has also been a preoccupation among the existential psychologists. For instance, the early construct of the *noogenic neurosis* (Frankl, 1981) referred to the origins of psychological distress as a loss of meaning. Meaninglessness as an outcome has been identi-fied as encompassing estrangement, hopelessness, lack of authenticity, failure to cope and emptiness (Orbach, 2008). Furthermore, demoralization is a proposed psychiatric construct to describe a state of existential conflict characterized by hopelessness, helplessness and loss of purpose and meaning in life and strongly associated with the desire for HD (Robinson, Kissane, Brooker, & Burney, 2015).

Seeking deeper meanings tethered to the desire for HD is aligned with recent develop-ments in the literature (e.g., Rodríguez-Prat & van Leeuwen, 2017). For instance, Nissim and colleagues (2009) identified three distinct categories of meaning buttressing the desire for HD in an advanced oncology sample. First, participants reported that HD was a hypothetical exit plan that allayed anxiety and brought some certainty to an ambiguous future. Second, the wish for death was identified as the only course of action available to escape the trap of being engulfed by overwhelming feelings of anxiety, helplessness or despair. The final group-ing was framed as a manifestation of "letting go." In the final days and weeks, participants felt they had reached their limit to continue living and came to some form of acceptance of their mortality. Others welcomed an imminent death, began to withdraw and sought to minimize external stimulation.

A relevant systematic review and meta-ethnography penned by Rodríguez-Prat and col-leagues (2017) identified five sub-themes of meanings underpinning the wish for HD. First, the wish to die may be a plea for immediate relief, which may speak to either intolerable suffering or a difficulty accepting the illness. Second, death can be seen as a way to avoid or end suffering. Suffering was reported to encompass solitude, terror, dependency, pain, futility, anhedonia and the need to protect the self from disintegration. Third, the wish to die is linked to altruistic desires to protect others by not being a burden. Death is preferable than being an encumbrance to others and thereby causing loved ones to suffer. Fourth, many people at the end of life seek to reaffirm their control of the situation, particularly as they lose functional capacity. In this way, MAiD may represent a way to reclaim some personal authority. Lastly, the authors report that individuals face two concurrent and competing motivations: people desire to continue living but find it impossible as the tasks of life that have previously brought meaning and value become inaccessible.

These last two studies are representative of a relatively small movement toward constructivist-informed inquiries into the desire for MAiD. Before considering the clinical implications of a meaning-based approach to MAiD, we give some attention to the role of the therapist, which may exist both in tension and in harmony with the goals of MAiD.

POSITION OF THE THERAPIST

What little has been written on the roles for psychologists in end-of-life care generally makes no mention of euthanasia (Haley, Larson, Kasl-Godley, Neimeyer, & Kwilosz, 2003) and, in fact, conversely provides guidance on assessment for suicide prevention (e.g., Neimeyer, 2005). Therapists are generally tasked with preventing the suicide of their clients and thus encounter a critical dilemma surrounding MAiD. What is the role (if any) for therapists working with patients who wish to end their lives when the traditional role has been one of preventing suicide?

In Canada, counseling someone to die by suicide or aiding a person's suicide without med-ical assistance are criminal offenses that carry prison terms. However, providing information on MAiD is not considered a criminal act. One can then infer that an ethical and legally respectful psychological intervention may include exploring the intersubjective meanings the person has concerning MAiD. However, any meaning-seeking interventions quickly lead to several complications.

To begin, it is incumbent on therapists to determine if they even have a part to play in a MAiD scenario. For example, Quebec law does not necessitate the involvement of a mental health professional in the eligibility process for MAiD. Each institution is at liberty to involve a therapist (e.g., social worker, psychologist) at its discretion.

If a therapist is asked to be involved in the evaluative process, this has profound implications. For one, the therapist becomes to some extent a gatekeeper in either facilitating or blocking access for the patient to MAiD. Working as part of a multidisciplinary team, the therapist may be asked to report back the outcome of the meeting. It would therefore be important to know the purpose behind or meaning of the referral. For instance, what outcome is the treating team seeking from the therapists' meeting? Knowing that the contents of a conversation with the therapist could potentially inform the decision for MAiD also opens the strong possibility for response bias. For example, patients may feel they have to mask their true psychological state to avoid being disqualified for MAiD.

The possibility of disqualification is raised in the case of severe clinical depression. In Canada, when non-terminally ill and severely depressed clients are imminently at risk of killing themselves, the law supersedes the rights of individuals. A therapist has a legal obligation to intercede, break confidentiality and inform the relevant authorities, depending on the severity and imminence of the threat of suicide. In this case, suicidality impairs people to the extent that they are deemed no longer competent to make their own decisions.

As is relates to MAiD, however, an early definition of rational suicide precludes the individual having severe emotional distress (Siegel, 1986). It therefore becomes important to consider the meaning the patient attributes to a conversation with a therapist. A conversation in which the goal is determining if a patient qualifies for MAiD is very different from one that explores the meaning that MAiD holds for the patient.

Moreover, the situation becomes even more obscure in the circumstances when the therapist plays no part in the question of access to MAiD. Psychotherapeutic treatment broadly defined can be construed as facilitating a process whereby patients discover new options in responding to a given impasse that they have not been able to readily circumvent. In the case of a psychotherapeutic intervention concerning MAiD, what new meanings can (or should) be made, and what would adopting those meanings imply? Is the desired psychotherapeutic conversation that centers on the intersubjective meanings of MAiD meant to create new options, and, if so, what might those options be? Constructivists work in the realm of reformulating meanings that are no longer serving the individual. In this sense, psychotherapeutic conversations with patients who have elected to go forward with MAiD may require therapists to embrace a certain paradoxical position in which they are tasked with facilitating the creation of options in the shadow of an impending death that removes all options.

CLINICAL IMPLICATIONS

This concluding section concerns ways to access the untold intersubjective meanings of MAiD. Conversations with individuals confronting the end of life with MAiD demand a high degree of sophistication and professional maturity. Patients could be potentially ambivalent and uncommitted to any discourse concerning MAiD. Clinical maturity thus includes a tolerance for powerlessness and ambiguity and detachment of the therapist from any preferred outcome.

To begin, therapists should attempt to differentiate state versus trait desire for HD. State desire would be defined as a temporary wish to die, whereas trait desire would be more longstanding and persistent. The literature surveyed in this chapter clearly suggests that the desire for HD can be unstable and uncertain and can oscillate between the state and trait poles. Returning to the compelling article by Nissim and colleagues (2009), the desire for HD can become more prominent at moments of great transition, such as the initial diagnosis or a poor test result. Clinical interviews that take place at these inflection points should keep in mind that expressions of despair associated with the wish to die tended to be transient, and, as general psychotherapy practice suggests, patients in the middle of a crisis should be discouraged from engaging in major life (or death) decisions. Similarly, people in severe multifactorial pain may not be in the best mindset to render meaning to their situation, and every attempt should be made to control for this pain before MAiD is considered (consistent with best palliative care practice, Tucker, 2012). However, if patients can endure the passage through their own despair, it may permit them to identify alternative sources of meaning that may make life sustainable. For example, a patient struggling with feelings of being a burden on others might consider MAiD; however, learning new ways to address the perception of being a burden might bring about a novel perspective, thereby altering the pursuit of MAiD.

On the other hand, the necessity of having a departure strategy tends to be a more sustained feature and suggests there may be underlying meanings around the need to control the final moments of one's life. Control is often a means to cope with anxiety, and there can be many influential meanings undergirding this coping structure. For instance, many of us have histories of abandonment, neglect or betrayal that leave deep imprints and tend to surface in watershed moments, such as the end of life (Back et al., 2008). The ways in which we internalize our histories often compel us to repeat rigid scripts, such as protective behaviors that may simply not match the present circumstances.

CONCLUSIONS

Meaninglessness inhibits fullness of life and is therefore equivalent to illness. Meaning makes a great many things endurable—perhaps everything.

(Carl Jung, 1963b, p. 340)

The appeal of MAiD seems to be driven in part by the anguish in facing an intolerable intrapsychic state of physical symptomatology. To date, the possible subjective meanings of patients requesting MAiD are only beginning to be mapped. Constructivist psychotherapy offers a compelling paradigm to advance this clinical and research agenda. Closely aligned with other forms of depth psychotherapy (Hollis, 2013), constructivists offer a process of tracking backward to discern the invisible stories that often govern a person's life (Neimeyer, 2009). While many patients requesting MAiD feel a profound loss of meaning and purpose in life (Wilson et al., 2016), constructivists are experts in rebuilding meaning. Shedding light on a patient's subjective world of meaning as it relates to the wish to die may lead to the creation of alternative options around the request for HD. As a starting point for deeper inquiry, one question to pose to people requesting MAiD is what MAiD represents to them.

Therapists may also be tasked with helping patients tolerate the *tension of opposites* (Jung, 1963a) between whether or not to proceed with MAiD, perhaps waiting until a third option presents itself, possibly created in the psychotherapeutic encounter. Therapists in this way may best position themselves in the role of companions accompanying patients, reflecting their experience and allowing them to come to a decision. Therapists may be able to help dying patients conceive of how to best align themselves with the circumstances of their living and dying when the latter presents difficult challenges that invite no simple solution.

Notes

1. MAiD exists in parallel with various other forms worldwide including rational suicide, physician-assisted suicide, physician aid in dying and euthanasia. While these end-of-life options vary in implementation, they generally share the same desired outcome and have many similar psychological facets. Consequently, we will use these terms interchangeably with MAiD.
2. An Act to amend the Criminal Code and to make related amendments to other Acts (medical assistance in dying) (formerly Bill C-14), 1st Sess, 42nd Leg, Canada, 2016 (assented to June 17, 2016).

References

Back, A. L., Young, J. P., McCown, E., Engelberg, R. A., Vig, E. K., Reinke, L. F., . . . Curtis, J. R. (2008). Abandonment at the end of life from patient and clinician perspectives: Loss of continuity and lack of closure. *Archives of Internal Medicine, 169*(5), 474–479.

Boer, T., & Lic, T. (2017). Does euthanasia have a dampening effect on suicide rates? Recent experiences from the Netherlands. *Journal of Ethics in Mental Health, 10*, 1–9.

Frankl, V. E. (1981). *Will to meaning: Foundations and applications of logotherapy.* New York: Meridian.

Haley, W., Larson, D., Kasl-Godley, J., Neimeyer, R. A., & Kwilosz, D. (2003). Roles for psychologists in end-of-life care: Emerging models of practice. *Professional Psychology: Research and Practice, 34*(6), 626–633.

Hollis, J. (2013). *Hauntings: Dispelling the ghosts who run our lives.* Asheville, NC: Chiron.

Jung, C. G. (1963a). *Mysterium coniunctionis* (R. Winston & C. Winston, Trans.). New York: Bolligen Foundation.

Jung, C. G. (1963b). *Memories, dreams, reflections* (R. Winston & C. Winston, Trans.). New York: Vintage Books.

Koopman, J. J. E., & Boer, T. A. (2016). Turning points in the conception and regulation of physician-assisted dying in the Netherlands. *The American Journal of Medicine, 129*(8), 773–775.

Kim, S. Y. H., De Vries, R. G., & Peteet, J. R. (2016). Euthanasia and assisted suicide of patients with psychiatric disorders in the Netherlands 2011 to 2014. *JAMA Psychiatry, 73*(4), 362–368.

Mystakidou, K., Rosenfeld, B., Prapa, E., Katsouda, E., Tsilika, E., Galanos, A., & Vlahos, L. (2005). Desire for death near the end of life: The role of depression, anxiety and pain. *General Hospital Psychiatry, 27*(4), 258–262.

Neimeyer, R. A. (2005). From death anxiety to meaning-making at the end of life: Recommendations for psychological assessment. *Clinical Psychology: Science and Practice, 12*, 354–357.

Neimeyer, R. A. (2009). *Constructivist psychotherapy: Distinctive features.* New York: Routledge.

Nissim, R., Gagliese, L., & Rodin, G. (2009). The desire for hastened death in individuals with advanced cancer: A longitudinal qualitative study. *Social Science and Medicine, 69*, 165–171.

Oczkowski, S. J. W., Ball, I., Saleh, C., Kalles, G., Chkaroubo, A., Kekewich, M., . . . Frolic, A. (2017). The provision of medical assistance in dying: Protocol for a scoping review. *BMJ Open, 7*(8), 1–5.

Orbach, I. (2008). Existentialism and suicide. In A. Tomer, G. T. Eliason, & P. T. P. Wong (Eds.), *Existential and spiritual issues in death attitudes* (pp. 281–316). New York: Lawrence Erlbaum Associates.

Oregon Health Authority, Public Health Division. (2018). *Oregon Death with Dignity Act 2017 data summary.* Retrieved March 31, 2018, from www.oregon.gov/oha/PH/PROVIDERPARTNERRE-SOURCES/EVALUATIONRESEARCH/DEATHWITHDIGNITYACT/Documents/year20.pdf

Robinson, S., Kissane, D. W., Brooker, J., & Burney, S. (2015). A systematic review of the demoralization syndrome in individuals with progressive disease and cancer: A decade of research. *Journal of Pain and Symptom Management, 49*(3), 595–610.

Rodríguez-Prat, A., Balaguer, A., Booth, A., & Monforte-Royo, C. (2017). Understanding patients' experiences of the wish to hasten death: An updated and expanded systematic review and meta-ethnography. *BMJ Open, 7*(9), 1–13.

Rodríguez-Prat, A., & van Leeuwen, E. (2017). Assumptions and moral understanding of the wish to hasten death: A philosophical review of qualitative studies. *Medicine, Health Care and Philosophy, 21*(1), 63–75.

Sands, D. C., Jordan, J., R., & Neimeyer, R. A. (2011). The meanings of suicide: A narrative approach to healing. In J. Jordan & J. L. McIntosh (Eds.), *Grief after suicide: Understanding the consequences and caring for the survivors* (pp. 249–281). New York: Routledge.

Siegel, K. (1986). Psychosocial aspects of rational suicide. *American Journal of Psychotherapy, 40*(3), 405–418.

Srinivasan, E. G. (2018). Bereavement experiences following a death under Oregon's Death with Dignity Act. *Death Studies, 43*(10), 647–655. doi:10.1080/07481187.2018.1511636

Stillion, J., & McDowell, E. E. (1996). *Suicide across the lifespan: Premature exits* (2nd ed.). New York: Routledge.

Tucker, K. L. (2012). Aid in dying: An end of life-option governed by best practices. *Journal of Health and Biomedical Law, VIII,* 9–26.

Wilson, K. G., Dalgeish, T. L., Chochinov, H. M., Chary, S., Gagnon, P. R., Macmillan, K., . . . Fainsinger, R. L. (2016). Mental disorders and the desire for death in patients receiving palliative care for cancer. *BMJ Supportive & Palliative Care, 6*(2), 170–177.

5
Grief After Non-Death Losses

Darcy Harris

Patricia and James met one morning at a coffee shop. Patricia needed a place to set her laptop down to work while she drank her morning coffee, and there were no tables available. James was sitting alone at a table and offered a chair and the tabletop to Patricia. Once they started talking, they hit it off very well. Patricia was 40 years old at the time, and James was 53. Over the next year, they dated, traveled together and met each other's extended families and close friends. They were such a good fit—even their dogs liked each other! They married and settled into a comfortable routine of sharing meals, walking the dogs, traveling and reading snippets of the paper to each other on Sunday mornings. Neither had children, and given their ages, they had discussed the possibility of either adopting an older child or being foster parents to share their loving home with a child in need.

One Sunday morning, James woke up and did not feel well. He was dizzy and felt weak. He called out to Patricia as he was getting out of the shower and then collapsed into a heap on the floor. Patricia called 911, and an ambulance came and took James to the emergency department of the nearest hospital. Patricia was told that James had suffered a significant stroke and that he would most likely survive, but he would probably not be able to speak, and he would not be able to use one side of his body. Once he was stable, James was transferred to a rehabilitation center to help him to gain as much function back as possible and learn to cope with the deficits that occurred as a result of the stroke.

Patricia was now 43 years old. They did not have children. Both sets of their parents were older and had significant health problems, so there was no extended family to assist her in caring for James. She made modifications to the house to accommodate a wheelchair and the special needs that James had for his personal care. She resigned from her position at work so that she could care for James, taking early retirement, which paid her less than half of her usual income. As time went on, fewer and fewer friends came over to visit; most of the time when the doorbell rang, it was someone from the home health agency arriving to provide care of some sort or to bring medical supplies that were needed. James could usually understand what Patricia said to him, but he would become very frustrated and agitated when she couldn't understand what he wanted or needed. Intermittently, James became confused and agitated, and Patricia worried about the possibility of his hurting himself when these times occurred. They no longer shared sexual intimacy. Patricia set an alarm several times through the night to assist James in changing his position in bed and to help him if he needed to use the bedside commode.

After several months of caregiving, Patricia slumped herself down in a chair in the corner of the bedroom while James slept. Tears flooded as she assessed her life—or what was left

    DOI: 10.4324/9781351069120-6

of it. She would never have children. She couldn't just run to the store to pick something up without making arrangements for someone to be with James. James could stay like this for years, or he could get worse, and she often worried that she would somehow neglect something important and cause a complication to occur. She felt completely exhausted and alone.

This scenario has many losses in it. However, none of the losses are because someone died; rather, the losses are ongoing, and they exist in and mingle with the everyday life of Patricia and James as time goes on. In this chapter, we will explore some of the various non-death, *living losses* that can occur, including some unique aspects of these losses and their implications.

GRIEF FROM A BROAD PERSPECTIVE

Early bereavement research focused on the concept of grief as a form of separation distress (Bowlby, 1998). Grief was viewed as the result of a broken attachment bond that occurred when an attachment figure died (such as a parent, child, spouse, partner). More recently, a substantial body of research (Field, 2006; Klass, Silverman, & Nickman, 1996; Stroebe, Schut, & Boerner, 2010) demonstrated that many bereaved individuals maintain an ongoing attachment bond with their deceased loved one(s) in the form of ongoing conversations, dreams, signs, a sense of the loved one(s) watching over them and/or guiding them as they continue to live and an often-intangible but real sense of the presence of the loved one(s) in their daily lives. These researchers concluded that the attachment bond isn't necessarily broken when a loved one dies. As the implications of these findings were gradually integrated into the literature, it became apparent that although *attachment style* has an impact on grief, the actual grief response is more complex than the basic construction of it as a variant of separation distress. Grief could no longer simply be defined in terms of a broken attachment bond or the loss of an attachment figure through death.

Bowlby posited that early-life attachment experiences led individuals to form "working models" of the self and the world. He suggested that significant losses can threaten these working models, leading to efforts to rebuild or restructure these models to fit the post-loss world. Expanding on Bowlby's work, Parkes (1975) described the concept of the "internal working model," extending it to that of the "assumptive world," which includes our interpretation of the past and our expectations of the future, including our plans and our prejudices. Later, Janoff-Bulman (1992) identified three major categories of the assumptive world construct. Harris (2011) further expanded on these three categories to incorporate the possibility of these assumptions anticipating both negative and positive scenarios. The three basic categories are:

1. *How an individual expects the world and others to relate to himself/herself.* An example of this assumption might be the view that the world is basically a good place and that people are generally trustworthy and have basically good intentions toward others.
2. *How an individual makes sense of the world and attaches meaning to it.* Often, this category includes the concepts of justice and cause/effect. For example, one common assumption in most Western societies is that if you work hard, you will be rewarded.
3. *How an individual perceives him/herself within the world and situates him/herself within a social context.* An example here might be the view that the individual has worth and value because all human beings have intrinsic worth and value.

The assumptive world provides the ability to predict, make sense of and determine responses to events that occur, ensuring a sense of stability and security in everyday life. Like the attachment system, the assumptive world is most likely formed very early in life and forms a core aspect of the individual. When one's assumptions about the world are shattered or rendered meaningless after significant life events occur, the assumptive world must be rebuilt in order to engage in life again (Harris, 2020). Certainly, the death of a loved one has great potential to cause such a disruption. However, other types of losses that may not involve death can also have the same outcome, with the need to rebuild and relearn one's assumptions about the world in a way that preserves a sense of coherence and safety. Certainly, losses of significant others in life can come about through death—but we also lose those we care about through life transitions, relationship dissolution and distance. We can lose objects that we value and endow with meaning. We can lose a sense of connection to our community, our country and our beliefs. We can even lose ourselves, a little piece at a time or all at once. At the core of all significant losses is the potential to shatter our assumptions about the world, and in this context, it is this overarching loss of a meaningful assumptive world that provides the main trigger for the grief response (Harris, 2020; Harris & Winokuer, 2016).

Returning to Patricia's life after James suffered his stroke, it is possible to consider the many assaults on her assumptive world that occurred. Her assumption about the world and others would be challenged as her friends no longer checked in with her, and her main sources of human contact were the professional caregivers assigned to assist with James's care. Her view of what life should be like and the plans that she and James had for their future disappeared in a single moment. Certainly, they were still comparatively young, and this kind of health issue was unexpected for James, who was active and in good health prior to the stroke. And finally, Patricia's view of herself changed from being a woman who had a fulfilling career and loving mutual relationship to a stay-at-home caregiver to her husband, who was now completely dependent upon her. In short, Patricia was grieving the many losses that had shattered her assumptive world.

Understanding the role of the assumptive world in everyday life provides a broad framework for appreciating the potentially adaptive role of grief in both death and non-death loss experiences. The rest of this chapter will briefly discuss different types of non-death loss experiences and their implications. The ability to have descriptive words for these experiences can be empowering for those who experience them, in addition to providing conceptual terms that are readily applicable to research and clinical practice.

NONFINITE LOSS AND CHRONIC SORROW

Many non-death loss experiences are ongoing in nature and have no foreseeable end. The loss itself will require ongoing accommodation, adaptation and adjustment for the rest of the lives of those affected. These ongoing loss experiences are *nonfinite losses*. In their writings, Bruce and Schultz (2001) describe several cardinal features of the experience of nonfinite losses:

- There is ongoing uncertainty regarding what will happen next. This uncertainty is often intermingled with a sense of ongoing dread and chronic despair.
- There is often a sense of disconnection from the mainstream and what is generally viewed as "normal" in human experience.
- The magnitude of the loss is frequently unrecognized or not acknowledged by others. Social misunderstanding and disenfranchisement are very common with these types of losses.
- There is an ongoing sense of helplessness and powerlessness associated with the loss.

The person who experiences nonfinite loss is repeatedly asked to adjust and accommodate to the loss. At the same time, because nonfinite losses are often not well understood, the experience may go unrecognized or unacknowledged by others. Support systems may tire of attempting to provide a shoulder to lean on in a situation that has no defined ending. Ongoing adjustment occurs as individuals with nonfinite losses try to reconcile the reality of the world they now face as a result of their loss and the world they had previously anticipated and envisioned.

Chronic sorrow is the response to nonfinite loss experiences. The ongoing grief in chronic sorrow is not a disorder such as prolonged grief or delayed grief, but rather a unique form of grief that is also ongoing in nature because the loss itself and its effects are ongoing (Harris, 2011). Chronic sorrow differs from prolonged grief disorder in that it occurs in a *living loss* (a non-death loss), and it is not an anomaly or a sign that something is wrong. The grief continues in an ongoing way because the loss is ongoing in nature; the loss itself and related factors continue to surface. Chronic sorrow can be manifest in individuals who experience nonfinite losses as well as in those who are close to these individuals. In fact, sometimes chronic sorrow resides primarily with those who journey alongside individuals with nonfinite losses, occurring as they have to continually adapt their lives to the new realities that occur with the nonfinite loss, in addition to painfully and helplessly watching their loved ones struggle and attempt to cope with their experiences in an ongoing way.

Chronic sorrow is defined by Roos (2018) as "a set of pervasive, profound, continuing, and recurring grief responses resulting from a significant loss or absence of crucial aspects of oneself (self-loss) or another living person (other-loss) to whom there is a deep attachment" (p. 25). The way in which the loss is perceived determines the existence of chronic sorrow. Chronic sorrow is the response to the ongoing loss experience, as the mourner is faced with a painful discrepancy between what is perceived as reality and what continues to be dreamed of as otherwise possible.

The scenario with Patricia and James provides a good example of nonfinite loss and chronic sorrow. James is very much alive but is unable to function as he did previously. The relationship between Patricia and James is permanently altered due to his difficulties in communicating and his ongoing care needs. Patricia's life now revolves around caring for James. The situation could potentially continue for many years, and there is no end in sight. It is unlikely that the grief that both Patricia and James are experiencing would be acknowledged because James is still alive and has the potential to live for a long time.

AMBIGUOUS LOSS

Perhaps the most dramatic experience of ambiguous loss in North America occurred after the events of September 11, 2001, when thousands of individuals who worked in the two towers of the World Trade Centre were trapped after planes flew into each of the two buildings, sending them crashing to the ground in an inferno of intense heat and debris. The majority of the loved ones of these individuals never received physical confirmation of their deaths, as all traces of DNA, articles of clothing, jewelry and personal effects were obliterated in the heat and destruction. For weeks after these events, pictures of missing loved ones were posted on bulletin boards, on telephone poles and in many public places. People walked around the local area holding pictures of their missing loved ones, hoping that perhaps someone would confirm that their loved one had been taken to a hospital or rendered confused by the events that had occurred and had taken shelter somewhere. There was grief, but also hope and uncertainty—without proof of their loved one's whereabouts or evidence of their death, it was impossible to know how to proceed.

Ambiguous loss is a particularly stressful kind of loss because it is not typically officially acknowledged, and there is no possibility of closure (Boss, 1999, 2009). Ambiguous losses always occur in the context of a relationship and descriptions of ambiguous losses occur as an absence/presence dynamic. There are two types of ambiguous loss:

1. A loved one is physically absent but psychologically present (e.g., kidnapped, lost at sea, missing, deserted, abandoned).
2. A loved one is psychologically absent but physically present (e.g., traumatic brain injury, dementia, autism, depression, addiction, chronic mental illness).

Ambiguous losses lack clarity and certainty. At times, as when someone is literally missing or is cognitively impaired, the loss remains unclear as people don't know if a loved one is dead or alive, absent or present. In situations of loved ones with cognitive impairment, when a brief moment of recognition or understanding can intermittently occur, the experience of loss and uncertainty is intensified. People can become frozen in the grief (which is a hallmark sign of grief in ambiguous loss) because there is no answer, no clear-cut defined loss and no way to recognize what has happened (Boss, 1999, 2009). People who experience ambiguous losses have difficulties describing their experiences, and those around them often don't know how to respond, so people often pull away and don't reach out to those who are affected by the loss. In our case study of Patricia and James, there is the loss of the relationship through James's intermittent confusion and difficulties communicating. James is still physically present, but the person that James was is no longer present. Patricia is left to grieve the emotional loss of someone whose physical care needs now govern her life.

INTANGIBLE LOSSES

Intangible losses are more abstract or symbolic in nature. These types of losses may involve the loss of hopes or dreams. They may be existential in nature, or they may involve a loss in beliefs about the world or others, loss of meaning, loss of faith or loss of a sense of spiritual connection. These losses often include profound changes in the view of self, and they can also be related to demoralizing situations, situations of abuse and neglect and experiences in which shame is prominent (Harris, 2011; Harris & Winokuer, 2016). While these losses are not readily observable or recognized by others, they are often profound and debilitating to those who experience them. These losses are sometimes referred to as *invisible losses* because of the lack of physical signs of an obvious loss to the casual observer. Many intangible losses are symbolic in nature, focused on hopes, dreams, beliefs and identity.

Intangible loses may include:

- Loss of sense of security or safety
- Loss/change in sense of self or in a sense of identity
- Loss of innocence
- Loss of self-esteem/self-confidence
- Loss of faith or hope
- Loss of familiarity
- Loss of connection to self or others

In contrast to intangible losses, tangible losses are those losses that are readily apparent, obvious to the observer or physically evident. Tangible and intangible loss can sometimes occur together:

- A violent attack leaves a woman unable to have children (tangible) and a new feeling of being unsafe (intangible).

- The death of a child can result in the loss of the child (tangible) and the loss of sense of identity for a parent or sibling (intangible).
- Moving to a new country can result in the loss of one's actual home and closeness of friends (tangible) and loss of familiarity or a sense of belonging (intangible).

Patricia and James are experiencing both tangible and intangible losses. The loss of her job and the changes in her income, routine and daily life are tangible losses, readily apparent to those who know of her situation. What is probably not acknowledged are Patricia's intangible losses—the loss of her hopes and dreams for their future, her identity as a competent working woman and her companion and confidante. James's tangible losses include all the physical adjustments and changes that have occurred because of the stroke, including his loss of independence and ability to care for himself. The intangible losses could include his loss of identity as Patricia's equal partner, his hopes and dreams for the future and how he once viewed himself.

IMPLICATIONS

Being able to name and describe experiences provides a sense of validation and empowerment to those who are caught in situations of ongoing, non-death losses. While the *Techniques of Grief Therapy* series was initially written for those who have experienced losses related to death, many of these techniques can be readily adapted to address non-death losses as well. Two key aspects of non-death loss are that it is often unacknowledged (and invalidated), and there are no rituals that can readily assist individuals to begin the process of rebuilding their assumptive world in the face of it. Adapting techniques that acknowledge its significance and support the painful work of rebuilding the assumptive world will provide a foundation of healing for those who experience living losses of all kinds. All significant loss experiences call us to attend to the aspects of our assumptive world that have been shattered and our need to engage in the grieving process as a form of reparative work. By acknowledging our losses and grief, we are then open to allowing healing and rebuilding to occur. It is important to note that grief doesn't just disappear because we tell ourselves (or others tell us) that it shouldn't be an issue. The bottom line is that no form of grief is unimportant to the person experiencing it.

References

Boss, P. (1999). *Ambiguous loss*. Cambridge, MA: Harvard University Press.

Boss, P. (2009). *Ambiguous loss: Learning to live with unresolved grief*. Cambridge, MA: Harvard University Press.

Bruce, E. J., & Schultz, C. L. (2001). *Nonfinite loss and grief: A psychoeducational approach*. Sydney, Australia: Maclennan & Petty.

Field, N. P. (2006). Continuing bonds in adaptation to bereavement: Introduction. *Death Studies, 30*(8), 709–714.

Harris, D. L. (2011). *Counting our losses: Reflecting on change, loss, and transition in everyday life*. New York: Routledge.

Harris, D. L. (Ed.). (2020). *Non-death loss and grief: Context and clinical implications*. New York: Routledge.

Harris, D. L., & Winokuer, H. R. (2016). *Principles and practice of grief counseling* (2nd ed.). New York: Routledge.

Janoff-Bulman, R. (1992). *Shattered assumptions: Towards a new psychology of trauma*. New York: Free Press.

Parkes, C. M. (1975). What becomes of redundant world models? A contribution to the study of adaptation to change. *Psychology and Psychotherapy: Theory, Research and Practice, 48*(2), 131–137.

Roos, S. (2018). *Chronic sorrow: A living loss* (2nd ed.). New York: Routledge.

Stroebe, M., Schut, H., & Boerner, K. (2010). Continuing bonds in adaptation to bereavement: Toward theoretical integration. *Clinical Psychology Review, 30*(2), 259–268.

6

Posttraumatic Growth and Expert Companionship in Grief Therapy

Richard G. Tedeschi and Lawrence G. Calhoun

The term *posttraumatic growth* was first used in print in the 1990s (Tedeschi & Calhoun, 1995) to describe the experience of positive change resulting from the struggle with a highly stressful or traumatic event. In this chapter, we will summarize three major elements to help guide clinicians who work with grieving persons: a general description of what posttraumatic growth (PTG) is, a therapeutic stance that we call *expert companionship* and some specific suggestions for dealing with PTG in grief therapy. (More extensive descriptions can be found in Calhoun & Tedeschi, 2013; Tedeschi & Calhoun, 2004; Tedeschi, Shakespeare-Finch, Taku, & Calhoun, 2018.)

MAJOR ELEMENTS OF PTG

Statistical studies of the major components, or, in statistical terminology, factors, of PTG tend to find that five consistently occur: a changed sense of self; changes in relationships; greater appreciation; the emergence of new possibilities or priorities; and changes in one's existential, religious or spiritual life. PTG arises in these five life domains as a result of the struggle to reconsider core beliefs that help people understand themselves, their world and their futures. The challenge to the core belief system, or the assumptions people make about their lives and their world, was described by Janoff-Bulman (1992) as a *shattering of the assumptive world*. When these core beliefs are challenged, better perspectives are needed, and the work of developing these perspectives leads to the positive changes that comprise PTG. In order to develop these changes, people who survive trauma need to appreciate their inherently paradoxical nature. PTG is gain that arises out of loss, and other paradoxes are involved in the factors of PTG as well.

A typical way to summarize the change in sense of self is the sentence *I am more vulnerable than I thought, but stronger than I imagined*. Life crises serve as an unavoidable reminder that difficult challenges are simply a part of life. However, simply having faced them can be a source of perceiving oneself as stronger than previously assumed.

Another change in self that some people report is an increased sense of empathy and compassion, especially for persons who experience the same kind of difficulty or loss. As one grieving parent said: *I've become more empathetic toward anybody in pain and anybody in any kind of grief*.

"You find out who your real friends are." Loss can place a strain on some relationships, and sometimes those relationships do not survive the test. However, what people experience as an

 DOI: 10.4324/9781351069120-7

element of PTG is an increased sense of closeness and intimacy with (some) others that can emerge from the struggle with loss. At the same time, relationships that do not stand the test of traumatic loss may be exchanged for the ones that do.

Another element of PTG is an increased sense of appreciation for what one still has. The loss of something can lead some people to increase their appreciation and gratitude for what they still have or for what they have regained. Out of grief can come gratitude and a determination to appreciate better each day what one is experiencing. This can produce a clearer sense of being present in the moment as each moment has value.

Changed priorities are another element of PTG. Things that used to be important no longer are, and things that were not before become so. New possibilities for how to live life may be revealed as very often, the old priorities can no longer be accomplished in the aftermath of loss.

A fifth element of PTG is the experience of changes in the existential or spiritual sphere that the person considers positive. This does not necessarily mean that people become more spiritual or religious—for some, becoming *less* orthodox or *less* religious is experienced as growth. New perspectives on the spiritual realm, what is means to be human and how to live life well and with meaning can arise out of the struggle with the necessity to revise the old system of beliefs.

THE *EXPERT COMPANION*

Well-trained clinicians are "experts." They have been trained in how best to help grieving and distressed people. However, bereaved persons may sometimes need a good *companion* more than they need an expert who only relies on a lot of therapeutic techniques. We are suggesting that the very best clinicians are those who are indeed *experts*, but whose expertise is primarily in how to be *companions* on what can sometimes be a long and very demanding journey of coping with loss. The wisdom lies in when to rely on one's technical and intellectual expertise and when simply to be an empathetic fellow human being.

PTG IN GRIEF THERAPY

As a first step, clinicians who practice expert companionship need to be knowledgeable about what PTG is. The brief and simple description provided earlier in this chapter may be useful, but clinicians need to know more and should consult the sources mentioned earlier. The essential therapeutic stance in expert companionship is to be a learner and a listener first. Each grief experience is different, and the expert companion treats each with respect, learning what is unique about this relationship that has turned tragic. It also involves honoring the perspectives of the griever, including views of proper ways to grieve and cope, the degree to which help is accepted, death and the afterlife that may be part of the person's cultural and religious traditions. At the same time, respectful questioning of these perspectives can lead to new ideas that may form the basis for PTG.

As expert companions listen and learn about the grief being described to them, they also need to be able to listen for and recognize themes of growth in what their clients are saying. And, when themes of growth are present, expert companions may choose to label those themes as such, even if the client does not use explicit PTG language—when the context and the timing are appropriate.

What if themes of growth never emerge? One reason may be that growth has not yet occurred, and the expert companion encourages the kind of reflection that can allow for this possibility. However, if the expert companion has reason to believe that some growth may be present but has not been articulated, then, if the context and the timing are appropriate, a gentle and carefully worded inquiry about the possibility of PTG may be useful.

CRUCIAL ADMONITIONS

It is very important to keep some things about PTG in mind when working with grieving clients. First, *PTG is not universal.* Although common, many persons deal with loss without experiencing growth in any form. To assume that all clients will have some form of PTG is a mistake and places an additional burden on people who are already suffering.

The experience of PTG does not eliminate the pain of loss. Do not make the mistake of assuming that the experience of PTG is going to produce a commensurate reduction in grieving and yearning for that which has been lost. Instead, it is better to help the bereaved person appreciate that their loss is borne more lightly when there is some recognition of a meaningful aftermath over the long haul. It is especially helpful for people experiencing loss to find a way to be of service to others as part of a meaningful mission that honors who they have lost.

PTG, if it occurs at all, tends to emerge over time—don't rush it. Although some people do, indeed, report PTG very early after the encounter with loss, this is not the case for most people. Expert companions recognize that PTG sometimes requires months or years of a careful process of learning about dealing with a particular loss. For the bereaved person, this process involves coming to understand something about what they are going through and will face in the future; developing ways to manage their emotional reactions to grief; finding people they can talk with honestly, including expert companions who are not professionals; developing a clear understanding of their revised life story; and finally, creating meaningful ways to be of service to others. This difficult path toward PTG can be made somewhat clearer with the presence of an expert companion.

References

Calhoun, L. G., & Tedeschi, R. G. (2013). *Posttraumatic growth in clinical practice.* New York: Routledge.

Janoff-Bulman, R. (1992). *Shattered assumptions: Towards a new psychology of trauma.* New York: The Free Press.

Tedeschi, R. G., & Calhoun, L. G. (1995). *Trauma and transformation: Growing in the aftermath of suffering.* Thousand Oaks, CA: Sage Publications.

Tedeschi, R. G., & Calhoun, L. G. (2004). *Helping bereaved parents: A clinician's guide.* New York: Brunner-Routledge.

Tedeschi, R. G., Shakespeare-Finch, J., Taku, K., & Calhoun, L. G. (2018). *Posttraumatic growth: Theory, research, and applications.* New York: Routledge.

Part II
Evaluating Grief

7

The Persistent Complex Bereavement Inventory (PCBI)

Sherman A. Lee and Evgenia (Jane) Milman

PURPOSE

Grief is one of the most emotionally painful but natural responses to losing a loved one. Although the vast majority of the bereaved eventually adjust to loss, a minority of these individuals experience protracted and debilitating reactions (Bonanno & Kaltman, 2001). Researchers have discovered that these difficulties in bereavement are not expressions of general psychiatric disorders, such as depression, posttraumatic stress and anxiety, but are unique to complications in grief (Boelen & Prigerson, 2007; Bonanno et al., 2007). Despite extensive research supporting the validity of a grief-specific disorder (Boelen & Prigerson, 2012), official recognition of this kind of condition was only comparatively recently introduced in the *Diagnostic and Statistical Manual of Mental Disorders* (DSM-5) (American Psychiatric Association, 2013) as persistent complex bereavement disorder (PCBD) in the *Conditions for Further Study* to facilitate research into protracted and debilitating forms of grief. The Persistent Complex Bereavement Inventory (PCBI) was subsequently developed to assist this line of empirical inquiry (Lee, 2015).

DEVELOPMENT

The PCBI was developed to measure symptoms of the DSM-5's pathological grief construct. Specifically, the PCBI mirrors the diagnostic criteria B and C for PCBD (APA, 2013, pp. 789–790). Criterion B does not have an official title but consists of symptoms such as yearning, sorrow, preoccupation with the deceased and preoccupation with the circumstances of the death. This section appears to reflect *core grief* reactions that occur when a person is separated from an attachment figure (Archer, 2008). Criterion C is divided into two sections. The first section of criterion C is named *reactive distress to the death* and consists of symptoms such as difficulty accepting the death, disbelief/numbness, difficulty with positive reminiscing, bitterness/anger, maladaptive self-appraisals and excessive avoidance (APA, 2013). The second section of criterion C is named *social/identity disruption* and consists of symptoms such as the desire to die, difficulty trusting others, loneliness/detachment, feeling empty, life role confusion and difficulty pursuing interests (APA, 2013). The PCBI does not measure criteria A (closeness to the deceased), D (significant distress or impairment), and E (abnormal reaction) because they seem to be diagnostic qualifiers as opposed to grief-specific symptoms.

DOI: 10.4324/9781351069120-9

FORMAT AND PSYCHOMETRIC PROPERTIES

The PCBI is a 16-item self-report assessment tool designed to measure PCBD symptoms (see Appendix to this chapter). Each PCBI item is rated on a 5-point scale (0=*none/not at all*; 1=*slight/rare, less than a day or two*; 2=*mild/rare, several days*; 3=*moderate/more than half the days*; 4=*severe; nearly every day*) and is based on a subjective report of how much or how often each symptom was experienced since the deceased's death. The PCBI items are grouped into three subscales that tap distinct facets of PCBD (core grief, reactive distress and social/identity disruption). When the three subscales are joined together, they collectively provide a measure of overall PCBD symptomatology.

The PCBI can be scored in a variety of ways. If the purpose of using the PCBI is to quantify the severity level of PCBD symptoms, then a dimensional approach to scoring is recommended. In this approach, individual item ratings are combined, by either summing or averaging them, to form subscale scores and a total scale score. Combining rating scores on items 1 through 4 will produce a core grief subscale score while combining rating scores on items 5 through 10 will produce a reactive distress subscale score. Combining rating scores on items 11 through 16 will produce a social/identity disruption subscale score while combining rating scores across all 16 items will yield a total scale score. The resulting PCBI scores can be viewed as points along a continuum of severity on which higher scores reflect elevated symptoms of PCBD.

If the purpose of using the PCBI is to formulate a "diagnosis" of PCBD, then a categorical approach to scoring is recommended. In this approach, individual item ratings are used to identify specific thresholds that, in conjunction with other criteria, aid in the diagnosis of PCBD. To meet the DSM-5's proposed criteria set and severity thresholds for diagnosis of PCBD, the following requirements have to be fulfilled: First, the deceased has to be someone with whom the bereaved had a close relationship (criterion A). Second, a rating of either 3 or 4 has to present in at least one of the PCBI item scores from items 1 through 4 and have persisted for at least 12 months after the death of the deceased for adults and 6 months for children (criterion B). Third, a rating of either 3 or 4 has to present in at least six of the PCBI item scores from items 5 through 16, and these scores have to have persisted for at least 12 months after the death of the deceased for adults and 6 months for children (criterion C). Last, the elevated PCBD symptoms, as defined by PCBI item ratings of 3 or 4, have to have caused clinically significant distress or impairment in important areas of functioning (criterion D) and appear out of proportion to or inconsistent with cultural, religious or age-appropriate norms (criterion E). The resulting categorical scoring approach should determine if the PCBI scorer meets the requirements for a PCBD diagnosis.

The PCBI exhibits solid psychometric properties. The instrument has demonstrated strong internal consistency reliability for the subscales (Cronbach's αs > .80; Lee, 2015, 2017a) and total scale (Cronbach's αs > .90; Lee, 2015, 2017a, 2017b; Lee, Callan, & Gibbons, 2016; Lee & Gibbons, 2017). The PCBI has also shown firm test-retest reliability for the subscales (intraclass correlation coefficients > .53) and total scale (intraclass correlation coefficient > .66) (Lee, 2015). Factor analytic studies support the validity of the instrument to measure grief symptoms on both specific (items and subscales) and global (total scale) levels (Lee, 2015, 2017a). These findings also support the adherence of the PCBI scales to the DSM-5's proposed criteria for PCBD.

The validity of the PCBI as a measure of dysfunctional grief has been demonstrated by its high correlations with a well-established measure of prolonged grief disorder (convergent validity) and relatively weaker correlations with measures of depression, posttraumatic stress and separation anxiety (divergent validity) (Lee, 2015). Moreover, studies have shown that the PCBI correlates, in expected ways, with measures of neuroticism, dependence, harmful health behaviors, negative religious coping, suicidal ideation and meaning-made, corroborating the DSM-5 and previous research on complicated grief (construct validity) (Lee, 2015, 2017a; Lee et al., 2016). The ability of the PCBI to predict different kinds of impairment, above and beyond measures of depression, separation anxiety and posttraumatic stress, provides additional evidence to support its validity and clinical utility (incremental validity) (Lee, 2015, 2017b).

CLINICAL APPLICATIONS

In a clinical context, the most straightforward application of the PCBI is for diagnostic purposes. However, the PCBI subscales also provide a nuanced characterization of a client's PCBD symptomology, which can be used to inform the course of treatment. To demonstrate how the PCBI can be implemented clinically in this manner, we discuss two cases selected from a research study conducted with a sample of bereaved adults. For the purposes of confidentiality, the participants' real names are not presented.

Nearly a year and a half ago Jenna, a woman in her 60s, lost her spouse to cancer. Around the same time, Rachel, a woman in her early 40s, lost her mother to an accident that occurred during surgery as a result of medical malpractice. Jenna's and Rachel's responses on the PCBI can be scored in a categorical manner to determine whether their PCBD symptomatology meets the threshold for diagnosis. Both indicated that at least several days a week, they experienced more than one symptom from the *core grief* (CG) subscale and more than six symptoms from the *reactive distress* (RD) and *social/identity disruption* (SID) subscales. In addition, Jenna and Rachel meet the remaining requirements for a diagnosis of PCBD, including being more than 12 months post loss, having a close relationship with the deceased and reporting functional impairment outside cultural norms. Collectively, this information suggests that Jenna and Rachel are both experiencing PCBD.

Jenna scored highest on the CG and SID subscales, with an average of 3.25 and 3.50, respectively. As its name suggest, the CG subscale of the PCBI represents the core of Jenna's PCBD symptomatology—a sense of being "stuck" in grief emotionally (e.g., "Felt a constant . . . yearning for the deceased") and cognitively (e.g., "Preoccupied with the deceased"). Meanwhile, her high score on the SID subscale suggests that Jenna's experience of being "stuck" in grief manifests in a diminished sense of identity and a consequent struggle to meaningfully re-engage with ongoing life. Indeed, she responded with "Nearly daily" to the statement "without the deceased, life was either meaningless [or] empty." A meaning-oriented intervention would allow the clinician to work with Jenna to fortify her sense of life purpose (MacKinnon et al., 2015; Neimeyer, Milman, & Steffen, 2021; Neimeyer & Alves, 2018). For example, the *Chapters of Our Lives* (Neimeyer, 2014) technique can serve as a means of exploring recurring themes driving Jenna's life narrative that may have been challenged by her mother's death (e.g., the primacy of family challenged by disconnection among family members post loss). This work provides a basis for establishing a direction for the next "chapter" of Jenna's life so the clinician can then encourage the pursuit of interests and social interactions that are compatible with this life direction (e.g., reconnecting with family by planning family dinners).

The RD subscale reflects a struggle to process the death event and its finality, both emotionally and cognitively (e.g., "Experienced disbelief or emotional numbness over the loss"). Jenna's score on the RD subscale was relatively low (average of 1.50), indicating that the death event is not a prominent feature of her PCBD symptomatology. Therefore, the clinician may choose not to emphasize the death itself as a principal focus of intervention. Furthermore, Jenna indicated "Not at all" in regard to the RD item "Found it difficult to have positive memories about the deceased." Accordingly, the clinician might leverage Jenna's willingness to engage in memories of her spouse as a means of facilitating re-engagement in life. For example, cognitive constructivist techniques such as the *Life Imprint* exercise (Neimeyer, 2012b) or *Correspondence with the Deceased* (Neimeyer, 2012a) could highlight life goals and traditions Jenna and her spouse pursued in their time together (e.g., shared sense of adventure). Behavioral activation, which is a prominent component of complicated grief therapy (CGT) (Shear, 2015) and cognitive behavioral therapy (CBT) for grief (Eisma et al., 2015), could then be employed to schedule specific activities that affirm or honor the ongoing impact her deceased spouse has on Jenna's life.

As is the case with Jenna, Rachel also endorsed an emotional and cognitive sense of being "stuck" in grief, with an average score of 2.25 on the CG subscale. However, unlike Jenna, it appears that Rachel's PCBD symptomatology is centered on the finality and the manner of her mother's death. This is indicated by an average score of 3.83 on the RD subscale. Indeed, Rachel responded with "Nearly daily" to all but one of the symptoms in the RD subscale, including items such as "Found it extremely difficult to accept the death" and "Had negative thoughts about yourself in relation to . . . the death (e.g., self-blame)." Further contrasting to Jenna's grief experience, Rachel's average score of 1.83 on the SID subscale is relatively low, suggesting that she continues to engage meaningfully in life. Accordingly, in Rachel's case, a clinician might focus on reviewing the experience of her mother's death, including its unexpected and potentially unjust nature, as well as the fact that it resulted from negligent action on the part of a presumably trusted medical professional. To this end, exposure techniques featured in CGT, CBT and meaning-oriented grief interventions (Eisma et al., 2015; Neimeyer et al., 2021; Shear, 2015) can be employed by the clinician. Such techniques would allow Rachel to explore and process the salient aspects of her mother's death while building her capacity to regulate her affective response to their distressing nature.

Despite sharing a diagnosis of PCBD, Rachel and Jenna's symptomatic profiles differ substantially. Thus, a review of their cases illustrates how the PCBI subscales can be implemented in a clinical setting to tailor the intervention approach to diverse presentations of grief.

References

American Psychiatric Association. (2013). *Diagnostic and statistical manual of mental disorders* (5th ed.). Washington, DC: Author.

Archer, J. (2008). Theories of grief: Past, present, and future perspectives. In M. S. Stroebe, R. O. Hansson, H. Schut, & W. Stroebe (Eds.), *Handbook of bereavement research and practice: Advances in theory and intervention* (pp. 45–65). Washington, DC: American Psychological Association.

Boelen, P. A., & Prigerson, H. G. (2007). The influence of symptoms of prolonged grief disorder, depression, and anxiety on quality of life among bereaved adults: A prospective study. *European Archives of Psychiatry and Clinical Neuroscience, 257*, 444–452. doi:10.1007/s00406-007-0744-0

Boelen, P. A., & Prigerson, H. G. (2012). Commentary on the inclusion of persistent complex bereavement-related disorder in DSM-5. *Death Studies, 36*, 771–794.

Bonanno, G. A., & Kaltman, S. (2001). The varieties of grief experience. *Clinical Psychology Review, 21*, 705–734. doi:10.1016/S0272-7358(00)00062-3

Bonanno, G. A., Neria, Y., Mancini, A., Litz, B., Coifman, K. G., & Insel, B. (2007). Is there more to complicated grief than depression and posttraumatic stress disorder? A test of incremental validity. *Journal of Abnormal Psychology, 116*, 342–351. doi:10.1037/0021-843X.116.2.342

Eisma, M. C., Boelen, P. A., van den Bout, J., Stroebe, W., Schut, H. A., Lancee, J., & Stroebe, M. S. (2015). Internet-based exposure and behavioral activation for complicated grief and rumination: A randomized controlled trial. *Behavior Therapy, 46*(6), 729–748.

Lee, S. A. (2015). The Persistent Complex Bereavement Inventory: A measure based on the DSM-5. *Death Studies, 39*, 399–410. doi:10.1080/07481187.2015.1029144

Lee, S. A. (2017a). Factorial structure of the Persistent Complex Bereavement Inventory: Testing a hierarchical factor model. *Death Studies.* doi:10.1080/07481187.2017.1348402

Lee, S. A. (2017b). *Persistent complex bereavement symptoms predict impairment above depression, posttraumatic stress, and separation anxiety: An incremental validity analysis.* Manuscript submitted for publication.

Lee, S. A., Callan, S. M., & Gibbons, J. A. (2016). School and religious factors impact the neuroticism-grief link in adolescents. *Death Studies, 40*, 601–606. doi:10.1080/07481187.2016.1198843

Lee, S. A., & Gibbons, J. A. (2017). The dark triad and compassion: Psychopathy and narcissism's unique connections to observed suffering. *Personality and Individual Differences, 116*, 336–342. doi:10.1016/j.paid.2017.05.010

MacKinnon, C. J., Smith, N. G., Henry, M., Milman, E., Chochinov, H. M., Körner, A., . . . Robin Cohen, S. (2015). Reconstructing meaning with others in loss: A feasibility pilot randomized controlled trial of a bereavement group. *Death Studies, 39*(7), 411–421.

Neimeyer, R. A. (2012a). Correspondence with the deceased. In R. Neimeyer (Ed.), *Techniques of grief therapy: Creative practices for counseling the bereaved* (pp. 259–261). New York: Routledge.

Neimeyer, R. A. (2012b). The life imprint. In R. A. Neimeyer (Ed.), *Techniques of grief therapy: Creative practices for counseling the bereaved* (pp. 274–276). New York: Routledge.

Neimeyer, R. A. (2014). Chapters of our lives. In B. E. Thompson & R. A. Neimeyer (Eds.), *Grief and the expressive arts: Practices for creating meaning* (pp. 80–84). New York: Routledge.

Neimeyer, R. A., & Alves, D. (2018). Seeking meaning in loss: An online narrative constructivist intervention for complicated grief. *Grief Matters: The Australian Journal for Grief and Bereavement.*

Neimeyer, R. A., Milman, E., & Steffen, E. M. (2021). The meaning in loss group: Principles, processes and procedures. In R. Neimeyer (Ed.), *New techniques of grief therapy: Bereavement and beyond.* New York: Routledge.

Shear, M. K. (2015). Complicated grief treatment (CGT) for prolonged grief disorder. In U. Schnyder & M. Cloitre (Eds.), *Evidence based treatments for trauma-related psychological disorders* (pp. 299–314). New York: Springer.

Appendix
The Persistent Complex Bereavement Inventory

Instructions: For each statement, indicate which number best describes how much or how often you experienced each activity since the deceased's death.

None	Slight	Mild	Moderate	Severe
Not at all	Rare, less than a day or two	Several days	More than half the days	Nearly every day
0	1	2	3	4

1.	_____	Felt a constant longing or yearning for the deceased.
2.	_____	Felt intense sorrow and emotional pain because of the loss.
3.	_____	Preoccupied with the deceased.
4.	_____	Preoccupied with the circumstances of the death.
5.	_____	Found it extremely difficult to accept the death.
6.	_____	Experienced disbelief or emotional numbness over the loss.
7.	_____	Found it difficult to have positive memories about the deceased.
8.	_____	Felt bitter or angry over the loss.
9.	_____	Had negative thoughts about yourself in relation to the deceased or the death (e.g., self-blame).
10.	_____	Avoided anything that reminded you of the loss.
11.	_____	Wished to die in order to be with the deceased.
12.	_____	Found it difficult to trust others because of the loss.
13.	_____	Felt alone or detached from others because of the loss.
14.	_____	Believed that without the deceased, life was either meaningless, empty, or could not go on.

| 15. | _____ | Experienced confusion over your role in life or felt like your identity was diminished because of the loss. |
| 16. | _____ | Experienced difficulty or reluctance to pursue interests or planning for the future because of the loss. |

Note. A total PCBI *mean* score can be calculated by summing all 16 items and then dividing that sum by 16. A Core Grief *mean* score can be calculated by summing items 1, 2, 3, and 4, and then dividing that sum by 4. A Reactive Distress *mean* score can be calculated by summing items 5, 6, 7, 8, 9, and 10, and then dividing that sum by 6. A Social/Identity Disruption *mean* score can be calculated by summing items 11, 12, 13, 14, 15, and 16, and then dividing that sum by 6. The PCBI is placed in the public domain to encourage its use in clinical assessment and research. No formal permission is therefore required for its reproduction and use by others, beyond appropriate citation of the present chapter.

8

The Social Meaning in Life Events Scale (SMILES)

Benjamin W. Bellet

PURPOSE

A wealth of extant literature on grief indicates that a mourner's ability to make meaning of loss has a major impact on bereavement outcomes (Holland, 2016; Neimeyer, 2016). To the extent that a mourner experiences difficulty in coming to terms with the meaning of a loved one's death, the loss and life after will appear threatening and senseless, manifesting as the distress and functional disability associated with problematic bereavement. Much has been done to advance the assessment of sense-making difficulties and their relation to grief outcomes. The well-validated Integration of Stressful Life Events Scale (ISLES) (Holland Currier, Coleman, & Neimeyer, 2010) assesses the extent to which a mourner has effectively integrated a loss's micro-narrative into his or her self-narrative. Difficulty in making sense of the loss as measured by the ISLES has proved consistently predictive of complicated grief (CG) severity (Burke et al., 2014; Lee, Feudo, & Gibbons, 2014), general distress and functional disability (Holland et al., 2010).

Although it is important to consider the intra-psychic meaning-making efforts of individual mourners, both clinical experience and a growing body of literature indicate that such efforts never occur in a vacuum. The social constructionist model of grief states that a mourner's attempts to come to terms with loss are always a "situated, interpretive, and communicative activity" (Neimeyer, Klass, & Dennis, 2014, p. 1). A mourner's attempts to make sense of the loss, memorialize the decedent and construct a new identity are affected by, policed by and validated within an intricate sociocultural environment. Cultural understandings and interpersonal interactions have the potential either to encourage and validate such efforts or to frustrate them by disenfranchising the mourner and devaluing the deceased (Doka, 2002; Neimeyer & Jordan, 2002).

DEVELOPMENT

The interpersonally derived "social meanings" described here are distinguishable from generic social support. The overall availability of social support has shown inconsistent (Murphy, Chung, & Johnson, 2002) and sometimes deleterious (Burke, Neimeyer, & McDevitt-Murphy, 2010) effects on bereavement outcomes, depending on whether such attempts are construed as helpful by the mourner. Moreover, support can take several forms, only some

DOI: 10.4324/9781351069120-10

of which bear on the attempts of the grieving persons to make sense of the loss or their lives in its aftermath.

The potential for mourners' social environments to serve either a healing or counter-therapeutic funttion calls for a more nuanced way of assessing social worlds as they apply to grief. We therefore sought to develop a measure that would examine the impact of the social environment at multiple levels (dyadic, community, and culture-level interactions) as they apply to the mourner's sense-making efforts.

FORMAT AND PSYCHOMETRIC PROPERTIES

The Social Meaning in Life Events Scale (SMILES) (Bellet, Holland, & Neimeyer, 2018) is a 26-item self-report instrument that assesses the degree to which social interactions help or inhibit an individual's efforts to make meaning of a life event. (See Appendix to this chapter.) Respondents indicate their level of agreement with each statement on a scale from 1 (*strongly disagree*) to 5 (*strongly agree*). The SMILES consists of two subscales that reflect the dual roles of social interactions as they apply to making meaning of an event. The social validation (SV) subscale assesses the extent to which social interactions facilitate and validate meaning-making efforts (e.g., "Talking to other people about this event has brought some clarity to the situation"). Higher scores on this subscale indicate a social environment conducive to and supportive of meaning-making efforts. The social invalidation (SI) subscale measures the extent to which the mourner's social environment frustrates or casts aspersion on the griever's sense-making attempts (e.g., "I feel more distant from others when I talk to them about this event"). Higher scores on this subscale indicate an interpersonal milieu that impedes sense-making efforts.

Due to substantive differences between social validation and invalidation, the SMILES should not be used as a composite of its two subscales (i.e., no total-sum score should be computed). An initial validation of the SMILES as it applied to loss of a loved one in a bereaved college student sample indicated that the subscales emerged as distinct and weakly related factors (Bellet et al., 2018). Strong internal consistency was observed for both the SV ($\alpha = .84$) and SI ($\alpha = .91$) subscales.

Convergent validity analyses of the subscales with bereavement outcome measures spoke further to the role of invalidation and validation as elements that exerted different effects on a mourner's meaning-making process. The SI subscale appeared to be more associated with negative outcomes such as CG severity scores ($r = .59, p < .01$) and decrements in over-all health scores ($r = -.25, p < .01$). Additionally, the SI subscale demonstrated incremental validity in predicting general health problems over and above the influence of general social support for grieving and entirely eclipsed the role of general social support in predicting CG severity, proving far more essential to an understanding of how social interactions affect grief symptoms. In contrast, the SV subscale was more highly associated with the positive outcome of posttraumatic growth scores (PTG) ($r = .50, p < .01$). The subscales also demonstrated discriminant validity in their significant but moderate associations with a measure of general social support, indicating that they are not simply measuring the presence of generic support or lack thereof. Overall, the SMILES assesses two distinct constructs that are important to the prediction of both negative and positive clinical outcomes.

The subscales of the SMILES also demonstrated sensitivity to the circumstances of the loss, another important consideration in therapy. Consistent with previous research indicating that violent or sudden losses put mourners at higher risk for social disenfranchisement (Jordan & McIntosh, 2011), mourners with such losses displayed significantly higher SI and lower SV scores than those who had experienced natural and expected losses (Bellet et al., 2018).

CLINICAL APPLICATIONS

The SMILES is best used by clinicians as a way of understanding potential stumbling blocks and resources within the client's interpersonal sphere in the search for meaning after loss, allowing for a fuller clinical picture. High SMILES-SI scores may portend higher risk for the exacerbation of CG symptoms and functional disability due to misunderstanding or stigmatization as a result of loss. High SMILES-SV scores may indicate the opportunity for the promotion of unsought benefit as a result of loss with the help supportive others. To demonstrate the application of the SMILES in a clinical setting, we present a case study from the original validation sample and describe clinical insights and courses of action that could be taken with the information gleaned from this measure. For the purposes of confidentiality, the participant's real name and identifying details are not used in this case study.

Beverly is a 19-year-old Caucasian female college student who lost a good friend to suicide 13 months prior to the date of the survey. She is experiencing a high level of CG symptomatology, as indicated by her score on the Inventory of Complicated Grief-Revised (ICG-R) (Prigerson & Jacobs, 2001), which is above the established cut score for a probable diagnosis of CG (Prigerson et al., 1995). In particular, Beverly indicates that she is often drawn to places and things associated with the decedent and has experienced a consistently high level of hyperarousal since the loss. She is also experiencing a marked level of functional impairment, which she attributes to the loss.

Although Beverly answered "yes" to an item that asked whether she had available social support figures in her life, her SMILES-SI score tells a more nuanced and problematic story. Beverly's SMILES-SI subscale score is more than a standard deviation above the validation sample's mean, indicating that many of Beverly's social interactions in reference to the loss (or lack thereof) have created difficulty for her in making sense of the death. A review of Beverly's item-level scores on the SMILES-SI reveals that she endorses in particular the notion that "no one really understands what this event means to me." Perhaps as a result of being misunderstood, Beverly also highly endorses the statement that she doesn't "want to burden others by talking about this event."

Beverly's SMILES-SV score is near the mean of the validation sample, indicating that although she feels misunderstood and unable to discuss her loss openly, she is not entirely without potential facilitators of her meaning reconstruction process. In particular, Beverly strongly agrees with the statement that "others can learn something valuable by hearing me talk about this event."

The clinical picture painted by Beverly's responses indicates that she has not yet made meaning of a loss that she feels others cannot understand or be bothered with. The fact that her friend died by suicide may well be a source of such difficulty, as Beverly may feel unable to approach potential support figures with the pain of a death that is unfamiliar and stigmatized in her culture's dominant grief discourse. Unsurprisingly, this feeling of isolation in grief is functionally debilitating and is accompanied by a marked sense of insecurity, which manifests as hyperarousal and draws her to reminders of the decedent.

In orienting Beverly to therapy, the therapist would do well to exemplify a nonjudgmental presence during sessions and invite her to expand upon her experiences of relating her grief narrative to others, with the goal of identifying and overcoming perceived barriers to more intimate sharing with selected others. If appropriate, the therapist might suggest seeking out suicide-specific grief support groups, either in person or online, where Beverly can safely validate her personal grief narrative within a wider interpersonal context. Another source of strength is found in Beverly's indication that she feels that her story, although hidden, has value from which others can benefit. If growth outcomes appear possible later in therapy, the therapist may encourage an exploration of a new role of actively reaching out to other survivors of suicide loss or engaging in other forms of advocacy along these lines. Beverly could then draw strength from a new identity as a storyteller who gives fellow mourners of stigmatized loss the gift of her experiences.

References

Bellet, B. W., Holland, J. M., & Neimeyer, R. A. (2018). The Social Meaning in Life Events Scale (SMILES): A preliminary psychometric evaluation in a bereaved sample. *Death Studies*. doi:10.1080/074811 87.2018.1456008

Burke, L. A., Neimeyer, R. A., Holland, J. M., Dennard, S., Oliver, L., & Shear, M. K. (2014). Inventory of complicated spiritual grief: Development and validation of a new measure. *Death Studies*, *38*, 239–250.

Burke, L. A., Neimeyer, R. A., & McDevitt-Murphy, M. E. (2010). African American homicide bereavement: Aspects of social support that predict complicated grief, PTSD, and depression. *Omega*, *61*, 1–24.

Doka, K. J. (Ed.). (2002). *Disenfranchised grief: New directions, challenges, and strategies for practice.* Champaign, IL: Research Press.

Holland, J. M. (2016). Integration of Stressful Life Experiences Scale (ISLES). In R. A. Neimeyer (Ed.), *Techniques of grief therapy: Assessment and intervention* (pp. 46–50). New York: Routledge.

Holland, J. M., Currier, J. M., Coleman, R. A., & Neimeyer, R. A. (2010). The Integration of Stressful Life Experiences Scale (ISLES): Development and initial validation of a new measure. *International Journal of Stress Management*, *17*, 325–352.

Jordan, J. R., & McIntosh, J. (Eds.). (2011). *Grief after suicide*. New York: Routledge.

Lee, S. A., Feudo, A., & Gibbons, J. A. (2014). Grief among near-death experiencers: Pathways through religion and meaning. *Mental Health, Religion & Culture*, *17*(9), 877–885. doi:10.1080/13674676. 2014.936846

Murphy, S. A., Chung, I. J., & Johnson, L. C. (2002). Patterns of mental distress following the violent death of a child and predictors of change over time. *Research in Nursing & Health*, *25*, 425–437.

Neimeyer, R. A. (2016). Meaning reconstruction in the wake of loss: Evolution of a research program. *Behavior Change*, *33*, 65–79.

Neimeyer, R. A., & Jordan, J. R. (2002). Disenfranchisement as empathic failure: Grief therapy and the co-construction of meaning. *Disenfranchised Grief*, 95–117.

Neimeyer, R. A., Klass, D., & Dennis, M. R. (2014). A social constructionist account of grief: Loss and the narration of meaning. *Death Studies*, *38*, 485–498.

Prigerson, H. G., & Jacobs, S. C. (2001). Traumatic grief as a distinct disorder: A rationale, consensus criteria, and a preliminary empirical test. In M. Stroebe, R. O. Hansson, W. Stroebe, & H. Schut (Eds.), *Handbook of bereavement research* (pp. 613–645). Washington, DC: American Psychological Association.

Prigerson, H. G., Maciejewski, P. K., Reynolds 3rd, C. F., Bierhals, A. J., Newsom, J. T., Fasiczka, A., . . . Miller, M. (1995). Inventory of complicated grief: A scale to measure maladaptive symptoms of loss. *Psychiatry Research*, *59*, 65–79.

Appendix
SMILES Items and Scoring Instructions

Please indicate the extent to which you agree or disagree with the following statements with regard to (a particular loss or the most stressful life event you experienced in the past two years). Read each statement carefully and be aware that a response of agreement or disagreement may not have the same meaning across all items.

Item	Strongly Disagree	Disagree	Neither Agree Nor Disagree	Agree	Strongly Agree
1. I worry that if I shared too much about this event, people might see me differently.	1	2	3	4	5
2. I have difficulty getting people to understand how hard this has been for me.	1	2	3	4	5
3. Talking to other people about this event has brought some clarity to the situation.	1	2	3	4	5
4. I would like to talk about this event, but I don't think others would understand.	1	2	3	4	5
5. This event is too complicated to talk about.	1	2	3	4	5
6. Opening up about what happened has helped bring resolution to the situation.	1	2	3	4	5

Item	Strongly Disagree	Disagree	Neither Agree Nor Disagree	Agree	Strongly Agree
7. I avoid sharing the story of this event with others to avoid their criticism and judgment.	1	2	3	4	5
8. I keep the details of this event to myself because they don't quite make sense.	1	2	3	4	5
9. Talking about this event has helped me make sense of what happened.	1	2	3	4	5
10. I feel more distant from others when I talk to them about this event.	1	2	3	4	5
11. No one really understands what this event means to me.	1	2	3	4	5
12. When I tell people about this event, I believe they feel closer to me.	1	2	3	4	5
13. I feel more distant from others when I talk to them about this event.	1	2	3	4	5
14. No one really understands what this event means to me.	1	2	3	4	5
15. Other people have shared with me useful perspectives on this event.	1	2	3	4	5
16. I feel like my role in this event is often misunderstood by other people.	1	2	3	4	5
17. I feel more confused about this event after I talk to other people about it.	1	2	3	4	5
18. Sharing my story about this event has brought about greater compassion in others.	1	2	3	4	5
19. I feel more uncomfortable around people since this event.	1	2	3	4	5

(continued)

Appendix (continued)

Item	Strongly Disagree	Disagree	Neither Agree Nor Disagree	Agree	Strongly Agree
20. This event only makes sense to others if I leave some of the details out.	1	2	3	4	5
21. Others can learn something valuable by hearing me talk about this event.	1	2	3	4	5
22. I don't want to burden others by talking about this event.	1	2	3	4	5
23. I have comfortably shared my own private story of this event with others.	1	2	3	4	5
24. Ever since this event, I don't feel like I fit in with other people the way I did before.	1	2	3	4	5
25. The way I've handled this event has served as a positive example for others in my life.	1	2	3	4	5
26. There are few people I can confide in about this event.	1	2	3	4	5

Note. This scale can be used to calculate two subscale scores (social invalidation subscale and social validation subscale). To calculate the social invalidation subscale, sum items 1, 2, 4, 5, 7, 8, 10, 11, 13, 14, 16, 17, 19, 20, 22, 24 and 26. To calculate the social validation subscale, sum items 3, 6, 9, 12, 15, 18, 21, 23 and 25. The portion of the instructions in parentheses may be altered to make the measure applicable to different groups of interest.

9

Quality of Relationships Inventory-Bereavement Version (QRI-B)

Jamison S. Bottomley and Robert A. Neimeyer

PURPOSE

Clinical wisdom and empirical evidence have both suggested that perceived closeness to the deceased prior to the death is associated with higher distress throughout the course of bereavement (Dyregrov, Frykholm, Lilled, Broberg, & Holmberg, 2003; Servaty-Seib & Pistole, 2007). As a result, it stands to reason that differences in grief reactions across numerous modes of loss are likely to follow more accurately the closeness of the personal relationship rather than the degree of genetic relatedness or kinship category (Cleiren, Diekstra, Kerkhof, & van der Wal, 1994). However, given its ease of measurement, the latter is far more commonly studied in bereavement research (Burke & Neimeyer, 2013), despite findings indicating that relationship category represents only a marginally adequate predictor of grief reactions (Servaty-Seib & Pistole, 2007).

An additional dimension of relationship quality that likely contributes to the expression of problematic grief reactions, presenting unique relational challenges to the mourner in the aftermath of a loved one's death, is pre-death interpersonal conflict with the decedent. The notion that the degree of conflict between the bereft and the decedent prior to the death influences the trajectory and manifestation of grief symptomatology dates back to early psychoanalytic theory. Psychoanalytic theories of grief posited that the loss of a conflicted relationship is associated with "pathological" grief, presumably because this dimension of the relationship complicates resolving attachment issues with the deceased and releasing the person through emotional extrication, or what Freud deemed *decathexis* (Freud, 1917). Such assertions have been confirmed by data linking conflict and bereavement complitcations, such as the identification of levels of distress related to "unfininshed business" (e.g., conflict, unresolved issues) with the deceased as a potent predictor of complicated grief (CG) in a large college student sample (Klingspon, Holland, Neimeyer, & Lichtenthal, 2015).

Given the evidence that closeness is a strong predictor of grief reactions following losses due to a variety of causes, and theoretical and empirical propositions that high levels of interpersonal conflict engender protracted and "pathological" bereavement trajectories, the accuracy and ease with which these two relational constructs are examined is of high importance for both research and clinical practice. Unfortunately, previous research in the field of thanatology has employed ad-hoc, intuitive measures of closeness and conflict, the validity and reliability of which are unsubstantiated. This warranted the construction of a

DOI: 10.4324/9781351069120-11

novel instrument that enhances the assessment of pre-death relationship quality between the mourner and decedent—aspects that greatly come to bear on grief outcomes.

DEVELOPMENT

One measure that examines different dimensions of relationship quality is the Quality of Relationships Inventory (QRI) (Pierce, Sarason, & Sarason, 1991), a psychometrically sound self-report questionnaire consisting of 25 items that inquire about specific aspects of a relationship with a particular individual. Despite the utility of the QRI in assessing the quality of relationship between the respondent and another indexed individual, the original instrument was not constructed with a pre-death mourner-decedent relationship in mind. Moreover, subsequent research that examined the factor structure of the QRI across living relationship types and among diverse ethnic backgrounds has yielded mixed results (e.g., Marques, Pinheiro, Matos, & Marques, 2015; Nakano et al., 2002; Reiner, Beutel, Skaletz, Brähler, & Stöbel-Richter, 2012; Verhofstadt, Buysse, Rosseel, & Peene, 2006), making the instrument's structure empirically equivocal. Therefore, in an effort to develop an instrument that could assess the pre-death relationship quality between a mourner and decedent and aid in the identification of those who might require therapeutic intervention following the death of an important relational figure, we sought to develop a variation of the QRI that could be utilized in the context of bereavement. Consequently, an adapted version of the original QRI was developed using past-tense language commensurate with the experience of bereavement, and this adapted version, appropriately entitled the Quality of Relationships Inventory-Bereavement Version (QRI-B) (Bottomley, Smigelsky, Floyd, & Neimeyer, 2017), was administered to a large sample of bereaved college students in order to clarify its factor structure.

FORMAT AND PSYCHOMETRIC PROPERTIES

The QRI-B (Bottomley et al., 2017; see Appendix to this chapter) is a 13-item self-report instrument that assesses the pre-death relationship quality between the bereft and an indexed decedent. Respondents are instructed to indicate the frequency or magnitude of each of the 13 statements using a 4-point Likert scale ranging from 1 (*not at all*) to 4 (*very much*). Although the original QRI (Pierce et al., 1991) assessed relationship quality on three dimensions (depth, support and conflict), an exploratory factor analysis of the QRI-B yielded two salient factors—closeness and conflict (Bottomley et al., 2017). The closeness subscale assesses the degree to which the relationship was characterized by warmth, support and trust prior to death (e.g., "To what extent could you count on this person for help with a problem?" "How positive a role did this person play in your life?"). Higher scores on the closeness subscale of the QRI-B indicate a relationship that was intimate, supportive and of great significance to the bereft. The conflict subscale, on the other hand, assesses the degree to which the pre-death relationship was characterized by discord and distress (e.g., "How upset did this person sometimes make you feel?" "How often did you need to work to avoid conflict with this person?"). Higher scores on the conflict subscale are indicative of a relationship that was largely conflictual and quarrelsome prior to the death.

The QRI-B assesses relationship quality across two distinct dimensions (closeness and conflict), so the instrument should not be used as an overall metric of relationship quality broadly. The QRI-B, therefore, is intended as an instrument that can yield scores reflecting the degree to which the pre-death relationship was close and/or conflictual, rather than an aggregate of these two constructs. The two subscales that comprise the QRI-B were negligibly correlated ($r = .12$), further supporting the notion that the closeness and conflict subscales should be examined independently. Furthermore, the closeness and conflict subscales evidenced strong inter-item consistency, with alpha coefficients of .95 and .88, respectively.

CLINICAL APPLICATIONS

Ongoing research in our lab has underscored the QRI-B's ability to predict bereavement complications along dimensions of pre-death relational closeness and conflict, above and beyond other relevant indicators of risk, suggesting that this is a reliable instrument in the realm of bereavement research (Smigelsky, Bottomley, Relyea & Neimeyer, 2020). However, although the QRI-B was developed to facilitate research into the impact of the relationship with the deceased, it can be broadly applied to clinical practice to advance the identification of potential avenues of meaningful intervention with the bereft, as illustrated in the following case examples.

Teresa is an 18-year-old Hispanic woman who is currently contending with the death of her grandmother to cancer four months prior to her symptom assessment. On the QRI-B, Teresa indicated that she had a close and supportive relationship with her grandmother (closeness = 32), leaning on her grandmother's wisdom for assistance with various problems or emotional support during times of distress. Against the backdrop of her grandmother's death, Teresa now struggles filling the interpersonal void that her grandmother once occupied and grapples with the ongoing realization of the death. With an elevated score on the Inventory of Complicated Grief-Revised (ICG-R) (Prigerson & Jacobs, 2001), indicating a likely diagnosis of CG, it is clear that intervention might be warranted to help Teresa reconstruct meaning around her grandmother's death and adapt to her life in its wake. Given the nature of Teresa's close relationship with her grandmother and her responses to specific items on the ICG-R, such as "always" *longing or yearning* for her grandmother and *feeling lonely* since her passing, an astute therapist might suggest the relevance of correspondence or legacy work. With regard to the former, the therapist could invite Teresa to construct an "unsent letter" to her grandmother in an effort to "say hello again" and renew the bond that was broken by the loss (Neimeyer, 2012). To do this, the therapist, recognizing Teresa's paralyzing grief, could begin by instructing her to hand write on a piece of paper a letter to her grandmother, beginning with the prompt, "I want to keep you in my life by . . .", although this opening prompt need not be prescriptive. In addition to inviting Teresa to have an ongoing correspondence with her grandmother in this fashion, the therapist might encourage her to write back responses as she imagines her grandmother might have, especially at times that call for her wise consultation. The therapist could augment this relational work by encouraging Teresa to undertake a legacy project in her grandmother's honor while also providing a clear source of solace and strength for her. Through this process-oriented work, Teresa could acknowledge the pain that was elicited by her grandmother's death while ultimately identifying and attending to potent memories and tacit gifts that were left for Teresa as a result (Attig, 2012). Doing so would respect the enormity of Teresa's grief while simultaneously providing space for her to express gratitude for the time they had together, ultimately restoring their bond and reconstructing the sense of meaning that was compromised by her grandmother's death.

When Monica, a 20-year-old Caucasian woman who lost her friend in a vehicular accident nine months prior, completed her assessment, it was clear that the relationship she had had with her friend prior to their death, although close, was less than ideal. With an elevation on the conflict subscale of the QRI-B (conflict = 20), Monica indicated that she would oftentimes need to work proactively to avoid conflict with her friend and that she was made to feel guilty about aspects of her friend's life on a fairly persistent basis prior to her untimely death. In addition to clearly meeting the established cutoff for a suspected diagnosis of CG, as indicated by her ICG-R score, Monica was contending with strong feelings of guilt and shame around the circumstances of her friend's passing, ultimately feeling a sense of responsibility for the tragic accident or an inability to prevent it. Because Monica and her friend's relationship was rather conflictual, in tandem with being particularly close, and against the backdrop of feelings of guilt and responsibility, a sensitive grief therapist might inquire about the possibility of "unfinished business" and offer a way of potentially resolving such lingering matters. One way unfinished business could be addressed and potentially mitigated would be by inviting Monica to "chair" her friend by holding an imaginal conversation in which she spoke directly to the symbolic presence of her friend and, subsequently, taking the position of her friend to offer a likely response (Neimeyer, 2012). In this manner, Monica could be coached to renegotiate the relationship in a manner that would yield greater clarity, harmony or reconciliation. Ultimately, this work, perhaps pursued across a few sessions, could allow her to make peace with the relationship as she moves forward and perhaps even draw on the better parts of the friendship as a living resource, without the burden of things that were left unsaid, which has encumbered her grief journey thus far.

References

Attig, T. (2012). Reaching through sorrow to legacy. In R. A. Neimeyer (Ed.), *Techniques of grief therapy: Creative practices for counseling the bereaved* (pp. 277–280). New York: Routledge.

Bottomley, J. S., Smigelsky, M. A., Floyd, R. G., & Neimeyer, R. A. (2017). Closeness and conflict with the deceased: Exploring the factor structure of the quality of relationships inventory in a bereaved student sample. *OMEGA—Journal of Death and Dying.* doi:10.1177/0030222817718959

Burke, L. A., & Neimeyer, R. A. (2013). Prospective risk factors for complicated grief: A review of the empirical literature. In H. S. M. S. Stroebe, J. van der Bout, & P. Boelen (Eds.), *Complicated grief: Scientific foundations for healthcare professionals.* New York: Routledge.

Cleiren, M., Diekstra, R. F., Kerkhof, A. J., & van der Wal, J. (1994). Mode of death and kinship in bereavement: Focusing on "who" rather than "how." *Crisis: The Journal of Crisis Intervention and Suicide Prevention.* Retrieved from http://psycnet.apa.org/psycinfo/1994-41119-001

Dyregrov, A., Frykholm, A. M., Lilled, L., Broberg, A. G., & Holmberg, I. (2003). The Göteborg discotheque fire, 1998. *Scandinavian Journal of Psychology, 44,* 449–457.

Freud, S. (1957). Mourning and melancholia. In J. Strachey (Ed. & Trans.), *The standard edition of the complete psychological works of Sigmund Freud* (Vol. 14, pp. 243–258). London: Hogarth Press (Originally published 1917).

Klingspon, K. L., Holland, J. M., Neimeyer, R. A., & Lichtenthal, W. G. (2015). Unfinished business in bereavement. *Death Studies, 39,* 387–398.

Marques, D., Pinheiro, M. R., Matos, A. P., & Marques, C. (2015). Confirmatory factor analysis of the QRI father's version in a Portuguese sample of adolescents. *Procedia-Social and Behavioral Sciences, 165,* 267–274.

Nakano, Y., Sugiura, M., Aoki, K., Hori, S., Oshima, M., Kitamura, T., & Furukawa, T. A. (2002). Japanese version of the Quality of Relationships Inventory: Its reliability and validity among women with recurrent spontaneous abortion. *Psychiatry and Clinical Neurosciences, 56,* 527–532.

Neimeyer, R. A. (2012). Chair Work. In R. A. Neimeyer (Ed.), *Techniques of grief therapy: Creative practices for counseling the bereaved* (pp. 277–280). New York: Routledge.

Pierce, G. R., Sarason, I. G., & Sarason, B. R. (1991). General and relationship-based perceptions of social support: Are two constructs better than one? *Journal of Personality and Social Psychology, 61*(6), 1028–1039. doi:10.1037/0022-3514.61.6.1028

Prigerson, H. G., & Jacobs, S. C. (2001). Traumatic grief as a distinct disorder: A rationale, consensus criteria, and a preliminary empirical test. In M. Stroebe, R. O. Hansson, W. Stroebe, & H. Schut (Eds.), *Handbook of bereavement research* (pp. 613–645). Washington, DC: American Psychological Association.

Reiner, I., Beutel, M., Skaletz, C., Brähler, E., & Stöbel-Richter, Y. (2012). Validating the German version of the Quality of Relationship Inventory: Confirming the three-factor structure and report of psychometric properties. *PLoS One, 7*(5), e37380.

Servaty-Seib, H. L., & Pistole, M. C. (2007). Adolescent grief: Relationship category and emotional closeness. *OMEGA—Journal of Death and Dying, 54*(2), 147–167. doi:10.2190/M002-1541-JP28-4673

Smigelsky, M. A., Bottomley, J. S., Relyea, G. & Neimeyer, R. A. (2020). Investigating risk for grief severity: Attachment to the deceased and relationship quality. *Death Studies,* doi:10.1080/07481187.2018.1548539

Verhofstadt, L. L., Buysse, A., Rosseel, Y., & Peene, O. J. (2006). Confirming the three-factor structure of the Quality of Relationships Inventory within couples. *Psychological Assessment, 18,* 15.

Appendix
The Quality of Relationships Inventory-Bereavement Version (QRI-B)

DIRECTIONS: Please select the item that corresponds with each question to describe your relationship with your deceased loved one.

	Not at all	A little	Quite a bit	Very much
1. How often did you need to work to avoid conflict with this person?	1	2	3	4
2. To what extent could you count on this person for help with a problem?	1	2	3	4
3. How upset did this person sometimes make you feel?	1	2	3	4
4. How much did this person make you feel guilty?	1	2	3	4
5. To what extent could you count on this person to help you if a family member very close to you died?	1	2	3	4
6. How positive a role did this person play in your life?	1	2	3	4
7. How significant was this relationship in your life?	1	2	3	4
8. If this person were still alive, how close would your relationship be with this person in 10 years?	1	2	3	4
9. If this person were still alive, how much would you miss this person if the two of you could not see or talk with each other for a month?	1	2	3	4
10. To what extent could you count on this person to listen to you when you were very angry with someone else?	1	2	3	4

	Not at all	A little	Quite a bit	Very much
11. How angry did this person make you feel?	1	2	3	4
12. To what extent could you really count on this person to distract you from your worries when you feel under stress?	1	2	3	4
13. How often did this person try to control or influence your life?	1	2	3	4

Note: This version of the QRI-B is reproduced with permission from Bottomley et al., 2017. All items should be scored using the 1 (Not at all) to 4 (Very much) format presented in the table. Items 2, 5, 6, 7, 8, 9, 10 and 12 can be summed to compute the closeness subscale. Items 1, 3, 4, 11 and 13 can be summed to compute the conflict subscale.

10
Death Imagery Scale

Joah L. Williams, Edward K. Rynearson
and Alyssa A. Rheingold

PURPOSE

For many mourners, reflection on the circumstances of a loved one's dying is a painful but often necessary step in integrating the reality of a loss (Neimeyer, 2019). When a death is sudden and traumatic, however, as in cases of homicide, suicide or fatal accidents, reflection on the dying story can supersede a mourner's ability to reflect on other, pleasant memories of a loved one's life. Not surprisingly, then, fixation on the dying story can dramatically impact the mourner's overall psychological well-being and, indeed, is a key feature of several bereavement-related mental health problems, including posttraumatic stress disorder and prolonged grief (APA, 2013; Shear et al., 2011).

In practice, recognizing both the extent to which survivors are experiencing intense mental imagery associated with a loved one's death and the elements of the story that are most disruptive to them can help guide clinicians in tailoring clinical interventions for survivors. The Death Imagery Scale (DIS) (Rynearson & Correa, 2008) was initially developed as a tool to help clinicians assess these various aspects of death imagery among traumatically bereaved families. However, it may also be useful with families grieving sudden, natural losses. Because most traumatically bereaved individuals will experience some degree of recurrent death-related imagery, the DIS can be a useful tool for a wide variety of clinicians and providers, not just those working with the most clinically severe survivors experiencing complications in mourning.

DEVELOPMENT

Clinicians and researchers have long noted that many bereaved persons, especially those surviving sudden, traumatic losses, experience recurrent, narrative replays of the action of their loved one's dying. These intrusive re-experiencing images of the event may be of the literal event as witnessed by the survivor or non-witnessed imagery in the form of fantastical representations of the death event (Blakley, 2009). Although the surviving family members may not have witnessed the death event, they may have intrusive images of the death that involve the deceased, the bereaved person him or herself and others who might have been directly or indirectly involved in the death. In one of the first clinical reports detailing these imagined replays of dying events, Rynearson (1984) observed that, among a sample of 15 homicide survivors, all survivors described experiencing intrusive reenactment imagery characterized

DOI: 10.4324/9781351069120-12

by vividly imaging the events of their loved one's dying. Rynearson also noted that this reenactment imagery often emerged in the form of nightmares, and, in many cases, survivors reported themes of attempting to save or rescue the victim in the context of these nightmares. Furthermore, all these survivors reported some degree of anger toward the person(s) responsible for their loved one's death, expressing in some cases a desire for retaliation and revenge.

Recognizing the clinical importance of these dying images and their association with psychological adjustment to a traumatic loss, Rynearson later developed a brief, self-report survey—the Death Imagery Survey—assessing reenactment, rescue and revenge imagery, along with reunion imagery. Like reenactment imagery, reunion imagery generally involves a preoccupation with the deceased and their role in the dying narrative, but these memories aim to restore an image of the deceased as they were before their death, effectively reversing the events of the death. Comparing treatment seekers and treatment refusers in a sample of 52 homicide survivors, Rynearson (1995) found that treatment-seeking survivors endorsed higher rates of reenactment imagery than treatment refusers ($p < .001$), further evidence that clinicians may benefit from assessing and evaluating death imagery when working with traumatically bereaved families.

In addition to the various aspects of death imagery already described here, clinicians have noted that many survivors preoccupied with their own role (or lack of a role) in the dying narrative, especially those preoccupied with their perceived inability to prevent the death or rescue their loved one from dying, may also experience intense guilt and remorse associated with their inability to rescue their loved one (e.g., Shear & Mulhare, 2008). Indeed, our clinical observations suggest that remorse imagery is more common than not among traumatically bereaved families, perhaps because traumatic losses are perceived as inherently preventable. Thus, an additional item assessing remorse imagery was eventually added to Rynearson's Death Imagery Survey, resulting in the DIS.

FORMAT AND PSYCHOMETRIC PROPERTIES

The DIS is not intended to be used as a diagnostic tool, per se. Rather, it is a tool designed to help clinicians better understand the extent to which clients may be experiencing various forms of death-related imagery. Although it is designed to be administered as a self-report measure, it can also be administered by clinicians as a semi-structured interview. The DIS consists of five items, each assessing a different facet of death imagery, including reenactment, rescue, revenge, reunion and remorse. The frequency of each form of imagery over the past month is assessed using a 4-point scale ranging from 0 ("none") to 3 ("daily"). Items can be summed to derive an overall score ranging from 0 to 15, with higher scores indicating more frequent imagery. Alternatively, items can be used individually to gauge the frequency of specific forms of imagery. The full DIS is available in the Appendix to this chapter. The authors recently developed an expanded, 19-item version of the DIS, and rigorous psychometric evaluation of this revised DIS is currently underway. For purposes of this chapter, however, we will present preliminary data on the original, five-item version of the DIS.

In a study using data from 130 treatment-seeking violent loss survivors from two clinics on the US West Coast (Baddeley et al., 2015), the DIS demonstrated good internal consistency ($\alpha = .74$). Among these survivors, reenactment, reunion and remorse imagery were the most frequently endorsed forms of death imagery (nearly 81.5% of the sample endorsed past-month reenactment imagery), with smaller numbers of participants endorsing rescue and revenge imagery. Those survivors grieving deaths due to homicide, suicide and motor vehicle crashes did not differ from one another in terms of past-month endorsement of reenactment, reunion, remorse or rescue imagery. However, compared to suicide survivors, homicide survivors were more likely to endorse some form of past-month revenge imagery ($p = .005$). All five aspects of death imagery were associated with several dimensions of bereavement-related distress, including depression and trauma-related intrusions, avoidance and hyperarousal symptoms (r's range from .18–.55). Reenactment, revenge, reunion and remorse imagery were also associated with prolonged grief symptoms (r's range from .35–.54).

CLINICAL APPLICATIONS

To date, the DIS has been used in two treatment outcome studies (Rheingold et al., 2015; Rynearson, Williams, & Rheingold, 2016). The DIS can provide clinicians with valuable insight regarding the nature and frequency of death imagery experienced by survivors in a way not captured by other assessment tools and aid in the development of treatment planning as is illustrated in the following case of a 34-year-old woman who was referred for assessment three weeks after the suicidal death of her boyfriend. When she presented for treatment, it became apparent that she was unable to quiet her mind's frequent replay of images of his hanging.

His death occurred in a separate city where he had been transferred months before. Before this move, their relationship of six months had been idyllic, with plans for "settling somewhere sunny and close to the water." While she was preparing for their reunion, a series of alarming phone calls occurred. "We had never been angry with each other before," she recalled, and because of their irresolution, there was no communication for a month before she learned of his suicide through a mutual friend. The notification of his suicide was sudden, traumatic and unanticipated. They had not talked about his apparent despair, and he left no note.

She associated "sun and a sandy beach" with his living image—an image now obscured by flashbacks of his hanging and her remorseful self-accusations that "I should have stopped him." Pertinent mental health review revealed a bright, successful software designer who denied developmental or family history of psychiatric disorder, including depression. She occasionally used alcohol and marijuana to calm her intermittent anxiety (including the weeks since his death), and her primary diagnosis included adjustment disorder (traumatic grief) with anxiety.

To assess the intensity and frequency of her acute dying imagery, a DIS measure was completed with the following results: Intrusive visual images of his lifeless and hanging body, interspersed with intrusive and remorseful thoughts of her failed obligation interrupted her concentration and triggered panic attacks multiple times during the day.

Reinforcing resilience was an initial objective in her treatment before dealing with the intrusive visual and cognitive aftermath of the traumatic death. Following several sessions of stabilization from panic and the traumatic triggers of her lover's death, she was encouraged to replace the dying imagery with memories of their positive and meaningful relationship. In subsequent therapy sessions while reviewing pictures of their shared activities, she began focusing on a memory system of meaning and coherence. By consciously and repeatedly choosing to replace reenactment imagery with meaningful memories of their relationship, she regained an autonomous and counterbalancing control over its prominence.

Her subsequent therapy did not require exposure and reframing of the reenactment imagery. After ten individual sessions (with continuing exercises of resiliency reinforcement, cognitive stabilization, a supportive interview with her family, preparation for returning to work, engagement with friends and meaningful activities), her reenactment and remorseful imagery diminished. A more specific technique of restorative re-exposure of the dying imagery could be applied with persistence of intense and frequent reenactment imagery but was not indicated in her management with this focused and time-limited intervention.

References

American Psychiatric Association (APA). (2013). *Diagnostic and statistical manual of mental disorders* (5th ed.). Washington, DC: Author.

Baddeley, J. L., Williams, J. L., Rynearson, E. K., Correa, F., Saindon, C., & Rheingold, A. A. (2015). Death thoughts and images in treatment-seekers after violent loss. *Death Studies, 39*, 84–91.

Blakley, T. (2009). Triggers, flashbacks, and fantasia: Intrusive death imagery following homicide loss. *Illness, Crisis, & Loss, 17*, 23–37.

Neimeyer, R. A. (2019). Meaning reconstruction in bereavement: Development of a research program. *Death Studies, 43*, 79–91. doi:10.1080/07481187.2018.1456620

Rheingold, A. A., Baddeley, J., Williams, J. L., Brown, C., Wallace, W. M., Correa, F., & Rynerson, E. K. (2015). Restorative retelling for violent death: An investigation of treatment effectiveness, influencing factors, and durability. *Journal of Loss and Trauma, 20*, 541–555.

Rynearson, E. K. (1984). Bereavement after homicide: A descriptive study. *American Journal of Psychiatry, 141*, 1452–1454.

Rynearson, E. K. (1995). Bereavement after homicide: A comparison of treatment seekers and refusers. *British Journal of Psychiatry, 166*, 507–510.

Rynearson, E. K., & Correa, F. (2008). *Accommodation to violent dying: A guide to restorative retelling and support* (Unpublished manuscript).

Rynearson, E. K., Williams, J. L., & Rheingold, A. A. (2016). Treating the narrative fixations of traumatic grief. *Grief Matters: The Australian Journal of Grief and Bereavement, 19*, 14–18.

Shear, M. K., & Mulhare, E. (2008). Complicated grief. *Psychiatric Annals, 38*, 662–670.

Shear, M. K., Simon, N., Wall, M., Zisook, S., Neimeyer, R., Duan, N., . . . Keshaviah, A. (2011). Complicated grief and related bereavement issues for DSM-5. *Depression and Anxiety, 28*, 103–117.

Appendix
Death Imagery Scale

The following is a list of images reported after the death of a friend or relative (as thoughts or visual "flashbacks" [i.e., wide awake] or dreams while asleep). Please underline the type of types of imagery experienced and check their frequency within the last month.

	Frequency			
	None	*Once/month*	*Once/week*	*Daily*
1. **Reenactment**: I experienced a fantasied replay of the dying (as thought, visual "flashback," dream).				
2. **Rescue**: I experienced a fantasy of rescuing the person from dying (as thought, visual "flashback," dream).				
3. **Revenge**: I experienced a fantasy of retaliation for this dying (as thought, visual "flashback," dream).				
4. **Reunion**: I experienced a fantasy of reunion with the deceased family member and/or friend (as thought, visual "flashback," dream).				
5. **Remorse**: I experienced a fantasy that I should have somehow prevented the dying from happening (as thought, visual "flashback," dream).				

Part III
Moving Through Bereavement

11
The Grieving Styles Grid

Robert A. Neimeyer

CLIENTS FOR WHOM THE TECHNIQUE IS APPROPRIATE

Participants in grief workshops, bereavement support groups and classes in the psychology of loss can benefit from this relatively "safe" way to explore their own grieving styles while comparing and contrasting them with those of others. However, this exercise is not intended to be a complete therapy and is not a substitute for more intensive personal work, often conducted in an individual or family context, especially in the immediate aftermath of tragic loss.

DESCRIPTION

As the conceptualization of grief has broadened and deepened, theorists, therapists and educators have become increasingly aware of the extent to which losses are processed differently as a function of gender, ethnicity, economic position, religion, age and other characteristics of bereaved individuals and the cultural contexts in which they live. This exercise provides a lively interactive structure for expressing and exploring the diversity of grieving styles in a small group of people, usually numbering between 8 and 30. It consists of four phases—*marker selection, grid work, small group processing* and *plenary group discussion*—which together total 60 to 90 minutes. Each phase is outlined here, followed by an illustrative case study and comments on possible variations.

Conceptual Framework

The Grieving Styles Grid invites participants to explore their position on two axes, each of which ranges along a continuum of *expressive vs. stoic* or of *continuing bonds vs. letting go*. The former captures preferences for the social expression versus the private experience of grief, noted in connection with discussions of gender roles (Doka & Martin, 2010) and ethnic variations in bereavement (Rosenblatt & Wallace, 2005). In contrast, the latter locates participants according to their emphasis on retaining versus relinquishing bonds with the dead, which reflects both cultural prescriptions (Stroebe, Gergen, Gergen, & Stroebe, 1992) and mourners' personal attachment styles (Kosminsky & Jordan, 2016). As they respond to the instructions that follow, participants ultimately position themselves on a two-dimensional grid that depicts four different grieving styles, as depicted in Figure 11.1, and gain deeper

DOI: 10.4324/9781351069120-14

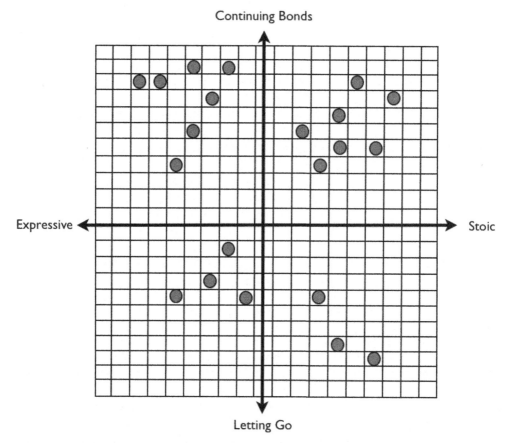

Figure 11.1 The Grieving Styles Grid, with the Vertical *Continuing Bonds vs. Letting Go* Axis and the Horizontal *Expressive vs. Stoic* Axis and Illustrative Marker Positions After Exercise

appreciation for how they and others make meaning of their loss and find orientation in it (Neimeyer, 2016).

Materials

In the "board game" version of the Grieving Styles Grid, the facilitator would provide either variegated markers such as small stones and shells of various colors, shapes and textures or small sand-tray-like figurines (human forms, animals, monsters, symbolic objects) along with a large tabletop-size matrix of at least 25 x 25 squares, ideally larger. Alternatively, in the "walking grid" variation noted in *Concluding Thoughts*, no materials of any kind are needed as participants themselves serve as the "markers," stepping up or back in response to instructions in a large room devoid of furniture or in a large, clear outdoor space. Each has its own advantages, as noted in the closing section.

Marker Selection

If a physical tabletop grid is used, the facilitator first invites participants to search for a distinctive marker from among a generous supply of possibilities attractively scattered across a colorful scarf on an adjacent table, encouraging them to select one intuitively that "represents them," rather than after thinking the decision through explicitly. After doing so, they gather around the table or tables on which the grid is placed and lay their markers in a starting position anywhere along the *vertical* (or north/south) axis of the grid in a single long line, facing any direction (see Figure 11.1).

Grid Work

To orient participants to the grid, the facilitator places simple index cards labeled *North*, *South*, *East* and *West* on the corresponding edges of the grid to avoid the evaluative implications associated with other directional markers like "up and down," "forward and backward," or even "right and left." Using compass points also enhances the metaphor of "mapping" one's grieving style, providing a preliminary vocabulary for processing the experience once it is completed. The facilitator first places the *West* and *East* cards on the left and right of the grid and then reads each of the questions in Appendix 11.1 slowly, pausing after each to allow participants to move their markers the number of spaces corresponding to their selected answers. In each case, the facilitator indicates whether participants may choose multiple answers (thereby moving the number of spaces associated with each) or the single most appropriate response for them. However, the axes on the grid are not labeled *Expressive*, *Stoic*, *Continuing Bonds*, and *Letting Go* until all questions for both sections of the grid work are completed to avoid conveying a response set to participants. A simple way to do this is to reveal these labels by writing them on the backs of the compass directional cards mentioned earlier and simply flipping them over after all moves on both dimensions have been made.

After participants have moved their markers up or back in response to the *Expressive vs. Stoic* (West/East) questions, they are asked to re-center their markers on the horizontal axis, preserving their distance from the vertical axis on which they started. The facilitator then indicates the *North* and *South* cards at the top and bottom of the grid, respectively, and continues by reading the *Continuing Bonds vs. Letting Go* questions in Appendix 11.1, again pausing after each to allow participants to move the appropriate number of spaces. The result is a dispersion of markers across the grid in a pattern that represents how extremely participants view their personal and cultural grieving styles on the two dimensions. The facilitator then draws together "affinity groups" on the basis of the proximity of their markers, attempting to include at least three participants in each group. Although these may correspond to the four quadrants of the grid, other configurations are also possible, such as groups that are more extreme or more intermediate in their grieving styles on one or both dimensions. Outliers are also possible—as participants themselves will note—but for the sake of the group work to follow, they should be placed with the nearest cluster of markers. A workable number of groups to form in this fashion will depend on the size of the larger group, with three to five probably being optimal. The entire grid work phase typically takes 15 minutes.

Small Group Work

With affinity groups formed, participants are asked to meet with others in their cluster in different rooms or in different corners of the larger room and discuss the questions in Appendix 11.2. These begin with each person sharing what attracted him or her to a particular marker or figurine to represent the self, providing a good icebreaker for the conversation to follow. Further questions then explore any surprises that arose for members with whom they found themselves grouped; how they felt as they moved more deeply into the grieving styles depicted in the grid, getting closer to or farther from others; and what personal, familial, social and cultural factors they discovered that might help account for their similarity. In particular, questions prompt both an appreciative and a critical perspective on each possible style, considering its advantages and disadvantages and inviting members to reflect on the degree to which they affirm it without ambivalence or with some degree of discomfort or resistance, suggesting the possibility of change. This phase of the exercise typically takes approximately 30 minutes.

Plenary Group Processing

Before closing, each affinity group will select one or more spokespersons to "report out" on the observations of their group to the whole group as it is reassembled in a circle. Reporters begin by emphasizing what their groups most want others to understand about their grieving styles and proceed to share surprises they encountered, cultural values their style implies and how comfortable or uncomfortable they were with the overall style they shared. After making sure that each group is heard, the facilitator invites more general discussion about personal variations on the group styles, participants' observations about the sharing of those in the other groups and what this implies about how each person or group would like to be supported in living out his or her own grieving style or attempting to change it. This final phase of the exercise can last from 15 minutes to half an hour or more.

CASE ILLUSTRATION

The 20 adult participants in a multi-session workshop on grief and bereavement were diverse in age, gender, ethnicity, religion and country of origin, but all were motivated to take part in the group by a range of personal losses (death of a parent or grandparent to disease, death of a pet, loss of a sibling in childhood, suicide of a friend). Having in previous sessions addressed these various losses, the Grieving Styles Grid was presented as an activity for exploring their culturally informed ways of responding to them psychologically and socially. In preparation for the session, the facilitator had pushed together three tables to form a square and spread a simple checkered tablecloth across them to create a large grid, with a paper sticker in the center to mark the intersection of the two axes. On a side table he had placed a scarf, forming a kind of "altar" on which he scattered approximately 150 small, colorful stones, which varied in their shape and texture, some polished, some rough, as well as other natural objects (small pinecones, seashells, etc.). Gesturing to this collection, the facilitator then invited participants to examine it, with the instruction to "intuitively allow your hand to select an object to represent you." This then became the marker that each participant placed on the unlabeled vertical axis of the checkered tablecloth.

Next, placing the East *and* West *cards on the far right and left of the grid, the facilitator read each of the first set of questions slowly, as participants stepped forward to move their markers the appropriate number of spaces. As the questions continued, the group appeared quiet and thoughtful, shifting the objects on the Expressive vs. Stoic dimension until they were dispersed in rough clusters at various distances from the vertical axis. As he shifted to the second set of questions, the facilitator first asked participants to re-center their markers on the horizontal axis, preserving the distance they had traveled from the vertical axis with the previous questions. Placing* North *at the top of the grid and* South *at the bottom, the facilitator then read the remaining questions as participants again moved their markers in response to instructions, this time dispersing them on the Continuing Bonds vs. Letting Go dimension (see Figure 11.2). When this was accomplished, the natural objects were distributed across the grid as displayed in Figure 11.1. The facilitator then grouped the markers into four sets, in this case corresponding to the four quadrants of the grid: Expressive/Continuing Bonds, Expressive/Letting Go, Stoic/ Continuing Bonds and Stoic/Letting Go. (In other groups, different clusters that vary in degree*

Figure 11.2 Moving around the Grieving Styles Grid

of endorsement of the same grieving styles might well emerge.) Participants were then asked to join their appropriate affinity group in one corner of the room taking their markers with them, pull their chairs into a circle and discuss the questions in Appendix 11.2.

Participants began by describing why they selected the natural object they had chosen to represent them. Steve, a Caucasian man in his late 20s, said the pinecone he held attracted him because it suggested life, was multidimensional and was ready to open up, as he was. Toni, a Hispanic woman in her 50s, held up a polished stone in a cubic shape with a tiger's eye coloration and noted that although she didn't like the "boxed-in" shape of the stone, the way it held light within its darkness struck her as expressive of her life and her loss. In his group, Dai Ming, a Chinese graduate student, said he selected a small seashell because he felt "closed off" and self-protective. Spirited discussion followed in each group about the commonalities in their grieving styles; how they understood their origins, advantages and disadvantages; and the degree to which members identified with or resisted the prescriptions of their family and culture and whether and how they would like to change.

After spending a few minutes visiting with each affinity group in turn, the facilitator reconvened them as a plenary group and invited the spokesperson for each small group to open the discussion. The Expressive/Continuing Bonds group, who named themselves the Open Books, consisted solely of younger Caucasian women. Unsurprisingly, they spoke first, extolling the virtues of open sharing of grief and associated emotions as well as remaining connected to the memory of their deceased loved ones. The single male representative of the Travelers group, endorsing an Expressive/Letting Go style, responded that although they, too, appreciated communicating about feelings, focusing so heavily on the loss seemed like a "downer" to them. For this reason, they preferred to think about more positive things and move on with life. One of the two older Caucasian women in the group agreed. Next, the spokesperson for the Little Statues, who exemplified a Stoic/Continuing Bonds orientation, noted their initial surprise in their group composition, as it comprised all the African American women in the workshop, as well as one Caucasian man and woman. The common denominator for them, they discovered, was a fundamental Protestant or Catholic faith, with its emphasis on ritual and an afterlife of reconnection, rather than prolonged expression of sorrow and personal practices of remembrance. Finally, the three members of the Stoic/Letting Go group, which described itself as Frozen, consisted of a Chinese man, a Pakistani woman, and a middle-aged white Southern woman. Though quiet at first, they shared their surprise at the inclusion of the latter in the otherwise Asian group, finding an explanation in the rural isolation in which she grew up. As a result, she, like her younger Asian counterparts, had internalized norms of processing experiences internally rather than socially, focusing on necessary practical tasks and roles, and moving on in the aftermath of loss. Heads nodded in appreciation as members of different groups developed a keener appreciation for the inner logic of different grieving styles, including their own.

CONCLUDING THOUGHTS

When conducted almost as a "board game," as in the version of the Grieving Styles Grid shown in Figure 11.2, participants are able to see at a glance how their placement positions them vis-à-vis other "players," who ultimately will form different affinity groups for further processing. An advantage of this version is the "self-distancing" perspective it encourages, as participants literally view their position from an outsider perspective in a broad overview. Processing that follows, therefore, tends to be somewhat more cognitive and conceptual, shifting between personal and cultural factors that together configure each small group's grieving style.

An alternative "walking grid" variation dispenses with markers and a literal grid and instead invites participants to form a line in the middle of an empty room or outdoors on a level field or court and step forward or back in response to question prompts, rather than moving a symbolic marker. Experience suggests that this variation is somewhat more "self-immersive," generating more emotion and self-awareness as the questions continue and participants move closer to or farther from one another. Small group processing then often includes somewhat greater emphasis on the feelings generated by the movement and the sense of bonding with others of the same style, but also less awareness of the distinctive clusters of others at greater distance from them. With awareness of this somewhat different "pull" for the two versions, facilitators could choose either for contexts as diverse as bereavement support groups, adolescent grief camps, university classes and professional training in grief and loss. In the more academic or professional contexts, assigning a brief, five-minute "free write" following the exercise can help deepen and personalize the learning, encouraging the learners to capture in words what most struck them about the diverse grieving styles encountered, including their own. In all cases, the Grieving Styles Grid tends to promote bonding within subgroups, understanding of differences and respect for the diverse ways in which people confront the universality of loss.

References

Doka, K., & Martin, T. (2010). *Grieving beyond gender*. New York: Routledge.

Kosminsky, P., & Jordan, J. R. (2016). *Attachment informed grief therapy*. New York: Routledge.

Neimeyer, R. A. (2016). Meaning reconstruction in the wake of loss: Evolution of a research program. *Behaviour Change*. doi:10.1017/bec.2016.4

Rosenblatt, P., & Wallace, B. (2005). *African American grief*. New York: Routledge.

Stroebe, M., Gergen, M., Gergen, K., & Stroebe, W. (1992). Broken hearts or broken bonds: Love and death in historical perspective. *American Psychologist, 47*, 1205–1212.

Appendix 11.1
Facilitator Questions for Grieving Styles Grid

DIMENSION 1: EXPRESSIVE VS. STOIC

1. (Can choose more than one) When you were a child, if you were crying over someone or something you lost, would close adults:

   - encourage you to talk about your feelings? Move 2 steps *West*.
   - provide you nonverbal comfort (e.g., a hug)? Move 1 step *West*.
   - leave you alone? Move 1 step *East*.
   - distract you or encourage you to "be strong"? Move 2 steps *East*.

2. (Choose the single best answer) At this point in your life, when you are feeling sadness or grief, if

   - you can name 3 or more people you'd open up to about it: Move 2 steps *West*.
   - you can name only 1 or 2 people you'd open up to about it: Move 1 step *West*.
   - there is no one you'd open up to about it: Move 1 step *East*.
   - it is hard to acknowledge to yourself that you are sad or grieving: Move 2 steps *East*.

3. (Choose the single best answer) When someone in your community* of family or friends dies, if the *majority* of people

   - share personal feelings about the one who died: Move 2 steps *West*.
   - say something like "I'm sorry for your loss": Move 1 step *West*.
   - say something like "He's with the Lord now" or "She's gone home": Move 1 step *East*.
   - say something like "God never gives us more than we can bear" or "This is God's way of testing your faith": Move 2 steps *East*.
     Community is defined as the participant's most relevant reference group, whether understood as ethnic group, extended family, social circle, etc.

4. (Choose the single best answer) When someone close to you in your community dies, would you

- write the bereaved a personal note of consolation: Move 2 steps *West*.
- send a standard sympathy card: Move 1 step *West*.
- say, "If there is anything I can do, just let me know": Move 1 step *East*.
- avoid the bereaved: Move 2 steps *East*.

5. (Can choose more than one) If you were struggling with severe grief over the death of someone, would you

- seek out a grief counselor or therapist? Move 3 steps *West*.
- seek a friend or family member to talk to? Move 1 step *West*.
- deal with your suffering by yourself? Move 2 steps *East*.

6. (Choose the single best answer) Which of the following best completes the sentence, "Sharing grief with another would be _____."

- a welcome relief for me: Move 2 steps *West*.
- awkward but possible for me: Move 1 step *West*.
- a burden for the listener, so I would tend not to do it: Move 2 steps *East*.

DIMENSION 2: CONTINUING BONDS VS. LETTING GO

1. (Choose the single best answer) The *most common* tendency of people in my community following a death would be to:

- Share spontaneous stories of the dead: Move 2 steps *North*.
- Hold the deceased in their hearts: Move 1 step *North*.
- Say goodbye to the deceased: Move 1 step *South*.
- Move on and put their energy elsewhere: Move 2 steps *South*.

2. (Choose the single best answer) Does your community have customs or rituals for memorializing the dead on special days of remembrance a year or more after the funeral?

- If yes: Move 2 steps *North*.
- If no: Move 2 steps *South*.

3. (Can choose more than one) In the months following the death of a loved one, are you likely to:

- Write an unsent letter to them to express how you feel? Move 2 steps *North*.
- Have an imagined "conversation" with them in your mind? Move 1 step *North*.
- Avoid conversations about them with others? Move 1 step *South*.
- Try to think of something else when they come to mind? Move 2 steps *South*.

4. (Can choose more than one) If you were left with a loved one's clothes, jewelry or possessions after they died, would you:

- Wear some of them publicly or display them in your home? Move 2 steps *North*.
- Pass them on as special mementos to others? Move 1 step *North*.
- Pack them all away in a closet, attic or basement? Move 1 step *South*.
- Donate all of them to charity or throw them away? Move 2 steps *South*.

5. (Choose the single best answer) If a loved one died, would you be inclined to:

- Keep photos of them in your home or on your phone to share with others? Move 2 steps *North*.
- Keep photos of them to view on your own? Move 1 step *North*.
- Keep photos of them but rarely look at them? Move 1 step *South*.
- Discard or delete their photos? Move 2 steps *South*.

6. (Can choose more than one) If a child, sibling or parent of yours died, would you

- Create a legacy project (e.g., scholarship, art project or web site) to honor them? Move 2 steps *North*.
- Donate, do good works or pursue acts of kindness in their name? Move 1 step *North*.
- Avoid activities or places that reminded you of them? Move 2 steps *South*.

Appendix 11.2
Questions Distributed to Participants to Prompt Group Processing

SMALL GROUP PROCESSING

Form several affinity groups of three to six people near you and move to different parts of the room. Then consider the following questions:

- If you chose a symbolic figure or marker to represent you on the board or tabletop, briefly describe why you chose it or what it reflects about you.
- Look around the group, noting similarities and differences in ethnicity, country of origin, age, gender, social class, rural vs. urban residence, sexual orientation or religion. Do you find yourself with the group of people you expected, or are you surprised in any way at the people whose grieving style is like your own? Why or why not?
- Discuss with others how you felt as you moved farther and farther into your position on the board or in the room.
- Consider the assumptions, values and strengths implied in your group's grieving style. What contextual, historical or family factors contribute to it? What is one thing about your community's grieving style you most appreciate?
- Consider any possible drawbacks or challenges associated with your group's grieving style. In your own life, do you find yourself embracing it or resisting it in some way? What reactions, if any, do members of your community have to this? If you could change one thing about your community's grieving style, what would it be?

PLENARY GROUP PROCESSING

- Choose one member of your group to report out to the larger group on your behalf. Collaborate in helping this spokesperson convey what you as a group most want others to understand about your grieving style.
- Have this spokesperson or another share what most surprised or interested all of you about the exercise.
- Open the floor to general discussion.

12
The Grief Dance

Andria Wilson

CLIENTS FOR WHOM THE TECHNIQUE IS APPROPRIATE

This can be an effective technique for adolescents and adults who are interested in cultivating meaningful storytelling from their grief after the death of a loved one as well as nonfinite, non-death-related losses. This activity might be inappropriate for individuals who are in the immediate aftermath of a traumatic loss or when positive reactions initiate anxiety or distress. The facilitator should create a safe environment for exploration of emotional engagement with self and others throughout the activity.

DESCRIPTION

The art of discovering meaning in life is self-given, the product of one's chosen attitude toward and willingness to derive sense and learning from experiences. The potential for suffering to engage humanity is universal. Inescapable brokenness will surely introduce itself should we choose to remain open and vulnerable to the love of others. Our attitude toward loss is a determining factor in our ability to accept and to create meaning surrounding our grief (Lichtenthal & Breitbart, 2012). The belief that human nature is motivated by the search for a purpose and meaning is captured thoughtfully by Holocaust survivor and psychiatrist Viktor Frankl (1992) who stated, "Man's main concern is not to gain pleasure or to avoid pain but rather to see a meaning in his life" (p. 117). For those ready to embark on restorative retelling and repair, the grief dance can foster growth and provide the mourner space to transcend loss through a self-guided narrative technique.

There is a growing body of research related to loss that demonstrates the powerful healing component of group experiential work as a successful approach that enhances body awareness and aids in the reconstruction of narrative through emotional release, relationship and repair (Dayton, 2004, 2015). As a college speech instructor with a theatrical and therapeutic background, I lean toward experiential techniques to create an atmosphere that decreases anxiety and allows for exploration, play and storytelling. I construct my classroom through structured group activities that are simple but remarkable in their ability to move students into action, regulate emotion, create meaningful bonds and foster self-understanding. Borrowing from sociometry, neuropsychodrama relational techniques by psychodramatist Tian Dayton (2004, 2015) and acceptance and commitment therapy (Hayes, Strosahl, & Wilson, 2012), I incorporate exercises that stimulate emotional integration of loss and meaning,

DOI: 10.4324/9781351069120-15

providing a safe space in which they can be shared and processed. Utilizing this approach, my students serve as therapeutic witnesses who can buffer, support and encourage each other through their storytelling assignments.

The grief dance is an activity I developed for students to creatively explore meaning making through their attitudes of acceptance and curiosity. By navigating their story through a variety of words, students are given the opportunity to engage their bodies through a series of steps—an intimate dance with self. This process allows group members to choose which words might apply to them and which might not, giving them freedom to choose their dance steps throughout their narratives or specific loss experiences. Through choice and movement, the students derive meaning from their loss and ultimately bring about a brief but restorative retelling to those present.

This activity was introduced as a warm-up to the commemorative speech preparation. Within this speech, students are given the option to embrace their stories through the construction of a self-narrative to share with the class, expanding on meaning and purpose as a result of their life experiences. My students come from hard places and have experienced significant losses throughout their lives. Many do not have a platform to explore and normalize their losses within a supportive community; therefore, I offer my class as a "living stage" to expose hurts, cultivate resiliency and make meaning from hard things. This activity offers the students a safe place to emotionally engage within themselves and with each other, shifting perspective and witnessing the strength of vulnerability from their peers. Pain expressed and witnessed by supportive group members can help assist the grieving with the reconstruction of their loss, creating a narrative that reframes suffering (Dayton, 2004).

EXAMPLE

I prepared the space by laying cards containing large, printed words on the floor, each related to a specific emotion that students previously had given in response to their upcoming speech, which was to commemorate someone or something special that they had lost. Once students entered the classroom, we discussed how freedom to choose one's attitude in the midst of hard things could be a gift. I invited students to accept their emotional response to their loss without critique—to befriend it, lean into it and ultimately become its dance partner. Only through collaboration and fellowship with the ache can one potentially expand into the discomfort, revealing growth and meaning.

Following a brief discussion, I began by demonstrating the activity through a personal example. I spoke about the loss of my sweet grandfather when I was 10. I began by standing on the word "sad," an emotion related to the initial loss of my grandfather. I explained that in this dance I had the freedom to choose my response to his death. I continued my dance by moving to the word "struggle," attempting to retain my relationship with my grandfather but having to move on without him. By adopting an attitude of love and connection with the memories of my grandfather, I accepted the loss and discovered its meaning. Acceptance ushered in feelings of kindness and humor—gifts my grandfather left me. These are the very gifts I consistently use in my teaching. The result of this grief dance was self-directed as I moved from the word "sad" to the word "struggle" and "humor" and then "connection," an ending point to my grief dance.

Whether the students were navigating the loss of a loved one or a nonfinite, non-death-related loss as part of their speeches, they began to explore their own meaning-making processes. I gave students time at each step to share with fellow students who chose the same word(s). The spontaneity involved gave little room for intellectualization and thus grew from a deeper connection of emotional revelation and witnessing. With the cognitive filter removed, the body has the freedom to speak through each word chosen. The clustering of individuals on certain words gave way to laughter, tears, hurt, connection and the building of resiliency.

As narratives were constructed and shared, the students' affect and emotions were exposed, and courage became contagious. "I didn't realize what my best friend gave me," 19-year-old Jamal said. "After he was shot, I thought I lost him forever but doing this . . . I see how he taught me so much. I'm a better friend and a better student because of him. It's like a part of him is still here with me." Another young student, Ebony, completed her last dance step on the word "strong," stating, "I was raped repeatedly as a child. It was terrible. I had a baby at 17, but through it all, I survived. I'm a survivor. I am strong. I can now teach my daughter how to be strong." This activity occurred rather quickly for students, their bodies moving toward acceptance through each chosen step, essentially inviting the loss to dance. The natural propensity for connectedness and belonging was revealed, and students became healing agents for each other.

Upon completion of the activity, students collectively processed their grief dance and its meaning discovered throughout the experience. This information was then incorporated as part of their speeches the following week.

CONCLUDING THOUGHTS

I was moved by my students' responses to the activity. Many stated that "dancing" with loss gave them opportunity to embrace their vulnerability, exposing and sharing themselves in a culture that has historically viewed emotional intimacy as a weakness, particularly among college-aged individuals. Grief witnessed and affirmed is powerful. The sharing of the experience itself promotes resiliency, growth, and healing. Choosing an attitude of acceptance, a bereaved individual can develop a healthier relationship with the loss and create space to move forward. Highlighting choice to the bereaved can empower them; although their loss was beyond their control, what is within their control is how they face their suffering.

The grief dance can extend to educational and therapeutic groups that desire to explore meaning making from grief after the death of a loved one as well as nonfinite, non-death-related losses. I hold to the belief that meaning can be created from hard things. The brokenness of grieving, while challenging and painful, can become a restorative narrative of healing and hope.

References

Dayton, T. (2004). *The living stage: A step-by-step guide to psychodrama, sociometry and experiential group psychotherapy.* Deerfield Beach, FL: Health Communications, Inc.

Dayton, T. (2015). *Neuro-psychodrama in the treatment of relational trauma.* Deerfield Beach, FL: Health Communications, Inc.

Frankl, V. E. (1992). *Man's search for meaning: An introduction to logotherapy.* New York: Simon & Schuster.

Hayes, S. C., Strosahl, K. D., & Wilson, K. G. (2012). *Acceptance and commitment therapy* (2nd ed.). New York: Guilford Press.

Lichtenthal, W. G., & Breitbart, W. (2012). Finding meaning through the attitude one takes. In R. A. Neimeyer (Ed.), *Techniques of grief therapy: Creative practices for counseling and the bereaved* (pp. 161–164). New York: Routledge.

13
Walking the Labyrinth

Jane Williams

CLIENTS FOR WHOM THE TECHNIQUE IS APPROPRIATE

Adults who can walk without assistance are candidates for walking the labyrinth. Finger labyrinths can be used by persons who are not ambulatory. Labyrinth walking addresses normal, complicated or conflicted grief; stress and burnout of hospital and hospice staff; children and adolescents experiencing first losses; and first responder grief.

DESCRIPTION

Grief can be isolating, especially in American and European cultures where there is typically little social support for the griever after a flurry of concern during the first weeks of bereavement. After an initial period of shock, the bereaved may be left with overwhelming feelings of loss and little cultural guidance, social support or spiritual resources to work through the mix of emotions. Lack of empathic relational and spiritual support often results in the mourner's withdrawal and hiding of intense emotions. Especially in early grief, mourners need a safe container in which to express and explore their loss experience.

A mourner can step into the labyrinth, walk the path and then step back out of the labyrinth, using it as a means of accessing yet also containing strong emotions within the kinesthetic experience of walking a defined path that requires nothing more than beginning and continuing on the journey.

Whereas a maze exists to confound and confuse the walker, the singular winding path of the labyrinth leads inevitably to the center without calling on the walker to choose at any point. Like walking meditation or mindfulness practice, it requires the mourner merely to put one foot in front of the other, eliciting a relaxation response and allowing the walker to connect to inner wisdom, flashes of awareness and new insights about his or her grief journey.

The 11-circuit Chartres labyrinth pattern (Figure 13.1), which is most often used in a spiritual context, describes the pathway as a path of prayer, and the symbolism of the pattern is related to its Christian heritage. Instructions for walking the labyrinth (see handout in Appendix to this chapter) use the ancient archetypal three-fold process of personal and spiritual transformation: Purgation/Releasing, Illumination/Receiving, and Union/Re-Entering.

Walkers set out from the entrance and, following the path, walk until they reach the center. After pausing in the center as long as they wish, they re-enter the same path that brought

DOI: 10.4324/9781351069120-16

Figure 13.1 Chartres Labyrinth

them in, walking it until they reach the entrance once again. Because of this single path design, the walker need not engage critical thought but can sink deeply into his or her experience. Walking the winding path often stimulates awareness of insights, remembrance of sacred scripture passages and memories that have been held out of conscious awareness but emerge in the silence and walking meditative experience.

The journey through the labyrinth becomes a metaphor for one's life—and one's grief. Feelings of not knowing the way through, feeling lost, feeling like one is not making progress, feeling like grief is lifting and then finding oneself plunged into its depths again are common in the grief experience—and in walking the labyrinth. Some mourners feel they are being accompanied on the path by the deceased or sense the presence of angels or a spiritual being as they walk.

A near-universal experience of comfort and safety in the center of the labyrinth is reported by walkers, with many experiencing it as sacred space where one is close to Holy Mystery or God. In this sacred space, deep emotions of grief—tears, regret, sadness, guilt, anger—are often released and may be offered to God or one's Higher Power. Mourners often report feeling comforted, accepted and "held in God's hands."

Walking the path back from the center, one may be aware of a release, a clearing out, a letting go of at least some of what one brought into the labyrinth walk and an opening up of space within oneself for healing or new opportunities in life. The simple accomplishment of having navigated the twists and turns of the path to arrive in the center gives one confidence on the path outward from the center that there is a path to follow—in one's life as in the labyrinth. And if one has felt an accompaniment on the path (by the deceased or a spiritual guide) or has felt held in God's heart or hands in the center, that experience has broken through the isolation of grief and become part of the memory—and hope—of one's journey through grief.

Yet healing one's grief is a process, and while a single walk offers comfort, release, insights and healing, it does not negate the need for additional grief work. Many persons who walk the labyrinth for grief work will find it helpful to walk repeatedly over time, reviewing, releasing and opening more deeply each time. Each labyrinth walk—even multiple walks by the same person—yields a unique experience. Absolutely essential to the labyrinth walk is to process the experience with one's therapist or another trusted person after the walk.

CASE ILLUSTRATION

Joy's three-year-old daughter, her only child, died nearly two months ago as a result of a rare viral encephalitis. Joy had been with her daughter every day during the final two months of Emmy's life when the toddler was on full life support and ventilator. Joy, a single mother, had struggled during that time to accept that Emmy was in an irreversible coma. With the support of her priest, the hospital chaplain, Emmy's physicians and a close friend, Joy was able to allow Emmy to be withdrawn from machines and take her last breath in Joy's arms.

Joy came to a hospice Day of Remembrance six weeks after Emmy's death to walk the labyrinth at the suggestion of her therapist who, having walked labyrinths herself, encouraged Joy to walk it as one tool for healing her grief. The therapist accompanied Joy to the event in order to support her by observing the walk and helping Joy process the experience afterward.

In a private space after the labyrinth walk, Joy's therapist asked her to share any ways in which the labyrinth walk and her present life experience were similar. Joy thought for a moment and then excitedly told her therapist that initially at the first turns she wanted to give up and walk away—coming to the turns felt like she was being blocked from where she wanted to go—just as she felt blocked in her desire to be with Emmy and to erase the past months' events. But as she paused at those turns, she began to feel like Emmy would want her to go on. She remembered a time when Emmy pulled her by the hand so they could wade in a shallow stream when Joy (who couldn't swim) wanted to back away. In the labyrinth, just as at the stream, Joy forced herself to continue on "because Emmy wanted me to." Next, the therapist asked what had occurred in the center. Joy remembered feeling like a small, lost child as she curled up and rocked, not wanting to cry. She said that at some point, she became aware that she wasn't so much rocking herself as feeling rocked and held. At that point, something inside her let go of deep sobs, and she just let it happen—something she had not been able to do since holding Emmy as she died.

"When I finally stopped and opened my eyes, I felt empty—but not hollow," Joy said. "I felt like Emmy was safe—and we would see each other again."

She remembered writing in her journal but didn't remember what she wrote. She opened to the page and showed her therapist what she had written:

I have been so afraid of forgetting Emmy, so afraid to go on with my life, afraid that it would mean I did not love her enough. I can never give her up, but I don't need to always dwell on her dying. I can dwell on the good memories, like that day at the brook when she told me I didn't need to be afraid, that she would "save me" if I fell in the water. Emmy will save me—save me from being alone in the world. I will always be her mother and she will always be my daughter—in this life and in the next.

Joy said that the walk from the center outward felt different than the walk to the center. Her experience of release added hope to the desolation of her grief—hope that the depth of feelings of loss and aloneness will not always be her constant companion and the affirmation that death does not erase connections. She felt more connected with Emmy through an ongoing non-physical relationship accessed through memory and perhaps in contexts like labyrinth walks. Although her grief work was not finished, for the first time since Emmy's death, Joy felt there was a reason to re-engage with living.

CLOSING THOUGHTS

Therapists who want to use the labyrinth for grief work should be familiar with it and have walked it themselves at least once. Clients should be offered brief information on how to use the labyrinth and what one might expect in the walk (see handout in Appendix to this chapter). Although the labyrinth can be valuable to clients when walked alone, most therapists will want to accompany the client to the site to observe the initial walk and use time afterward to help the client debrief and integrate what occurred with the grief work already done. Just as journaling only for emotional release without seeking meaning or insight in what is written is often unproductive, walking the labyrinth without unpacking what was learned on the journey lessens the impact of the walk. Questions that are helpful to consider when debriefing include *What metaphors came to mind during the walk? Are there any insights that became clear at any point? What words or phrases may have arisen during the walk? Did you feel alone in your walk? Were there any feelings of hope, comfort, strength that you felt during your walk or in the center?*

A second option for harvesting the benefit of a labyrinth walk would be to have the client walk without the therapist present and then journal or create a collage or other form of art in response to the walk. The journal or art can then be taken to the next therapy session and processed.

In some instances when the client is hesitant to walk the labyrinth or fears emotional release, the therapist might agree to walk behind or beside the client—not talking but as a companion whose nonverbal presence strengthens the client to continue. After completing the walk, client and therapist can debrief the experience as described earlier. The therapist may ask if the client would now feel positively about walking the labyrinth alone—at this time or in the future.

Labyrinths available to the public are widespread. One tool for locating labyrinths can be found at http://labyrinthlocator.com/home.

Recommended Readings

Artress, L. (2006). *The sacred path companion: A guide to walking the labyrinth to heal and transform.* New York: Riverhead Books/Random House.

Bloos, I., & O'Connor, T. (2002). Ancient and medieval labyrinth and contemporary narrative therapy: How do they fit? *Pastoral Psychology, 50*(4).

Cunningham, M. (2012). *Integrating spirituality in clinical social work practice: Walking the labyrinth.* Boston: Pearson Education.

Hong, Y., & Jacinto, G. (2012). Reality therapy and the labyrinth: A strategy for practice. *Journal of Human Behavior in the Social Environment, 22,* 619–634.

Appendix
Instructions for Walking the Labyrinth

Prepare to Walk: Take off your shoes . . . briefly journal a snapshot entry of where you are in your life and what concerns you in this moment . . . pause at the entrance . . . take a slow deep breath . . . then walk at your own pace . . . remember that everything that happens on the labyrinth is a metaphor for your life situation.

Begin Your Journey: The labyrinth path is a single meandering way that leads to the center. There are no intersections or choices. Simply paying attention to staying on the path will invariably lead you to the center. The way in is the way out. You may encounter others on the path who are walking at a different pace. You can step around them or slow your own pace. Others will be traveling out as you walk in. Again, just step aside to let them pass and then continue on your path.

The Three-Fold Spiritual Path: Walking into the labyrinth on the path to the center is a *letting-go* process in which you may feel thoughts slow down and dissipate more easily than with sitting meditation. You may feel lost on the meandering path and wonder if you have lost your way. Be present to whatever you experience with each step.

Arriving at the center is often an experience of stepping into safe or sacred space. Indeed, the center for many walkers is connected with Holy Mystery—sometimes a feeling of being held in the hands of God. It is a place of *receiving* where one can be open to gifts of insight, clarity and the freedom to experience deep emotion. Kneel, stand, sit and stay for as long as desired.

When ready, you will step onto the same path on which you entered, but it will feel quite different from the walk in. This is a time for *integrating* what you have received so far and bringing it with you into your life in the world. You have experienced something transformative (whether it is yet in your awareness or not) that will make itself known more clearly over the ensuing days.

Reflect on Your Journey: Before you step off the path, you may wish to turn to face the center, say a prayer, make a ritual gesture or just pause. After the walk, take a few moments to write in your journal or use art materials to reflect on the insights you have gained or the questions that remain.

Come Again: Each labyrinth walk is unique for each person, and each walk by the same person is likely to be a completely different and deepening experience. So come and walk the labyrinth whenever you can. The sacred path awaits you.

14
Drawing It Out

Cindy S. Perkiss

CLIENTS FOR WHOM THE TECHNIQUE IS APPROPRIATE

Adults, children, and adolescents who have symptoms of trauma in the aftermath of a death can benefit from the opportunity to engage the traumatic imagery associated with the event through both artistic and somatic means. However, this approach could be inappropriate for those clients who do not have adequate coping mechanisms to deal with difficult emotional material.

DESCRIPTION

Symptoms of traumatic grief may include intrusive memories, avoidance of things or situations related to the deceased or events surrounding the death, emotional numbing, physical and/or emotional symptoms of hyperarousal or shut-down and other emotional and somatic complaints. These trauma responses impede the person's ability to navigate the process of grieving and need to be addressed before it is possible to grieve for the person who has died. Many processes that accompany bereavement (remembering the person who died, developing a continued attachment to the deceased, reminiscing, meaning making etc.) are triggers for traumatic reactions.

Trauma art narrative therapy (TANT), developed by Dr. Lyndra Bills (2012), is a structured, creative, cognitive exposure and narrative resolution technique. The structure of the process requires that the activities be followed in the order prescribed, with the traumatic event first being drawn in a non-chronological time sequence. The therapist then assists the client in reordering the drawings and narrating the event, which leads to integration of emotion and novel meaning making for the event. According to Bills, this makes resolving a traumatic experience possible. A useful paper size to work with is 11 x 17 office paper (used in this example) or 12 x 18 drawing paper. Colored markers with large tips were also used and are generally recommended because they help keep a client more grounded.

Somatic experiencing (SE), developed by Dr. Peter Levine (Levine & Frederick, 1997), is a body-oriented approach to the healing of trauma. Through tracking bodily sensations, as well as thoughts and emotions, a person can develop responses to counteract the experience of incomplete fight, flight or freeze responses. A major focus of SE is on the nervous system, helping restore or establish a more fluid rhythm between the sympathetic branch (accelerates heart rate, constricts blood vessels, increases blood pressure) and parasympathetic branch (slows heart rate, increases digestive and gland activity, relaxes sphincters) of the autonomic nervous systems.

DOI: 10.4324/9781351069120-17

Two of the major tools in somatic experiencing are titration and pendulation, which are used throughout the drawing process presented in this case. Titration is the slowing down of emotional or physiological responses to enable the client's system to process and help integrate what happened at a pace not originally possible. Pendulation is movement from more distressing or activating material to more settling or deactivating material. In addition, SE often leads to the creation of a corrective and healing experience, which may facilitate the release of stuck physiological and emotional states and provide greater meaning making for the client.

As both a somatic experiencing practitioner and someone certified in trauma art narrative therapy, I have found it useful to combine the art sequencing and narration of TANT with the body-focused nature of SE.

CASE ILLUSTRATION

Jennifer, a 37-year-old married woman with two children, was referred to me because of concerns about her daughter. Jennifer saw many similarities between herself as a child and her daughter's current struggles but stated that her own mother had helped her get through many situations. She described her mother as "easy to talk to, accepting of me and someone who encouraged me to be myself." She died when Jennifer was 26 years old, three months after being diagnosed with lung cancer. At the time of her death, Jennifer's mother, a nonsmoker, was 58 years old and had always been a steady presence in Jennifer's life. Jennifer's father had not coped well after his wife's death and was now in poor physical and emotional health, and Jennifer had become his primary caregiver, overseeing his medical, emotional and practical needs. Much of our initial work focused on better navigation and delegation of caregiving responsibilities for her father, helping with parenting issues and improving self-care and emotional regulation. However, whenever she spoke of her mother, tears came to Jennifer's eyes, and it was difficult for her to continue speaking.

A year and a half into our work together, as Mother's Day approached, Jennifer began to talk more about the grief and trauma connected to her mother's death. By now, she was more able to balance the demands in her life, and she was feeling stronger and more capable of focusing on her own emotions. She described feeling stuck in the shock and trauma of her mother's illness and death and, 12 years after, was still unable to talk about her mother without great difficulty. Jennifer also reported intrusive memories of the day her mother died and an overall sense that a part of her was frozen at the time of her mother's death.

When her mother became ill, 26-year-old Jennifer became her mother's caregiver and the "main functioning adult" in the household. This continued after her mother's death, with Jennifer moving into the role of her father's caregiver, with no one available to help take care of Jennifer and her own grief.

Using the general structure of the TANT process and the titration and pendulation of SE, I encouraged Jennifer to draw her experience of the time surrounding her mother's death, the place where she felt most "stuck." Over the course of three sessions, she drew five pictures. The first picture depicted a "safe point" before the traumatic event occurred, when nothing specifically traumatic was happening, even if there was sadness because of the situation. Jennifer drew a snapshot of the day before the death, with the house being "clean, peaceful, pretty and bright." She also stated that "things felt very separate," with people sitting in different places, each in his/her own world. The second drawing depicted a "safe point" soon after her mother's death, when it was clear that the actual event of the death was over. For Jennifer, this was the day after her mother's death as she was looking in the closet for something to wear to the funeral. Having these two pictures drawn first anchored the experience with the knowledge that there were bookends around the actual event of her mother's death. This is part of the structure of TANT and is also an example of the pendulation of SE (moving from less difficult to more difficult material).

The third picture was of Jennifer and her mother immediately after her mother's death. Jennifer was holding her mother's hand, and she described how torn she felt between wanting to stay and be with her mother and experience this time and feeling the responsibility of dealing with the practical details with no other functional adult around. We then laid out the three pictures in chronological order, beginning to create a more coherent narrative and, frequently, slowing the discussion to allow for processing of this intense material (titration). After this therapy session, Jennifer reported spontaneously talking with her children about her mother and telling them stories, something that had previously been too difficult. She reported feeling more present with her memories and her enjoyment in sharing them with her children.

At our next session, as we looked at the three pictures, I asked Jennifer what happened after the funeral, which generated two additional drawings. The first was of the immediate family sitting in the living room after the funeral—once again separate, with each person in his/her own world. She described feeling intensely alone and disconnected, which reflected much of her experience while taking care of her mother through the time of her illness and death. When asked what she wished could have happened, Jennifer stated that she wished there had been a shiva for her mother—the Jewish mourning ritual in which family members gather for a period of up to seven days and are cared for by friends, neighbors and others close to those who are grieving. In addition, there are often prayer services each day and time for reminiscing about the deceased. This would have allowed the death of her mother to sink in a bit more, and she would have been comforted and provided for by a community of caring people. This did not occur, and Jennifer recognized that as soon as her mother became sick, she split off her emotions in order to manage the tasks of ministering to her mother and then supporting her father.

This last picture of a shiva gathering became a corrective and healing experience for Jennifer (often part of the SE treatment). As she imagined that time of shiva and was given the time and space to process the emotional experience it would have provided (titration and pendulation), Jennifer was able to be more in the present, coming out of the shock and disconnection around the trauma of her mother's illness and death. She was then able to reminisce about her mother and tap into a sense of continued attachment, which she could now access for comfort and guidance. In addition, when her father died a few years after this series of drawings, Jennifer recognized her need for care and support. She made sure that shiva was observed so that she and her family could experience the range of emotions that were present and begin the process of grieving.

CONCLUDING THOUGHTS

Traumatic grief can be an overwhelming and isolating experience. Helping clients understand the trauma-related nature of their symptoms and provide ways to develop a more coherent and manageable trauma narrative can offer powerful tools for healing. The structured nature of TANT, combined with the interventions of SE, provides clinicians with creative interventions to help clients enter into traumatic material with support, helping guard against flooding and promote greater capacity to hold and process emotionally difficult material. This case also speaks to the importance of a supportive community for help in dealing with trauma as well as bereavement.

References

Bills, L. (2012). *Trauma art narrative therapy: The Handbook.* Camp Hill, PA.
Levine, P., & Frederick, A. (1997). *Waking the tiger: Healing trauma: The innate capacity to transform overwhelming experiences.* Berkeley, CA: North Atlantic Books.

Part IV
Articulating Ambiguous Loss

15

What Have You Lost?

Robert A. Neimeyer

CLIENTS FOR WHOM THE TECHNIQUE IS APPROPRIATE

This simple but subtle technique is especially relevant for people who are seeking to identify and validate a range of primary and secondary losses related to the death of a significant person, as well as more ambiguous losses that commonly go unrecognized. Although it can be practiced in individual therapy, it is particularly appropriate in group work, where it can foster greater understanding of both self and others. However, it could be inappropriate in early sessions of therapy following bereavement, when the source of the client's suffering is clear and when broadening or deepening awareness of various life losses could be experienced as callous or irrelevant.

DESCRIPTION

Though we rarely pause to consider it, every person, every place, every project and every possession we love, we will one day lose—at least in an earthly sense. And with this unsettling recognition comes the awareness that occasions to experience grief extend far beyond the death of a family member or another significant attachment figure to include a litany of losses that may be ambiguous or abstract, chronic or cultural, intimate or invisible. When one considers the ubiquity of these "nonfinite" losses associated with the dissolution of close relationships, deterioration of health, disruption of beliefs and diminution of one's sense of self (Harris, 2020), it becomes quickly evident that only a small percentage of deeply grievous life transitions are "enfranchised," in Doka's (2002) sense of being socially validated and given ritual support. Others, however life vitiating, are typically borne privately and silently, and even the person experiencing their effects might well struggle to acknowledge them or give them words.

"*What have you lost?*" is a straightforward but surprisingly powerful technique that enhances participants' awareness of their losses and, with this, their needs. It proceeds by fostering reflection upon and sharing loss experiences with an attentive and empathic partner, whether this is the therapist or another member of a group, as in the context of bereavement support. It begins with a mindful moment of centering breath work with closed eyes, after which participants open their eyes to meet the gaze of their partner, as one slowly repeats the question "What have you lost?" with the other giving a brief answer of a word or two or phrase, without elaboration. Pausing for two to four seconds, the questioner then simply and

DOI: 10.4324/9781351069120-19

softly responds, "Thank you," pauses for another two to four seconds and repeats the question. The partner then responds with another loss, and the cycle of questioning continues at an unhurried pace, with the disclosures commonly broadening, deepening and reaching toward more unacknowledged, intimate and fundamental losses as the exercise continues for five minutes. In a group application, partners then switch roles and repeat the exercise before being ushered into another brief interlude of two minutes of mindful breathing to re-center and then open their eyes to discuss what they have learned and observed. The exercise is commonly emotional as the respondent delves more and more deeply into previously unarticulated and ambiguous losses, as these are simply named and claimed in the nonreactive presence of a partner who receives them with gratitude, with no attempt to solve or soothe them. As a result, respondents typically feel safely "held" in a vulnerable moment and are better able to respond with self-compassion and a greater awareness of their needs. Reciprocally, the questioner often is touched and encouraged by the bravery and candor of the respondent, being brought into contact with the ubiquity of loss and implicitly encouraged by example to reflect on his or her own.

CASE ILLUSTRATION

In preparation for their own future roles as grief therapists, a group of 20 learners participated in a three-month training program, which included weekly reflections on their own losses using a variety of therapeutic techniques. To invite greater recognition of the role of ambiguous losses (Boss, 2009), nonfinite losses (Harris, Chapter 5) and chronic sorrow (Roos, 2018) in their clients' lives as well as their own, the group leader introduced the "What have you lost?" exercise.

The room grew hushed as the leader ushered participants into a brief moment of mindfulness, during which they closed their eyes and concentrated on slowing and deepening their breathing while also quieting their inquisitive minds. Opening their eyes to one another with the partner they had chosen, one person in each dyad followed the softly voiced instruction to ask, "What have you lost?" as the second offered a single brief response to the recursive question, which in each instance was met by a slight pause and a simple "Thank you." Soon the losses were whispered into audibility: My grandfather . . . . My cat . . . . My sister . . . . My friend to an overdose . . . . My career . . . . My father after the divorce. Gradually, the responses began to shift toward less visible or obvious losses: Family traditions . . . . A sense of home . . . . My ability to say no to people . . . . Safety . . . . Trust. Many of the uttered responses were intimately concrete: My sense of invulnerability after the cancer . . . . My uterus . . . . My ability to have children. Some were more abstract but no less transformative: My language . . . . My culture . . . . My belief in God . . . . My identity. Tears flowed in many dyads, and as participants accepted the invitation to change roles and then to shift into ten minutes of processing of the experience with their partners, disclosures and insights continued to deepen. The exercise concluded with spontaneous expressions of gratitude and more than a few hugs before selective sharing in the larger group consolidated the learning. In the end, the experience underscored the universality of loss and unwelcome changes in our lives and the legitimacy of naming and claiming them and, in doing so, embracing our right to grieve.

CONCLUDING THOUGHTS

For nearly all participants, the simple, unhurried prompting provided by the recursive questioning of an appreciative partner evokes a deepening stream of self-reflection as the respondent voices a series of losses rarely spoken and often unacknowledged, even by themselves. The result is usually a profound sense of validation and self-compassion, sometimes ushering in clearer recognition of contemporary needs or possibilities that could redress different dimensions of the loss or help ease the associated grief. Likewise, participants commonly report that the exercise opens their hearts to compassion for the suffering of others, which they are surprised to learn frequently parallels their own. The simplicity of the repeated question and the brevity of the responses seem to lift the need to provide superficial comfort or to elaborate on a single loss, instead tapping into deepening currents of reflection that flow toward a sea of previously unarticulated experience.

In group applications, participants frequently benefit from a brief modeling of the exercise with a volunteer, to convey both the brevity of the desired response (as opposed to a long discussion in each round of questioning) and the simple and repeated pausing and "thank you" that give this technique much of its power. Further meaning making about the encounter can be facilitated by the simple suggestion that participants journal about the experience after processing it in dyads, taking care to establish safe conditions for doing so at a private space and time, with a plan for also setting aside the journaling and actively re-entering the social or natural world. For example, one middle-aged woman wrote of her loss of identity with the childhood death of her Hispanic grandmother and how the "series of subsequent losses has shaken the grounds of my identity even more." The result of her partner's careful questioning, she said, was "eye-opening. . . . I began to realize that it was not a question of *who* I had lost, but *what*," a "what" that included her identification with a culture now only abstractly anchored in her last name, as well as a sense of security and connection to family and community with the loss of the "glue" of her *abuela*'s presence and nurturing of relational bonds. Although relevant in a group setting as a follow-up to dyadic discussions, the optional task of journaling for 30 to 60 minutes can be especially helpful in consolidating meaning making when a client responds repeatedly to the "What have you lost?" prompt in individual therapy without the benefit of the mirroring provided by a partner.

A further extension of the technique is to follow this initial round of questioning with another, simply shifting the question to "*How would you like to change?*" Whereas the loss query tends to bring to light a great range of life-altering events, circumstances and consequences that are beyond the participants' control, this second series of recursive questions, asked in the same format and in similar depth, tends to invite agency and hope: *To strengthen my ties with my relatives . . . . To forgive my sister . . . . To leave a position I know is wrong for me . . . . To stand up for myself more . . . . To forgive myself and let go.* Research on a weekend retreat regarding "unwelcome change" that used this second exercise to consolidate insights and galvanize action demonstrated the capacity of even a relatively brief intervention of two days to reduce grief-related suffering, enhance meaning making and increase grief-related growth (Neimeyer & Young-Eisendrath, 2015). An alternative question could be "*What have you gained?*", asked in the same structure and cadence. In summary, voicing and validating not only the tangible deaths of loved ones but also the intangible that punctuate and follow them can be a first step toward identifying the changes we might now embrace to heal, and the sometimes unacknowledged growth and opportunity that loss can also usher in.

References

Boss, P. (2009). *Ambiguous loss: Learning to live with unresolved grief.* Cambridge, MA: Harvard University Press.

Doka, K. J. (Ed.). (2002). *Disenfranchised grief: New directions, challenges, and strategies for practice.* Champaign, IL: Research Press.

Harris, D. L. (Ed.). (2020). *Non-death loss and grief: Context and clinical implications.* New York: Routledge.

Neimeyer, R. A., & Young-Eisendrath, P. (2015). Assessing a Buddhist treatment for bereavement and loss: The Mustard Seed Project. *Death Studies, 39,* 263–273. doi:10.1080/07481187.2014.937973

Roos, S. (2018). *Chronic sorrow: A living loss* (2nd ed.). New York: Routledge.

16
Letters to Love, Time and Death

Robert A. Neimeyer and Kathleen Rogers

CLIENTS FOR WHOM THE TECHNIQUE IS APPROPRIATE

Adults who struggle with either death-related or non-death-related losses can find this technique helpful in voicing their anger, confusion, grief and other turbulent feelings associated with the violation of their assumptive world and the loss of connection to someone or something they once held dear. It can also provide a vehicle for expressing and exploring the cascade of secondary losses issuing from an ambivalent or destructive relationship. Because it involves writing to Love, Time, Death or another abstraction, it may not be appropriate for clients with cognitive disabilities or highly concrete styles of thinking or for children and young teens. It also could be premature for those in the early aftermath of trauma, when emotion regulation and self-care might be higher priorities.

DESCRIPTION

In the movie *Collateral Beauty*, actor Will Smith plays Howard, a once-charismatic advertising executive immersed in a prolonged, pervasive and preoccupying grief after losing his young daughter to a rare disease and whose previously successful company verges on bankruptcy as a function of his brooding withdrawal. In his self-isolation and ruminative bitterness about the loss, he spends his time writing angry letters of protest to Death, Time and Love, each of which he feels betrayed him through taking from him what he most loved or by making false promises that were shattered, along with his illusions, with his daughter's dying. As the film moves forward, Howard's partners hire actors to personify each of these roles and challenge him directly, in a desperate plot to save the company in which each of them has invested most of their professional (and personal) lives. Significantly, however, each of them also faces a profound loss of his or her own: the undisclosed terminal illness of one partner, an ugly divorce and estrangement from his child for another and the age-related infertility of the third. Ultimately, each is led by interactions with these same actors to acknowledge and constructively address these very specific but sometimes ambiguous or invisible losses and to take constructive action in relation to them, as Howard also does with his own.

Like Howard, people grieving a loss may find clarity and insight by personifying and addressing those abstract entities implicated in their distinctive losses, whether these are finite and death related or nonfinite and arising from other forms of unwelcome change or transition (c.f. Harris, 2020). I (RAN) have found letters to these personifications especially

DOI: 10.4324/9781351069120-20

fruitful in helping people name and claim the more pervasive and ambiguous losses that are largely silenced and disenfranchised (Doka, 2002), as well as those that are associated with longstanding conditions, such as progressive illness or disability, that engender chronic sorrow (Roos, 2017), though they are also quite relevant to those that stem from bereavement. Although such abstractions as Love, Time and Death serve as appropriate "recipients" of such letters for many people, virtually any abstract entity that represents a lost part of the assumptive world or an agent viewed as responsible for this might also be chosen. For example, one young woman whose apartment was broken into not once but twice addressed her "goodbye" letter to a lost sense of Security, while a victim of sexual assault wrote consolingly to her own Naiveté. Alternatively, a gay man wrote an angry letter to Society to protest the conditions that contributed to his years of closeted sexuality and self-loathing, and a woman who was spiritually disillusioned after the tragic death of a special friend wrote of her crisis of faith directly to God. As in other clinical applications of dialogical self theory (Konopka, Hermans, & Gonçalves, 2019), each of these abstract principles, sentiments or personifications of externalized "others" also can be regarded as "I-positions" within the individual's inner world, which can be accessed, addressed and voiced in a way that fosters meaning reconstruction in the context of grief therapy (Neimeyer & Konopka, 2019).

Concrete instructions for these letters can be paraphrased as follows:

Consider a loss of your own, whether through death or some other form of unwelcome transition such as a relationship breakup or abandonment, traumatic event, geographic dislocation, serious illness in yourself or another or an important change or loss in your career or identity. Then write a one- or two-page letter to Death, Time, Love or another abstract entity about this just as if it were an actual person, expressing your feelings, questions or sense making about the loss.

Of course, like all other techniques in grief therapy, this one should be offered only when the client has demonstrated a clear *need* to voice or sort through strong feelings about the loss and a clear *readiness* to do so in this written form (Neimeyer, 2019). This implies that it typically would be suggested by the therapist in an open, provisional way, allowing the client to consider whether it would be useful or intriguing or, alternatively, irrelevant or premature. The following case study conveys the use of this technique with a woman who was clearly ready to express a range of troubling reactions to the sudden death of her previous partner and father of her child and to reconstruct the meaning of love in the turbulent aftermath of a violent and destructive relationship.

CASE ILLUSTRATION

Some months after the unexpected death of her estranged partner and father of her young child, Kathleen accepted the invitation to write a letter to Love about the impact and implications of this loss for her. She wrote:

Oh, Love. It's not just what you did. It's what you let him do.

You let him gut me, like a gasping-flopping-dying fish, my hopes strung out of me like clots of blood in a gush of saltwater. You let him slice through my sternum, crack apart each separate shelf of my rib cage, grab my heart and tear it, still beating, from my gaping chest.

I threw up for two weeks when I discovered he lived nearby with a twenty-two-year-old he'd met while we were still married. I lost twenty pounds. For a year, I cried an ocean, hiding my tears from our son.

And then Death stormed in and swallowed him down, and my hollow self shattered completely, collapsed in a cold cast metal tub under a stream of lukewarm water because the shower was the only place I could howl my rage and anguish without upsetting my son.

Love, you left me crouched on the side of a crater larger than my world. Bottomless, sheer-sided, no path up or down—all space and dark and empty and cold. You left me walking through the endless minutes of my life on a sheet of glass above that endless Dark. You left me as thin as tissue, bleached white, colorless, formless, depth-less, mass-less. You left me surrounded by and enclosing nothing.

Love, you looked the other way the first time he cheated on me. You convinced me to accept his lies as truth. Love, you made excuses when he threatened to cut me with the knife he always carried in his pocket. You pretended I should bear all things. You pretended you meant forgiveness and forbearance for everything. That, to be worthy of you, understanding and helpfulness should extend even to a person creating violence.

Love, oh Love, you forgot that fences make good neighbors. You dissolved all boundaries, all safety, all self-protection. All skin, all muscle, all bone, even the enclosed sacs of organ. You ate everything.

I will never let you in like that again. You will be contained. You will be reasonable and safe. You will be kind, gentle, courteous, compassionate. You will never again drive me, half-crazy with loneliness, to believe I can save a person who shows no signs of wanting to be saved. I will never again stay, because of Love, in a situation where I am in physical or psychological danger from another person's behaviors or attitudes.

I love to love—light, color, form, my son, my friends, blue-green, the way a sunny breeze feels against my freckled cheek, Helvetica, a mockingbird's lilting song. I love to love, and I love this universe I live in and so many beings in it. But Love, you will not be self-sacrifice leading to the grave.

Love, you should be joy and flow and the magic moment when creation streams from my fingers. You should be laughter and happy tears and serenity and contentment and the long, slow, wet walk from a rocky mountain river after a long day chasing dragonflies. You should be kites and bedtime stories, popcorn and constant questions, the arc of graphite across the first page in a new sketchbook and the click of utensils against a half-empty blue bowl. Love, stay smaller than I thought you were, smaller than you pretended to be. Be the subtle and the comic and the simple and the plain.

Love, come down to where I am—in this rocky place, still strewn with debris and healing scars. Become this small thing with me—the smooth pebble, the white whorl of a broken shell, the lift of living bone and the shift of a hip sliding into a dance. Become, o Love, the quiet, the silence, the still. The soft breath of sleep in the early dawn light, the first sip of tea, the flash of a grin.

Be content, o Love, with all this every day.

—Kathleen

In reflecting further on the thoughts engendered by this exercise, Kathleen went on to write:

The act of writing this particular letter, to a personified version of romantic love, helped greatly in two main areas—achieving closure of a traumatizing, violent relationship and mourning the losses suffered during and after that relationship ended prior to his death.

Writing the letter allowed me to safely acknowledge the roles played by my personal cognitive distortions surrounding romantic love in the series of decisions I made to remain in relationship with this particularly damaged, and dangerous, individual. It then allowed me the space to recognize those cognitive distortions for what they were and to pivot *toward envisioning a healthier version of romantic love (one more authentic to my values, beliefs and personality).*

It was written following extensive trauma-focused therapy as an exercise; if this particular exercise had been completed before I felt "safe enough" to bring deep intentionality and self-awareness to the exercise, it would have failed to help resolve issues remaining from that relationship and might also have served to reinforce unhealthy attitudes about romantic love. Using this approach might require a thorough understanding of the individual's life history and careful monitoring of how the letter functions for them.

By externalizing and personifying Love and writing directly to, rather than about it, Kathleen was able to adopt a self-distancing rather than self-immersive or self-incriminating perspective on a complicated relationship and a complicated loss. In doing so, she not only affirmed her life-saving decision to leave a destructive partnership but also reconstructed the meaning of love to be something life enhancing rather than life vitiating. Her further reflections on the value of the exercise close by emphasizing the critical role of timing in the introduction of such deep work, a caveat that is all the more important as such writing typically takes place in the privacy of the client's life, rather in the immediate context of a therapy session in which a counselor can support or direct the client's process to help ensure its salutary impact.

CONCLUDING THOUGHTS

Although, as Kathleen's poignant letter illustrates, writing to a relevant abstraction in the wake of tangible and intangible losses can in itself voice, validate and revitalize the writer's meaning making regarding her or his experience, it is also possible to augment this technique in a number of ways in the context of grief therapy. For example, it can be useful to precede this technique with five minutes of the "What have you lost?" exercise described in Chapter 15 as a way of helping clients identify silent and secondary losses entailed by a primary one, thereby accessing highly relevant content that they can spontaneously draw upon as they formulate their letter to Death, Time, Love or another abstraction. In addition, as with symbolic correspondence with the deceased (Neimeyer, 2012a), the client can also be encouraged to draft a response letter back to the self, in this case from the standpoint of the entity to which they are writing, adding a second step that often deepens the work. Giving voice to such a germinal dialogue need not be dependent on writing as a medium, as clients who prefer to dictate the letter can be encouraged to use widely available smartphone technology to do so, optionally responding with a return voice memo from the personified recipient of the client's missive. Likewise, as a substitute or supplement to a written or dictated exchange, chair work (Neimeyer, 2012b) might be used to perform the two positions spontaneously as each engages the other under the therapist's orchestration. Finally, visual expressive arts might be enlisted to depict the personified abstraction to whom the client is writing or speaking, permitting further meaning making regarding the character of the abstraction and how it might change in shape or form in response to the exchange. In this way, visual modalities might complement the verbal and enhance a client's ability to build new meaning bridges between different I-positions from which to view a troubling life event.

References

Doka, K. J. (Ed.). (2002). *Disenfranchised grief*. Champaign, IL: Research Press.

Harris, D. (Ed.). (2020). *Counting our losses*. New York: Routledge.

Konopka, A., Hermans, H. J. M., & Gonçalves, M. M. (Eds.). (2019). *Handbook of dialogical self theory and psychotherapy: Bridging psychotherapeutic and cultural traditions*. London: Routledge.

Neimeyer, R. A. (2012a). Correspondence with the deceased. In R. A. Neimeyer (Ed.), *Techniques of grief therapy* (pp. 259–261). New York: Routledge.

Neimeyer, R. A. (2012b). Chair work. In R. A. Neimeyer (Ed.), *Techniques of grief therapy* (pp. 266–273). New York: Routledge.

Neimeyer, R. A. (2019). Meaning reconstruction in bereavement: Development of a research program. *Death Studies*, *43*, 79–91. doi:10.1080/07481187.2018.1456620

Neimeyer, R. A., & Konopka, A. (2019). The dialogical self in grief therapy: Reconstructing identity in the wake of loss. In A. Konopka, H. J. M. Hermans, & M. M. Gonçalves (Eds.), *Handbook of dialogical self theory and psychotherapy*. London: Routledge.

Roos, S. (2017). *Chronic sorrow: A living loss* (2nd ed.). New York: Routledge.

17

The Human-Animal Bond

Sara Gody Jackson Bybee

CLIENTS FOR WHOM THE TECHNIQUE IS APPROPRIATE

Animals, specifically pets and companion animals, can be used in therapeutic interactions with patients and families at the end of life and in bereavement, regardless of age or ability. Even clients with allergies can benefit from animal-assisted therapy as it can be performed with water animals, hairless animals and reptiles. Although animal-assisted therapy can be utilized with people of all ages and backgrounds, it is not appropriate for patients in critical care, who do not like animals, have had negative experiences with animals or who feel that having an animal present will not aid their therapeutic process.

DESCRIPTION

Animal-assisted therapy (AAT) is defined by Pet Partners as a "goal oriented, planned, structured and documented therapeutic intervention directed by health and human service providers as part of their profession" ("Pet Partners," n.d.). Unlike animal-assisted activities (AAA) that are not performed by a qualified practitioner, AAT is directed by physicians, occupational therapists, physical therapists, certified therapeutic recreation specialists, nurses, social workers, speech therapists or mental health professionals ("Pet Partners," n.d.). The goal of AAT is to utilize the human-animal bond to improve emotional, cognitive, physical and or social well-being. The animal interaction is viewed as a necessary part of treatment and aids the client in meeting his or her therapeutic goals.

Clinicians who decide to utilize AAT carefully select a therapy animal and receive education and training in how to work with the animal as a therapy team. The animal must receive regular medical care, be properly groomed and obey all the rules and regulations of the certifying agency. The therapy animal must also be up-to-date on vaccines and have periodic retesting to make sure he/she is still able to perform the duties of animal-assisted therapy.

The clinician begins by asking the patient if he or she would find it helpful to work with a therapy animal. The clinician provides information regarding how other patients have found the presence of a therapy animal helpful in their therapeutic process. If the patient is not interested or does not think that the inclusion of a therapy animal would be beneficial, the clinician resumes standard therapeutic approaches. If the patient is interested, the next step is to explain how the animal will be utilized to help the patient meet his or her treatment goals. The clinician and the patient work together to form a treatment plan that addresses the most

DOI: 10.4324/9781351069120-21

important issues as well as clearly outlining how the therapy animal will aid in reaching these goals.

During sessions in which the therapy animal is present, the clinician should check in with the patient to make sure he or she feels comfortable with the animal. Clinicians can "speak" for their therapy animal as a way of communicating how the relationship between patient and animal is progressing. For example, saying "It looks like Fluffy is very calm and relaxed with you" can encourage the patient to further develop the relationship with the animal but may also relax the patient. When it is time for a session to end, it is important that the clinician allows time for the patient to say goodbye to the therapy animal in addition to the clinician. Patients may feel more attached and bonded with the animal after a session in which they felt particularly supported, and it is important to hold space for that relationship.

The modern form of AAT began in the 60s with Boris Levinson, a psychologist in New York, who utilized his dog Jingles in his therapeutic work. Research demonstrates the effectiveness of animal-assisted therapy with the elderly (Walsh, 2009), including patients on hospice and those with memory loss (Geisler, 2004). The effectiveness of utilizing animals in therapy has also been documented with children and adolescents, veterans, prison inmates, psychiatric patients (Walsh, 2009), those suffering from autism or chronic/terminal illnesses (Parish-Plass, 2008) and those with severe physical impairments (Geisler, 2004). This list is not exhaustive.

Although the scientific evidence for the use of AAT has only recently begun to grow, AAT has been documented to have both physical and psychological benefits. Parish-Plass (2008) found that interactions with animals reduce anxiety, blood pressure and heart rate, which leads to a reduction in stress and an increase in the general sense of pleasure. In addition to the physical benefits gained from interactions with animals, a number of emotional and psychological benefits have been touted. Both McLaughlin (2015) and Parish-Plass (2008) remark on the nonjudgmental nature of animals and how this aids social interaction. In addition, the presence of an animal instills trust in the client. When clients observe the interaction between the therapist and the animal and see the nurturing and positive way that the therapist interacts with the animal, they feel less threatened and are encouraged that therapy will be a safe place.

Another theme that emerges in the literature is that of nonverbal communication. In a study by cited by Walsh (2009), Cain administered a questionnaire to 60 families with a variety of pets. She found that "most family respondents believed that their pets understood when they talked or confided in them and that their pets were sensitive to their moods, as conveyed in their tone of voice, body language or tears. Family members reported that their pets were "'tuned in' to their feelings, whether happiness, excitement, tension, sadness or anger" (Walsh, 2009, p. 484). In addition, clients often receive physical comfort from animals that let them stroke their fur or embrace them. In fact, when working with children, "the animal may serve as a transitional object when the client is in need of physical comforting through touch and it is inappropriate between the child and the therapist" (Parish-Plass, 2008, p. 15).

CASE ILLUSTRATION

In his early 90s, Earl was a Vietnam War veteran with a smile that could light up the room. He was living in the Veterans Affairs Nursing Home and had recently been placed on hospice after being diagnosed with chronic obstructive pulmonary disease (COPD). My therapy dog, Bailey, and I were asked by Earl's hospice team to visit him to provide him some comfort after his recent diagnosis. Growing up, Earl had dogs, and thus the hospice organization thought it would be beneficial for him to come into contact with a therapy animal.

The first time Bailey and I visited Earl, he seemed surprised and delighted to be receiving a canine visitor. He smiled and asked many questions about Bailey: What kind of dog is she? How old is she? What is her name? Bailey sidled up to him and sat right next to his wheelchair so that he could reach out and pet her without straining. She stayed at his side the entire visit, pushing his hand up with her head to encourage more caresses.

Bailey served as a conversation starter between us, and Earl was able to use the experience with Bailey to invoke memories of his own past. During the next few visits, he began talking about his dogs and what it was like to grow up with dogs. He told me stories about playing in the woods with his dogs and how he missed owning a dog. This helped him start reviewing his life and looking back at all he had done. He began telling me more about the war, his job and what life was like for him. After speaking for a while about memories from his past, Earl invited Bailey to play bingo with him. She sat by his feet the entire time, available for puppy kisses and caresses anytime Earl felt he needed them. Bailey and I only visited Earl a handful of times. He died shortly after our visits began, and I believe that the comfort and opportunity for life review provided by the human-animal bond helped him come to terms with his prognosis and die peacefully.

CONCLUDING THOUGHTS

In conclusion, animals can be powerful partners for improving the emotional, cognitive and physical facets of a client's life. Performed by qualified professionals, animal-assisted therapy integrates the use of the animal into the client's treatment plan. Studies have demonstrated the benefits of utilizing animals in healthcare and therapeutic settings. Animals decrease blood pressure, stress, heart rate and anxiety and can even lengthen one's lifespan. The psychological benefits of animal-assisted therapy are just as profound: Animals promote social interaction; encourage clients to open up emotionally; help the client feel safe; and improve self-esteem, empathy and the client's sense of control. I encourage clinicians to think about how the integration of animals may further the therapeutic process of their clients.

References

Geisler, A. (2004). Companion animals in palliative care: Stories from the bedside. *American Journal of Hospice & Palliative Medicine, 21*(4), 285–288.

McLaughlin, E. E. (2015). Animal-assisted therapy as a trauma intervention. *Master of Social Work Clinical Research Papers*, Paper 496.

Parish-Plass, N. (2008). Animal-assisted therapy with children suffering from insecure attachment due to abuse and neglect: A method to lower the risk of intergenerational transmission of abuse? *Clinical Child Psychology and Psychiatry, 13*(1), 7–30.

Pet Partners. (n.d.) Terminology. Retrieved from https://petpartners.org/learn/terminology/

Walsh, F. (2009). Human-animal bonds II: The role of pets in family systems and family therapy. *Family Process, 48*(4), 481–499.

Part V
Practicing Self-Care

18

MyGrief.ca Online Support

Shelly Cory, Christopher J. MacKinnon,
Andrea Warnick and Fred Nelson[1]

CLIENTS FOR WHOM THE TECHNIQUE IS APPROPRIATE

As novel online psychoeducational tools, MyGrief.ca and KidsGrief.ca are appropriate resources for a culturally diverse adult population grieving the death of spouses, parents, siblings, children and other significant family members or friends and those supporting a grieving child. The websites are written at the sixth-grade reading level, and users need access to the internet and a basic level of computer skills to navigate them. However, currently MyGrief.ca addresses only death that is non-traumatic in nature and non-complicated grief. KidsGrief.ca includes content on sudden death, suicide and medical assistance in dying (MAiD).

DESCRIPTION

In 2004 the Canadian Virtual Hospice (CVH) (www.virtualhospice.ca) was launched with a mandate to curate and disseminate evidence-informed content and an array of interactive online supportive services for people living with life-limiting illness, their families and others in the health-care network (Chochinov et al., 2015). CVH has evolved to include several new websites and multiple social media channels with content encompassing the trajectory of illness through to bereavement. It has been identified as the most comprehensive internet resource for palliative care in the world. Content and services are available in English and French, reflecting Canada's bilingual context. Recently, CVH launched several new platforms, but particularly relevant for this chapter are MyGrief.ca, which addresses the challenges of bereavement for adults, and KidsGrief.ca and the French version, DeuildesEnfants.ca, with modules for adults who are supporting grieving children.

Representing a significant health concern, bereaved adults often suffer from co-morbid health problems, increased use of health-care resources, periodic hospitalizations and even mortality in the first two years after a death (Stroebe, Schut, & Stroebe, 2007). Those seeking formal support in bereavement often encounter noteworthy obstacles, including a general lack of understanding by those in their social system as well as professionals whose knowledge of grief may be limited. Many in isolated or rural settings cannot easily access specialized bereavement support services. Others do not have the financial means to consult

DOI: 10.4324/9781351069120-23

a mental health practitioner. Inspired by personal loss and the experience of growing up in a rural area with limited health services, CVH Executive Director Shelly Cory envisioned an accessible tool that provided equitable access to trusted content in an engaging, interactive format. MyGrief.ca is the world's first evidence-based, psychoeducational tool to provide online loss and grief support. It was developed through funding by the Canadian Partnership Against Cancer and the commitment of national grief experts.

A comprehensive literature review, environmental scan, readiness analysis and development team comprising research and clinical experts and bereaved family members informed MyGrief.ca. This resource largely adopts a constructivist or meaning-based framework to understanding bereavement adaptation (Neimeyer, 2019). Content is presented in text-based, interactive and video formats. The video clips include grief narratives representing diverse ages, relationship to the deceased, cultures, genders and sexual orientations. While the tool design is based on a logic model, tool functionality facilitates self-directed navigation.

The nine learning modules are organized as follows: (1) *Grieving an expected loss* covers the time, events, tasks and features in the period prior to death that can have definitive impact on the bereavement experience; (2) *Understanding grief* highlights common and less-common bereavement responses, including physical, cognitive, behavioral and emotional reactions; (3) *How has this loss affected my family and me?* facilitates consideration of changes in the familial and social hemispheres following loss; (4) *Moving through grief* addresses changes in identity, fostering constructive continuing bonds with the deceased and factors that contribute to grief stagnation; (5) *Making sense of intense emotions* covers the difficult affective landscape of bereavement, highlighting constructive ways to respond to feelings; (6) *Managing difficult situations* characterizes grief triggers, as well as offering thoughts on navigating complex social situations; (7) *Caring for yourself* tackles the unexpected challenges of self-care, including shame, limit setting and unrealistic expectations of self and others; (8) *Do I need more help and where do I find it?* outlines severe grief reactions that usually merit a professional consultation; and lastly, (9) *When life starts to get better* focuses on the challenges of committing to the future and making new plans in the aftermath of death.

An evaluation by the University of Victoria and First Nations University indicated that MyGrief.ca exceeded user expectations (Courtney, 2017). Respondents indicated that the resource was easy to navigate, included high-quality information and could easily support existing university-level and volunteer education programs. Of note, MyGrief.ca is being used in bereavement support services and health-care provider training and has been commended for rendering complex concepts in easily accessible language and responding to grievers' need for a sense of universality and shared experience.

KidsGrief.ca is the first of a series of planned expansions to MyGrief.ca. It responds to the fact that too often children and youth do not receive the grief support they need. Children in bereavement who are not adequately supported may be more at risk of a variety of adverse emotional and psychological impacts across their lifespan. KidsGrief.ca helps adults recognize children's and youth's grief, prepare them for anticipated death and provide them with well-informed grief support. Topics such as suicide, medically assisted death and preparing children for funerals are also covered. KidsGrief.ca was developed through funding provided by the Canadian Internet Registration Authority Community Investment Program and Hope & Cope, a community support service based in Montreal, Quebec.

Unique in the world, MyGrief.ca and KidsGrief.ca complement existing services and provide comprehensive, accessible tools where barriers to in-person support and education exist, extending evidence-informed grief programming well beyond its existing confines.

CASE ILLUSTRATION

Barbara is a social worker located in a rural community in Atlantic Canada. Her mandate in working for a public health authority includes bereavement support for the community. She is seeking a resource that would strengthen an existing ten-week bereavement support group she has facilitated for many years, with a focus on parental grief following the death of a child.

She begins by perusing the content of MyGrief.ca in preparation for her group. To begin, she identifies several content areas that would be pertinent. She decides to organize the themes of each session around the nine modules of MyGrief.ca. She elects a semi-structured approach that allows participants to ultimately move the group discourse in directions that are most pertinent to them. After the group begins, she invites participants to work through each module sequentially between sessions while encouraging them to inspect additional content according to their own sensibilities. She further urges participants to identify topics or questions stemming from MyGrief.ca they may wish to bring to the next group session.

Barbara also identifies content areas that may be of interest and can be used to facilitate more in-depth conversations in the group, including: (1) an element from module three that covers changes in parenting role, (2) material from module five focusing on intense guilt and anger common to parental bereavement and (3) content from module six that focuses on navigating demanding social situations as bereaved parents.

Barbara also decides to present several video narratives that grapple with the death of a child. Specifically, she chooses the videos of Aimee and Mishi. This couple experienced the death of their young daughter Stella from a highly aggressive brain cancer. Barbara begins several of the group sessions by sharing a three- to five-minute video segment of Aimee and Mishi. She has several clinical goals in mind: to encourage engagement and interaction in the group by viewing a profound and touching testimonial, to prompt participants to reflect on commonalities and divergences in experiences of loss and to invite comment on Aimee and Mishi's responses to grief that may help participants inform their own responses to loss.

Further, Barbara identifies video segments from fellow social worker Fred Nelson, one of the grief experts who contributed to MyGrief.ca. Fred's video provides a professional perspective on bereavement, and Barbara is particularly interested in highlighting content that provides guidance on when to seek formal support. Her clinical goal here is to prepare a bridge for some participants who may need additional formal grief support when the group concludes. Barbara encourages both the bereavement support participants and those she is counseling individually to access MyGrief.ca between sessions as a source of support and education. She knows that doing so will reinforce what they have covered in sessions and that viewing the videos will help decrease the sense of isolation and normalize the experience of many parents following the death of a child. Lastly, she refers grievers who have other children to explore KidsGrief.ca to better understand their children's grief experience and find guidance for conversations and providing support.

CONCLUDING THOUGHTS

MyGrief.ca and KidsGrief.ca address critical gaps in reliable, thorough and effective online supportive resources for people who are grieving, parents supporting grieving children, health-care providers, educators and other professionals. Rendered into a highly usable format in accessible language, the tool supplements detailed descriptions of bereavement within a constructivist framework with coping strategies and video testimonials from a diverse group of grieving people. It in no way is designed to supplant or replace professional intervention, but rather can be used as either a compliment to current services or an accessible tool where no such services exist. Additional MyGrief.ca modules that target traumatic and complicated grief reactions are in the planning stages.

Note

1. The authors wish to acknowledge the following individuals involved in this project: Harvey Max Chochinov, Eunice Gorman, Darcy Harris, Robert A. Neimeyer, Susan Cadell, Marney Thompson, Nadine Gariepy-Fisk, Bev Berg, Elder Betty McKenna, Jacquie Dorge, Pam King, Sylvie Lalande, Tanny Nadon, Serena Hickes, Lisa Toye, Antonietta Petti, Camara Van Beeman, Candace Ray, C. Elizabeth Doherty, Joan Hamilton, Courtney Teetaert, Stephanie Rabenstein and Suzanne O'Brien.

References

Chochinov, H. M., Harlos, M., Cory, S., Horst, G., Nelson, N., & Hearson, B. (2015). Canadian Virtual Hospice: A template for online communication and support. In J. C. Holland, W. S. Breitbart, P. B. Jacobsen, M. J. Loscalzo, R. McCorkle, & P. N. Butow (Eds.), *Psycho-oncology* (3rd ed., pp. 253–258). doi:10.1093/med/9780199363315.003.0033

Courtney, K. (2017, February). *Evaluation report: Methadone tool, my grief tool, living my culture & indigenous voices tools* (Unpublished Technical Report). University of Victoria, Victoria, Canada.

Neimeyer, R. A. (2019). Meaning reconstruction in bereavement: Development of a research program. *Death Studies, 43*, 79–91. doi:10.1080/07481187.2018.1456620

Stroebe, M. S., Schut, H., & Stroebe, W. (2007). Health outcomes of bereavement. *The Lancet, 370*, 1960–1973.

19

Differentiating Grief and Depression

Elizabeth Sheppard Hewitt

CLIENTS FOR WHOM THE TECHNIQUE IS APPROPRIATE

Clients seeking treatment who have experienced clinical depression before facing significant loss require differential diagnosis and treatment of the former condition before focusing on the latter. Clients who maintain good strategies for managing depression, even with this history, may be responsive to an earlier focus on grief therapy.

DESCRIPTION

Bereaved clients with a history of major depression are at high risk for depressive recurrence in the context of loss (Friedman, 2012, p. 1856). Regardless of treatment history, those who have faced depression commonly experience great challenge in stabilizing mood. Some may have attempted suicide or become fearful of their own pervasive thoughts encouraging self-harm. While any client can be overwhelmed by loss, those still working through the complexities of stabilizing depression may find the additional weight of loss too much to bear.

A pre-existing diagnosis of depression does not in itself necessitate treating depression before grief. Many clients with a clinical depression have developed great skill in managing symptoms and have adaptive strategies that keep the illness stable despite life challenges. For these individuals, discussion about the impact of depression on their ability to cope with loss may be valuable to address their adaptive strategies and resilience to date. It may also serve to acknowledge that loss can overtax even the best coping strategies and to recruit the client as a partner in ensuring that loss does not allow depression to regain ground. For such clients, recognition that they can contribute to their own wellness may help restore a locus of control and facilitate development of hope.

Symptoms of depression may be best differentiated from loss by the existence of significant cognitive distress. The bereaved client rarely identifies low self-esteem and feelings of worthlessness as primary issues (Bonanno & Kaltman, 2001; Bonanno, Wortman, & Nesse, 2004). As well, bereaved clients may wish to be reunited with a deceased loved one but rarely develop a complex suicide plan or experience persistent suicidal ideation consistent with the diagnosis of clinical depression (Friedman, 2012). Bereaved clients may experience extended periods of wellness but may be triggered by significant dates such as birthdays and Christmas. Depression, in contrast, tends to be more pervasive (APA, 2013). Indicators specific to depression also include prolonged and significant inability to complete activities of daily

DOI: 10.4324/9781351069120-24

living, existence of guilt unrelated to loss and reports of seeing or hearing the deceased person (Auster, Moutier, Lanouete, & Zisook, 2008). Perper (2014) details some of the variables differentiating the two conditions (see Table 19.1).

If the presenting distress appears to be primarily related to the depression, stabilization of the pre-existing condition becomes the initial treatment focus. A treatment approach addressing stabilization of depression as the first treatment objective might include:

- Assessment of presenting issues and clarification of primary issue
- Development of a treatment plan with the client
- Education regarding the challenges inherent in the diagnosis to empower and normalize
- Medication (as appropriate) to assist in restoring sleep and appetite, increasing energy and decreasing safety risk
- Optimization of positive self-soothing and grounding strategies to address depression and loss
- Externalization of the illness to negate feelings of shame over inability to operate at a pre-illness level
- Behavioral activation, structuring the client's day with manageable goals
- Individual therapy to address impact of low mood on hope, personal safety, self-esteem, ability to cope with loss and inability to meet systemic demands
- Challenging of negative thoughts to facilitate all the steps required
- Collaboration with other treatment providers to ensure shared treatment goals
- Ongoing assessment to determine stabilization of depression in order to determine the next stage of treatment

Biological and safety needs (Maslow, 1943) addressed through stabilization of the pre-existing illness facilitate advancement into higher-level therapeutic goals. With the depression stable, safety risk is decreased, and clients may now be better equipped to consider maintaining a connection without suicide. Likewise, they may now be able to process and

Table 19.1 Differential Diagnosis of Grief and Depression

Clinical indications of Typical Grief	Clinical Indications of Major Depression
• May have tendency to isolate but generally maintains emotional connection with others	• Extremely self-focused, feels like an outcast or alienated from friends and loved ones.
• Hope that grief will end (or get better) someday	• Sense of hopelessness, believes that the depression will never end
• Maintains overall feelings of self-worth	• Experiences low self-esteem and self-loathing
• Guilt, if present is focused on "letting down" the deceased person in some way	• Guilt surrounds feelings of being worthless or useless to others (not related to the loss)
• Loss of pleasure is related to longing for the deceased loved one	• Pervasive anhedonia
• Suicidal feelings are more related to longing for reunion with the deceased	• Chronic thoughts of not wanting to live
• May be capable of being consoled by friends, family, music, literature etc.	• Often inconsolable

explore complex emotion associated with loss in a mindful way. Accessing and unearthing the complex emotion associated with loss without stabilization is risky and can be too overwhelming to be therapeutic.

Treatment goals must be responsive to the client's needs. If the depression appears to be more stable, bereavement can become a greater treatment focus. If symptoms return, safety and depression-management strategies must then become the focus.

CASE ILLUSTRATION

Sarah was a 45-year-old happily married mother of two young stepchildren. Her physician had diagnosed her with major depression disorder (MDD) ten years previous and had treated her symptoms successfully through the years with medication until three months ago.

Sarah was adopted as an infant. Her adoptive family were reported to be very intelligent but showed little emotion. In contrast, Sarah was very sensitive and expressive. She reported growing up feeling like an outsider and worried that her parents regretted adopting her. She described her father as highly critical and never felt able to please him.

Nine months previous to referral, her father became ill and was hospitalized. The illness was not serious, but he died unexpectedly one evening while Sarah was alone with him. His final words to her were critical. While sad at the loss of her father, Sarah was able to continue working and functioned well for six months. Then suddenly, she could not get out of bed, cried continuously and was irritable, self-isolating and angry. She was placed on extended leave from her job as a secretary, and despite medication trials by her physician, her symptoms did not resolve.

Three months after this abrupt change, her physician referred her to our mental health clinic for medication evaluation, diagnostic clarification and treatment. Psychiatry completed a thorough assessment and diagnosed Sarah with MDD with anxious distress and symptoms of bereavement. Medications were adjusted, behavioral activation was encouraged, and clinical social work was consulted to treat the depression and grief.

At our initial session Sarah identified her goals for treatment as returning to work, feeling better able to manage her depression and coping with anger and grief. She identified depression and grief as the barriers to a successful return to optimal daily functioning and employment. Her husband was worried, and so was she.

Upon assessment, I determined Sarah's primary symptoms to be depression related to the pervasive cognitive component, profound worthlessness. She also expressed active suicidal ideation, feeling she had nothing to offer anyone in her family and was a burden to all. She exhibited classic depression symptoms, including sleep disturbances, irritability, lack of interest in previously enjoyed activities, feelings of alienation, loss of appetite, challenges maintaining activities of daily living and difficulty getting out of bed (American Psychiatric Association, 2013).

While grief was the catalyst for her mood decline, it appeared to overtax coping strategies used to manage depression. She reported that her current symptoms were similar to a previous relapse eight years earlier that was unrelated to loss. We agreed on a treatment approach that included initially addressing depression to free up energy to address the loss. Sarah reported that having a clear treatment plan helped her feel an increase in control.

Initial steps addressed Sarah's sense of powerlessness in the face of such life upheaval. She described feeling as if she were in a deep hole and could not escape. Responsive to a narrative approach (White & Epston, 1990), Sarah came to view her symptoms (negative thinking, anxiety and panic upon leaving the home, irritability, isolative behavior, suicidality) as manipulations of the illness. These symptoms were viewed as ways the illness could facilitate its objective of taking away her personal power and creating hopelessness. By the end of the first session, Sarah reported a resurgence of hope in the knowledge that she could resist the illness and mobilize resilience.

Sarah was seen for therapy every two weeks for three months. She began to skillfully identify which thoughts were hers and which were part of the illness. By challenging negative thoughts, she began to feel more in control. The medication assisted in increasing her energy, which she redirected into fighting depression and returning to work. Despite this progress, the anger and sadness remained. It was now time to address the grief.

Sarah reported that the grief became more tangible with her depression better managed, resumption of activities of daily living and return to work. She was better able to discern where the depression ended and the grief began, and the grief was substantial. In therapy, Sarah began to recognize that the anger she had thought to be a symptom of depression was still present. She soon recognized that she was still angry that her father had been critical and that despite her working hard to please him, it was never enough. With anger came tremendous guilt. How could she be angry with someone she loved who had died? Interestingly, before stabilization of the depression, Sarah was not aware of her anger toward her father and subsequent guilt. It was only while addressing the grief that this emerged.

Unable to confront her father directly, I encouraged Sarah instead to experiment with "corresponding with the deceased" (Neimeyer, 2012). We discussed writing a letter to him, communicating her inner conflict and unresolved anger and hurt. We discussed over many sessions what Sarah might do with the letter and finally settled on the use of ceremony. Sarah would read the letter aloud in her backyard at the fire pit with her supportive husband present and, once done, she would burn it, symbolizing release from the despair, anger and pain.

Sarah struggled to write her letter until one day she was ready. She took a notebook to a city park and quickly wrote ten pages. That evening, she read her letter aloud to her father, crying, yelling and releasing words she had never shared until that moment, then burned her letter as planned in the fire. She described the feeling of freedom from pain, anger and despair as she watched it burn and a peace that wrapped around her like a blanket. The next morning, Sarah and her husband dug out the ashes from her letter and in a gesture of love, carefully placed them around the large oak that grew in her garden, her father's favorite tree.

Sarah came to see me for her next session a week after the ceremony. The change in her was dramatic. She looked ten years younger, and as she described the ceremony, she smiled for the first time since we had begun treatment six months before. While still grieving the loss of her father, she reported feeling better able to manage the simplicity of loss without the complications of anger and depression. We met for two further sessions, exploring the pain of loss and strategies to remain connected to her father despite his passing.

A year later, I happened upon Sarah in the hospital parking lot, and she shared with delight her success at moving through the pain of loss, feeling more connected to her husband and stepchildren and garnering a promotion at work. She had found her way out of the hole.

CONCLUDING THOUGHTS

Clients with a pre-existing diagnosis of clinical depression who face significant loss can be challenging to treat. Gaining a greater understanding of the predominant diagnosis triggering debilitating symptoms is key in developing a successful treatment plan. Stabilizing the pre-existing illness before addressing bereavement issues in detail decreases risk to personal safety, reinforces the framework for adaptive coping strategies and enables the client to proceed with hope and resilience.

References

American Psychiatric Association. (2013). *Diagnostic and statistical manual of mental disorders* (5th ed., text rev.). Washington, DC: Author.

Auster, T., Moutier, C., Lanouete, N., & Zisook, S. (2008). Bereavement and depression: Implications for diagnosis and treatment. *Psychiatric Annals, 38*(10), 655–661.

Bonanno, G. A., & Kaltman, S. (2001). The varieties of grief experience. *Clinical Psychology Review, 21,* 705–734.

Bonanno, G. A., Wortman, C. B., & Nesse, R. M. (2004). Prospective patterns of resilience and maladjustment during widowhood. *Psychology and Aging, 19,* 260–271.

Friedman, R. (2012). Grief, depression and the DSM-5. *New England Journal of Medicine, 366,* 1855–1857.

Maslow, A. H. (1943). A theory of human motivation. *Psychological Review, 50*(4), 370–396.

Neimeyer, R. A. (2012). Correspondence with the deceased. In R. A. Neimeyer (Ed.), *Techniques of grief therapy: Creative strategies for counseling the bereaved* (pp. 259–261). New York: Routledge.

Perper, R. (2014). *Grief, depression and the DSM-5.* Retrieved from http://therapychanges.com

White, M., & Epston, D. (1990). *Narrative means to therapeutic ends.* New York: Norton.

20
Concentrated Eye Gazing

Antonio Sausys

CLIENTS FOR WHOM THE TECHNIQUE IS APPROPRIATE

Bereaved individuals (adolescents and adults) grieving both death- and non-death-related losses presenting sleep disruptions and negative anticipatory thinking can benefit from this individual concentrated eye-gazing technique. Those suffering from glaucoma should be sensitive to pain and modify the practice as needed.

DESCRIPTION

Tratak—eye gazing—(Sanskrit त्राटक—"to look, or to gaze") is the sixth and last of the *Shat-karma* (purification techniques) included in the old *Hatha Yoga Pradipika*, intended to prepare the mind and the body for accessing higher levels of consciousness. Concentrated gazing is included in the *Yoga for Grief Relief* program (Sausys, 2014), a somatic psychotherapeutic protocol using yoga techniques to address the physical, mental and spiritual symptoms of grief toward the re-identification process that follows an important loss. The program follows its own inherent rhythm, a progression of steps for transforming grief. First, it helps us prepare to be present for the full palette of our feelings, then it promotes the proper flow of life force, creating optimal conditions for healing. Next, it stirs the emotional heart, deepening our connection with our emotions, and then it provides an outlet for the ones we want to release. Subsequently, it offers some control over the emotional roller coaster of grief so that balance can then be achieved. Through relaxation, the deep release of internal and external stressors follows, readying the mind to access new programming. We then have a more direct, unobstructed pathway to the depth of our spirit for creatively redefining our new identity.

Eye gazing is useful to help balance the pineal gland that is often heavily taxed during the grief process. The insomnia many grievers experience—or its opposite, oversleeping—is the result of an imbalance in the melatonin the gland produces, which is involved in the sleeping cycle. Engaging the optic nerves is a way of addressing this disturbance since the gland reacts to light registered through these nerves.

1. Sit comfortably and extend your right arm with your fist closed and your thumb pointing up, the thumbnail facing you. If you need support for the arm, place the closed fist of your left hand at the right armpit. You may also bend the right knee and use your knee to support the arm (see Figure 20.1).

DOI: 10.4324/9781351069120-25

Figure 20.1 Establish a near focal point with the thumbnail of your right hand, shifting each minute to a more distal focal point about 10 feet (3 meters) away

2. Locate a distant object (at least 10 feet or 3 meters away) at eye level as a focal point, and place your thumbnail within the line of vision between your eyes and the distant object of focus. The object being focused on should be relatively small, such as a doorknob, a rock or a drawn black dot.
3. Focus on your thumbnail for 1 minute.
4. Shift your focus to the distant object for 1 minute.
5. Shift back to your thumbnail.
6. Repeat the process of switching the focus three times (six times in total). Avoid blinking throughout the exercise if you can.

Suggested time: Including 1 minute of focus and three switches between focal points, the practice takes 6 minutes. For improving sleep, it can be practiced half an hour before going to bed and then again half an hour after waking up.

Benefits: Concentrated gazing stimulates the optic nerves, which prompts the functions of the pineal gland. The resulting balanced levels of melatonin tend to regulate many biorhythms, including the sleep-wake cycle. It helps regulate stress by influencing the fight-or-flight reaction and modulates the immune system. It increases nervous stability, mitigates insomnia and relaxes the anxious mind. It improves the memory and helps develop good concentration and strong willpower.

Precautions: Always avoid unnecessary strain and be tolerant of different experiences such as seeing two thumbs or two distant focal points—these experiences change with time.

Contraindications: As noted previously, those suffering from glaucoma should be sensitive to pain and modify the practice as needed by reducing the time focusing or the number of changes between focal points.

Many practitioners report falling asleep before completing a full round of concentrated gazing. With steady practice, cosmic rhythms soothe the body, helping it remember when to sleep and when to stay awake. The wisdom of healthy grieving lives more in the spirit than in the mind. Working with the pineal gland is important for its connection with *ajna* chakra, the third eye, where we view life through awakened intuitive knowledge. Our spirit knows that things end, and our bodies are accustomed to processing endings constantly, yet it is our minds that want the things we are attached to be with us forever.

Concentrated gazing also offers a symbolic opportunity to take a look at how we want to transition through the next steps of our lives. The two focal points, one close and one distant, serve as symbols of the situations we go through when grieving. When the old reality is not there any longer and the new one is not yet known, our controlling minds have a hard time waiting. The negative anticipatory thinking indicative of the limbic system's involvement in grief makes us perceive the projected new reality negatively. It fills us with ideas such as thinking that no one will love us as much or that no job will ever suit us in the same way. That might be true or completely false, and we can't know yet. In the meantime, we can only trust the journey and accept that change will come. Shifting focus from the thumbnail (our present situation) to the chosen distant point (the new reality to be discovered) symbolizes the journey ahead.

Deciding on what could be the distant focal point can be very useful in determining the next steps of the journey. You can choose a picture representative of how you would like to feel in the future, the house you would like to have or the job you would like to get. Place it in the distance, so when you switch to that focal point, you are adding intention and meaning to your practice. Deciding where to start and where to end (with the distant or close focal point) can add strength to your ability to meet yourself where you are and to your precision in designing your future.

Sometimes the eyes get tired or strained when practicing this technique. If this happens, rub the palms of your hands together, then bring the cupped hands to your eyes and enjoy the warmth and darkness that can soothe them (see Figure 20.2).

CASE ILLUSTRATION

John, a 41-year-old firefighter from California, was actively involved in fighting the devastating Sonoma County fires that took over 5,000 private homes plus several other buildings in the course of just three days. In the early hours of the fire and while he was on a break, he attempted to escape the flames that were menacing his house, packed some cash and few documents in a box and rushed from of his house in his van with his wife and two-year-old son. A tree had fallen down his street, so they got out of van and jumped over the fallen tree. As he turned back, he saw his house and van go up in flames. He lost everything he owned. His sleep cycles were already disturbed due to his working schedule, but now, he was unable to fall asleep, and if he did, he would wake up few hours later, unable to go back to sleep. I suggested he practice concentrated eye gazing half an hour before going to bed and after having woken up as well as during the times he awoke in the middle of the night. The technique helped him stabilize his sleep cycle. Then I suggested that he cut out an image of the home he would like to rebuild, including as many details as he could when making his choice. Next, I proposed he substitute the picture he

Figure 20.2 After completing the concentrated gaze exercise, rub hands together, then place them on your eyes to soothe them prior to sleep

had cut out for the distant focal point he was using to combat the negative anticipatory thinking that was preventing him from thinking that a possible new home would ever be as beautiful, spacious and cozy as his burnt house was. To his surprise, after few times of practice, he wanted to add more details to his picture. I suggested that he create a collage, in which he not only added details he was able to find in magazines but also drew some personal items and features that he found by tapping into his creativity and his heartfelt desires for the future. John readily accepted the suggestion and began literally to envision a new and more satisfying future, one built on a more restorative cycle of sleep.

CONCLUDING THOUGHTS

The pineal gland is actively involved in the human sleep cycle through its production of melatonin. Because the gland is photoactive—it reacts to the presence or absence of photons or particles of light—activating the optic nerves through concentrated eye gazing can be a powerful aid to assist grievers with their altered sleep patterns. From a somatic psychotherapeutic standpoint, challenging the ocular segment of the body armor can result in changes in the way we view our lives and their development (Reich, 1949), therefore affecting the negative anticipatory thinking grievers often experience. In addition, the relationship of the gland with the so-called "third eye" in Kundalini yoga (Satyananda, 1996) implies that by working on this spiritual center, we can access intuitive knowledge that can assist grievers in comprehending the true depth of the impermanence of all things and how we relate to them.

References

Reich, W. (1949). *Character analysis.* New York: Farrar, Straus, and Giroux.

Satyananda, S. (1996). *Asana pranayama mudra bandha.* Bihar, India: Yoga Publications Trust.

Sausys, A. (2014). *Yoga for grief relief: Simple practices for transforming your grieving mind and body.* Oakland, CA: New Harbinger Publications.

21

Dance and Movement for Therapist Self-Care

Sara Gody Jackson Bybee

FOR WHOM THE TECHNIQUE IS APPROPRIATE

Dance or movement can benefit bereaved individuals of all ages, races and ethnicities. It may be least appropriate in the earliest days or weeks of bereavement, when straightforward supportive interventions might be most valuable. It would also be inappropriate for individuals with a physical injury or those who experience pain with movement.

DESCRIPTION

Dance therapies began in the United States when the American Dance Therapy Association (ADTA) was formed in 1966 under the leadership of Marian Chace. At St. Elizabeth's Hospital in Washington, she worked with returning war veterans who were suffering from "war neuroses" or most likely what we now identify as posttraumatic stress disorder. She aimed to mirror her patients' movement to help gain an understanding of what their gestures might symbolize. The method that she developed began with a group standing in a circle, each person taking turns in leading an improvised movement while the rest of the group mirrored this action. Since the development of this initial method, dance/movement has been used to help people from a wide variety of backgrounds with varying needs.

Dance movement therapy or DMT is defined by the American Dance Therapy Association as "the psychotherapeutic use of movement to further the emotional, cognitive, physical and social integration of the individual" (ADTA, 2015).[1] Body movement helps individuals express their thoughts and feelings using a creative foundation. Sometimes, thoughts and feelings that may be too difficult to describe in words can be more adequately accessed and portrayed through a movement or series of movements. Things that may not be present in one's consciousness may, in fact, be opened up through movement. As Penfield (1992) states in her chapter on the use of DMT, "Movement gives direct access to the unconscious" (p. 167).

Although structure is important in the therapeutic process, too much structure, such as through imposed exercises, can produce rote movement or behavior instead of helping clients on their journey of discovery (Payne, 1992). DMT can be used individually, in a group or with families. A group environment can encourage meaningful connections with others and serve as emotional support. Listening to music while in the group can promote a feeling of

DOI: 10.4324/9781351069120-26

group unity and may also facilitate the invocation of a memory (Payne, 1992). For individuals pursuing movement as a means of self-care, creating a movement or series of movements that might illuminate a thought or feeling can be useful in gaining a better understanding their internal struggles. Movement that is created in the format of dance therapy is typically not presented to the public. The movements that arise from spontaneous interactions cannot usually be replicated. However, if an individual is creating movements to express him- or herself, these movements can be replicated, and sharing this creation with others can often be cathartic and help one not feel as alone in his/her experience.

Research has demonstrated the effectiveness of dance and movement with individuals with developmental, medical, social, physical and psychological impairments. In a meta-analysis of studies using dance and movement as a therapeutic modality, dance/movement was supported as an effective evidence-based intervention for the following populations or disorders: anxiety, at-risk youth, autism in both children and adults, breast cancer, cystic fibrosis, depression, dementia, eating disorders, elderly, fibromyalgia, Parkinson's disease, rheumatoid arthritis, schizophrenia, somatoform disorder and stress (Koch, Kunz, Lykou, & Cruz, 2014). In addition, dance movement therapy has been identified as being "of great help in transcending the difficulties surrounding those who are coming to the end of their life and facing the imminence of death" (Payne, 1992, p. 14). Since grief, loss and end-of-life topics are often addressed by clinicians, exploring one's own feelings about death through movement can be a wonderful self-care activity.

CASE ILLUSTRATION

Working with children who have suffered some type of trauma, including physical and sexual abuse, is a job that is often associated with vicarious trauma and quick burnout. After hearing countless stories from my clients about childhood sexual abuse, I began to feel like every story I heard was the same. My disgust and hatred grew for brothers, cousins, uncles, fathers and even mothers who had sexually abused their loved ones. I knew if I was to be able to continue this work, I had to find a way to express my feelings about what I was seeing and hearing. Dance has always been a way for me to express myself in a creative and unscripted manner, so I thought I would give it a try.

First, I sat down and thought about the words that come to me when I think about childhood sexual abuse. I also thought about the key words that some of my therapy clients used when talking about their abuse, and I jotted these down. My list included disgusted, scared, ashamed, embarrassed, mad, sad, intrusive, nightmares *and* flashbacks. *I then thought about the progression of the client's treatment in working through the sexual abuse and the feelings that arise as they come to terms with what happened to them. I wrote down* warrior, strength, strong, unstoppable, determined *and* powerful. *From these lists of words, I created small movements. For* scared, *a turn of my head to look over my shoulder; for* ashamed, *curling in a ball and rocking back and forth. I eventually combined the movements to make a sequence. I used the progress I have noticed in therapy as a sort of storyline to guide the choreography. I decided to start with the scared, embarrassed girl who has intrusive thoughts and nightmares and eventually transform her movement into that of a strong and powerful warrior. Although I was the therapist for many of these girls and thus knew that they improved and were stronger than they were when the abuse began, somehow dancing the story instead of merely hearing it was much more powerful. I was able to direct my anger at the perpetrators into my movement, and it helped me no longer carry that weight with me. The warrior that emerged was not only that within my clients who were stronger and wiser than before but also the warrior within a therapist who braved the path with them.*

CONCLUDING THOUGHTS

In conclusion, dance has been used for decades as a therapeutic intervention. It has been used effectively with clients of all ages and with many different presenting problems. Dance can be used not only by clients but also by clinicians as an individual artistic expression. Dance is a powerful tool that can help clinicians tell their stories and make meaning of these stories. Although dance movement therapy can only be practiced by a certified dance movement therapist, I encourage practitioners to open their minds to the possibility that dance might be beneficial as a means of self-care. Consider a small exercise in which you create a movement that embodies how you are feeling instead of describing it in words. Perhaps consider playing a song that is meaningful for the current struggle and see if any movement is elicited. As is poignantly stated by the ADTA, "Whether the issue is the will to live, a search for meaning or motility, or the ability to feel love for life, dance/movement therapists mobilize resources from that place within where body and mind are one" (ADTA, 2015).

Note

1. In this chapter, DMT will be used to describe any type of dance or movement used in a therapeutic manner. I am not a trained DMT therapist but have used dance and movement to work through my own feelings as a clinician.

References

American Dance Therapy Association. (2015). *ADTA informational brochure*. Retrieved from https://adta.org/

Koch, S., Kunz, T., Lykou, S., & Cruz, R. (2014). Effects of dance movement therapy and dance on health-related psychological outcomes: A meta-analysis. *The Arts in Psychotherapy, 41*, 46–64. Retrieved from www.sciencedirect.com/science/article/pii/S0197455613001676

Payne, H. (Ed.). (1992). *Dance movement therapy: Theory and practice*. London: Brunner Routledge.

Penfield, K. (1992). Individual movement psychotherapy: Dance movement therapy in private practice. In H. Payne (Ed.), *Dance movement therapy: Theory and practice* (pp. 163–181). London: Brunner-Routledge.

Part VI

Fostering Compassion

22
Forgiveness Therapy

Judy Chew

CLIENTS FOR WHOM THE TECHNIQUE IS APPROPRIATE

Offering the "moral gift" of beneficence, empathy and altruistic concern in forgiveness therapy can benefit adults interested in releasing the burden of resentment and anger toward their injurer(s). However, this requires the client to recognize the humanity of the offender (e.g., personal history, sociocultural pressures) and contextually scrutinize the hurtful behavior(s). The process is contraindicated for clients who confuse a "moral gift" with condoning injurious behavior or who believe it relieves responsibility or assumes reconciliation.

DESCRIPTION

Enright and Fitzgibbons (2000) define forgiveness as letting go of resentment toward a wrongdoer. In their approach, the offender is offered a "moral gift" of undeserved compassion, generosity or beneficence. This classic process model of forgiveness has four phases. The "uncovering" phase invites the injured individual to express valid and natural feelings arising from the experience. Attention in the first phase is placed on developing insight into the impact and extent of the injury. Work then flows into the "decision" phase of therapy, which aims to help the client clearly define the meaning of forgiveness (including what is *not* meant by forgiveness). With knowledge and understanding, the client is better able to consider the possibility of forgiveness. This leads to the "work" phase, in which the client reframes the experience through sufficient insight or cognitive understanding of the offender. Having a broad understanding of the offender's life context (e.g., personal history, trauma or mental health issues) creates the conditions for the client to offer a "moral gift" as a culmination of the work phase. The final phase of forgiveness therapy—the "deepening" phase—weaves existential themes into therapy. Themes may include insight into the mystery and meaning of suffering, a renewed purpose in life, deeper connection with others and diminished negative affect (Enright & Fitzgibbons, 2000). One of the benefits of the four-stage process model is that it allows the client to offer forgiveness regardless of the offender's presence or availability.

This traditional therapeutic model can be enriched by viewing forgiveness through a feminist lens (McKay, Hill, Freedman, & Enright, 2007). A feminist perspective considers the client's social locations, influential gender role messages regarding anger and forgiveness and the power differential between client and offender. It introduces the importance of collaboration in the therapeutic relationship and the use of unbiased, non-pathologizing language and

DOI: 10.4324/9781351069120-28

explores sources of choice and empowerment for the client (McKay et al., 2007). It also examines the sociocultural pressures (e.g., patriarchy) that impacted the offender and resulted in a vulnerability to mental health issues and predisposition to misuse of power.

CASE ILLUSTRATION

Ling is a 23-year-old woman who recently left her hometown to begin a career. She sought counseling to address intense feelings of shame, resentment and sorrow toward her mother. Her mother's neglect, harsh criticism and outbursts of rage included prohibiting Ling from using hot water for any purpose, such as drinking or bathing. Her mother's mental health problems eventually resulted in the loss of a job in a textile design company. Ling said she was ashamed of her mother and also of her responses to her mother, which included taunts, arguments and physical altercations. During one altercation, Ling contacted the police, who escorted her mother to the hospital where she was diagnosed with paranoid schizophrenia. After the hospital discharge, Ling's mother lived on the street, insisting that it was "for the good of the family."

Our counseling work spanned a year, with a focus on resolving what Courtois (2004) describes as "complex trauma." Ling also exhibited signs of "chronic sorrow" (Roos, 2002) and spoke of feeling powerless and pessimistic about the possibility of positive change. She grieved the longstanding disconnection with her mother and not being able to share life milestones with her. She regretted not being able to care for her as she aged. Yet as we worked through the first three phases of forgiveness therapy, Ling was able to forgive herself and make a decision to forgive her mother.

Then Ling's mother died suddenly, and she discontinued counseling for a month to attend to family affairs. She returned determined to continue the forgiveness process; as a part of the "work phase," I introduced Ling to the concept of a "moral gift." The idea captivated her, but she requested the term "moral gift" be changed to "gift from the heart." This better reflected Ling's hopes—for her, the term "moral gift" felt too much like a "Chinese daughter's obligation."

Taking a compassionate and curious stance, I invited Ling to describe what she knew about her mother's childhood. She tearfully told me she had just learned new details from extended family who attended the funeral. Ling's mother had been abused by her own parents, who were humiliated that she was born a girl. They often used scalding water to force obedience and discipline. As a result, Ling's mother became a frightened and withdrawn child. Her pursuit of education and marriage became her path to freedom.

I validated Ling's openness and courage as she learned of her mother's horrific childhood. We discussed how trapped her mother would have felt living in a home where parents exerted their power and tyrannized her. I affirmed Ling's sorrow for her mother's traumatic past and acknowledged Ling's desire to keep her heart open as she pondered her mother's adult choices. I wondered aloud how her mother's "symptoms" of paranoia might be understood as a protection strategy. Ling's eyes teared as she shared the insight that her mother's extreme fear and prohibitions concerning hot water was a way of protecting—at one and the same time—both her "childhood self" and Ling from harm. Her mother's eventual decision to live on the street may have been a gesture of self-sacrifice that enabled the family—and Ling—to live more freely. Ling's breathing relaxed as she acknowledged a growing empathy and respect for her mother. She understood that her mother's behaviors were not to be excused or forgotten but situated in context.

As our sessions closed, I invited Ling's feedback on her expanding view of her mother. She produced a quilt of textile fabrics originally designed by her mother. After her mother chose to live on the street, Ling sewed the pieces together and took the quilt to her mother for warmth. Sometime later, after Ling located her in the Chinatown alleyway, her mother lifted the quilt out of a rusted grocery cart and said through a cracked-tooth smile: "Look, Ling Ling, was I not right in giving you your name? You are a daughter of understanding and compassion. Now don't argue with your mother this time." Ling sighed with tears of relief: "Understanding and compassion are the gifts from my heart to my mother. There is no argument."

CONCLUDING THOUGHTS

Forgiveness as a therapeutic approach holds potential benefits, but scholars underscore the need for therapists and clients to clearly identify and understand what is meant by forgiveness (Enright & Fitzgibbons, 2000; Freedman & Zarifkar, 2016). The offering of a "moral gift" can be augmented by a feminist perspective. This approach examines relevant client social locations such as gender, class, spiritual or religious affiliation, sexual orientation and ethnicity. It also supports a therapeutic process that considers sources of power, victimization, oppression and marginalization for the client. Efforts to identify and restructure biased principles and methods are crucial. Further empirical research needs to examine the integration of feminist principles with forgiveness therapy models to empower clients (McKay et al., 2007).

Throughout the counseling process, we need to ensure that forgiveness is a healing option rather than a disempowering obligation.

References

Courtois, C. (2004). Complex trauma, complex reactions: Assessment and treatment. *Psychotherapy: Theory, Research, Practice, and Training, 41*, 412–425. doi:10.1037/0033-3204.41.4.412

Enright, R., & Fitzgibbons, R. (2000). *Helping clients forgive: An empirical guide for resolving anger and restoring hope*. Washington, DC: American Psychological Association.

Freedman, S., & Zarifkar. (2016). The psychology of interpersonal forgiveness and guidelines for forgiveness therapy: What therapists need to know to help their clients forgive. *Spirituality in Clinical Practice, 3*(1), 45–58. doi:10.1037/scp0000087

McKay, K., Hill, M., Freedman, S., & Enright, R. (2007). Towards a feminist empowerment model of forgiveness therapy. *Psychotherapy: Theory, Research, Practice, Training, 44*(1), 14–29.

Roos, S. (2002). *Chronic sorrow: A living loss*. New York: Brunner-Routledge.

23
Writing a Letter of Condolence

Lisa L. Clark and Jessica Sawyer

CLIENTS FOR WHOM THE TECHNIQUE IS APPROPRIATE

Writing a letter of condolence to adults in bereavement is nearly always appreciated and appropriate, especially when such letters are sincere and personal rather than clichéd expressions of sympathy. Moreover, they can benefit the writer as well as the recipient, as they provide a format in which caring individuals can offer compassionate support to others in their social network. However, they are best viewed as a supplement to rather than a substitute for caring actions of a practical and face-to-face kind, especially when the loss is experienced as devastating by the bereaved.

DESCRIPTION

Two emotions are consistently triggered when witnessing the suffering of another: empathic concern and emotional contagion (Decety & Cowell, 2014). Empathic concern is the emotion from which the desire to provide compassionate support to bereaved family members, friends or co-workers arises. It's an "other-focused" emotion produced by witnessing another's suffering and involves such feelings as sympathy, compassion and tenderheartedness. In contrast, emotional contagion occurs when personal distress is experienced through observing someone's distress, motivating egotistical behaviors such as avoiding a grieving individual and making comments that comfort the giver rather than the bereaved. Empathic concern is more likely to be triggered than emotional contagion when confronted with someone's grief if a person is competent in expressing supportive words.

Continuing bonds theory defines grieving as a process of reconfiguring the relationship with a deceased loved one such that there is an ongoing bond that will endure throughout the bereaved person's life (Klass & Steffen, 2017). Contributing memories that link the deceased to the bereaved through compassionately written expressions of condolence may support and strengthen the construction of an ongoing bond. In addition, learning and practicing effective empathic communication skills may result in perceived and actual improved competence in empathic communication (Winefield & Chur-Hansen, 2000; Yedidia et al., 2003).

The *Writing a Condolence Letter* exercise can be utilized in an individual or group setting. A notecard that is blank on the inside and perhaps has a meaningful photo or artwork on the front should be selected by each participant. The message should be handwritten,

DOI: 10.4324/9781351069120-29

communicated honestly and transparently, in words that are authentic to the writer. Seven components should be considered in the body of the letter:

1. *Acknowledge the death while avoiding euphemisms and refer to the deceased by name.* The writer is conveying courage to face the loss and grief alongside the bereaved person.
2. *Express heartfelt sympathy.* Don't default to clichéd consolation.
3. *Share special qualities or traits that characterized the deceased.* If the deceased was personally unknown to the writer, qualities or traits of the loved one that were shared by the bereaved person or others who knew the deceased can be incorporated into the letter. Should the writer have no personal information about the deceased, the message can acknowledge and validate the meaning and importance of the deceased individual to the bereaved person.
4. *Share a favorite memory of the deceased person.* A detailed, written description of a shared moment in time with the loved one validates the bereaved person's suffering by reinforcing the significance of the life that has ended, not just to the recipient of the letter but to the writer as well. Communicate emotions that were felt in the moment the memory was created and also the emotions that are experienced when remembering it. If the recipient of the letter was previously unaware of the memory that is shared, the gift of a new memory is given to the mourner. A grieving mother said, "I can't make any new memories with my child. However, when you share a memory *you* have with my child, you create a new memory for me."
5. *Remind the bereaved person of his or her personal strengths and special qualities.* Communicating strengths and qualities is a reminder to the grieving person of personal resources that might be called upon to cope with the loss.
6. *Offer to help in a specific way.* Taking responsibility for determining a specific supportive action to offer a grieving person communicates genuine and sincere altruism, rather than a vague offer to help.
7. *End with a thoughtful hope, wish or expression of sympathy.*

CASE ILLUSTRATION

I was asked to make a presentation to staff at a large children's cancer hospital regarding what to say and do in times of sorrow. Staff are frequently confronted with deaths of current or former patients and experience distress when they are unsure about how to appropriately communicate with a bereaved family. The objective of the presentation was to provide tools to staff to empower them in expressing condolences compassionately.

The one-hour presentation was publicized as a "Lunch and Learn" via institution-wide email. Participants were required to register for the event and invited to bring their own lunches. Approximately 80 employees from multiple departments across the institution attended. Upon entering the room, participants were given a notecard and a pen. A PowerPoint presentation was utilized during a discussion of the reasons it can be difficult to express condolences, including the need to "fix" another's grief, fears of upsetting the bereaved person by mentioning their loss, feelings of vulnerability when we see someone's grief and our feelings of discomfort when we see another person grieving. The discussion also explained the goal in expressing condolences and covered examples of appropriate and inappropriate things to say and do. The final section of the presentation focused on writing a condolence letter. The seven components of a condolence letter were explained, and examples of each component were provided. Participants were then asked to participate in a letter-writing exercise.

Participants were given the following instructions: We are now going to do a brief exercise to practice writing a condolence letter. Think of or imagine someone you know who has experienced a loss. Don't worry about how long ago the loss occurred. I would like for you to write a condolence letter to that person using the seven components that have been presented. A PowerPoint slide with the seven components discussed will be showing throughout the exercise for your reference. You will have approximately 10 to 12 minutes to complete your letter.

Once the participants completed their condolence letters, we processed the experience with the group through a series of questions. How was this experience for you? What emotions did you have as you wrote your letter? What did you feel when you recalled and shared a memory of the deceased? Were there any components of the letter you struggled to write? Several participants were deeply moved by the experience and verbalized relief that they had been able to express their emotions in their writing. I invited volunteers to read their letters to the group, and several participants came forward to do so. After each letter was read, I thanked the writer and then asked the following questions of the group: Are there any thoughts you would like to share with (the reader) after having heard the letter? What particular part of that letter impacted you?

As an illustration, Jessie, who was herself a survivor of a life-threatening illness and a young mother, wrote:

Dear Jane,

My deepest condolences to you, your family, and to everyone else who loves Emily. She is greatly missed and will forever remain a beautiful light in our lives.

I will never forget the first time she visited my house with you that summer evening. There was a tiny moth that had flown into the kitchen and become trapped by the window. I remember how we chased that bug all over the house, laughing, as Emily and I were trying to save it from the cat. I can still see Emily's beautiful smile as she released it in the backyard, saying that it could now be free to fly home. I will always think of her whenever I see a moth and how her smile lit up the night as it flew out of her cup.

I would very much like to treat you to a coffee soon to share your tears, your strength, and more stories. Keeping you in my daily thoughts,

Love always, Jessie

Reflecting on the exercise afterward, Jessie noted:

In Lisa's presentation, we were allowed to "imagine" a bereaved parent, which is what I did. In doing it this way, the similes of personal losses emerged in my letter naturally. The moth represented both the loss of a young girl (my friend and fellow horseback rider, who was treated at St. Jude) and an ambiguous loss of my best friend (which was very recent for me and extremely difficult). The cat represented cancer and the lengths that families will go to save their children from the disease, but with smiles and hope. And Emily released the moth into the night because moths always fly into the Light and because to me the Light is our true home. I didn't realize the deep meanings behind that imaginary condolence letter until I was done writing it. So in a way I practiced a kind of condolence that I will likely write to many people I know personally and professionally and as a fringe benefit also honored my own losses.

CLOSING THOUGHTS

When people feel empowered to write personally meaningful letters of condolence to the bereaved, they are better able to avoid the sense of being overwhelmed by emotional contagion and to step toward the other's pain in a genuine expression of empathic concern. This simple but heartfelt action can strengthen the mourner's bonds not only with the deceased but also with living representatives of a compassionate community. At the same time, it reinforces the supporters' capacity for caring communication and sometimes pays hidden dividends in honoring their own losses, including those shared with the bereaved.

References

Decety, J., & Cowell, J. M. (2014). Friends or foes: Is empathy necessary for moral behavior? *Perspectives on Psychological Sciences, 9*(5), 525–537.

Klass, D., & Steffen, E. (Eds.). (2017). *Continuing bonds in bereavement.* New York: Routledge.

Winefield, H. R., & Chur-Hansen, A. (2000). Evaluating the outcome of communication skill teaching for entry-level medical students: Does knowledge of empathy increase? *Medical Education, 34,* 90–94.

Yedidia, M. J., Gillespie, C. C., Kachur, E., Schwartz, M. D., Ockene, J., Chepaitis, A. E., . . . Lipkin, M. (2003). Effect of communication training on medical student performance. *Journal of the American Medical Association, 290,* 1157–1165.

24
Thematic Analysis

Judy Chew

CLIENTS FOR WHOM THE TECHNIQUE IS APPROPRIATE

Accessing journal entries of the deceased offers a window for meaning making in bereavement work. Journals can shed light on the qualities, values, choices, experiences and feelings of the writer. Journal reflections that chronicle significant experiences can promote an understanding of the life of the deceased and ease the pain of those who grieve. Thematic analysis of journal entries is suitable for individuals who possess the cognitive and emotional resources to explore the inner life of the deceased. This approach is contraindicated when the process of analysis and discovery may be emotionally premature or highly charged with negative complexities or is attempted without necessary emotional support.

DESCRIPTION

Thematic analysis is based on the premise that humans seek meaning and want to make sense of life (van Manen, 1990). Such analysis is commonly associated with qualitative research that examines everyday lived experience. Expressive writing and putting experiences into words can help the writer through traumatic or private pain (Pennebaker & Smyth, 2016). With this in mind, it may be possible that the reader of these written expressions can derive healing benefits. Thematic analysis can be adapted for psychotherapy work with those who grieve. The following guidelines and questions are offered to promote this therapeutic endeavor:

- Read and reread the journal in its entirety to familiarize yourself with its content, bearing in mind the questions "What is going on here that is meaningful? What is the big picture about?"
- Look for aspects that are meaningful and interesting, such as certain emotions, choices or relationships. Some guiding questions include: "What is this an example of? What appears to be happening here? What is being conveyed?" Colored Post-it notes can be placed on the journal pages or a bulletin board to capture a sentence or a few words of importance.
- Engage in a deeper review and reflection of the selected information to identify overarching or broader themes. Flash cards, mind maps or tables can be used as visuals to

DOI: 10.4324/9781351069120-30

promote a list of potential themes. What is each theme about? Reflect on the significance of the findings. Identify any contradictions, discrepancies or questions.

- Review the themes to explore their relationship to each other. Describe each in a couple of sentences. What are the patterns and relationships that emerge from this review? Does the relationship between the themes reflect an overall narrative or storyline? Are there any surprises or contradictions? Elaborate on the storyline.

From a constructivist perspective, bereaved individuals "strive to organize life events according to personally significant ideas so that they can understand, anticipate, and to some extent control their world" (Neimeyer, Laurie, Mehta, Hardison, & Currier, 2008, p. 30). The guidelines for thematic analysis and accompanying questions allow for a therapeutic stance of anticipation and discovery. The client's own journaling of personal responses throughout this thematic analysis may be valuable in therapeutic conversation. The case study that follows captures this application of thematic analysis.

CASE ILLUSTRATION

A graduate student named Eduardo sought counseling to deal with the "moral angst" he reported after the "complicated" death of his biological father (Geraldo) two years earlier. Geraldo's mental health issues and addictions had separated father from son when Eduardo was an infant. Just one year before being diagnosed with terminal cancer, Geraldo transitioned from male to female (Geraldine). Eduardo briefly visited Geraldine before she died, and after what Eduardo described as a "painful reunion and farewell," he began to read her journal, given to him as a "goodbye gift." Geraldine had encouraged him to read it "only if and when [he] felt ready."

After the funeral, Eduardo was certain that Geraldine's death would have little, if any, impact on him. He said he "gave up hope of ever having a father long ago." Yet Eduardo began to read the journal, and when he did, "waves of confusing emotions" prompted him to seek counseling. He wanted to "make sense" of what was going on inside him.

Working from a constructivist perspective, I established a working alliance of respect and empathy while also inviting a collaborative approach to the client's discovery of meaning (Neimeyer, 2009). I affirmed Eduardo's pursuit of understanding and peace of mind and encouraged him to trust the trajectory of his life experience. I also acknowledged the timeliness of his search for clarity.

Our early work focused on Eduardo's years of not caring that he had been "abandoned and left behind" by his father. To his surprise, after spending a week with Geraldine's journal, Eduardo reported a surge of sadness. He said he was now confused, not able to either comprehend or morally accept his father's decision to transition. He also wondered if his father found peace in both this life and the "afterlife." Eduardo expressed a desire to get acquainted with this "new person" in order to make some sense of the death of a parent that was no longer his father. Yet this very desire was accompanied by fear. Eduardo said he worried that this exploration might negatively impact his academic performance and also threaten his moral and spiritual values. I assured Eduardo of my support in his quest and encouraged him to be confident that he could navigate wisely and arrive at a place of satisfactory meaning (Neimeyer, 2009). I affirmed his courage in visiting Geraldine in her last days and told him I was curious to know how he decided to read her journals, given how "mindboggling and overwhelming" it was. Eduardo admitted that the Geraldine he was "getting to know" through the journal entries seemed content with her life and spirituality. She apparently accepted her untimely death, and this both puzzled and intrigued him.

As sessions continued, Eduardo said he was buoyed by the emotional support and growing confidence he drew from our working relationship. He continued rereading the journal with a "more open mind," one less fearful and judgmental of Geraldine. When he wondered how he might understand Geraldine's thoughts "in a more organized fashion," I encouraged him to consider thematic analysis and offered practical ideas for the process. He returned with a colorful bulletin board full of poignant themes. He reported starting his own journal to express how the newly discovered themes impacted him. Through my open-ended questions, he shared how his moral or spiritual perspectives were shifting. Eduardo also reported that a major theme in the journal was Geraldine's lifetime of feeling in the wrong body—Geraldo had been "at odds with himself and the world." Clearly, the decision to embrace a transgendered identity was not merely a lifestyle choice (Norwood, 2013). Geraldine's journal also described the themes of pain, guilt and loss as a parent who left Eduardo behind. Newfound peace emerged as a theme as she both transitioned and faced the cancer prognosis. She was able to love herself and feel whole, spiritually transformed by a loving Creator (Reinsmith-Jones, 2013). Eduardo tearfully told me that Geraldine had also expressed "immeasurable joy" in their brief reunion, and the theme of self-forgiveness punctuated the final journal entries.

Eduardo said he was more accepting of his father's gender change. Geraldo/Geraldine was the same human throughout life; the transition did not involve the replacement of one person with another (Norwood, 2013). As he shook his head, Eduardo admitted to the mystery of it all but smiled as he said, "Until we meet again. Rest in peace, Geraldine."

CONCLUDING THOUGHTS

The death of a parent is often a complex experience, and the loss of a transgendered parent can add to the challenge of disentangling narratives and meaning making in the grief journey. Fresh conceptualizations are often needed for uncharted emotional territories. Crossing culturally unfamiliar territory requires the accompaniment of an empathic, nonjudgmental and creative therapist.

Eduardo's determination to understand Geraldine's death required him to ponder life choices that she made in the quest for inner peace. A reflective, thematic analysis approach was well suited for Eduardo, given his strong contemplative capacity in both exploring Geraldine's journal and probing the depth and meaning of his own emotions. Our psychotherapy sessions provided opportunity for expression, feedback and validation of his growing awareness. Through this meaning-making process, Eduardo reported gradual spiritual clarity and psychological peace.

Thematic analysis is suited for clients who desire to enrich their understanding of the deceased through careful review of journals. This method can be effectively broadened to optimize its application across a range of grief experiences and client presentations. Existing digital recordings may be examined to identify salient themes of the life of the deceased. Additionally, interviews with friends, colleagues or relatives of the deceased can be conducted and explored with the guidelines outlined. Due care needs to be taken in decision making around out-of-session exercises. A sense of safety is an ethical requirement. Thus, efforts should be made to minimize (re)traumatization. Similarly, the content of other sources of material related to the deceased, such as a suicide note or text messages, is better suited for carefully timed collaborative work in the therapeutic hour. For other clients, there are benefits that can be derived from a thematic analysis of published books or movies on grief/loss that are pertinent to them, such as loss of baby, child, sibling, parent or spouse. Care and respectful pacing from the therapist are crucial. A spirit of collaboration and willingness to provide options for "goodness of fit" are recommended. Ultimately, it is our clients who choose their preferred path in the pursuit of meaning making after loss.

References

Neimeyer, R. (2009). *Constructivist psychotherapy*. New York: Routledge.

Neimeyer, R., Laurie, A., Mehta, T., Hardison, H., & Currier, J. (2008, Spring). Lessons of loss: Meaning-making in bereaved college students. *New Directions for Student Services* (121), 27–39. doi:10.1002/ss.264

Norwood, K. (2013). Grieving gender: Trans-identities, transition, and ambiguous loss. *Communication Monographs*, *80*(1), 24–45. doi:10.1080/03637751.2012.739705

Pennebaker, J., & Smyth, J. (2016). *Opening up by writing it down* (3rd Ed.). New York: Guilford Press.

Reinsmith-Jones, K. (2013). Transsexualism as a model of spiritual transformation: Implications. *Journal of GLBT Family Studies*, *9*(1), 65–99. doi:10.1080/1550428X.2013.748509

van Manen, M. (1990). *Researching lived experience*. London: Althouse Press.

Part VII
Working With Emotion

25

Balancing Caring and Daring

Jakob van Wielink, Leo Wilhelm and Denise van Geelen-Merks

CLIENTS FOR WHOM THE TECHNIQUE IS APPROPRIATE

As a technique that is appropriate for practically all clients, balancing caring and daring is equally relevant to death and non-death losses. However, when the loss is experienced as traumatic by the client, therapists should not press the "daring" agenda too quickly.

DESCRIPTION

Parents can become "secure bases" for their children, a term John Bowlby adopted from Mary Ainsworth, when they are available, provide a sense of security and warmth and at the same time challenge them to explore the world, to set out on their own and to stand on their own two feet. Bowlby did not limit his attachment theory to the relationship between parents and children; he expanded its scope to the relationship between therapists and clients. Kohlrieser and his colleagues (2012) then added a concept to the idea of the secure base that is highly relevant for practical therapy situations: a balance between "caring" and "daring." "Caring" here is all about the sense of security and trust that the therapist provides, which is necessary as a basis from which to "dare" clients and challenge them to take new steps and grow. A proper balance and alternation of security and challenge are required for successful therapy. Therapists who present themselves as secure bases are able to provide their clients with security and trust while at the same time challenging them to develop themselves further (Wielink, Wilhelm, & van Geelen-Merks, 2020).

Therapists should provide 100% caring as well as 100% daring. One without the other will result in either a lot of warmth but very little progress (in the event of mostly caring and little daring) or a lot of action but little actual change and the risk of boundaries being pushed too far (in the event of a lot of daring but little caring).

The Dual-Process Model (Stroebe & Schut, 2010) describes the oscillation or pendulum swing from being focused on the loss to being focused on restoration. This model illustrates the complexity of dealing with loss. The left-hand side of the model contains aspects that have to do with being occupied by or dwelling on the loss. The right-hand side, the one focused on restoration, contains aspects that have to do with taking on new things, moving on, looking for distractions etc. Grieving is defined as the pendulum swing between the two orientations. The movement of the pendulum varies from person to person and from one moment to the next. The model does not express any value judgments of either focus; neither

DOI: 10.4324/9781351069120-32

Figure 25.1 Dual-Process Model

is better than the other. It also does not present solutions; it does not narrow in on any one desirable final situation.

Combining a balance of caring and daring with a balance between being focused on the loss and being focused on restoration results in an approach featuring four different quadrants, as depicted in Figure 25.2.

For each intervention, the therapist has the choice of these four quadrants. From the security of the therapeutic secure base, the therapist is able to challenge the client to explore other quadrants as well, insofar as the client's attachment style, resilience and coping allow.

CASE ILLUSTRATION

Vera sat in the waiting room, withdrawn into herself. She was small in stature and looked fragile. It took some effort for her to drag herself into the office. Ever since Vera lost her job due to the company's bankruptcy a year and a half ago, she had spent her days sleeping and watching TV. She felt unable to get up and exercise, meet up with friends or go out to find a new job. "I feel miserable," she said. "I had been working for the department store for ages. I began as junior sales assistant when I was 16, and I am now 56. I worked there for 40 years, as part of various departments, eventually becoming team leader. I loved working for this company." Vera's cheeks flushed and her eyes lit up as she talked about her time working in the store. "You really had a great time working there, huh? I can tell; you light up when you talk about it," the therapist remarked. She asked Vera to talk about back then, when things were good. Vera was relieved to be "allowed" to dwell so fully on this situation that she so yearned for. By aligning herself with the client in this way, the therapist created a comfort zone that helped the client feel like her loss and her story were accepted. Vera tended to be highly loss oriented in her coping, understood in the terms of the Dual-Process Model. The objective of the therapy was to help Vera regain perspective and open up to the future, but first, the therapist was able to create rapport by

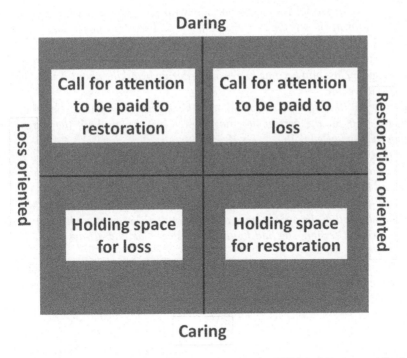

Figure 25.2 Quadrants of the Combination Between the DPM and Caring and Daring

aligning herself with her client. The therapist asked questions now and then, and Vera related her story. She had started out as junior sales assistant. She was then transferred to the women's fashion department, where she eventually became senior sales assistant and coordinator. For years and years, she had the same group of co-workers, with whom she would often go dancing on Saturday nights. She sighed. Those were good times. "What was so great about it?" the therapist asked. "It was nice to have such a great time together. But also, we were all involved in creating the look and feel of the store. In those days, a sales team had a lot of input regarding the product range. We were the store, essentially. That's what it felt like. I was proud of our window displays, of our range. . . . We all were; we shared that sense of pride." Vera stopped for a moment. Her gaze became distant. "Yes, those were good times." "What is it like for you to think back on those times?" the therapist asked. "It's nice to recall those memories. They are so clear in my mind. Those were the best times of my life. A lot changed later on." The atmosphere in the store changed. The employees were allowed to provide less and less input regarding the product range, and a number of co-workers left. "How did that feel?" "Not great. I still felt very responsible for the look of the place. I always made sure that my department looked tip-top, but a lot of my younger co-workers didn't care about that. They were just going through the motions." "Who did you draw strength from at the time?" "Who did I draw strength from? No one, really. It felt as though no one cared about the look and feel of the store anymore." "How do you feel about that, looking back on it now?" "It's unbelievable. The company was doing poorly. People felt that the store became less and less appealing. I don't get why management didn't listen to those of us on the shop floor more." "So, would I be correct in saying that there was a time when you really enjoyed working for this organization but also a time when things weren't so great?" "Yes, that's true. It had been going downhill for a while. Noticeably so. I tried incredibly hard to maintain the standards of the old days, but it was impossible."

Clients who have been focused solely on a loss for a long time can have a tendency to roman-ticize the past. Vera primarily missed the elements that she had good memories of. She did not pay attention to the rest. The therapist made sure to ask her about "forgotten" or "unpleasant" details so that the story would be complete once more and be more real. The therapist stayed on the side of being focused on loss and became increasingly daring by asking about details that the client was inclined to leave out.

By telling the story and through the therapist's questions, clients learn to re-examine their relationship with the thing or the person they have lost. They explore both the things they miss and the things they struggled with.

Vera indicated that she missed the contact with her co-workers and the pride she felt for the store. To her, these were important elements. She did not miss the feeling of being misunderstood or the travel time and the regular working hours.

The therapist was daring by asking whether this loss had brought Vera anything. Maybe it created room for something that she did not have room for at first? Vera did not have an answer right away, but by the next session, she had found the answer. She had always wanted a dog because she loved animals.

The therapist then asked her to come up with ideas for how to find meaning in life in the future, based on the elements she missed and the things she would have liked to see changed. After some initial uncertainty, Vera began to enjoy thinking of new possibilities.

Two years later, Vera was working as a volunteer at an animal shelter. She had recently finished a course to become a licensed animal caretaker, and thus, the shelter had started pay-ing her a small amount for her help. Moreover, she was the proud owner of Murphy, a black Labrador.

CONCLUDING THOUGHTS

Clients will progress at their own pace. Sometimes, a lot of endurance is required from thera-pists for them to stay present and provide caring, especially when the direction that the client should be moving seems very obvious to the therapist. It can be quite daring for both thera-pist and client to take the time and wait for room to be cleared for a changed perspective. Trying to force things when the client is not yet ready for such a change may result in the opposite: withdrawal. Sometimes, the only way forward is by taking two steps forward and three steps back. Therapists who are familiar with their own internal movements and are able to draw strength from their own secure bases are better equipped at observing and enduring this process.

References

Kohlrieser, G., Goldsworthy, S., & Coombe, D. (2012). *Care to dare—unleashing astonishing potential through secure base leadership.* San Francisco: Jossey Bass.

Stroebe, M. S., & Schut, H. (2010). The dual process model of coping with bereavement: A decade on. *Omega, 61*(4), 273–289.

Wielink, J. P. J. van, Wilhelm, L., & van Geelen-Merks, D. (2020). *Loss, grief and attachment in life transi-tions. A clinician's guide to secure base counselling.* London/New York: Routledge.

26

Externalizing Conversations

Carolyn Ng

CLIENTS FOR WHOM THE TECHNIQUE IS APPROPRIATE

The technique is applicable for adults and adolescents who are struggling with life-threatening or life-limiting illnesses. Such struggles may include their awareness of their impending death and the resultant death anxiety. However, people may not be ready for externalizing conversations soon after receiving bad news about their illness or after having experienced a medical crisis. This technique also would be unsuitable for people at the end of life, when they start showing such signs of dying as agitated delirium with cognitive impairment. Like-wise, it would also be inappropriate to use this technique when they show at-risk tendency (e.g., suicidal risk) that requires risk assessment and intervention instead.

DESCRIPTION

Many people perceive death to be an emotionally laden topic that inevitably leads to serious or even morbid conversations. Yet using externalizing conversations, a technique from narra-tive therapy (White, 2007), can actually empower people with critical illnesses to take a more proactive role in response to the illness or even their impending death. These conversations create a space in which people are invited to redefine their identities and/or their relationship with the struggles identified (Carey & Russell, 2004) so that they can perceive themselves differently and experience their lives anew, though the illness and its threat remain. At times, especially with adolescents and young adults, externalizing conversations may even turn such heavy topics as death and dying to something approached with playfulness and humor instead of intimidation and taboo (Ng, 2015).

To facilitate such externalizing conversations, the structure of *NETS* (name, elicit, take a stand, step forth) may act as a guiding frame to invite people with critical illness into these conversations:

1. Name the struggle.

As people with critical illness share about a struggle (e.g., hopelessness resulting from a terminal condition) during the therapy, we may invite them to give a name to this struggle in a way that fits well for them and their experiences. We may also invite them to personify

DOI: 10.4324/9781351069120-33

this identified struggle, such as describing its unique features or characteristics. Such a naming process is important because this makes their own problem-solving strategies, skills and ideas, which have been developed over the course of their lives, readily available and relevant as they address their current predicament (Carey & Russell, 2004). Here are some sample questions:

- If you were to give this struggle a name, how would you like to call it?
- How did you come to decide on this name?
- I wonder what the stories behind this name could be.

2. *Elicit its effects on the person.*

After naming the identified struggle, we may proceed to invite people with illness to further share some stories about the identified struggle and the influence that it has had on them and their lives. By placing the identified struggle into storylines, we may start to shed some light on how it has come to have those influences on their lives (Carey & Russell, 2004). Here are some sample questions:

- Does its name actually tell people about its characteristics?
- When did you notice that [the struggle's name] had entered into your life?
- How has [the struggle's name] been influencing you or your day-to-day life thus far?
- What would you say about such influences—positive, negative, mixed or. . . ?
- Are there times or situations in which you appreciate its presence in your life?
- Were there times that you wished for its absence from your life? If so, when?

3. *Take a stand in relation to this struggle.*

As people become more aware of their relationship to and interactions with the identified struggle, as well as its impacts on their lives, we may then invite them to consider how they would like to move on from there. They may choose to keep things status quo or make some changes they deem necessary or helpful to reclaim their lives from the influence of the struggle (Carey & Russell, 2004). Their perspectives and decisions may change as the therapy proceeds as well. Here are some sample questions:

- How much would you want to allow [the struggle's name] to continue to influence your life as before?
- How would you like to position [the struggle's name] in your life then?
- What kind of relationship would you prefer to have with [the struggle's name] at this stage? How come?
- What would [the struggle's name] think or say about having such a relationship with you?
- How would having such relationship with [the struggle's name] make a difference to your life?

4. *Step forth accordingly.*

As we "de-center" the struggle in people's lives through externalizing conversations (Carey & Russell, 2004), we may get in touch with other aspects of their lives that have been obscured by the effects of the struggle. The focus of exploration then becomes people's knowledges of life skills that are relevant to addressing the struggle and helping them step forth in life. We may also invite them to identify significant others who can testify to and support their efforts in this process. Here are some sample questions:

- What would it take for you to keep [the struggle's name] in such a position?
- How would you go about developing or maintaining such a relationship with [the struggle's name]?
- How determined or eager are you to make that happen?
- When you are able to make that happen, what will it say about you as a person?
- Would [the struggle's name] be surprised to see you doing so? How come?
- Who would come alongside you and bear witness to your efforts?
- Do you foresee any possible obstacles ahead? If so, how will you handle them?

CASE ILLUSTRATION

In one of my conversations with Nas, aged 23 with relapsed chronic myeloid leukemia, she described herself as "a dying patient" and revealed her struggle with death anxiety. As such narrations are often opportunities for externalizing conversations, I invited her to name her struggle. She then named it "the Crush" because she felt she was being crushed inside, and she cried upon learning she had incurable pulmonary fibrosis. Subsequently, I further invited her to share how "the Crush" had affected her and her life since then. Initially, she felt she had been victimized by "the Crush" as it bothered her to the extent that she could have "no life." In her own words, she described such a state: "I'd be very tried and down, just want to sleep. I'm very lethargic, don't like to go out or chat with friends, but just want to stay home and don't want to go to school. There's no life at all. . . . I'd have no friends and become lonely."

While I listened to Nas, my heart ached for her, as I believed Nas did not need to continue living under the shadow of "the Crush," and I doubted that she wanted to spend her remaining days in such a manner. As I explored with Nas how much she would like "the Crush" to continue bothering her, she replied, "That's not what I want. . . . I'm getting tired of sleeping and having no life. I want to wake up and have life, which is something I value more." As I gradually invited Nas to reflect on how she had been responding to "the Crush" and how she would like to reclaim a life that she valued more, she started to generate different knowledges and skills in handling the visits of "the Crush." These knowledges and skills included doing something active like going out for a walk or cooking her favorite food at home, as well as talking to someone she trusted and releasing her tears without suppressing them or dwelling on "the Crush."

Interestingly, in one of our later conversations, Nas revealed that somehow "the Crush" had not come to her and bothered her for a period of time, ever since we had the externalizing conversations about it. She reckoned that was "something surprising." While I was amazed and curious about her experience, I invited Nas to elaborate further on what might have contributed to it. She shared that "now I don't bother to google about the pulmonary fibrosis. I just live how I'm supposed to live, work, study and whatever." I also explored with Nas how her life had been different without "the Crush." I was heartened to hear her sharing that "this period without 'the Crush' is good. I can eat well, but I'm getting fat." She laughed. "I enjoy myself, smile most of the time instead of being gloomy and am able to concentrate on my studies more. Now I wake up very early. My daily routine has been different. . . . What I value most is my life. That's the kind of life I want."

CONCLUDING THOUGHTS

Externalizing conversations do not solely focus on people's struggles but can also be used for positive internalized qualities like resilience. Such conversations open up space for people to tell alternative stories of their multidimensional lives that widen their perspectives and options for action to enable significant changes to happen. These conversations are especially needed when people are labeled "dying patients," and illness and threat of death seem to have taken center stage in their lives rather than just being one of their life chapters (Cincotta, 2004). Instead of thinly constructing their life stories as if illness and death are the only things happening in their lives, externalizing conversations help elicit people's alternative stories and preferred identities that they might have neglected when a critical illness intruded into their lives, especially when it made their days numbered. Regardless of where they are in their journey of life and how gravely ill they may possibly be, very often, people continue to want to live and experience life until their very last day. Their rich life stories, therefore, continue to evolve and deserve to be explored and witnessed by the surrounding helping professionals.

References

Carey, M., & Russell, S. (2004). Externalizing: Commonly-asked questions. In S. Russell & M. Carey (Eds.), *Narrative therapy: Responding to your questions.* Adelaide: Dulwich Centre Publications.

Cincotta, N. (2004). The end of life at the beginning of life: Working with dying children and their families. In J. Berzoff & P. R. Silverman (Eds.), *Living with dying: A handbook for end-of-life healthcare practitioners* (pp. 318–347). New York: Columbia University Press.

Ng, C. (2015). Consulting young people about living with cancer. *The International Journal of Narrative Therapy and Community Work, 2,* 51–57.

White, M. (2007). *Maps of narrative practice.* New York: Norton.

27
The Castle

Riet Fiddelaers-Jaspers

CLIENTS FOR WHOM THE TECHNIQUE IS APPROPRIATE

The technique is suitable for children, adolescents, adults and seniors who seek insight into their survival mechanisms after a meaningful loss. It is also useful in a group setting for demonstrating and asking thought-provoking questions. However, it could be inappropriate for clients with a recent loss, those not yet capable of reflecting on their coping styles and for adults and seniors who think that playing with such "toys" is childish.

DESCRIPTION

I use the metaphor of the castle to help clients examine the survival strategies they developed after a meaningful loss. The original story, "The Gate to My Heart," is the story of my mother and me (see Chapter 33). I always change the story slightly so that it touches on the story of my client. In this chapter, I use the version entitled "The Gate to Your Heart," written for children and teenagers (see later in this chapter). I prefer, if possible, to sit on the ground or on a pillow, as does my client. But a table and chairs will also do. In front of us is a castle made of wood, cardboard, paper or plastic. I have cards with symbols; Duplo, Lego or Playmobile figures; figures of guards or knights; a vicious-looking or three-headed dog or something similar; a bunch of different-size keys; and some soft or small things like feathers, a tissue, a tiny box, a shell and so on.

For the castle exercise, read the story aloud for the client(s). Wait a few seconds after finishing reading before going further to give clients an opportunity to take it in. Start a conversation by asking questions. In a group, you can aim these questions directly at the participants.

The goal is to help them recognize the way they cope with loss, understand their survival strategies and make contact with their pain and their vulnerability.

Telling the Story: "The Gate to Your Heart"

I have a heart, just like you do and everybody else does. My heart is a kind of castle with a big, thick door in front: the gateway to the world. In front of this door is a sturdy guard; he can open the gate, and he can close it. I'm the one who tells the guard what to do: to open or to close the door.

When I came into the world, the door was open. I was safe in the arms of my mother; she smiled at me and cuddled me. I gave her the greatest gift I had to give at that moment: my

DOI: 10.4324/9781351069120-34

beautiful smile. I started to bond with her, and after some time, I also smiled at other people. I let people into my heart. But very soon, I learned that sometimes I needed to close my heart for a while to protect myself. While I was living my life, I met people who weren't very nice at all, and I had some painful experiences. I told the guard to close the door again.

Maybe you also know how to close your door very quickly. Then you have had the experience, just as I did, of someone causing pain in your heart. Maybe your parents got divorced, or you had to move to another city, even though you didn't want to move; maybe you had to leave your country because it wasn't safe there anymore or you were bullied; maybe someone you love very much is very sick or has died. You can feel a lot in your heart: anger because of what happened, sadness because someone left or died, homesickness, guilt, shame or abandonment.

When there is chaos inside me, my guard doesn't know what to do anymore. Maybe you've said to your guard, just as I did, 'Keep the door closed; it hurts too much when someone disappoints or abandons me." Nobody is allowed in anymore because I don't want to feel this pain again!

But do you know what the strange thing is? If you keep the door locked so you don't feel the pain anymore, life is less joyful. Because joy and sadness belong together. Most of your sadness comes from the beautiful and wonderful things you have experienced.

You can choose for yourself: keep the drawbridge up or down, keep the door to your heart open or closed, even if it is exciting or stressful. You can treasure the memories, thinking of all the beautiful things that happened even if there was fighting or sadness sometimes. You can save the beautiful memories in your heart. Nobody can take them away from you. They're yours! Open the door of your heart. Not all the time, just time and again (Fiddelaers-Jaspers, 2011–4; Fiddelaers-Jaspers & Kinkkelder, 2018; Fiddelaers-Jaspers & Visser, 2017; Visser & Fiddelaers-Jaspers, 2016).

Letting the Castle Do the Work

When people suffer a meaningful loss and are confused as to exactly what is happening to them and why they are reacting in such a manner, words are not the only and often not the best way to make contact. The senses provide better access to internal processes through images, touch, colors and shapes. Using symbolism, the castle illustrates the story "The Gate to Your Heart." Certainly, children and adolescents, and often adults, recognize the image and become curious. Are they able to raise the drawbridge and lock the gate? In other words: can they identify with the metaphoric safety and reliability of the castle? Most often, the answer is yes. This enables them to make contact (maybe for the first time) with their deep, hidden feelings of pain, distress, grief and loneliness. The use of metaphors and images helps prevent clients from being overwhelmed with emotion and allows them to maintain their boundaries. It offers them the opportunity to tell their story in their own words.

Major events in life cause the gate to slam shut, and later this happens even when a threat is presumed (Fiddelaers-Jaspers & Noten, 2015). The goal is to protect something vulnerable that has often disappeared from the conscious mind. The gate has been locked, and a guard has been placed outside. The vulnerable piece or aspect has been severed and now resides in the courtyard of the castle. The gate and the guard are the gateway to the outside world. These defense mechanisms ensure that one can carry on with life by pretending that the pain is not there. The client now continues life in "survival mode."

The Guard Dog at the Gate

Working with specific symbolic images helps clients to tell their story, protecting them from the threat of doing so just as knights wear armor and a helmet for defense. Like a vicious guard dog that stands in front of the gate and is trained to approach strangers growling, the client is unable to judge whether the person approaching has bad intentions or not and so keeps everyone at a distance. Deep within, clients know exactly how to do just that: by using angry looks, making use of humor, acting irritated, being uninterested, acting as if they are busy or always caring for others instead of being vulnerably engaged with them. (See Figure 27.1.)

Returning to the exercise, the therapist can leave keys lying in front of the castle as a cue to talk with the client about locking and unlocking the gate. (See Figure 27.2.)

- Which key fits your lock?
- Who is allowed to use the key?
- When do you unlock the gate?
- What do you need to unlock the gate?

When someone sets the gate ajar and allows us to see inside, we will be touched by what we see and will learn a lot about the inner world of the client. If the client is prepared to really face the loss, the therapist can acknowledge this and start to emerge. The guard dog can then take a break more often, and the knights no longer have to stand guard all the time. These are the first steps toward healing. (See Figure 27.3.)

Figure 27.1 The dog guarding the gate

Figure 27.2 The keys to the gate

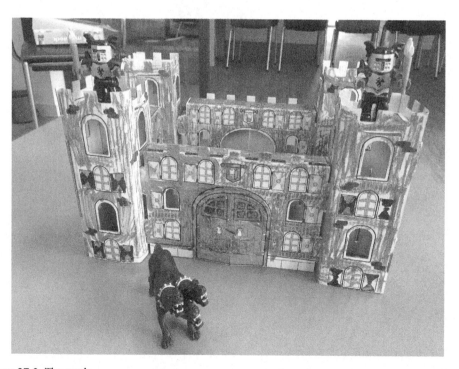

Figure 27.3 The castle

CASE ILLUSTRATION

Duke was nine years old. His parents were in the middle of a divorce. Even though his parents were trying hard to move through the process as peacefully as possible, his teacher, John, noticed that Duke was becoming quieter and more withdrawn. He also had difficulty dealing with unexpected situations. One day, during his lunch break, Duke got involved in a fight, something quite uncharacteristic for this boy. The teacher advised Duke's parents to find him a therapist. During treatment, the therapist made use of the castle because she knew that Duke loved knights. "Let's make sure that the castle is really safe, shall we? Which knights do we need to do that?" The therapist made contact in a playful manner with the fortified castle Duke had built inside himself because he was so sad that Daddy was moving out. He put the knights in a line in front of the gate. Along the battlements, he placed cannons and spear throwers. The therapist used questions:

- *How do you stop people from coming in through the gate, Duke?*
- *Who is allowed to look through a crack in the door?*
- *When do you say to your guard dog, "These are good people; they can come in"?*
- *For whom do the knights step aside so that the gate can open a little?*
- *I have a bunch of keys here, big and small. Which key fits the lock of your castle?*
- *When do you open the gate a little?*
- *What do you need to set the door ajar?*
- *Would you like for Grandpa or John to be there to help?*

When the gate metaphorically opened a crack, the therapist looked with Duke at what was in the courtyard. Duke had put some blue stones there that symbolized tears, a doll to symbolize his father and a card on which the word "Loneliness" was written. After some thought, he put a stone down, too, because the things that were happening at the moment were so heavy. He felt that his mother was sad all the time and that he had to comfort her. He put a tissue in the courtyard too.

- *Who is allowed to see your tears, Duke?*
- *Who is allowed to comfort you?*

Duke had been sitting with a Duplo clown in his hand for some time. When the therapist asked him about it, he told her that the clown made sure he didn't cry. Together, they put the clown on one of the towers because the joker also kept people at a distance. They both laughed at this clever tactic; humor is a very important aspect of this work. Duke wanted to take photos of "his" castle before ending the session to help him remember. The therapist could later make use of metaphoric language when referring to the clown, the key, the guard dog or the knights.

CONCLUDING THOUGHTS

Combining working with the castle with the story "The Gate to Your Heart" is an easily accessible and effective way to give more insight into survival strategies. It is also a gentle method, which looks at these strategies and tries to figure out why they are necessary. The use of keys empowers the client to take control and tentatively examine their hidden pain. Playfulness is a very important element when working with traumatic loss (Hughes, 2007). The first steps are taken to acknowledge the grief and the pain and to talk about it. This is an excellent tool for children, adolescents and often for adults too. It can also be used as a tool for explaining to adults how survival mechanisms work in children and adolescents.

Acknowledgements

Photography credits: Studio Chaos/Riet Fiddelaers-Jaspers.
Thanks to Gijs Visser (*Practice for Young People GO!*), who developed the technique of the castle based on the story "The Gate to Your Heart."

References

Fiddelaers-Jaspers, R. (2011–4). *Met mijn ziel onder de arm* (Wandering with a wounded heart; Between welcoming and saying goodbye). Heeze: In de Wolken.

Fiddelaers-Jaspers, R., & Kinkkelder, R. (2018). *De prins en het kasteel* (The prince and the castle). Heeze: In de Wolken.

Fiddelaers-Jaspers, R., & Noten, S. (2015[4]). *Herbergen van Verlies (Containing meaningful loss).* Heeze: In de Wolken.

Fiddelaers-Jaspers, R., & Visser, G. (2017, April). Als kinderen muurtjes bouwen (When children build walls). *PraxisBulletin, 34*(8), 9–14.

Hughes, D. A. (2007). *Attachment-focused family therapy.* New York: Norton.

Visser, G., & Fiddelaers-Jaspers, R. (2016, September). Verscholen achter dikke muren (Hidden behind thick walls). *Pedagogiek in Praktijk (PIP), 97*, 28–31.

28
Redecision and Reaffirmation

Gilbert Fan and Geok Ling Lee

CLIENTS FOR WHOM THE TECHNIQUE IS APPROPRIATE

Clients in individual or group therapy who have unwanted feelings that they want to release will benefit most from this experiential therapy. This therapy is most useful to clients who are stuck with painful feelings that hinder them from moving on constructively. However, it is important not to force clients into a confrontation with negative emotions for which they are unready or to press them to release such emotions prematurely, before their purpose and meaning are considered.

DESCRIPTION

Lee (1995) argued that every individual has the internal resources to "let go" of preoccupations, struggles and a need to control and to work toward a harmonious self, something that has special relevance for those facing death and bereavement. For Chinese people, doing so is coherent with their cultural belief in *tian-yi*, meaning accepting "the Will of Heaven or the Supernatural." Thus, letting go involves making meaning of one's life experience in a larger frame. Conversely, the inability to let go may generate anxiety or psychosomatic manifestations such as irritability. This concept stems from Eastern philosophical viewpoints on affliction, which is a negative emotion caused by maladaptive psychological attachment (Lee, Fan, & Chan, 2015). Letting go in the context of illness, therefore, promotes the acceptance necessary to acquire harmony and inner peace (Mok, Martinson, & Wong, 2004). For the bereaved, letting go helps facilitate closure in the wake of unresolved losses. Field and Wogrin (2011) wrote a case study of a woman who asked for forgiveness of her own limitations from her deceased father through the many letters she wrote. A similar Chinese custom is to write on kites or papers placed inside balloons to be released to the sky for the deceased (Chow & Chan, 2006).

Redecision or reaffirmation therapy is a simple technique using colored paper, pencils and envelopes. The overall goal is to let go of negative experiences, drawing on clients' inner resources. The therapist asks clients to choose a colored paper, pencil and envelope that they like best and one colored pencil that they dislike most. The colored paper is then folded in the shape of a booklet, as depicted in Figure 28.1.

The therapist then asks the clients to identify and share the strongest feeling that they want to either release, take better care of or transform. Next, the clients are asked to choose

DOI: 10.4324/9781351069120-35

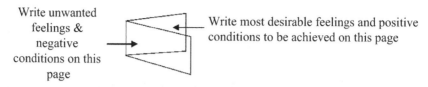

Figure 28.1 Folding of Colored Paper Containing Unwanted and Desired Feelings

a colored pencil they dislike most to write this most unwanted feeling. The therapist assists clients in doing this by encouraging them to think back to their previous coping attempts, reflecting on what troubled them, what worked and what failed. Clients then write the strongest unwanted feeling on the front side of the folded paper provided (see Figure 28.1). Clients next write down the two or three conditions in which this unwanted feeling can emerge most frequently. The therapist then discusses these conditions thoroughly with the clients to ascertain that this is, indeed, the most unwanted feeling. If clients are not able to name the unwanted feeling, the therapist helps the clients explore the closest possible unwanted feeling that fits the clients' descriptions.

The therapist needs to assess the clients' willingness to let go of these most unwanted feelings. Should it be unrealistic for the clients to do so, the therapist examines which of the clients' inner resources can "take care of" the strongest unwanted feeling, without the intent to eliminate it. The therapist then asks the clients what is the most desirable feeling or experience that they hope to achieve to replace the most unwanted feeling. At this juncture, the therapist asks for the two or three conditions that could bring out this desirable feeling most frequently. The therapist invites the clients to use a colored pencil that they like the most to write down this most desirable feeling or experience. Conversely, the therapist could help the clients strengthen the letting go by checking with them to see if they need to utilize any inner resources to protect themselves in its absence (e.g., the therapist may ask a client, "When anger is no longer with you, what would you like to have more of to take its place, to protect you?" The client might answer: "Forgiveness").

The therapist should demonstrate to the clients metaphorically how the unwanted feeling (e.g., anger) has blocked them from achieving the preferred feeling (e.g., forgiveness) by first asking that clients continue reading the unwanted word until they begin to feel that emotion and then showing how the feeling on the front page of the booklet covers the feeling on the following page. The therapist then turns the page to the preferred word and emphasizes how learning to experience this alternative emotion (e.g., forgiveness) also can protect one from the unwanted feeling (e.g., anger). The therapist then reverses the fold of the paper so that the preferred feeling is on top and the unwanted feeling beneath, providing a visual analogue for how either feeling can effectively displace the other.

If clients can begin to let go of the unwanted feeling realistically, they can perform a ritual by tearing off the portion of the paper that contains that unwanted feeling. Clients are encouraged to say what they feel as they tear the paper (e.g., Client: "Anger has been with me for a long time. It need not be there anymore. I don't need it to protect me anymore"). This constitutes what we would term *redecision*.

Clients who need to work further on their unwanted feeling and desirable feeling or experience are asked to place the colored paper into an envelope. They are encouraged to look at the colored paper to reflect further about the function of the unwanted feeling at least three times in the week that follows and journal their thoughts or feelings about it or call their therapist for an individual therapy session.

Clients who have no unwanted feelings to let go of can think of the most desirable feelings that they would like to keep. They then repeat the therapy process but focus only on the most desirable feeling and how to generate or extend it. This constitutes what we term *reaffirmation*.

CASE ILLUSTRATION

The redecision/reaffirmation technique can be illustrated by the following composite transcription of a client, Mr. Chan, who struggled with resentments regarding his harsh treatment by his parents when he was a child, as well as a combative attitude toward teachers, employers and now doctors who disappointed him. Now in his 60s and facing a progressive, incurable cancer, he realized that he wanted to release this legacy of anger and have greater equanimity in his final months or years of life.

> MR. CHAN: *Anger has been with me for a long, long time. It need not be there anymore. I don't need it to protect me anymore.*
>
> THERAPIST: *When anger is no longer with you, what would you like to have more of to take its place—to protect you?*
>
> MR. CHAN: *To be able to forgive. If I can forgive, my anger disappears.*
>
> THERAPIST: *Let's see. I'd like you to bring forgiveness into this room now. Can you close your eyes and get in touch with "forgiveness"?*
>
> MR. CHAN: *[Pause.] Yeah. It's here, all right [spoken softly].*
>
> THERAPIST: *Can you share how you feel when you can forgive?*
>
> MR. CHAN: *It is like I'm floating on a cloud, freely moving on and looking down at myself. I see myself smiling, looking comfortable. Feeling peaceful inside.*
>
> THERAPIST: *Can you take this picture with you when you wish to forgive?*
>
> MR. CHAN: *[Opening his eyes.] Yes, I can.*
>
> THERAPIST: *Where's anger now, when you can forgive?*
>
> MR. CHAN: *It just stands out there, looking at me. It is like anger is a stranger to me when I forgive.*

The client was instructed to write "forgiveness" on the remaining portion of the same folded paper to bring home with him, to keep as a reminder that he had this internal resource. If Mr. Chan had not been able to work through some issues—for example, if forgiveness was the only identified internal resource but was not strong enough to displace the anger—then he could have been asked to place the folded paper in an envelope and to take it home for further reflection, perhaps with the instruction to look for any other inner feelings or states that seemed to be present when he became angry and then began to shift away from into a better mood (e.g., assertiveness, redirecting his attention, soothing himself through listening to music). After identifying these, he could be instructed to write these on additional pieces of paper provided for this purpose and add them to his envelope of resources for dealing with anger in the future. On occasions when his resentment returned, he could then take out each and consider how he could draw on that to let go of the anger, retaining the option to request another session with the therapist for guidance or to share and consolidate his insights if this would be helpful.

CONCLUDING THOUGHTS

This experiential therapy of redecision or reaffirmation is most suited to a group setting as clients in a group share, learn and grow with one another. However, caution is to be exercised to ensure that clients are not coerced into encountering or releasing an unwanted feeling or embracing a desired one when they are not ready.

References

Chow, A. Y. M., & Chan, C. L. W. (2006). Bereavement care in Hong Kong: Past, present and future. In C. L. W. Chan & A. Y. M. Chow (Eds.), *Death, dying and bereavement: A Hong Kong Chinese experience* (pp. 253–260). Hong Kong: Hong Kong University Press.

Field, N., & Wogrin, C. (2011). The changing bond in therapy for unresolved loss: An attachment theory perspective. In R. A. Neimeyer, D. L. Harris, H. R. Winokuer, & G. F. Thorton (Eds.), *Grief and bereavement in contemporary society: Bridging research and practice* (pp. 37–46). New York: Routledge.

Lee, G. L., Fan, G. K. T., & Chan, S. W. C. (2015). Validation of Chinese and English versions of the Holistic Well-being Scale in patients with cancer. *Supportive Care in Cancer, 23*(12), 3563–3571.

Lee, R. P. L. (1995). Cultural tradition & stress management in modern society: Learning from the Hong Kong experience. In T. Y. Lim, W. S. Tseng, & E. K. Yeh (Eds.), *Chinese societies & mental health* (pp. 40–55). Hong Kong: Oxford University Press.

Mok, E., Martinson, I., & Wong, T. (2004). Individual empowerment among Chinese cancer patients in Hong Kong. *Western Journal of Nursing Research, 26*(1), 59–75.

29

Figurative Stories

Riet Fiddelaers-Jaspers

CLIENTS FOR WHOM THE TECHNIQUE IS APPROPRIATE

Adolescents, adults and seniors can benefit from using Duplo or alternative figurines and other materials such as wooden blocks, glass pebbles, little treasure chests etc. to make visible how the personality can sometimes split off traumatic aspects of a profound loss. However, this technique could be inappropriate for clients with a recent loss and is probably too complicated for children and for clients who are cognitively impaired.

DESCRIPTION

Psychological splitting is a natural response to traumatic loss, whether this takes the form of the death of an important person, a divorce, an attachment trauma or an early childhood trauma like child neglect (Ruppert, 2011, 2012). When a client has faced a meaningful loss and is incapable of dealing with it, the result is a state of helplessness and powerlessness. Torn by the contradiction between reality as it was and reality as it now is, the whole personality can unconsciously split into parts in order to manage the chaotic and terrifying experience. However, such survival strategies have great impact on traumatized persons and on those with whom they are in close contact.

Splitting allows clients to dissociate from what is happening here and now and distracts them from what is currently causing the trauma feelings to resurface. The surviving part constructs and guards the split-off event in order to deny and avoid the traumatic loss and the painful memories and traumatized parts of the self that are associated with it (see Figure 29.1). At the time the trauma took place, this survival mechanism was lifesaving, but later in life, these strategies become limiting, disturbing and sometimes self-destructive.

Therapists see a variety of ways of managing traumatic loss, like all kinds of addiction: to alcohol, drugs, gaming, medication, work, sex and food. Likewise, clients also practice avoidance strategies like minimizing contact, intimacy, caring for others instead of themselves and avoiding situations that trigger the overwhelming feelings associated with the trauma.

However, the emotional pain that was experienced as a child has remained in the body; it has been frozen or trapped there. And this means that in most cases, the emotional needs associated with the loss will not be able to be met as an adult. We call this the traumatized part. It can be triggered suddenly and unpredictably, and it is eager to be released. But the survival mechanisms prohibit this. As they relate to childhood needs and wants, they needn't

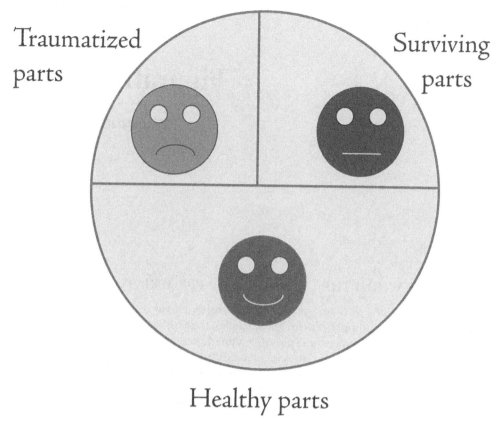

Figure 29.1 Splitting Off of the Personality

(*Source*: Ruppert, 2011; Broughton, 2013)

be experienced again but only have to be released and let go. In each person, there is a healthy part, which has the ability to engage in self-reflection, regulate emotions and seek help.

For the figurative stories technique, you will need a scaled up version of Figure 29.1, a so-called tablemat version (or you can draw it on a big piece of paper); Duplo, Lego and Playmobile or other figurines; treasure boxes (or some other symbol of loyalty and treasures/talents); wooden warriors or something similar (symbols for the loss, hurt and damage); and whatever else is needed to symbolize the aspects as described next. One advantage of Duplo and Lego figurines is that they have movable arms and legs, allowing them to assume different positions relevant to the self-states they are chosen to depict (Fiddelaers-Jaspers, 2017).

Basic rules for the exercise include the following:

- *Symbolize the splitting off of the personality by using three figures*: (1) the mature client with healthy abilities and choices who is able to reflect, whom we will call the *observer*; (2) a child figure for the traumatized parts, whom we will call *the little one*; and (3) the survival strategies, which we will name *the survivor*. The survivor can be visualized in a great variety of ways, following the client's lead: perhaps choosing a symbol for each, such as a boxer, clown, doctor, miniature wine bottle, sword, princess, sportsman, professor and so on.
- *Visualize the loss or damage and the treasures they might conceal*. The so-called damage figure might look like a warrior, but it can as easily be represented by empty liquor

bottles (a parent with alcohol addiction); a witch (the angry stepmother); a coffin, skeleton or car (death caused by an accident) and so on. A tiny treasure box, gem or heart can symbolize the gifts or strengths the child still retains. (See Figure 29.2)

- *Avoid confronting the client directly with the traumatic loss* (Levine, 1997) by talking to him or her in the third person. "What does this little boy long for?" The *observer* has an overview, looking from a distance at the unfolding image. The therapist can ask, "What does the observer see, looking at what is happening here?" "What would he or she like to change now?"
- *Keep it simple.* Sometimes there are so many figures and symbols on the table that the client and therapist can't see the forest for the trees. Ask clients what they would like to focus on and put away the rest.
- *Take pictures.* Prompting the client to takes a photograph of the scenario keeps the constellation in memory and permits the therapist and client to go further in the next session, using the image to set up the constellation on the table once more.
- *Respect the material.* As soon as the figures are on the table, they have a soul; they become a family. Don't swipe the figures into the box at the end but ask clients themselves to

Figure 29.2 The Warrior and Treasure Chest

return the figures to the storage container. At that point, if they want to swipe, the thera-pist should let them do so. Sometimes brusquely clearing the table permits emotional release and brings some laughter and humor into the room.

- *Sit next to each other* so you see the same picture as the client or sit at a 90° angle to each other at the corner of the table, conveying a sense of being "on the client's side" rather than opposed to them across the table. It is also important that both have the same view on the constellation.
- *Use silent moments, without hurry.* This work takes time.
- *Attune to the body of the client* to know what your next step will be.
- *Trust that this process doesn't stop after the session.* Let time do its work.

CASE ILLUSTRATION

Peter was 55 and the headmaster of a primary school. He was searching for help because he was suspended by the members of the board. A complaint of sexual harassment had been made against him by one of the teachers. Peter, married and already a grandfather, had fallen in love with this teacher. After the first incident, he was given a warning, but then one evening, he once again sought physical contact. During the investigation, Peter was forbidden to enter the school.

He didn't understand what had gotten into him as he had always been faithful to his wife and loved her very much. According to him it felt like a trance. During the first sessions, Peter and the therapist talked about his family history. Peter's parents were hardworking retailers; there was no time for emotions, cuddling or comfort. He had inherited the retailer's mentality: to always be there for the customers. And so he grew up as a friendly, helpful man, never saying no.

Because Peter was in need of an overview of his confusing situation, the therapist took a tablemat version of Figure 29.1 and a bowl filled with figures, treasure boxes and other materi-als and symbols. He asked Peter to choose a figure for his healthy, adult part, who was capable of reflecting, even when it was painful to look, and to place this figure on the mat in the cor-responding section.

Then the therapist invited him to choose a little boy, a symbol for the little Peter, and to place it on the traumatized part. He depicted Little Peter as sitting, his arms reaching out. The figure he chose for his father was carrying a box filled with things for the shop, standing with his back to little Peter. Peter placed his mother behind a shopping trolley. The shop always came first, and little Peter felt neglected. But nevertheless, a treasure chest was placed in the constellation for his parents because Peter was loyal, like most children are, no matter what. Peter could not take his eyes off the scene on the mat, and his eyes filled with tears. "What is happening, Peter?" After some time, he said, "I am deeply moved. He is so alone. . . . No one is comforting him." Peter had problems with attachment. He reached out, and his parents didn't react. He felt no safety and compassion, and he concluded: I have to do it on my own in life.

The therapist invited him to fill in the survival section by choosing an appropriate symbolic figure. Peter chose a doctor figure: "There, that's me. I'm the rescuer, the man who is always helpful and nice." Then he picked up a block of wood as a symbol for the impregnable fortress he made of himself. "Why is this man so helpful if he is longing for attention himself?" Peter looked surprised: "That's the way I am." The therapist made a connection between the little boy who was reaching out and wanted to be loved. "He had nothing more to give but himself." He pointed at the doctor. "This one is also reaching out but thinks he is not good enough, so he reaches out with his full hands. He gives to get attention and love. But he doesn't show his inside; is that right?" Peter stayed quiet and took another long look at the picture on the table. The therapist was silent too. Peter's body (eyes, breathing, muscle tone) was leading the constellation. The therapist told him why people developed survivor parts and how they helped them survive when there was no other way out. A little boy needs his parents and depends on them. "I think the survivors deserve a treasure chest, don't you?" "What happened during this man's youth is serious; it was damaging for the development of the little boy. Shall we place this wooden warrior with the traumatized parts to symbolize that?" (See Figure 29.3.) Peter cried: "Am I really crying because of something that happened 50 years ago? I cannot believe it, but still it makes me very sad." Before the session ended, Peter took some pictures of the constellation.

At the next session, Peter told the therapist that he had done a lot of thinking, and this time he didn't share his experiences with his wife, and he did not show her the pictures as it was still too fragile. With help of the pictures, the constellation was placed on the table again. The therapist said, "You see, Peter, little Peter had no other options, but as he gets older, there are other possibilities. The question is: Is the mature Peter making use of these possibilities, or is he abandoning little Peter himself?" Peter was visibly moved, and the therapist waited a while. When Peter took his eyes off the constellation and made contact again, the therapist asked, "Is it okay for you to focus on the situation you're faced with now? And let's do it outside this constellation, so we keep an overview. The mature Peter will help us."

The therapist took the Peter figure out of the healthy part and asked Peter to choose a figure for the teacher he fell in love with and to place these figures facing each other in the way he experienced the relationship. Peter let the mature figure reach out to his female colleague. The therapist asked him if he could try something. He took the little Peter out of the traumatized parts and put him in front of the grown-up figure, reaching out. "Who was longing for love and attention, this adult or the little boy that appeared?" Again, Peter cried. "And who is standing here? Is this the colleague, or is it the little boy's mother?" The therapist took the mother figure and put her in front of the teacher. (See Figure 29.4.) Now the therapist had to wait because

Figure 29.3 Peter's Family Constellation

Figure 29.4 Peter's Constellation of Reaching Out for Love

inside Peter, a lot was happening. After a while Peter said, "I'm beginning to understand. It wasn't my mature and reasonable self but the five-year-old boy who wanted to be held and cuddled. I didn't understand. Normally I can easily resist a beautiful woman. But she could look at me very intensely, as if she saw the real me. She always asked if I was well, and she was nice to me and warm, with eyes full of love. Yes, if I had grown up with a mother like her, maybe I would have led a different life." The therapist asked him to stop talking and take time to take in the image. It was enough for one day. Peter needed time to take it in.

CONCLUDING THOUGHTS

Using figures that can be posed to depict the splitting off of the personality is a profound method for working with traumatic loss. It benefits not only clients who find it difficult to verbalize their pain but also clients who talk too much. Using simple figurines, the client doesn't need a lot of words, as the image does the work. It is also useful for therapists who cannot endure long periods of silence. It's very helpful for clients to visualize the mechanism of the split to understand what is happening and why they behave as they do. The client is able to look at the image because the method helps prevent the client from being retraumatized. The therapist talks about Peter and about the little boy, and doesn't use "you," "your mother" and so on. That is of great help to enable the client to look at what happened and to endure the unfolding of the image before his or her eyes.

In this work, healing comes from honoring the survival mechanisms developed by clients because they helped them to survive when there were no other options. After this, it becomes necessary to downgrade these survival strategies, as they don't need to be removed, but they no longer need to work so hard. People use their best qualities for the survival mechanisms so, where possible, they can rebuild the good parts of these strategies into a resource. Peter had a great talent for helping other people and also for setting and maintaining his boundaries. These were positive qualities when they were in balance and not being used to avoid the pain, helping others when it was necessary and not overstepping his boundaries by doing more than was necessary. A healthy boundary was created without locking himself in and the other person out: boundaries in contact. Healing also means bringing together all the split parts and staying in contact with each of them. Clients will experience the sadness and the pain and find out they are not falling apart. And over time, they are better able to face their loss and feel that they have more energy at their disposal.

References

Broughton, V. (2013). *The heart of things. Understanding trauma: Working with constellations.* Steyning: Green Balloon Publishers.

Fiddelaers-Jaspers, R. (2017). *Verlies in beeld (Loss in sight).* Heeze: In de Wolken.

Levine, P. A. (1997). *Waking the tiger: Healing trauma.* Berkeley: North Atlantic Books.

Ruppert, F. (2011). *Splits in the soul: Integrating traumatic experiences.* Steyning: Green Balloon Publishers.

Ruppert, F. (2012). *Symbiosis and autonomy: Symbiotic trauma and love beyond entanglements.* Steyning: Green Balloon Publishers.

Part VIII
Utilizing Imagery

30
Mindful Photography

Jessica Thomas

CLIENTS FOR WHOM THE TECHNIQUE IS APPROPRIATE

Adults (including young adults and teenagers) who are anticipating the death of a loved one and those who are providing end-of-life care for a loved one can benefit from this mindful photography reflective practice. Practicing mindful photography and reflecting on self-made images is a process that allows caregivers to create the space that is needed to process and integrate thoughts and feelings, revealing a much deeper sense of awareness, acceptance and meaning. Depending on individual preferences, this method can be integrated into therapy for the final reflective stage of the method. It may be less appropriate for caregivers of loved ones following a major medical trauma or those who are anticipating the loss of someone with whom they have had a traumatic relationship.

DESCRIPTION

Preparedness for the death of a loved one is an important contributor to caregiver well-being, bereavement outcomes and possibly even spiritual growth. Awareness, acceptance and meaning making are key to a positive death experience and contribute to a shift in existential and spiritual perceptions. Accepting the impending loss of a loved one can prepare one for the loss, thus positioning one to cultivate meaning and gain insights. Caregivers and their dying loved ones face the profound spiritual dimensions of loss, pain and death. Mindfulness practices can provide a format for reconnecting with individual spiritual practices, thus forming new meaning and understanding of self and others (McBee, 2009).

Photography can be practiced in a way that is therapeutic and may increase awareness and opportunity for meaning making. The practice of mindful photography involves letting go of expectations, becoming attentive to moment-to-moment awareness and accepting that which is present. In the process of mindful photography, psychological components surface as one becomes receptive to feelings and sensations, thus allowing the eyes to open more fully to the present moment (Zakia, 2013).

As people physically and mentally slow down, they can begin to confront the anticipated death, come to greater comprehension of their relationship with the dying person and create meaning from the experience while their loved one is still living. Perception, thinking and feeling become interconnected within the act of making images. Meaning emerges as clients reflect on the self-made images and connect them with their inner experiences as

DOI: 10.4324/9781351069120-38

represented by the objects photographed. It is for this reason that we sometimes refer to this method as the *Within and Without* technique.

This form of therapeutic photography utilizes two modes of expression through four sequences that were inspired by Betensky's (1995) phenomenological art-based approach. Each sequence builds on the other to mediate the experience of anticipation and increase awareness and deep reflection, thereby positioning one to cultivate the meaning of one's experience of caregiving and anticipating the death of a loved one. As a therapeutic method, *Within and Without* is grounded in a process that brings light to the wholeness of one's experience through two modes of expression: visual imagery and reflective journaling. In the fourth and final sequence, the therapist facilitates a phenomenological inquiry through reflective dialogue with clients about their photographs, thereby allowing deeper meaning and an expanded life narrative to emerge.

Within and Without can be an effective method to confront thoughts and feelings associated with end-of-life caregiving and anticipating the death of a loved one. This method can be a catalyst for spiritual insight as existential awareness grows, and reflections on the meaning and purpose of life surface (Thomas, 2016). The steps that follow can be prescribed to clients as an independent practice and processed in therapy for the fourth and final sequence. Detailed instructions are offered here, followed by a case study.

1. *Opening Up.* Sequence 1 takes place as clients allow an opening to engage freely through direct experience. Clients approach photography independently, without directive and structured assignments, enabling them to connect with this medium of reflection.

Clients begin by sitting quietly through three deep breaths. Next, they slowly begin a mindfulness walk, with a special focus on their embodied experience (inner) and their visual experience (outer). Intuition and playfulness are encouraged; so as to inspire pre-reflective and embodied experience in the context of caring for a dying loved one or anticipating the death of a loved one.

2. *Making Contact.* Sequence 2 is observed as a conscious shift toward a more intentional approach that begins the creating process. Clients engage mindful photography, whereby they consciously create an image in the context of caring for a dying loved one or anticipating the death of a loved one.

Clients begin by sitting quietly through three deep breaths. Next, they slowly begin a mindfulness walk, with a special focus on their embodied experience (inner) and their visual experience (outer). Clients become visually attuned to the aesthetic qualities of their experience (color, shape, texture) and allow a sense of resonance to occur with their environment that invites them to make an image.

3. *Emotional Resonance.* Sequence 3 invokes deep awareness through the act of reflection and intuiting. At this stage, the images are carefully looked at and perceived by the creator in fresh ways, as if for the first time. Clients are encouraged to spend time with their photographs while suspending preconceived ideas about them and to journal about their experience of mindful photography without prematurely interpreting their images.

Clients begin by preparing their images for reflection, either by setting out prints or by uploading them to view on their computer screen. Next, they will prepare to journal either in a notebook or by typing on a computer. With a special focus on their emotional experience, clients will carefully reflect on the self-made images. Clients then write a reflective journal entry about the experience of mindful photography, the moment they made the image and what struck them in that moment.

4. *Authentic Insight.* In the final stage, Sequence 4, the therapist intervenes as a condition for clients to expand their meaning-making process. This stage integrates a procedure that Betensky (1995) calls "What do you see?" This question contains phenomenological aspects: individual perception, feeling, and seeing. The therapist calls the question forth in a conscious effort, in Betensky's words, to "connect the artwork with the inner experience which was the prime mover in the artwork process that brought forth visual art expression" (p. 17).

Clients bring their images and journals to a therapy session. They will prepare the photos by presenting them either in print or on their computer. The client and therapist both consider the images one by one as the therapist facilitates a reflective discussion about each image with the leading question: *What do you see?* After each image has been reflected on separately, the client and therapist will look at the images as a whole while the therapist asks, *Now, as you look at these images together as a whole, what do you see?*

CASE ILLUSTRATION

Janet is an in-home caregiver for her husband of 25 years, who is dying of amyotrophic lateral sclerosis (ALS). Figure 30.1 presents one of Janet's photographs and journal entries representing Sequences 2 and 3, followed by an excerpt from the final sequence of the method, Authentic Insight.

Figure 30.1 Rocking Chairs

Emotional Resonance. What is it? We've not always had rocking chairs. These are our first, bought just this spring. They stand for something. For companionability? For quiet? For wordless understanding? For recollection? For making meaning of our nearly twenty-five years? Fact is, as I contemplate the invitation of those chairs and my focus on them, I realize they make me wistful. They let me be wistful. Dan is holding his own; I am so grateful. But I am feeling a sense of loss so much of the time. And even though he is still very much with me, I am feeling a palpable loneliness. Ah, is that the clutch, that new, different, deep-down clutch?

Authentic Insight. Looking at this image, those chairs symbolize for me an invitation. An invitation to take it seriously and to live it, not to feel as though I am trapped or at a dead end, but that I can sit and I can be quiet, and he can sit with me. I am entering this practice, but I am also deliberately answering this period of time with him. That is the attraction of the chairs and being invited outside and being invited into what is coming.

CONCLUDING THOUGHTS

Within and Without is a mindful photography reflection practice and therapeutic method that was inspired by my own experience and subsequent research on mindful photography and end-of-life caregiving. *Within and Without* can be an effective method to mediate difficult thoughts and feelings associated with end-of-life caregiving and anticipating the death of a loved one. In addition, this method can act as a catalyst for meaning making and spiritual growth.

The combination of mindfulness and creative expression engages clients' ability to open up to their experiences of anticipatory loss through the lens of the camera. By opening up, clients explore their experiences and understand them more fully. Authentic insight surfaces as the clients create meaning based on direct experience and learn how to perceive that experience and trust themselves through the process. The clients' photographs serve as mirrors of their lived experience as caregivers to their dying loved ones, but it is not until their reflections in Sequences 3 and 4 that the images gain personal and transformative significance.

References

Betensky, M. (1995). *What do you see? Phenomenology of therapeutic art expression*. London: Jessica Kingsley.

McBee, L. (2009). Mindfulness-based elder care: Communicating mindfulness to frail elders and their caregivers. In F. Didonna (Ed.), *Clinical handbook of mindfulness* (pp. 431–445). New York: Springer.

Thomas, J. (2016). *Mindful photography and its implications in end-of-life caregiving: An art-based phenomenology* (Doctoral dissertation). Sofia University, Palo Alto, CA.

Zakia, R. D. (2013). *Perception and imaging: Photography—a way of seeing*. Burlington, MA: Focal Press.

31
My House After Loss

An Hooghe, Nele Stinckens and Nils Van Uffelen

CLIENTS FOR WHOM THE TECHNIQUE IS APPROPRIATE

This exercise is appropriate for adults and youngsters who would benefit from a reflection on how their identity and interaction with others has changed after the loss of a loved one. Some ability to reflect with some distance is needed. Therefore, it might be less suitable shortly after a loss or for clients who find it hard to think in a metaphorical way. This reflection on self can be used in individual therapy (spread over multiple sessions) as well as in group therapy.

DESCRIPTION

After the death of a loved one or other major losses (e.g., illness, injury, separation, job loss), most mourners describe that they have fundamentally changed. The person before the loss is no longer the same as who they become after the loss. The way mourners are in relation to others could also change profoundly. In this reflective exercise, clients are asked to represent themselves metaphorically as a house since the loss of their loved one (Stinckens, 2010). The inside of the house symbolizes what they keep at home (furniture, etc.) and what "rooms" (aspects of the self) they include within them. Loss usually requires a redevelopment and reconstruction, changing the organization and arrangement of the "rooms." The outside of the house shows how they relate themselves to their environment. This exercise comprises three phases as follows.

1. *Guided Reflection*

The therapist invites client to focus their attention inward, to close their eyes and listen to what the therapist has to say. A brief meditation exercise, poem or song can precede this. The therapist tells the client that since the loss, he or she might have changed as a person, in terms of both what is inside (emotions, thoughts, priorities, sensitivities etc.) and what is outside, what other people notice (one's appearance, self-presentation etc.): "Imagine that you were a house, with an inside and an outside; what would this house look like?" Sometimes it is important to emphasize to clients that it is not about the house of their dreams or the house they live in now, but rather that the house is a metaphor to represent themselves as a person.

"Let's start with the outside: you as a person, symbolized as a house, in relation to your outside world." Calmly and slowly, the therapist gives some examples: "Maybe you experience

DOI: 10.4324/9781351069120-39

yourself as a chalet, an igloo, a castle, a farm, a glass house, a mansion, or a tree house." After some silent time, the therapist elaborates on four major aspects of the house (location, size, style and accessibility), with a number of questions or examples: "Do you experience yourself, for example, as a house standing by itself or, rather, as an apartment or as a rowhouse? Does your home stand in a quiet area: in the countryside, perhaps on a dead end street or in a forest? Or in the hustle and bustle of a city?" In between, the therapist repeats that the intent is to represent themselves, as a person, as a house and that the image does not have to be realistic: "It can also be a house on stilts in the center of the city or a glass house on the water." Then the therapist focuses on the size of the house: "Is your home a small house or maybe a little attic room or a big chic villa or apartment building?" The therapist leaves time for reflection and then goes on: "Possibly, there are images coming to your mind, or you might already have a detailed picture of yourself as a house. Now take some time to sit still with the style of your house. Does your house have a classic look, or is it modern architecture? Is your house round or rather square or made in different blocks? Maybe there is a difference between the front of the house and the back. Perhaps your house also has a garden house that is separate from it. Perhaps your house has a garden with flowers, trees or bushes? Are there striking details on the outside of your house?" Finally, the therapist focuses on the accessibility of the house: "Is your home close to the street or rather remote? Is there a fence around your house or maybe a secured door with a code? Is there a driveway to your house? Does your house have many or few windows that allow others to look inside? Are there several doors? Do you have a bell at the door or a knocker, or is the door always open?"

After a longer silence, the therapist switches to the inside of the house. "Is your house one big room (a loft or large room) or does it have different rooms? Are there different floors, maybe even an attic or basement? Are there any rooms or places in your home where you receive guests, or where you retreat or unwind? Are there any rooms in your house that you prefer not to be in or that are forbidden for others to access?" Next, the decor of the house is discussed: "See how your house is designed on the inside. What style does your house have? Are there many colors, or is there a dominant color? Is it rather minimalistic or with a lot of wood or rather a rough or metal surface? Is it cozy in your house? Maybe there is a fireplace. Is your home orderly and tidy or rather a mess or cluttered? Are there any plants or flowers in your house? Are there any pictures, paintings or mirrors? Are there any rooms that need to be redecorated or remodeled or perhaps empty?" Then the therapist focuses on the light intensity. "Is there a lot of light in your house, or is it rather dark? Is your home illuminated with fluorescent lamps or a rather warmer light?" Finally, the therapist focuses on other sensations, such as the smells that may be in the house—"The smell of food or fresh flowers or a stench that comes from somewhere"—and on possible sounds in the house: "Music that sounds in the house or in certain rooms, or a silence . . . maybe a soft or rather a loud silence."

2. Drawing the House

In the next phase, the client is invited to draw the house that has just been visualized. The therapist prepares several large sheets of paper and all kinds of drawing material (crayons, paints, and pens). Usually, the client chooses to create a separate drawing for the outside and the inside. Often the image is enriched with all sorts of details during the process of drawing.

3. Discussion of the Process and the Drawing

In dialogue with the therapist or with other group members, the client is invited to tell something about this self-exploration process. "How was it for you to start this exercise? Did a picture come straightaway, or did it take a while? Were you happy with the images that came? Were there things that surprised you?" The focus then shifts to the process of putting the visualization into a drawing. "How was it to draw this? Were there any changes or updates during drawing?" An important part of this exercise is that the therapist (and fellow clients) also share their impressions about the drawing with the client. In this way, the therapist can indicate what surprised him or her about the drawing and link that to themes that were already discussed in previous sessions. The added value of the exercise in a group context is especially visible in this phase, with reflections of others coming in the form of recognizing similar aspects in the client's description and their own (e.g., the change in accessibility of the house to the environment, the need for intimate rooms or the importance of home security). Finally, the recognition of resilient elements in the drawing or possible differences in perceptions of how someone is in a group and how this same person designed the outside of his or her house seem to be important therapeutic ingredients.

CASE ILLUSTRATION

Nils lost his 16-year-old daughter Charlotte seven years ago. Since her death, he has been through a process of intense self-reflection, part of which took place in a professionally led support group for bereaved parents with whom he completed the My House exercise. In the discussion of his drawing, he focused on how he has changed in the past years in relation to his environment. There was a changed access to his house, which can only be visited by people with authentic interest and time. In response to this contribution, we asked him to write a short text appropriate to his drawing.

Becoming Me

It was a long search. Seeking the criteria this spot had to meet. A place at the water—the house will reflect beautifully in it—the everlasting rippling will bring the sound of peace without monotony. The sun will bewitch it with stars. The spot is at a distance, but not too far away. Far enough from the confusing overloaded human world and at the same time close enough to pay a visit without too much effort. Via a path, a dead-end side road. This exit off the main road leads to a unique combination of nature's beauty. Warmth, colours and relief will surprise the visitors who want to explore purposefully. The path is only viable for those who want to take the time and want to discover what the promenade can offer.

The house is standing along this path. The house reflecting "me." Built on an open spot bounded on the water side. A hundred years old oak tree spreads its branches protectively over the house. Only this tree interrupts the view over the water and the landscape surrounding the house. An extensive thatched roof offers protection against too much sun or rain. Enjoyable to take shelter in when necessary. The rectangle roof is supported by four tree-trunks. Their age and strength emit safety and security. The house only has one wall, the other three sides are open. No windows or doors, attractive to visit. Looking in and looking out are in no way blocked. Under the roof is standing a big, long table, on high table legs, surrounded with many stools. The table invites visitors to eat together, to talk, to laugh, to drink, to meet each other. Seats around the open fire are waiting for readers or thinkers, staring at the flickering flames. The only wall is furnished with small frames in diverse materials and measures. The frames both invite memory and serve as inspiration. They show all significant quotes and mental images of guests to this house.

It is a house where each time renewal, surprising moments and new encounters take place. Those people passing by can discover the side path and enrich the building of the house. The oak offers relaxation and awareness.

About his experience with this exercise, for himself and in conversation with the other bereaved parents, Nils related the following:

> To my surprise, my image came on its own, spontaneous without much thought. As a result, the drawing exercise represents the power of the image, an image that lasts for a long time. An image is a thousand words. The interaction with the other parents was all the more impactful because they also call for imagination and thus create dialogue through another approach.
>
> I carry the image with me every day. It makes me more conscious about how I am in life. Open but selective towards other people, more conscious of what makes sense and is useful. A stark contrast to the former house, classical, as society wanted: house, garden, baby. . . . Thank you, Charlotte, for removing the walls and finding a better fit. You would find it a lot more fun.

CONCLUDING THOUGHTS

In working with the bereaved, we have experienced that My House can be a very powerful and profound reflective exercise. Through images, drawing and dialogue, one can form and give words to how one has changed since the loss, both in relation to oneself and in relation to the environment. The three different phases of the exercise appear to be important. The slow process of visualisation gives clients time to reflect on themselves and their interaction with the outside world. For many clients, the transition to the drawing makes it more detailed and tangible. The dialogue with the therapist or other bereaved clients helps anchor and deepen the self-exploration process and often is what is needed to share these experiences with others, like family members and friends.

As a extension of this exercise, the therapist can invite clients to reflect on how they want to change, rebuild, reshape or redecorate their house, on the inside or the outside. For example: "How would you like your house to look in five years? How would you like to make it stronger (again), or how would you like your access gate to be different, to have more control over your interaction with your family and friends?" The resulting metaphors often recur throughout therapy, giving clients a vocabulary for discussing their ongoing reconstruction of their lives following loss.

Reference

Stinckens, N. (2010). Wat heb ik in huis? In M. Gundrum & N. Stinckens (Eds.), *De Schatkist van de therapeut, Oefeningen en strategieën voor de praktijk* [The therapist's treasury: Exercises and strategies for practice]. Leuven, Belgium: Acco.

32
The Virgin Island

Geok Ling Lee

CLIENTS FOR WHOM THE TECHNIQUE IS APPROPRIATE

This experiential and imagery exercise may be useful for patients who have been recently diagnosed with life-limiting illnesses and their key family caregivers. The ultimate goal of the exercise is to harness resilience in patients and their families (alternatively known as clients here) so that they can continue to live with their loss or onset of the illness, their grief associated with the loss of health and their changed lives as a consequence. The technique could be used in an individual, marital or group context but may be less appropriate in the latter setting for clients who may not be ready for deep emotional exploration in the presence of others, or who might prefer only more limited therapist attention.

DESCRIPTION

Many patients with advanced cancer and their families express shock, denial, sadness and even anger when they are given the bad news of their diagnosis. These emotional expressions are manifestations of their grief over the loss of health and other impending losses, ultimately including death. In an Asian context, Chinese clients tend to report psychosomatic symptoms (e.g., fatigue and sleeplessness) rather than depression. Families tend to revert to their usual coping strategies and styles, which might be maladaptive, with the aim of achieving equilibrium within self and within the family.

The classic transactional model of stress and coping by Lazarus and Folkman (1984) introduced the concepts of emotion-focused and problem-focused coping strategies for adapting to a significant life stressor such as a life-limiting illness. Folkman (1997) added the concept of meaning-focused coping efforts, with subsequent literature discussing the role of meaning making and meaning reconstruction as coping methods to deal with loss and grief (Gillies & Neimeyer, 2006; Neimeyer, 2016). In addition, the concept of relationship-focused coping efforts sheds light on what types of strategies are used to manage a relationship during a stressful period (O'Brien & DeLongis, 1996). This is particularly true in an Asian context, where secrecy within the family may not be an uncommon strategy used to manage the grief accompanying the onset of a life-limiting illness. In short, the various theoretical models make clear that there is more than one way of coping with loss and grief, and accordingly, therapists need to understand the dominant coping style, personality and beliefs that shape their clients' grief work.

DOI: 10.4324/9781351069120-40

The Virgin Island provides an experiential exercise for clients to work through their current "mood" terrains as they elaborate on their coping preferences after hearing a short, unexpected scenario. Obstacles are introduced to them as they share about their coping efforts to ascertain their strength, perseverance and creativity in resolving difficulties. At times, efforts may be needed to enable the clients to consider and expand their repertoire of coping strategies in a way that is more appropriate for their current predicament.

A typical session starts with the therapist reading a synopsis such as the following passage:

Seawater is seeping into your small vessel as your boatman rows close to the shore of an island. He has asked you to wade through the shallow waters toward this Virgin Island while he rows away to get help to mend his boat. There is no other sign of life or other islands within sight. There is also no satellite reception around the area for any form of telecommunication. Getting help is uncertain, but your boatman must find help so that the two of you are not stranded at sea or on this island. All you have with you is a backpack with a knife, a change of clothes, a medicine box with some pain reliever and diarrhea tablets and bandages. Your boatman also gave you his spare flashlight. Should he arrive at the island after sunset, he will flash his light to guide you to his boat.

The therapist then asks the clients to briefly check within themselves, then with their family or their group members, about their mood before they each proceed separately to describe and draw the Virgin Island as they imagine it to be on a sheet of paper using oil pastel crayons. Following this, the therapist asks questions to help the clients explore what they will do on the island to pass time while waiting for the boatman to return. Barriers are also introduced to the clients by asking, for example: (1) What if you are hungry and you need to find food on the island? (2) What if you suddenly fall into a pit as deep as your height? (3) What if you get lost and find yourself going in circles to the same spot? (4) What if the boatman never returns to pick you up?

Clients' accounts of their imagined experiences could, of course, feature multiple variations, but in each case, it is important for the therapist to identify the coping styles that need to be affirmed, addressed, maintained, enhanced or changed. There may also be a need to address clients' values and beliefs about what they can or cannot do, their existence and meaning of life, their sense of control and confidence in themselves. As the session continues, clients may be able to associate their experience on the island with their experience with cancer and the boatman with their physician. The therapist will then explore with the clients key lessons and how they can transfer what they have learned from the exercise to how they intend to continue living with life-limiting illness. The session usually ends with the recognition that living with cancer is a journey with no one standard map and that it is necessary for them to map their own unique journey.

CASE ILLUSTRATION

Jenny and John, aged 40 and 43, respectively, participated in a group session during an annual three-day residential retreat for patients living with cancer and their family caregivers. They have two children, aged 10 and 12 years old. John was recently diagnosed with advanced lung cancer, and the prognosis was bleak. Jenny had been suffering from depression since John's diagnosis, and she had refused to let John out of her sight for a single minute since that time.

In the session, John drew the Virgin Island in great detail, rich with color and content. In his picture, the island was full of resources such as a river, fish, coconut trees and a thick forest. John indicated that he would love to go on an adventurous exploration of the island, given that he was "freed" from the responsibility of the family. Even if there were dangerous animals in the dense forest, he would prepare himself with a hand-made spear and was ready for battle. Working on her own at the same time, Jenny drew the Virgin Island in a grayish tone. There was a beach on the left, front bottom and a cliff on the far right, top corner. Jenny mentioned that she would not have traveled with the boatman without her family, especially her husband. When Jenny was asked to describe more about what she would do on the island without her husband, Jenny had great difficulty imagining what to do without having John around, and she could not see herself living without him. She further added that John was always her lifeline, and he would protect her from hunger and danger. Upon hearing what Jenny said, John hesitated and then agreed that he would stay with her on the beach and venture only a short distance to find food and water for Jenny. When questioned about his furrowed brow and the hesitation, John responded that he felt a heavy burden on his shoulders and wondered when he could be "freed." The therapist then asked how they felt about their contrasting views of the scenario and coping strategies—how John would love to venture around and look for opportunities and resources, while Jenny would only remain on the beach, when paradise could lie just behind the bushes. This was when John responded that he could sense Jenny's anxiety and fear over losing him to cancer, but he also felt the fear of failing her as he could not change his current situation and mode of operating in life.

I then asked Jenny the sense she made of John's sharing and challenged the couple to consider what needed to happen so that they could break free of their usual patterns or even reverse roles. Jenny replied that she was aware of the burden she placed on her husband who was sick but, at the same time, acknowledged that it was a comfortable and familiar role for her. I concurred and emphasized to Jenny and John that change was never easy, and the decision to shift resided in them. I also highlighted the importance of identifying, respecting and accepting their differences in views and coping efforts as individuals and as a couple. I then ended the session by inviting them to reflect on how they would want to map and continue their unique journey with cancer, remembering their respective positions as depicted in the exercise.

CONCLUDING THOUGHTS

Living well in the face of impending death is hard work for both patients and their family members. Yet it is necessary to live well so that both the patients and the family can maintain some quality of life while living with an illness so that the negative impact of the loss can be reduced and the subsequent grief can be better managed by the bereaved. It is essential for a therapist to work with clients to help them achieve a new equilibrium, cope with the loss constructively and manage their grieving process. The Virgin Island, as an experiential and imagery exercise, is useful for clients who have difficulties getting in touch with the personal aspects of their loss and grief. This technique is also useful for marital work in which differences between partners can be explored, understood and appreciated. However, therapists must be cautious in a group-work setting that clients are not coerced into working on the emotional aspects of grief when they are not ready, especially given the public context of the work and the difficulty devoting close attention to all participants.

References

Folkman, S. (1997). Positive psychological states and coping with severe stress. *Social Science and Medicine, 45*, 1207–1221.

Gillies, J., & Neimeyer, R. A. (2006). Loss, grief and the search for significance: Toward a model of meaning reconstruction in bereavement. *Journal of Constructivist Psychology, 19*, 31–65.

Lazarus, R. S., & Folkman, S. (1984). *Stress, appraisal and coping.* New York: Springer.

Neimeyer, R. A. (2016). Meaning reconstruction in the wake of loss: Evolution of a research program. *Behaviour Change, 33*, 65–79. doi:10.1017/bec.2016.4

O'Brien, T. B., & DeLongis, A. (1996). The interactional context of problem-, emotion-, and relationship-focused coping: The role of the big five personality factors. *Journal of Personality, 64*, 775–813.

33

The Gate of My Heart

Riet Fiddelaers-Jaspers

CLIENTS FOR WHOM THE TECHNIQUE IS APPROPRIATE

Adolescents and adults who are dealing with surviving a loss, especially of a traumatic sort, can benefit from this technique, which uses the therapist's personal storytelling and recursive questions to prime clients' attention to how they manage their pain. It is especially useful for young people seeking to make themselves invisible and unapproachable as they avoid everything that might touch their pain and loss. However, it could be inappropriate for clients with a recent loss, not yet capable of reflecting.

DESCRIPTION

I use telling a personal story to gently encourage clients to self-reflect on their own lives and losses. The story, which might be entitled "The Gate to My Heart," is the story of my mother and me, but of course other therapists should modify it in a way that touches on their personal lives as therapists. If you don't recognize the "gate," the story doesn't work. Maybe your "gate" looks like a zipper, a glass wall, a brick wall, a blanket or a glass dome. Maybe your father was the one you've missed, rather than your mother. Just make it your own story to communicate authentically and to invite a (reticent) client to do the same.

After modifying the story to make it your own, read it aloud. Just wait some seconds after finishing the reading before you ask any questions, to give clients an opportunity to take it in. In a group, you can ask who recognizes some things in the story. In couples therapy, each person can share and tell each other what their "gate" looks like. In an individual session, you can talk this over with your client.

After this, give instructions to do the Buddha exercise described later in this chapter, and take time to allow it to have an impact. Rushing through it will guarantee that nothing useful will happen. The attention and the silence are very important.

Step 1: Telling the Story: "The Gate to My Heart"

My heart is the gateway to the world. I can open the gate and I can close it. That is my choice to make.

DOI: 10.4324/9781351069120-41

I came into the world with my heart open to make contact with others, completely vulnerable. My mother held me in her arms, cherished me and I gave her the greatest gift I had to give at that moment: my smile. I started to bond with her and with others I met during my life.

I let people into my heart. And I quickly learned that sometimes I needed to close my heart for a while so as to protect myself. I also discovered that I could be hurt in my intimate contacts and I learned to take that risk by falling down and getting back up.

As a child I reached out to others and often there was no response. That hurt, very much. I decided to oil the hinges of my gate so well that the gate could be closed within a fraction of a second and no one would be let in. Letting others in meant there was a chance that I would be hurt once again, abandoned once again. I started to protect myself from such hurt. And so my heart became a fortress. I wouldn't let anybody come closer; the gate closed at the slightest hint of possible pain. I did not realize how quickly the gate closed, how I made myself invulnerable so as not to feel the pain. This became normal to me. By doing it this way, I was denying myself the genuine encounters that make life worth living. Slowly I came to realize that I will only be able to live my life to its fullest, if I open my heart to all the experiences and dare to take that risk. I needed help from others to ensure that my gate could once again be opened. In the beginning, the gate was only slightly ajar, but as time passed it opened further and further. Sometimes it groans and squeaks a lot, but there are people who help me oil the hinges. That leaves the choice up to me: open or closed. To live life to its fullest, well-oiled hinges are needed. I do not close my heart so often any more. I opened the gate to let life and others in. Not always, just time and again.

(Fiddelaers-Jaspers, 2015)

Step 2: Time for Exploration

Before starting the inquiry, ask what the "gate" of the client looks like. It might be a different metaphor than the hinged door used in my story.

The therapist asks the questions, and the clients take time to answer, not with a long story, just the words that come up. The therapist listens very carefully, like a Buddha, and gives clients some time to search inside themselves for the answer, rather than coaching them for particular responses, after which the therapist moves on to the next question. The cycle of the following questions is repeated three times, just the same questions again and again.

- When does your gate close?
- Why might it be good to close the gate?
- Why might it be good to open the gate?
- In what way has your gate helped you in your life?

After the cycle of asking the four questions three times, you might ask in what way the gate is influencing the client's contact with you or others in the group at this moment.

Alternatively, in a group setting, the therapist can pair clients, having each ask the cycle of questions three times and then reverse roles.

Using this technique, people are touched by the metaphor of the gate. They share their metaphors: "My gate is a giant zipper that opens and closes very quickly"; "My gate looks more like a fence with bars"; " I live under a kind of glass dome most of the time"; "My gate is a one-way screen." Sometimes people share that their gate is not closing; it's always open. Then it is time to talk about the importance of being able to close the gate because it is exhausting if everyone and everything may come in. Oiling the hinges is important so you can decide yourself if the gate has to open or to close.

CASE ILLUSTRATION

Mary, a 50-year-old teacher, came because she couldn't bear her own survival strategies anymore. She had a bad relationship with her mother, and her father, whom she adored, worked hard and was almost never at home. Mary lost her mother when she was 15 without saying goodbye. She couldn't cope, and her father was not able to be there for her. Mary never had a relationship or friends and lived for her students, becoming a marvelous teacher. She knew intuitively which student needed help. And now, for the first time in her life, there was a colleague, Sarah, who cared for her. Sarah told her to seek some professional support so she can open up more to develop more trust in people.

In one of the sessions, the therapist read the story "The Gate of My Heart" aloud. Mary was very touched by the story. She recognized the big, thick door that was closed most of the time. Then the therapist began working with the questions.

THERAPIST: *When does your gate close?*
MARY: *It's closed all the time!*
T: *Why might it be good to close the gate?*
M: *Because no one can be trusted.*
T: *Why might it be good to open the gate?*
M: *I don't think this is good; I like to have it closed.*
T: *In what way your gate has helped you in your life?*
M: *It helped me a lot. It protected me against the world.*
T: *Very good, Mary. Let's do it another time.*
SHE STARTED THE SET OF QUESTIONS AGAIN.
T: *When does your gate close?*
M: *It's closed most of the time. Only when I work with my students the gate is open. . . . And, of course, when I'm in contact with Sarah.*
T: *Why might it be good to close the gate?*
M: *To protect myself. And maybe to feel safe.*
T: *Why might it be good to open the gate?*
M: *To let some people in, people like Sarah and most of my students. I love them!*
T: *In what way your gate has helped you in your life?*
M: *It helped me survive in the situation as a child and a teenager when I did not feel the love of my mother. I missed my father, I felt guilty when my mother died, and I was all alone. I did not know how to cope.*

After this the therapist asked the same questions again, and Mary's answers suggested there might have been another shift.

After this exercise, the therapist reflected with the client. What was her experience? What happened inside? What was helpful in the exercise?

Afterward, the therapist might ask, "What was the first moment you remember when you decided to close the gate? What happened?" The therapist talks about painful moments in life when it is necessary to find a way to survive. People tell about being neglected, not been seen as a child, never being permitted to be a child, losing someone they loved, a divorce, an illness and so on. In Mary's case, she had felt all alone her whole life and couldn't remember feeling cherished, protected or bonded with her mother. And how she loved her father, was looking out for him. When he came home, she would run toward him, telling him as much as she could in between his car and the front door. That was her moment with her father. Mary still talks very fast.

Then the therapist talks about how the client survived and how important that was to keep them from going crazy. They survived by being the strongest, acting like a clown, being the smartest, always helping others, withdrawing from contact, always being kind or working very hard. Mary became a very reticent person, working as hard as she could for her students, helping them in every way possible. And she drank a lot to dim the pain inside. After some sessions, Mary could see how she had acted in the past and why this was necessary. It was the first step in changing her behavior by looking at her hidden pain.

CONCLUDING THOUGHTS

The story "The Gate of my Heart," followed by the inquiry, is a potent and effective exercise to empower grieving clients and deepen their self-exploration of survival strategies they are using. For the therapist (or partner in group work), it is an exercise in accurate listening, using the silent moments with the conviction the client can make productive use of these. In this, the therapist makes a critical difference by being a witness to the process of the client, using his or her body (breath, tension of the muscles, eye contact, expression) to hold a metaphorical mirror to the client's introspection. This helps clients examine their survival strategies and why they do what they are doing: to cover the unbearable pain of a deep loss. This can then be the first step toward change, as the client attends to the loss and begins to endure the pain.

References

Fiddelaers-Jaspers, R. (2018). *De poort van mijn hart* (The gate of my heart: surviving and coming alive again in 33 poems). Heeze: In de Wolken.

Fiddelaers-Jaspers, R. (2019). *Met mijn ziel onder de arm* (Wandering with a wounded heart; Between welcoming and saying goodbye). Heeze: In de Wolken.

Part IX
Revising Personal Meaning

34

Recomposing the Self in the Wake of Loss

Agnieszka Konopka and Robert A. Neimeyer

CLIENTS FOR WHOM THE TECHNIQUE IS APPROPRIATE

This method is especially relevant for clients who feel lost in the complexity of a difficult transition and are in need of creating a map of the "landscape of loss" to have an overview, see connections between involved elements and explore new directions of change. It is appropriate for people who need to recognize and validate varied aspects of themselves affected by loss and access potential new sources of meaning in order to reconstruct their identity. It is also useful for cases in which as yet unverbalized or unspeakable aspects of experience need attention. For clients who are overwhelmed by emotions, composition work can enhance emotion regulation, helping create a working distance from tumultuous feelings. However, it can be inappropriate for clients overregulating their emotions, for whom externalization provokes further detachment, unless a therapist is able to facilitate the directly felt embodied experience in such cases.

DESCRIPTION

Though people often strive for unity, the self is a multiple entity, consisting of many often significantly different self-aspects, called *I-positions*, as has been elaborated in the model of dialogical self theory (Hermans, 2018; Hermans & Hermans-Konopka, 2010). According to this theory, not only different self-aspects as internal positions (e.g., I as anxious, I as professional) but also significant others as external positions (e.g., my mother, an imagined hero) are part of the society of mind and can entertain more or less dialogical relations. The experience of bereavement and transition can challenge and change a variety of I-positions and their organization (Neimeyer & Konopka, 2019), sometimes significantly rendering such relations between these aspects problematic (e.g., as when one part of the self rejects another needy or vulnerable part or when a mother blames herself for her child's death). On the other hand, people may potentially respond to a loss from a broad range of I-positions. While answering from a single habitual or rigid position can limit or block the process of self-reconstruction, looking at such experience from different positions can open unexpected possibilities for recomposing one's self and life in a new, meaningful way. As practitioners, we may need to stimulate the accessibility, differentiation and integration of a broad range of I-positions to facilitate the process of recomposing one's self and finding new meaning.

DOI: 10.4324/9781351069120-43

Composition work (Konopka & van Beers, 2019; Konopka, Neimeyer, & Jacob Lenz, 2017) stimulates these processes by symbolizing, externalizing, voicing and composing a variety of self-aspects in the form of a small landscape made of stones or other natural materials placed on a large sheet of paper or in a box with sand. Used in a grief therapy context, this symbolic landscape represents a multi-logical, dynamic field of loss, reflecting the qualities of separate elements, their differences, their relations and the overall pattern. A composition allows one to explore separate elements in the context of a broader self-organization. It supports exploring new configurations by shifting different positions or including new ones and checking the affective resonance of such changes. Introducing nonverbal, figurative elements can be helpful for attending to preverbal, bodily sensed meanings, reflecting implicit I-positions that can be important sources of innovation and adaptation.

The practice of composition work includes the following general steps, which can be introduced in a flexible way and can include various more specific interventions:

1. *Defining and Symbolizing I-Positions*

This process usually begins with defining a broad spectrum of relevant self-aspects and representing them by stones. After explaining and giving examples of such self and other aspects (e.g., I as mother, I as a lover, my child), the therapist invites the client to identify and symbolize with stones all relevant I-positions that have been affected in some fashion by a loss. Even a brief discussion of why a particular stone was chosen to represent a particular I-position (selecting a tiny white stone to represent hope or a jagged, sharp-edged stone to represent oneself as warrior) can be revealing, and help clients name and claim aspects of themselves that otherwise go unrecognized.

2. *Composing All Elements*

When a client has selected symbols of each position, he or she is invited to make a composition, placing them on a large sheet of paper or in a box of sand in a way that reflects their relations. For example, physical closeness of the symbols could represent psychological closeness of different aspects or placing one above the other on the page could represent dominance of one over another. Clients may also draw lines on the paper or in the sand to represent walls, bridges, conflicts or lines of influence or label the various elements.

3. *Exploring the Composition*

Once a composition is made, the therapist facilitates its exploration by asking additional questions related to: (a) separate positions (e.g., *Are there positions that are broken, isolated by the loss of . . . ? Are there positions that are liberated, enhanced? Which parts are potential sources of wisdom or support?*); (b) relations between positions (e.g., *Are there any conflicts between positions?*); and (c) voicing positions and their relations (e.g., *Which position needs to be heard now?*).

During the process, a therapist optimally bridges exploration with direct affective experience (e.g., *When you place this part here, how does that feel?*) and notes perceived micro-acts, like the way of holding a stone (e.g., *I noticed that you stroked that stone, almost caressing it. How does that feel?*) or shifts in expressions (e.g., *I see your face nearly freezing now*).

4. *Making a Shift*

When a composition is explored, it may be relevant to facilitate a possible shift by asking questions related to a preferred direction of change (e.g., *What change would be needed in the composition to rebalance it or make it feel better in some way?*). A person can change the position of some parts of the composition and check the affective resonance of such a shift. A feeling of relief is an important signal of a needed change.

5. *Learning, Actions and Further Processing*

At the end of a session, the therapist may focus the client's attention on learning (e.g., *What did you learn from your composition?*), practical actions (e.g., *What practical steps would be required to rebalance your composition in the way you depicted it?*) and possible further processing in the form of journaling (e.g., *Write a dialogue between two I-positions, before and after the shift*).

CASE ILLUSTRATION

Gene sought counseling following the loss of his job in a corporate reorganization several months before. During a composition work session (Figure 34.1), he depicted several different positions involved in the transition and composed them. Loss of his job broke his positions "I as successful" and "I as partner," isolating them from other figures such as "My partner" and "My children" and resulting in harsh self-criticism. The brokenness and isolation of Gene's "Successful" and "Partner" positions were reflected in a bodily felt feeling of weakness and heavy loneliness, emerging when he held the stones representing them in his hands. However, he noticed that at the moment his "Playful child" position needed the most attention and he was invited to hold the stone in his hands, he had an impulse to throw it away. Exploration of this impulse resulted in discovery of a voice that said, "Go away from here. Don't be so soft and needy. You have serious things to do in life," which he connected to the position of his father, which he represented by a heavy, dark stone. Asked to show their relation through the stones, he placed the father on top of the playful one. In doing so, he experienced an overburdening heaviness in his chest and expressed

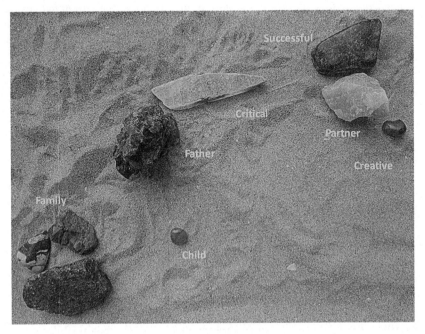

Figure 34.1 Gene's Initial Composition of I-Positions Following the Loss of His Corporate Career

Figure 34.2 Gene's Reconfigured Composition, Giving a More Central Place to His Child Position, with Greater Distance from Paternal and Critical Voices

in the voice of the playful child, "Your pressure suffocates me, I cannot breathe. I have no space here." Hearing these words and seeing the composition from the perspective of the playful child, Gene felt intense tiredness and grief and began to weep openly for the first time. As he allowed his tears to flow, he softly, compassionately cradled the small stone representing the child in his hands. As he drew the stone closer to his chest, he felt a growing warmth around his heart. Voicing the symbolic act by saying, "There is a place in my heart for you" prompted Gene to make a shift in the composition (Figure 34.2), in which he gave a more central role to the child while keeping his father and the self-critical voices at a distance. As he did so, he sighed, saying "I can breathe now." Concluding the session, Gene planned to make a small step toward this shift by writing a letter and perhaps even talking to his father from his child and compassionate side and seeking a career more in keeping with his previously marginalized playfulness and creativity.

CONCLUDING THOUGHTS

Voicing different externalized positions allows one to hear some of these voices for the first time and, in this way, to validate that which was previously not validated. Accessing, validating and expressing neglected parts silently and invisibly involved in loss may help access unmet needs. Inviting into the dialogue those positions that are supportive resources can be empowering as the client expresses acceptance or understanding from external figures living or dead, accesses the wisdom of another aspect of the self or physically shifts the stones into different, more balanced configurations.

Differentiating the terrain of loss by specifying the various internal and external I-positions involved enhances awareness of what precisely was lost and, paradoxically, also of what was gained through the experience. It is often revealing for clients to see which parts of a composition were diminished, broken or forgotten and which were potentially liberated or enhanced, which may result in their acknowledging the ambivalent and complex meaning of loss, whether this arises through the death of a significant other, the demise of an important relationship, the erosion of health or the sudden dismissal from an identity-defining career.

The landscape of loss and transition is like the famous Japanese garden *Ryoan-yin*, which can be viewed from many angles. Viewing it from one singular point allows you to see only some stones and only from one side. It is impossible to see all stones from one perspective while standing on the ground. When a beholder looks from another viewing point, he or she suddenly discovers a new picture. We use composition work, the three-dimensional representation of the inner landscape of self, to allow a client to view the loss and transition from different angles, literally rotating the composition on a tabletop to reveal different aspects and experience their associated meanings. For example, one client, Will, who had lost an adult son to suicide four years before, had thrown himself into his work in the aftermath of the tragedy as a means of coping. Viewing his composition from table level, however, from the standpoint of the stone reflecting his I-position as a salesman, Will recognized with a sense of shock that he was unable to see the small stone representing his son, which was relegated to the far periphery of the composition and obscured by other stones, and felt a powerful surge of guilt and longing. Invited to rearrange the configuration to reflect a more satisfactory arrangement, he brought in a previously distant metal orb representing God, granted a central place to a heart stone, and arranged his dead son, current wife, her children and his own previous cut off and mysterious creative self into a close constellation around this loving and spiritually informed core.

Alternatively, clients can be encouraged to take a meta-position, a "helicopter view" of the composition from above, to see juxtaposed positions and to become more aware of their relations and new meaning bridges. We literally invite clients to look at their compositions from these ground-level and meta-level perspectives, taking photos from the various reference points and describing them. Such practices can liberate clients from a limited or habitual perspective, offer possibilities of finding new meanings and directions, help articulate what was previously unarticulated, differentiate otherwise vague and homogeneous fields of experience and in this way support the process of recomposing one's self in the wake of loss.

References

Hermans, H. J. M. (2018). *Society in the self: A theory of identity in democracy*. New York: Oxford University Press.

Hermans, H. J. M., & Hermans-Konopka, A. (2010). *Dialogical self theory: Positioning and counter positioning in a globalizing society*. Cambridge, UK: Cambridge University Press.

Konopka, A., Neimeyer, R. A., & Jacobs-Lenz, J. (2017). Composing the self: Toward the dialogical reconstruction of self-identity. *Journal of Constructivist Psychology*. doi:10.1080/10720537.2017.1350609

Konopka, A., & van Beers, W. (2019). Compositionwork: Working with dialogical self in psychotherapy. In A. Konopka, H. J. M. Hermans, & M. M. Gonçalves (Eds.), *Handbook of dialogical self theory and psychotherapy: Bridging psychotherapeutic and cultural traditions*. London: Routledge.

Neimeyer, R. A., & Konopka, A. (2019). The dialogical self in grief therapy: Reconstructing identity in the wake of loss. In A. Konopka, H. J. M. Hermans, & M. M. Gonçalves (Eds.), *Handbook of dialogical self theory and psychotherapy: Bridging psychotherapeutic and cultural traditions*. London: Routledge.

35

Memory Reconsolidation

Jakob van Wielink, Leo Wilhelm
and Denise van Geelen-Merks

CLIENTS FOR WHOM THE TECHNIQUE IS APPROPRIATE

This technique is appropriate for practically all clients suffering prolonged and painful grief. However, for clients in the recent aftermath of a traumatic loss, suffering too great a distress directly re-envisioning past experiences, this technique may be contraindicated. Clients contending with normative symptoms of grief without indication of ingrained self-limiting patterns of belief or behavior may benefit less from this technique.

DESCRIPTION

A loss in the present can (subconsciously) trigger memories of previous losses, ranging from concrete losses, such as the death of a parent or a move from a family home, to more nebulous losses, such as the loss of a secure childhood or a reliable parent. Working with such memories can be facilitated by first identifying significant points of transition using a lifeline procedure and then directly evoking and modifying them using memory reconsolidation. Here we describe the two main phases of this process.

Lifeline. Creating a timeline of clients' lives can provide them with insight into such events (Wielink, Wilhelm, & van Geelen-Merks, 2020). These can include moments and periods of loss and failure but also moments of joy and success. These kinds of moments are known as transitional moments: i.e., moments that caused the client's life to take a particular turn. Placing significant transitions on a timeline, clients can use plusses and minuses to indicate their negative and positive impact on their lives. This puts the event story of the loss itself as well as the back story of someone's life context (Neimeyer, 2019) in a bigger context, potentially opening it to different meanings.

This lifeline can then be elaborated by indicating the relative intensity of each impactful event. The positive and negative events are marked above and below the time axis, respectively, at distances that indicate their relative intensity. The various highs and lows indicate the differences between how impactful the client felt the events to be. The various events are then connected by a line indicating when they happened, creating a kind of landscape with highs and lows and steep declines and inclines.

The lifeline provides insight into events that had an impact on the client. Each impactful experience leaves behind an imprint, registered in a physical reaction, intensity of emotion, shortness of breath, anxiety, physical pain or even a particular emotion being shut down, all of which are stored in memory with the experience. In other words, each time the client goes

DOI: 10.4324/9781351069120-44

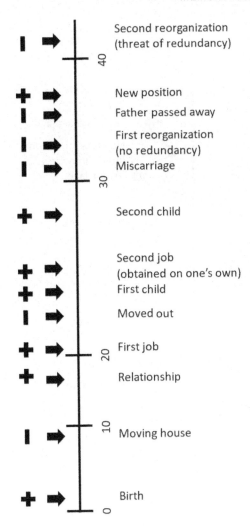

Figure 35.1 Lifeline Featuring Impactful Events on Both a Personal and a Professional Level

through a similar experience, the same emotional and physical responses can be brought back up. As a result, a certain deep-seated conviction can be formed, a certain perspective, cognitively as well as physically and emotionally. For example, a client may have a (subconscious) belief that the act of saying goodbye is frightening because he was once caught off guard by the intensity of his mother's grief when his grandmother died. When an impending goodbye approaches, this client may begin to sweat, start to feel uneasy and want to get away as quickly as possible. A wide range of such beliefs and associated behaviors can arise in the context of loss or threat of loss, persisting long beyond the lives of the significant figures implicated in the construction of the client's original reactions.

Memory Reconsolidation

The technique of memory reconsolidation can help replace these kinds of limiting imprints with beneficial experiences. As it turns out, the neural areas in which the consolidated memories have been recorded can be overwritten (Ecker, Ticic, & Hulley, 2012). For a long time,

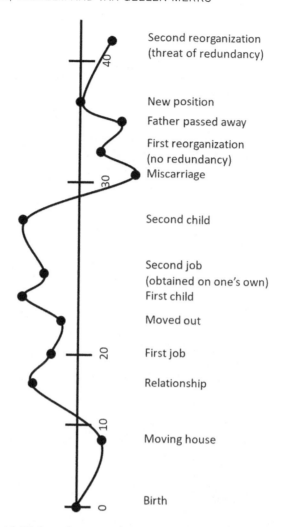

Figure 35.2 Lifeline with Highs and Lows

scientists thought that the brain's neuroplasticity only applied to making new neural pathways and thus storing new memories and learning new behaviors. As a result, therapy had to involve making clients sufficiently aware of the beneficial new behavior and repeating it often enough so as to make it stronger than the old subconscious patterns. However, it turns out that the neural pathways of these old experiences in someone's subconscious can be reopened; the imprint attached to the memory, which has limiting effects in the present, can then be modified or overwritten with a beneficial experience, after which the memory can be reconsolidated.

Ecker, Ticic and Hulley describe a three-step approach and a validation step to achieve this:

1. Reactivate the imprint by putting the client in a similar situation as during the initial experience to activate the relevant neural area.
2. Challenge the imprint by confronting it with a contrasting experience, which contradicts the client's initial expectation. This opens the synapses of the neural area and

enables that area of the brain to absorb new information as a modification of the old information.

3. Delete or overwrite the old imprint by providing a new experience that contradicts the old expectation (this can be done by simply repeating the experience used in step 2). According to the research, the neural pathway remains open to new information for about five hours after step 2, before it closes back up and reconsolidates.

The validation step is as follows: after the three steps are completed, the client is fed the same triggers as in step 1, to determine whether the reactions and symptoms that the old imprint would have triggered have, in fact, disappeared.

The three steps of memory consolidation can only be used if the client is first made aware of the limiting imprint and of a contradictory positive experience that can be used to disprove the limiting experience because the two are irreconcilable at a conscious level. Using the experiences on the lifeline, the following steps can be helpful in ensuring such awareness:

1. *Identifying the symptom.* What does the client experience exactly, and when does it occur?
2. *Unlocking/retrieving the previous experience.* What limiting imprint lies at the heart of the symptom?
3. *Identifying a contradictory experience.* Apart from the subconsciously established imprint with its limiting effect, which causes the client's symptoms, the client also has examples and experiences that prove the contrary. These often date from much later and have been recorded in the conscious brain but not in the subconscious brain. As a result, the availability of the disproving experience merely at a conscious level is not sufficient.

If the disproving experience and limiting imprint can be unlocked in the client's consciousness at the same time during their emotional reliving of the initial experience, memory reconsolidation will take place; the initial imprint will be overwritten with the new, positively impacting experience.

CASE STUDY

Irene's mother had passed away over a year ago, and she missed her terribly. She had been sleeping poorly, and things had not been going well at work; she had always been bad at saying no to assignments, but now, her issues with staying focused were preventing her from getting anything done. And yet Irene felt unable to tell her supervisor that she wanted to refuse or relinquish work. After all, who would do it if she did not? Everyone was busy; no one had room for more work. And if the work she would normally do didn't get done, she would feel terrible about that.

Irene's lifeline quickly revealed that she had a lot of responsibility in her own family from an early age. She had two younger brothers, and her mother was ill, so she ended up managing the household. She was never shown any appreciation for that. She herself feels that it was obvious for her to do so because who else was supposed to do it? Although Irene always tried to do her best, her mother was hard to please. She was always criticized, and the criticism was expressed by her mother being disappointed in her. This disappointment was something that Irene had no way of getting away from because refusing to help would have meant risking her mother's rejection.

The therapist asked Irene to finish the following sentence: "I must not say 'no' to people, because if I do . . ." "I would be disappointing my mother," she finished. She was visibly affected by this; her hands, which at first had rested comfortably in her lap, were now uneasily clasped together. She used a tissue to dab at her tears, sighing audibly. The therapist and Irene then formulated a sentence together to put on a card for her to read to herself several times a day, every day, between therapy sessions. This is the final sentence they settled on: "I must always please everyone because I must not disappoint them, just like how I must not disappoint my mother." This enabled Irene to become conscious of her subconscious imprint, thus completing steps 1 and 2 of the preparatory process.

In the next session, the therapist asked Irene how it had gone, reading the sentence on the card every day. "Very confronting," she admitted. "I now realize that I am incapable of setting boundaries . . . especially with people who somehow remind me of my mother." She then offered a story of her own accord: a male co-worker had asked her to take on some of his work, and though it took a few moments for her to get the words out, she had simply said no. The co-worker had accepted her refusal and said, "Fair enough, you're busy too." This situation served as step 3, meaning that the therapist could now initiate steps 1 through 3 of the memory consolidation process.

The therapist asked Irene to think back on a situation at work in which she felt incapable of saying no to her supervisor even though she wanted to, to imagine that situation vividly and to let the corresponding feelings in. This is step 1. The reactivation of this emotional memory was taken further by the therapist asking, "How old do you feel in this situation? Can you go back to a similar situation in your childhood that reminds you of this one?" This immediately triggered a reaction in Irene, who first sobbed restrainedly and then let her tears flow freely. The therapist reaffirmed the original imprint: "You must not say no because, if you do, you would be disappointing your mother." Reliving this experience opened the neural pathway for the original experience and formed the basis for the memory consolidation process.

The therapist then initiated step 2, by bringing up the disproving experience that the client had recently: "Now imagine your co-worker coming up to you, asking you if you would take on some of his work. Take a deep breath and say no." By presenting both of these contradictory experiences, which cannot both be true, to the client's conscious mind at the same time, the synapses of the relevant neural area were opened up, resulting in a time window of around five hours during which the original experience could be overwritten.

The therapist refrained from passing judgment on the various positions. It was up to the client to decide whether to actually overwrite the old imprint with the new, positive experience. In short, clients are the ones who carry out step 3 by themselves. Their therapists can aid them by repeating the contradictory positions, wording them differently every time, and thus inviting the client to keep experiencing the kinds of emotions these different positions trigger. This way, the client ends the overwriting process and, with it, step 3.

In this case, Irene sighed deeply, relaxed into her chair, sobbed one more time; then she blew her nose and sat up. "Yes," she said, and she was quiet for a bit. "Yes," she repeated, and a smile appeared. Letting this new experience in made it easier for her to say no. She was better able to stand up for her own needs at work, refuse work and find a new balance.

CONCLUDING THOUGHTS

Mental suffering that is being caused by a painful emotional imprint can be relieved via memory consolidation. However, if multiple imprints lie at the heart of the mental suffering, each imprint has to be treated separately.

In determining imprints, the limiting experiences behind them and suitable disproving experiences, it is important for the therapist not to pass judgment on the desirability of any one of the positions. The process is not about challenging limiting convictions at a cognitive level. The therapist's role is to support and stimulate, enabling contradictory experiences to be unlocked within the client's consciousness at the same time. Only then will clients be able to initiate memory reconsolidation themselves, overwriting the original experience. There are various methods for doing so; the one described here is only one of many. Various techniques from Gestalt to neurolinguistic programming (NLP) to systemic and many other methods can be used.

It is important to realize that the original imprint, though it has since become limiting, was initially intended to protect the client from worse damage. Consequently, it has served an important and positive purpose in their survival. Every symptom the client describes always turns out to be less bad than what would have happened to them had no such survival behavior been created, such as the rejection by a central attachment figure in Irene's case.

References

Ecker, B., Ticic, R., & Hulley, L. (2012). *Unlocking the emotional brain*. New York: Routledge.

Neimeyer, R. A. (2019). Meaning reconstruction in bereavement: Development of a research program. *Death Studies, 43*, 79–91. doi:10.1080/07481187.2018.1456620

Wielink, J. P. J. van, Wilhelm, L., & van Geelen-Merks, D. (2020). *Loss, grief and attachment in life transitions. A clinician's guide to secure base counselling*. London and New York: Routledge.

36
The Identity Constellation Exercise

Christopher J. MacKinnon, Dina Szynkarsky
and Leigh Stephens

CLIENTS FOR WHOM THE TECHNIQUE IS APPROPRIATE

This psychotherapeutic written exercise may be useful with adolescents or adults amid life transition including, but not limited to, loss or bereavement. It may be particularly welcome with clients seeking to shed light on the impact of relationships in shaping personal subjective constructions of identity in the aftermath of loss. The technique may be less interesting or applicable for more pragmatic and concrete-oriented clients, as well as those who approach grief with more instrumental coping styles.

DESCRIPTION

Life can be conceptualized as a series of losses and transitions. Some of these transitions—divorce, career loss, immigration, diagnosis of illness or death—are usually unplanned and complex to navigate and carry the risk of stagnation or complicated adjustment. The obstacles to productively traversing a transition can be a particular challenge when one's sense of identity is called into question (Neimeyer, 2009). Becoming a stranger to oneself in the midst of major life change is a common occurrence in the experience of bereavement. Loss can provoke a crisis of meaning as one seeks to make sense of what may become incompatible and contradictory internalized narratives of personal identity (Neimeyer & Sands, 2011). Of note for our purposes, constructivist notions of personal identity are often linked to the social world, particularly how identity is shaped by the relationships we find meaningful.

The playwright Robert Anderson (1968) foreshadowed the contemporary thanatological domain of the *continuing bond* when he proposed that the death of a meaningful relationship does not per se terminate the influence of the relationship itself. The continuing bond as it is presently defined embodies the presence of an ongoing inner relationship with the deceased person (Stroebe, Schut, & Boerner, 2010). As a result, the implicit or explicit influences of the relationship with the deceased can impact the grievers' sense of self and may be targeted with tailored clinical intervention such as the psychotherapeutic exercise described next.

The *Identity Constellation Exercise* is a modified version of a technique developed by James Hollis (2015) and is easily rendered, parsimonious and flexible. It seeks to bridge the notions of personal identity reconstruction in bereavement with the continuing bond, as well as constructivist notions of sense and meaning making. Consequently, it can be applied in general

 DOI: 10.4324/9781351069120-45

psychotherapy as well as grief therapy, but we have found it to be particularly helpful in the latter context. The clinical objectives of this technique include (1) fostering sense making of subjective experience and personal identity, (2) identifying implicit relational forces that may be impacting bereavement, and (3) setting targets for future therapeutic intervention. The exercise takes approximately five minutes to complete and may be best implemented in session to allow for a deeper consideration of the results in partnership with the therapist.

To complete the exercise, the client will need a blank piece of paper and a pencil or pen. The therapist invites the client to draw a large circle with a dot placed in the center. This circle symbolizes the client's relational life, a figurative *personal solar system* with the central dot representing the point of power. Said another way, the center of the circle is the locus of greatest influence. The client is then invited to draw a series of sub-circles within the solar system, relative in size and distance from the center based on the following factors. Each sub-circle represents a relationship in the client's life, including any meaningful or influential relationship with those both living and dead. The size of each sub-circle represents the quantitative space the relationship holds in terms of daily life, defined not only by time spent with the person but also by time invested in thinking about the relationship. The distance that each sub-circle occupies from the central dot is the relative power it exerts on the client. For example, a large sub-circle placed on the periphery of the solar system could represent an acquaintance who shares an adjacent cubicle daily at work but who has little to no impact on the client's life. Conversely, a small sub-circle placed close to the central dot would denote a very powerful and ongoing relational impact but one that does not occupy a large place in the client's daily life. Layering and overlapping of sub-circles may transpire and should be encouraged. The exact meaning of sub-circles overlapping can be left for the client to identify.

Assessment and interpretation of the resulting image can vary according to the clinical judgment of the therapist, in step with the needs of the client. The therapist may wish to ask the client's permission to display the constellation in the consultation room so both may view it concurrently.

Here are several clinical prompts that may elicit deeper reflections from the client.

- How does it feel to look at the constellation?
- What does the present constellation say about who you are?
- Which part of the exercise is/was the most surprising, interesting or troubling for you?
- What is the meaning of any overlapping sub-circles?
- If you wish to see changes in your constellation, what would they be, and what would need to happen?

After the initial composition and assessment, the constellation can be revisited by having the client add newly identified imprints resulting from these prompts. Some clients may wish to add sub-circles for dominant emotions such as shame, guilt, betrayal or other feelings correlated with the loss. Problematic behaviors that may be hindering coping may also be added (e.g., excessive avoidance coping behaviors). Sub-circles may also be added to encompass other areas of influence such as work, religious beliefs or pragmatic issues (e.g., financial stresses). The client can append to the constellation intrusive images or recurring thoughts that may be indicative of trauma or ruminative coping. Lastly, the client may be invited to compose another constellation, perhaps between sessions, that might represent a state of being prior to the loss. Alternatively, the client can arrange a *preferred future constellation* that maps out the ideal state of being and could suggest targets for psychotherapeutic emphasis.

CASE ILLUSTRATION

Reginald self-referred for bereavement and psychological support subsequent to the death of his father, with whom he shared a particularly close attachment. He presented with significant feelings of anxiety, lethargy, indecisiveness, self-criticism and despair. In addition to the death of his father, Reginald was confronting a loveless marriage in which, for many years, both he and his wife had led largely parallel lives. To complicate matters, he had begun a secret romantic relationship with a co-worker in the weeks after his father's death.

Through further assessment, it became clear that Reginald had been coping with the emptiness of his marriage by turning to his father for support in a common collusion and triangulation pattern. Conversations with his father had acted as a periodic pressure valve, temporarily relieving the tension Reginald experienced in the marriage. With his father now dead, this means of coping was removed, and Reginald found himself with mounting anxiety, unable to decide whether to leave the marriage or confront his spouse about their difficulties. "I am out of control," he exclaimed between tearful bursts; "I never imagined I would be this person, engaged in a secret relationship. I don't understand why I am doing these things, or why I can't make a move forward. I am simply stuck."

Reginald was creatively inclined and responded with a certain enthusiasm when the idea of the identity constellation was proposed as a possibility to help him make sense of his own reactions. He completed the exercise in session and leaned the drawing on the back of an empty chair so both he and the therapist could view it simultaneously. It took several moments for Reginald to begin to speak, and the therapist encouraged him to take his time as he took in the image.

He spoke first about the relationship with his father. While no longer occurring in the physical plane, his father now assumed a frequent place in Reginald's thoughts. Reginald further disclosed some recurrent disturbing images of the moments just prior to his father's death in palliative care that manifested in repetitive nightmares.

The therapist noted some overlap in the sub-circles of his father and his son named Jeff. Reginald explained that this denoted the valuable role that his father had played in Jeff's life. He described the compensatory role his father had played in childcare, as his wife was often not at home. In eliciting more details from Reginald, he shared some of the strain he felt to keep the family together for Jeff's sake and prevent divorce. He further identified a sense of personal inadequacy to address these parenting questions. Discussing the nature of the overlap between Jeff and his father opened the path for Reginald to introduce the question of how his son was managing the death of his grandfather.

Moreover, the secret romantic relationship with the co-worker emerged as surprising for Reginald, assuming considerably more space and influence than he had initially realized. It overlapped with his wife, whose small sub-circle was initially placed in an incidental position at the margins of the constellation. Reginald suggested that the nature of the overlap was in part due to the fact that when he was with his co-worker, his wife was sometimes on his mind.

In a follow-up prompt, the therapist invited Reginald to identify any feelings in response to the exercise or emotions that could be added do the constellation itself. "If I am to be brutally honest, I think I am completely enveloped by a sense of failure. It takes a far bigger place in my life than I want it to." The therapist helped Reginald deconstruct this feeling, with the client largely identifying with the word shame. Reginald then added a light gray sub-circle representing his shame that notably encompassed all the sub-circles, centering on the romantic relationship with the co-worker. He signaled this as his greatest failure in life, mumbling, "I am mortified to confess that this happened."

After a final prompt for feelings by the therapist, Reginald added a sense of panic that came upon him when he started thinking about the co-worker and his relationship with Jeff. "I can't seem to be able to make any movement forward. I just freeze up and keep repeating the same old pattern, going back to her again and again. I don't want to keep going like this, living in secret, and I am not even sure that I want this relationship. It is so confusing. I am also petrified that Jeff will discover the truth. What will he think of his father then?" A dark gray circle of panic was then added to the constellation, superimposed on the feeling of shame and the relationships with his son and co-worker.

At the conclusion of the consultation, Reginald took his constellation home after being encouraged by the therapist to make any refinements to the drawing he deemed appropriate to better capture his situation. He returned for the next session with a revised constellation (Figure 36.1). In the initial portrait not shown here, his wife, represented by the small sub-circle with the heavily weighted outline, occupied a space on the outermost reaches of the constellation. This sub-circle was subsequently moved and was now adjacent to the center of power. "I don't think I wanted to admit to myself how big a space she was taking in my life." He expressed that while she occupied little to no place in his daily life (e.g., they slept apart, had not been intimate in years and hardly spoke), he was being influenced by and defined in opposition to the impact this relationship had on him. He reported that his sense of who he was (i.e., his identity) was largely dependent on his wife. "I always thought of myself as someone who got things done. This tether between my wife and me changes my sense of self. I want to get back to the person I was, the person with a lot of motivation and energy."

Reginald, in collaboration with his therapist, agreed that addressing the future of the marriage was the immediate priority in their work. He agreed that making sense of and productively responding to his overwhelming shame and anxiety would be useful places to begin. Other therapeutic targets included processing the possible traumatic aftereffects of his father's death and finding useful ways to approach the relationship with his bereft son.

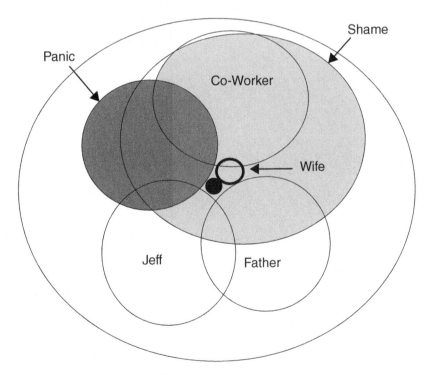

Figure 36.1 Reginald's Identity Constellation

CONCLUDING THOUGHTS

The *Identity Constellation Exercise* is a relatively straightforward, efficient and cogent psychotherapeutic technique that can easily render visible the implicit forces that are impacting and shaping an individual's grief experience and subjective sense of personal identity. An assessment method that may be employed across the course of treatment, it can be used collaboratively to highlight the various spheres of influence on a client's symbolic personal constellation. Moreover, it can permit a more conscious rendering of topics of import, concomitantly illuminating the path for future therapeutic work.

References

Anderson, R. (1968). *I never sang for my father.* New York: Dramatists Play Service.
Hollis, J. (2015). *Hauntings: Dispelling the ghosts who run our lives.* Accredited workshop presented at the C. G. Jung Society of Montreal, Concordia University, Montreal, QC.
Neimeyer, R. A. (2009). *Constructivist psychotherapy.* New York: Routledge.
Neimeyer, R. A., & Sands, D. C. (2011). Meaning reconstruction in bereavement: From principles to practice. In R. A. Neimeyer, D. L. Harris, H. R. Winokuer, & G. F. Thornton (Eds.), *Grief and bereavement in contemporary society: Bridging research and practice* (pp. 9–22). New York: Routledge.
Stroebe, M. S., Schut, H., & Boerner, K. (2010). Continuing bonds in adaptation to bereavement: Toward theoretical integration. *Clinical Psychology Review, 30*(2), 259–268.

37

Voice Dialogue

Jakob van Wielink and Anita Bakker

CLIENTS FOR WHOM THE TECHNIQUE IS APPROPRIATE

Voice dialogue is a method suitable for working with nearly all adult clients dealing with loss and grief in various forms. However, this method can cause confusion in younger children, in severe cases of trauma and when dealing with psychiatric issues that involve decreased ability to self-reflect.

DESCRIPTION

Voice dialogue is a powerful method developed by psychologists Hal and Sidra Stone (Stone & Stone, 1986). Its theoretical foundation is in Carl Gustav Jung's developmental psychology, which describes how people's personalities are developed through reconciliation of various (sometimes contrary) aspects of the psyche.

Voice dialogue, also known as *Psychology of the Selves*, is based on the assumption that everyone harbors a number of different selves, each with its own words, opinions, convictions, feelings and perceptions. Some of these selves are more dominant than others. The more dominant identities, the so-called *primary selves*, usually develop early on in life and enable us to avoid feelings of pain or loneliness and to maintain our footing in the world. For example, people might develop a strong, responsible self or an overactive people-pleaser self. On the other hand, it makes sense for us to minimize contact with those aspects of our identity that cause us to confront pain. The latter aspects of ourselves that we do not allow or struggle to allow to find expression are known as *disowned selves* and are often the polar opposites of our primary selves.

When loss occurs, the primary selves' survival strategies may sometimes be insufficient; they are no longer able to shield us fully from the experience of grieving. People may experience a sensation like being frozen and unable to deal with the new situation. Another possibility is for people's primary selves to manifest even more strongly and urge us to be even more strong, optimistic or withdrawn. Without our noticing, our primary selves can take over and intensify the survival behavior we have developed in the past. A highly impactful loss can also cause parts of ourselves that we did not know of to reveal themselves, making us fearful and insecure. Examples of feelings that may be involved in the process are anger, shame and guilt. Some of our inner selves will be more focused on moving on, whereas others will be more focused on the loss, as suggested by Stroebe and Schut's (2010) Dual Process Model.

DOI: 10.4324/9781351069120-46

A therapist can help clients regain (more) control during periods when their control has been fundamentally challenged by the experience of loss. In voice dialogue, the therapist does so by helping the client integrate various selves by literally engaging in dialogue with each of them and addressing them as separate people. It is hugely important for the therapist to actually be emotionally present during the sessions and to welcome each side that reveals itself in a respectful manner. If the therapist can succeed in being a secure base (see Chapter 25 on *Balancing Caring and Daring*), this will provide clients with the necessary security to truly meet the various selves they harbor inside.

Voice dialogue directs therapists to work with what is known as the client's *central position*, in which they talk to the client directly and to which they return after every conversation with one of the client's various selves. This position allows the various selves to be examined from an autonomous position and integrated properly. In voice dialogue, this aspect of the patient is known as the *aware ego*.

A typical session starts in the central position and uses that to explore the loss that the client wants to focus on. As the therapist, ask the client which voice, which self, arises, and assign that self its own spot in the therapeutic space, perhaps sitting in an empty chair, standing in the corner of the room or crouching to one side. Allow the client time to truly become attuned to this part; approach this new self as an independently thinking, feeling person and engage in a dialogue with it.

Here are some examples of questions you could ask to invite a different self:

- Who inside of you is stopping you from being sad?
- Who inside of you would have preferred to stay with your old employer?
- Who inside of you actually wants to give up?
- Who inside of you feels depressed?
- Who inside of you wants to move on and sees new opportunities?
- Who inside of you still feels attached to the past and does not want to say goodbye?
- Who inside of you sees the good in the loss that you suffered?
- Who inside of you is lonely?
- Who inside of you gives meaning to your loss?
- Who inside of you is relieved?
- Would you let me talk to the person who feels so terribly angry?

To begin a dialogue with a part of the client's self, start out by asking questions that allow you to meet and get to know that self a little bit. Once you are introduced, start asking questions that focus more on the self's feelings and thoughts regarding the loss, as well as its function and its reasons for manifesting or not manifesting. Talk to the selves about the client in third person to reinforce the notion that you are talking to just one part of them. After each exploration of a particular self, have the client return to the central position to establish some distance and perspective on the dialogue that just occurred. While they are in the central position, ask them about their experiences and responses to what has happened. Once you have assessed one self from the central position, you can then turn to another.

CASE STUDY

Johan was a 45-year-old man who was losing his manager position due to a company restructuring. He was having trouble coming to terms with his new situation and felt downcast, tired and listless ever since he heard that he was going to lose his job. What made things even harder was the fact that some of his fellow managers had been asked to fill different positions within the company after its restructuring, whereas Johan had not been offered any replacement position.

Johan told his therapist that losing his job felt like a kind of failure; on the other hand, he also admitted that he did not think the position of manager really suited him and that he preferred to do something else. He was clearly confused by all his contrary feelings.

His therapist suggested exploring his loss further by engaging in dialogues with various parts of himself that had to do with his loss, and he agreed to engage in this experiment with his therapist. To begin, his therapist asked Johan about the first thing that popped into his head when they talked about his impending job loss. Johan said that he felt incredibly ashamed. When asked to assign the part of himself that felt so ashamed a position in the room, Johan grabbed a chair and placed it in such a position that it was half-hidden behind the flip chart in the room and, at the therapist's request, occupied it.

The therapist then started the conversation by saying, "It is great to have you here with us; I would like to get to know you better." Johan then voiced the part's response:

SHAME (SOFTLY, ALMOST IN A WHISPER): *That's okay, if I can just stay seated back here.*
THERAPIST: *That's perfectly all right. You are welcome here. Would you like to tell me how you feel about the fact that Johan is going to be fired?*
SHAME: *I am ashamed that Johan did not perform better and am very scared of what the people in his life are going to say.*
THERAPIST: *You are worried about other people's opinions?*
SHAME: *Yes, of course. I am afraid they will think he is stupid, that he is a failure.*
THERAPIST: *Which is the last thing you would want, right?*

They talked for a little while, during which Shame told some more about some situations that he was present for. When the therapist asked him how long he had been a part of Johan, Shame shared that he had been with Johan for as long as he could remember, sharing a memory in which Johan's father was angry at his son's bad performance on the football field.

SHAME: *I think I became a part of Johan on that football field and never left. I make sure that Johan does not do things that will make people think of him in a certain way.*
THERAPIST: *You have been taking care of Johan for as long as you can remember. You so badly want him to make a good impression on other people. . . . You must care about him a lot.*
SHAME: *I don't want people to reject him. I don't want him to be a disappointment, so I'm always there to keep an eye on things.*

The therapist narrowed in on Shame's comment that people were absolutely not allowed to see Johan express weakness. Shame explained that he so badly wanted Johan's father to be proud of his son. The only way to accomplish that was for him to allow Johan to take very few risks and always be aware of other people's opinions.

Finally, the therapist thanked Shame for being present and asked Johan to come back and take a seat in the central position. Johan confessed that he felt very shaken by how familiar the voice of shame sounded to him. The struggle to obtain recognition in particular felt very familiar to him. The discussion of his relationship with his father had hit him hard. He became very sad. When asked to invite this sadness into the room as well, Johan took a chair and placed it in the far corner of the room. He took a seat, and as he focused on his sadness, a withdrawn, stooped figure emerged, sitting at the very edge of his seat. He came across as very young and vulnerable, so the therapist asked him how old he was. Warily, Sadness looked at the therapist. Very young, he said. Tears streamed down his cheeks. The therapist could tell that she would not need to ask very many questions this time around. She told Sadness that it was good to see him, that it was okay for him to cry and that he could share things if he wanted to but did not have to. *After a while, Sadness said the following: That's really nice because Johan does not let me be present most of the time. I don't have a lot to say—there is just so much sadness in me. He cried a little more, softly.*

When Johan was back in the central position and talked to his therapist about this experience, he slowly became livelier. It appeared as though he had found room for a different, more light-hearted energy, so the therapist asked him if maybe there was someone who was glad about losing his job. Johan smiled, grabbed another chair, and placed it to the right of his central position. He took the seat, and the therapist ended up talking to a self who felt relieved, a self who saw plenty of new opportunities and who liked to focus on those rather than anything else. This self felt a lot more optimistic about the future and could not wait to find a job that was more suited to Johan.

The therapist and Johan had a final chat in the central position. Johan indicated that it was a great relief to be allowed to meet his sadness. He also said that he now understood the role that his shame had played in his life a lot better, as well as how this side was part of his past and how he now linked it clearly with his relationship with his father. Johan identified fully with his shame, and unbeknownst to him, the shame had completely taken over his life. The therapy session provided him with insight; his shame would not go away just like that, but there was more to him than that. He was now aware that he had options.

CONCLUDING THOUGHTS

The power of voice dialogue lies in the fact that it makes people aware that they need not identify exclusively with certain parts of themselves. All of us have various, sometimes contrary parts of ourselves that give meaning to loss in their own way. These various sides can exist simultaneously. It can be very freeing to experience that depression and sadness can be part of our identity while at the same time having access to parts that want to move on and discover new opportunities. Voice dialogue can also allow clients to access any feelings or thoughts that they have been experiencing but have a hard time allowing in their daily lives. In summary, such work allows clients to examine their various selves from a more compassionate, accepting point of view. There is no pressure to interpret things or find solutions. We need only follow, take time, provide room and be close and present to the ongoing dialogue.

References

Stone, H., & Stone, S. (1986). *Embracing ourselves: The voice dialogue manual.* Novato, CA: New World Library.
Stroebe, M., & Schut, H. (2010). The dual process model of coping with bereavement: A decade on. *Omega, 61,* 273–289.

Thanks to Ruud Zuurman, Director of the Institute for Transformational Psychology.

38
Symbolic Reframing
Judy Chew

CLIENTS FOR WHOM THE TECHNIQUE IS APPROPRIATE

In death-related grief work, the exploration and use of personally relevant symbols can assist clients in meaning making and loss adaptation, especially when they are troubled by unfinished business with the deceased. Symbolic intervention as a reframing strategy may be contraindicated in situations in which the client interprets the approach as premature or sees it as an external requirement. Clients' reluctance to part with possessions may also reflect a lack of readiness for revision of self-identity.

DESCRIPTION

Symbols are an integral part of communication, and therapeutic use of symbolic associations can help clients both access and stabilize certain experiences (Combs & Freedman, 1990). Use of symbols in grief work may promote client adaptation to loss during the four key process tasks of grieving: coming to terms with the reality of the loss, working through grief, adjusting to life in the absence of the loved one and creating a sense of ongoing connection with the loved one while moving ahead in life (Worden, 2009). A client's chosen symbols offer perspective on the life of the deceased person and create space for the bereaved individual to interact with the deceased.

A symbol is anything (object, concept or action) that represents or stands for something else, whether it is an idea, belief or material entity. Therapeutic skill requires alertness in perceiving when clients may be thinking or acting symbolically; when this occurs, symbols have many uses. Milton Erikson's notion of "utilization" refers to therapeutic integration of the client's presenting "problems" with discovery of symbolic solutions (Combs & Freedman, 1990). "Reframing" is a therapeutic skill that enables clients to recognize how their own perceptions, actions or strategies may be symbolic. To facilitate this symbolic reframing, Combs and Freedman (1990) suggest use of the following questions: In what ways could the situation be a symbol for a solution or part of a solution? What positive intentions or motivations are reflected in and could be symbolized by the situation? What might this situation symbolize other than a problem? Use of these questions can enhance the collaborative work of counselor and client to explore, identify and apply symbols as a way forward in grief therapy.

DOI: 10.4324/9781351069120-47

CASE ILLUSTRATION

Adele sought counseling to address a surge of painful emotions linked to the tragic death of her son Nathan eight years earlier. Her grief was prompted by her need to move from the family home where they were last together. Nathan had returned to live at the house following his release from prison, but after a verbal altercation, Adele had "kicked him out." A short time later, his body was found in an abandoned home. Nathan had accidently died from carbon monoxide poisoning while trying to start an old stove.

Adele's review of her past eight years suggested that she had done much to cope and adjust to Nathan's death. Her life was enriched by a support system, career and hobbies, and she remembered her son in meaningful ways. She believed that she had survived and even thrived after this tragic loss, but now the decision to move out of her house ignited new sparks of grief. After placing her house on the market, Adele again felt heartbroken over Nathan's absence, and she spoke of unfinished business "eating away" at her. She described some of her coping behaviors as "bizarre and ridiculous," which left her bereft and frightened. Her situation brought to mind Stroebe and Schut's (1999) term "oscillation," the "alternation between loss- and restoration-oriented coping, the process of juxtaposition of confrontation and avoidance of different stressors associated with bereavement" (p. 215).

I acknowledged Adele's experiences and informed her that it is common to experience something left unsaid, unfinished or unresolved in a relationship with a loved one who has died (Klingspon, Holland, Neimeyer, & Lichtenthal, 2015). I invited her to describe what she meant by unfinished business. Adele tearfully shared her "preoccupation" with setting a place at the table for Nathan and continuing to hide a spare house key for him outside. She said this was "illogical" and that there was "no chance he would unlock the door and come back in." At the same time, Adele was inconsolable at the thought that she would have to "leave him behind for good" once she moved out of the house.

Our therapeutic work focused on the meaning and memories that her home represented, and I asked Adele to elaborate on her concrete expressions of love toward Nathan within her house. I invited Adele to assume a respectful stance toward her current behaviors and to remain curious as to what she might discover through them. I then drew from the work of Combs and Freedman (1990), who identify the benefits of reframing client symbols, inviting Adele to reflect on how her present gestures or activities might serve as restorative symbols (i.e., solutions). She began to recognize the positive dimensions, however small, that were symbolized by her behaviors.

In one particular session, Adele arrived with a photo album and Nathan's key. As an avid photographer, she had warmed to the idea of creating an album that featured photos of the rooms in the house and the front porch area where Nathan's key was hidden. Weiser (2004) suggests that a photograph in therapy can promote healing as "a moment of time, being held, and . . . frozen forever" (p. 26). Photographs can also serve to deepen therapeutic conversations and perspectives, connect the past with the present and gain access to knowledge that is unconsciously available (Weiser, 2004).

Adele still wept as she described her pending move as a reminder of Nathan's loss and her shattered dreams. Yet she referred to her album of rooms as a visual reminder of the 18 years she did share with him. She observed that her place-setting behavior was "not crazy" but a "gesture of a mother's love." She said that holding the photo album allowed her to talk more easily about what she felt. She described the pain in her heart and being unable to say goodbye, to no longer see Nathan's face or hold his hand—the agony of a mother torn from her son. I affirmed her experience of pain and acknowledged her efforts and responses as not unique to her; I said that others have felt the same and that she made sense. Adele nodded and said she no longer viewed her gestures and behaviors as "entirely crazy." Her movement from symptom or problem orientation to a more generous self-assessment illustrated the potential and power of symbolism. It also underscored how Adele's behavior had to be understood in context and that others had similar experiences (Klingspon et al., 2015).

I continued to affirm Adele's fresh (reframing) perspectives and wondered if her heart and home would always remain lovingly open toward Nathan. She enthusiastically agreed. Then Adele held the key out in her hand and said, "Nathan will be in my heart always—wherever I go. Do I really need to have this hidden key?" Her rhetorical question was accompanied by more tears and freshly discovered insight. A peaceful energy emanated from Adele as she expressed the immeasurable value of retaining the album and key as cherished keepsakes (symbols) of her steadfast love for Nathan. Toward the end of our conversation, Adele opened herself to the finality of Nathan's death. She said, "I have come to accept Nathan's death better this time around. Now my heart feels bigger, like a huge, spacious room that is full of love for him. Now I just might be able to make the move. And I don't even have to bring the whole house with me!"

CONCLUDING THOUGHTS

The exploration and use of symbols in grief work holds possibilities that can be enriched by reframing strategies. Within the context of a collaborative approach, therapeutic questions can promote the client's discovery of fresh (and multiple) meanings for behaviors and feelings that are initially experienced as primarily distressing or symptomatic. This can then open the client to new possibilities and choices in life after loss.

Adele's experience of grief and her self-described "bizarre behaviors" understandably became more acute and distressing during the major life transition of moving out of her house. This aftershock destabilized her early post-grief identity that had been established until that point in time. In therapy, Adele was willing to confront her renewed longing for Nathan and do the further grief work required to begin the next chapter of her life after the death of her son.

A strong therapeutic alliance and mutual respect are foundational in grief work when symbolic intervention is considered. The quality of the relationship needs to include therapist flexibility. The reconstruction of post-grief identity is complex, requiring the therapist to assess client safety, ego strength and readiness to explore the meanings of grief responses. The use of symbols and reframing can help clients access their own inner wisdom and creatively adapt, adjust—and continue to grow—after loss.

References

Combs, G., & Freedman, J. (1990). *Symbol, story & ceremony: Using metaphor in individual and family therapy*. New York: Norton.

Klingspon, K., Holland, J., Neimeyer, R. A., & Lichtenthal, W. (2015). Unfinished business in bereavement. *Death Studies, 39*, 387–398. doi:10.1080/07481187.2015.1029143

Stroebe, M., & Schut, H. (1999). The dual process model for coping with bereavement: Rationale and description. *Death Studies, 23*, 197–224.

Weiser, J. (2004). Phototherapy techniques in counselling and therapy: Using ordinary snapshots and photo-interactions to help clients heal their lives. *Canadian Art Therapy Association Journal, 17*, 23–53. doi:10.1080/08322473.2004.11432263

Worden, W. (2009). *Grief counseling and grief therapy: A handbook for the mental health practitioner* (4th ed.). New York: Springer.

39
Coin Therapy

Gilbert Fan

CLIENTS FOR WHOM THE TECHNIQUE IS APPROPRIATE

Cognitively clear patients with life-limiting illness as well as bereaved persons who are facing anxiety and depressive moods may benefit from this experiential exercise. Coin therapy is most useful to clients who ruminate on the negative side of their life circumstances and who are visual learners. Conversely, it is contraindicated for those who are more verbal learners or whose severe physical distress requires management before a brief psychological intervention can be effective.

DESCRIPTION

Patients facing death as well as bereaved individuals often suffer from anxiety and depressive moods (Boelen & Prigerson, 2007; Mitchell et al., 2011; Stroebe, Schut, & Stroebe, 2007). It is therefore encouraging that a meta-analysis of 116 intervention studies on cancer patients receiving psychoeducational and psychosocial interventions demonstrated that they had lower levels of such distress than those without intervention (Devine & Westlake, 1995). A special report in future oncology on group psychotherapy at the National Cancer Centre Singapore outlined the relevance and importance of experiential psychotherapy to Asian populations, who tend to have limited vocabulary to articulate the impact of serious illness or stressful life events (Khng, Woo, & Fan, 2016).

Coin therapy is a simple technique to demonstrate to clients the negative impact of over-worrying or focusing on only one side of their life experience. This therapy can be done with many patients in palliative care and bereaved clients in individual group settings (both of whom hereafter will be referred to simply as "clients"). In the exercise, clients are shown a one-dollar Singapore coin (or a familiar coin of similar configuration from other nations) placed on the palm of the therapist's hand, and they are asked to describe what they see on one side of the coin (e.g., the flowers on a Singapore dollar coin).

Clients tend to be very descriptive at the start of their conversation, typically relating concretely what they see (e.g., describing the image and reading the words or numerals on the coin's face). The therapist then encourages the client to provide further details by asking the question "What else do you see?" a couple of times. Worry-prone clients are prone to wander into abstract and evaluative thinking and elaborate about the coin as a national currency,

 DOI: 10.4324/9781351069120-48

what products the coin can buy, its diminishing purchasing power over time etc. In contrast, non-worriers tend to stop at the descriptive aspects.

Next, the client is asked, "What's on the flip side of the coin?" At this juncture, clients may experience uncertainty as they are unsure of what to do: whether to imagine the flip side, to flip the coin physically or, alternatively, to report only a generic description of what appears on the other side. The therapist then instructs the client to flip the coin and to describe what appears on the reverse. The therapist can then invite the client to formulate the lesson or moral of the exercise for living with illness or loss in his or her own terms. This simple prompt may lead many clients to recognize and voice that they need to look "on the other side of the coin" to see the positive parts of their lives that are overshadowed by their difficult circumstances. When further prompting is required, the therapist can bring to the client's attention the fact that sometimes an intense focus on the negative aspects of living leads us to miss out on many of the positive aspects of life, as we hardly explore this other side. At this juncture, it is often possible to ask the client, "Do you know that you have a choice in your life to look at the positive aspects in just the way you flipped the coin over?"

The therapist then encourages the client to look at both sides of the coin on a need-to-know basis, clearly examining the negative features associated with the illness or loss but without staring at these for prolonged periods. Returning to the coin demonstration, the therapist then instructs the client to explore both sides of the coin without holding the coin upright or turning it over. If the client gets stuck at this point, the therapist assists by placing the coin upright on a level tabletop, standing it carefully on its edge. With the coin positioned in an upright manner, clients can shift their heads in order to look at both sides. The therapist then asks the client, "What do you have to do to look at both sides of the coin?" Clients often observe that they need to shift their gaze or change their perspective to do so. The therapist can then emphasize that the effort to look at both sides of the coin comes from themselves. The coin represents life circumstances that are not likely to change, so the effort to change must come from the client. The therapist can then suggest that the client can look at either side of the coin on a need-to-know basis. To live life realistically, one has to explore both the negative and positive aspects of one's life fully and meaningfully. The last question that the therapist asks the client could be "How many sides do you see in this coin?" There are actually three sides, with the third being the rim on which the coin is balancing. The therapist can then note that the less-noticeable side is often neglected and that special effort might be required to see the coin and life in a more three-dimensional manner.

CASE ILLUSTRATION

Roger, age 45, had advanced cancer of the colon. He was referred for counseling as he had been depressed for the past five years. He had low mood and spoke very little, so extended talk therapy proved difficult, especially during his relatively brief visits to the clinic for treatment. For this reason, during one of our consultations, I took out a Singapore one-dollar coin, placed it on my palm and asked Roger to tell me what he saw on the coin. He was very concrete as he described to me the delicate details on the coin. When encouraged to elaborate on his description, Roger went into a prescriptive mode and talked about abstract knowledge, such as how the one-dollar coin can be used, what it can be used to buy, how a dollar doesn't go as far as it once did and so on.

Roger hesitated when I asked him what was on the flip side of the coin, staring hard at it without touching it or asking me to turn it over. In this fixed tendency to get stuck in his problem-solving behavior, Roger was typical of many depressed clients. I then flipped the coin and asked him what he saw on the reverse. Roger was able to describe what he saw. I then asked him whether he had gotten stuck looking at one side of the coin for the past five years of his life. He broke down and cried, sharing that it had been a long time since he had noticed or given attention to the other side. He acknowledged that he was too focused on his negativity to recognize any positivity in his life. I used my hands to gesture how he focused on one side and neglected life on the other side, which was invisible as the coin lay in my palm. I then told Roger that it was not too late to look at the other side.

I asked Roger whether he knew how to look at either side of the coin. He stared blankly at me. I then placed the coin upright on a table. I encouraged Roger to look at both sides of the coin. He began to reach for the coin, but I stopped him. I told Roger that the coin represented his life circumstances, which were difficult to change. Roger then shifted the position of his head to look at both sides of the coin. I asked Roger to tell me why he was doing that. Roger replied that in order for him to see both sides of the coin, he had to move his head to change his field of vision. I asked Roger what this implied for him. Roger was able to verbalize to me that the effort needed to come from him. I concurred and stressed to Roger that the decision to make a shift resided with him. He could learn from books and counselors, but ultimately, the choice was in his hands.

CONCLUDING THOUGHTS

Coin therapy can be adapted to be used with diverse currencies. It is better done with a coin than a bank note, which is too complex in its detail, lacks an edge on which to balance and, most importantly, lacks the metaphoric power of "looking at the other side of the coin," which exists as a saying in many languages. Coin therapy works best with clients who are visual and experiential in their focus and learning. It can be especially helpful for clients who are worriers, those who have anxiety and depressive moods, and those who are stuck in difficult and intractable circumstances of illness and loss.

References

Boelen, P. A., & Prigerson, H. G. (2007). The influence of symptoms of prolonged grief disorder, depression, and anxiety on quality of life among bereaved adults: A prospective study. *European Archives of Psychiatry and Clinical Neuroscience, 257*(8), 444–452.

Devine, E. C., & Westlake, S. K. (1995). The effects of psychoeducational care provided to adults with cancer: Meta-analysis of 116 studies. *Oncology Nursing Forum, 22*(9), 1369–1381.

Khng, J. N. W., Woo, I. M. H., & Fan, G. (2016). Experiential group work for cancer patients shaped by experiences of participants during group intervention. *Future Oncology, 12*(24), 2817–2822.

Mitchell, A. J., Chan, M., Bhatti, H., Halton, M., Grassi, L., Johansen, C., & Meader, N. (2011). Prevalence of depression, anxiety, and adjustment disorder in oncological, haematological, and palliative-care settings: A meta-analysis of 94 interview-based studies. *The Lancet, 12*(2), 160–174.

Stroebe, M., Schut, H., & Stroebe, W. (2007). Health outcomes of bereavement. *The Lancet, 370*(9603), 1960–1973.

Part X
Reaffirming Attachment

40

The Transition Cycle

Jakob van Wielink and Leo Wilhelm

CLIENTS FOR WHOM THE TECHNIQUE IS APPROPRIATE

This technique is not just appropriate for practically all adult and adolescent clients; addressing the themes of the Transition Cycle in working with both death and non-death losses also is relevant in order to put the loss in perspective. It may be inappropriate for young children, who could have a hard time understanding the sequence of concepts of which the Transition Cycle is composed.

DESCRIPTION

Every contact, every relationship, every connection we forge with others will eventually come to an end. The way we say goodbye, cope with loss, grieve and are able to give meaning to such events is about more than just the contact, the person or the relationship that we are saying goodbye to. It is also about how we connect with one another: how we connected with this one person but also how we become attached to people in a more general sense. The Transition Cycle provides insight into how themes in life such as attachment, resilience, bonding, experiencing intimacy, loss, saying goodbye, grieving, integrating the loss, reconstructing meaning and (re)discovering our calling—the unique contribution we are propelled to make to the world, coming from who we are at our core level—are connected to one another (Wielink, Wilhelm, & van Geelen-Merks, 2020). On a macro level, the Transition Cycle is a representation of life from the cradle to the grave: from the moment that we are first welcomed into the world when we are born, via attachment (whether of a secure or insecure nature), bonding and embracing intimacy in meaningful (partner) relationships, to saying goodbye, loss, grieving, giving meaning in old age and fulfilling one's calling, thus coming full circle to a new welcoming, a new beginning in the next generation. However, the Transition Cycle also represents the dynamics of every (brief) meeting in life on a micro level: every first meeting, every connection and every goodbye. Every meeting with other people activates our attachment pattern; every loss, every goodbye resonates with the separation anxiety we all experienced as children when our attachment figures were unavailable to us.

The cyclical nature of the Transition Cycle represents the fact that after each loss, there is still potential for new—and even deeper—connections to be forged. Addressing these themes explicitly during counseling allows people to gain an insight into their attachment patterns:

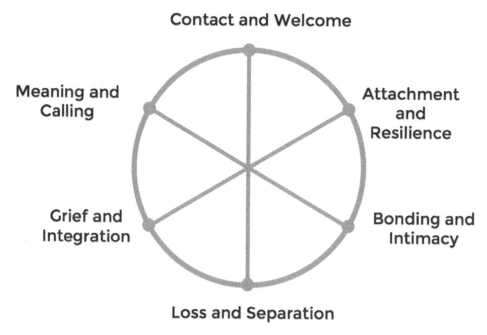

Figure 40.1 Themes on the Transition Cycle

patterns that can be beneficial or problematic for integrating loss into a life story that will always go on.

By working on these themes during counseling and learning to recognize the dynamics between the themes and the ways in which these themes continue to affect them in the present, clients may be able to put their loss into the right context. There are many ways of working with the Transition Cycle. We will outline one here. First, the counselor provides an explanation of the various themes and the way they relate to one another. The counselor then lays out cards with the themes on them in a circle on the floor and asks clients to stand on the theme that they feel is most important at that point in their counseling journey. While standing there, clients are given the opportunity to go back to situations throughout life in which they had to deal with that particular theme by imagining situations in which that theme generated particularly strong feelings within them. From that physical place and empathetic point of view, they may then also be able to consider the other themes and move to the other cards to envision a particular theme and become aware of its effects. The model provides a way in to settle on a diagnosis and to explore a client's request for help but also to help them obtain in-depth insight.

CASE STUDY

The development of a more efficient government frequently involves the merger of various government agencies. One such department, which performed economic analyses, was one that was merged, in this case with another economic agency. This was a massive change for the 450 employees in total. They not only immediately gained a large number of new co-workers, but there were also a lot of management changes. Moreover, they moved to a new building, a brand new open-plan office with flexible workstations and lockers in which everyone was to stash their personal items. This massive transition was supervised by a team of consultants. Apart from providing support for the strategic process and the selection of new supervisors, the consultants also organized workshops for the employees. During these workshops, the consultants prepared the employees for the transition as best they could. They explained all the practical matters and allowed the employees to express their own wishes and ideas for how the new municipal organization ought to be set up. There was an artist who created a triptych with the aid of those employees who wanted to be involved, depicting each of the merging units. This artwork was then put up in the new building. For most of the employees, the transition was relatively painless. After some initial awkwardness, they quickly found their footing in the new setting.

However, not all of them coped quite so well. Take Sharon, for instance. Sharon was HR manager. Several months had passed since the merger when she first contacted the therapist, after being referred by the occupational physician. She had been feeling anxious and tired and incapable of doing her job ever since she suddenly broke down sobbing during a team meeting.

During their first meeting, the therapist noticed that Sharon was very friendly toward her, complimenting the therapist's workspace and website. It became immediately apparent how Sharon acted within the theme of welcome. She had a tendency to welcome others; she ensured that the contact was easy and comfortable. When the theme of welcome and how that played a part in her family growing up came up later on in the conversation, Sharon shared that she was the oldest of four. Her parents had an in-house store, with just a single door separating the living room and the little storeroom behind the counter. "Welcome" was a concept mostly geared toward customers. As soon as the shop's doorbell rang, Sharon's mother would jump up immediately. It was as though everything in the living room was put on hold, and the entire focus shifted to what was going on in the store. This way, Sharon was exposed to the notion that it is important to welcome customers, regardless of what you are doing or of your needs, from a very early age. "How does this theme play a part in your work right now?" Sharon smiled before she answered. "I've realized that I do the exact same thing. I'm always there for others. As soon as people enter my office, I stop whatever I'm doing and take the time to listen to them. And if they have a question that needs answering, I get on that immediately."

In a subsequent session, the therapist wrote the various themes of the Transition Cycle on letter-size sheets of paper and laid them out on the floor in a circle. She then asked Sharon to come and stand on "welcome." "We spent some time talking about this theme last time. You told me a little about it then. Could you please recall that?" "Yes, I remember. For me, 'welcome' is mostly about welcoming customers." "And what about a welcome for you?" Sharon's breath caught at that. She blushed. "I don't know what to do with that question. . . . It's almost like I can't even contemplate that idea." Sharon was now connecting with the pain that was part of the theme of welcome for her. The therapist confirmed the notion: "That is how you have always experienced the theme of 'welcome.' It is easy for you to welcome others, but you feel uncomfortable with being welcomed yourself. Is that right?" Sharon nodded. Without going in depth, the therapist then switched to the next theme, attachment. "Please go stand on the theme of attachment. How does that make you feel?" Sharon took a deep breath. "It might sound odd, but it makes me feel a bit nervous, a bit uneasy. Like I should be doing something." The therapist reiterated: "So when you switch to the theme of attachment, you feel nervous; you feel uneasy, like you should be doing something." "Yes. It's a feeling of having to be at the ready, needing to get to work. Like it's not enough for me to just be there; I need to be doing something about it." She teared up.

Standing on the various themes not only activated Sharon's cognitive abilities but also allowed her to become more aware of her physical and energetic reactions. Her body and energy experienced unease, although there did not seem to be an identifiable reason for that, cognitively speaking. Sharon was made aware of her unconscious reactions so she could examine them. In Sharon's case, a major attachment pattern she had developed was the fact that she aimed to please others. She had a deep (unconscious) belief that if she pleased others, they would like her and stay with her.

When Sharon examined the theme of goodbye later on, she experienced fear. It took her back to an experience she'd had long ago, when she was only five. When she woke up, at around seven in the morning, there was nobody home. She panicked and crawled into her parents' bed. Around seven thirty, the neighbor stopped by to check on her. Her parents had gone to the hospital for the birth of the baby; Sharon's two-year-old brother had been taken to the neighbors' because he had been awake when her parents left. The matter was never discussed, least of all later on that day when Sharon's parents came home with her new baby sister.

For Sharon, the changes at work had unconsciously triggered old patterns and hit upon old pain. She had been working hard for months to help ensure a successful transition: making formation plans, supporting the management team, encouraging her co-workers, providing advice on team building etc. She had been putting everyone else first, taking perfect care of everything that needed to be done but paying too little attention to her own needs.

CONCLUDING THOUGHTS

The themes of the Transition Cycle are also present at a micro level in the moments of contact between counselor and client, from welcoming and forming attachments through sharing intimacy and saying goodbye. During counseling sessions, these themes affect not only the client but also the counselor. Consequently, it is important for counselors to be aware of and recognize how the themes resonate with them.

The themes can be used throughout the entire counseling process. For example, if the client's initial request for help is about loss, it might feel obvious to focus just on that theme. However, loss cannot be considered properly outside the context of the other themes. The counselor has the option of inviting the client to further explore the various themes at any point during the counseling process and when mining the client's request for help in a more in-depth manner.

References

Bowlby, J. (2005). *A secure base*. Abingdon: Taylor & Francis.

Wielink, J. P. J. van, & Wilhelm, L. (2020, May). (Re)discovering calling in the wake of loss through secure bases. *AI Practitioner. International Journal of Appreciative Inquiry, 22*(2), 13–18.

Wielink, J. P. J. van, Wilhelm, L., & van Geelen-Merks, D. (2020). *Loss, grief and attachment in life transitions. A clinician's guide to secure base counselling*. London and New York: Routledge.

41

Creating a Sensory Portal

Diana C. Sands

CLIENTS FOR WHOM THE TECHNIQUE IS APPROPRIATE

Supporting the development of a healing continuing bond (CB) with the deceased by drawing on sensory memories is appropriate for use with bereaved adults and can be modified for use with bereaved adolescents and children. It is particularly helpful with those who have experienced violent, sudden and traumatic loss—for example, due to suicide—and in those bereavement cases in which there are challenges in continuing bonds formation. It would not be indicated for clients uncomfortable with the CB concept, and prior clinical work would be required if the relationship with the deceased involved conflict. When indicated, sensory portal work can be implemented in individual and family counseling and in group settings.

DESCRIPTION

The process of realignment from having the loved one as a living person to having a reconstructed, ongoing presence in the bereaved person's life lies at the heart of grieving. This clinical intervention draws on continuing bond (CB) theory (Klass & Steffen, 2017), sensory and body trauma theory (Ogden, Minton, & Pain, 2006) and expressive arts as a medium for creating a sensory portal to support healthy CB development. Sensory memories persist in subtle ways within the psyche long after the death of a loved one and can be awakened through linking objects, thus providing entry to a vast world of recollection. Significant linking objects are items that belonged to the deceased or that bring them to mind. These objects can awaken deep currents of knowing and meaning embedded in sensory perceptions. A three-dimensional object collage can become a tangible touchstone between the present moment of loss and liminal space, to support the construction and enrichment of an ongoing bond with the deceased.

The complex process of constructing a CB evolves and deepens over time as the griever creates an internalized relationship with the loved one that grows and changes, even as they do. Through the process of constructing a CB, the loved one, although physically absent, remains a comforting presence in the bereaved person's life, which can enhance functioning (Sands, 2014). The loved one's finest qualities, values and beliefs become a resource to support decision making and sustain the sense of self as the griever navigates the overwhelming changes that accompany loss.

DOI: 10.4324/9781351069120-51

Sensory knowledge precedes intellectual understanding and is our first and primary way of knowing the world. There are five sensory perceptions: sight, hearing, touch, smell and taste and the sensory modalities of light, temperature and pressure. Linking objects can evoke many nuances of the person who used and touched the object, whether it be a pair of sunglasses, a hat, a wallet or a lingering scent on an article of clothing. These objects speak the language of the heart and can transport the griever to times and places that mark the way they were. Such objects are imbued with deep sensory memories and a significance that is greater than the nature of the object itself. Linking objects bring together sensory, emotional, cognitive and meaning experience. For example, a worn teddy bear may bring to memory not only a loved child's face at a particular moment in time but also a mélange of sensory memories: the color, smell and texture of the child's skin; the sound of shared laughter; and one's own presence in that moment (Sands, Jordan, & Neimeyer, 2011).

The process of constructing a sensory portal begins prior to the counseling session, with participants gathering a range of small objects, photos, cards and clothing. In a group setting, participants are invited to reflect on and share their grief as they weave an interactive narrative about their experiences of their loved ones' continuing presence. The French term *sillage* refers to the lingering impression made in a space after someone has been and gone. This felt sense of presence may be found in dreams, a particular piece of music playing or the appearance of feathers, coins, birds or other animals at synchronistic moments. Gently, a client's stories are drawn together to create a flexible space of possibility for creation of a sensory portal. Referring to the felt sense, Gabaldon (1997) commented:

> We come and go from mystery. . . . But a breeze passing in a still room stirs my hair . . . in soft affection. I think it is my mother. . . . Our rational minds say, "No, it isn't." But another part, an older part, echoes always softly. . . "Yes, but it could be."
> (Gabaldon, 1997, p. xi)

It is this felt sense of the beloved's presence that we seek to capture through the sensory portal process.

Participants then select a shadow box picture frame of white, black or timber that can be painted and remove the back panel in preparation for placing their objects. A bountiful supply of art materials is available, including colored cardboard, paints, pencils and a selection of shells, feathers, crystals, ribbons and seedpods.

A guided visualization moves participants into their bodies, soothing and focusing attention on their hearts and their connection with the loved one. Participants arrange and reflect on their items and, when ready, select a piece of the loved one's clothing or colored cardboard to form the background. Adhesive putty can be used to position objects within the frame in order to achieve a satisfying arrangement. Emotional support may be required if objects, clothing or photos need to be cut or reconfigured in order to fit. Glue guns, photo stickers and staples secure objects into place. Participants may want to add to or rearrange their work at a later time. Throughout, the therapist offers support, creating a space for quiet, absorbed creativity and allowing the process to unfold with minimal words. The time frame for constructing a sensory portal collage can be an hour or more, depending on the size of the frame and the degree of complexity.

Following construction of the collage, the therapist employs questions to prompt reflection and deepen narrative formation: How do they feel within their bodies? What stood out for them as they did this? What was the significance of objects selected, their placement and juxtaposition? Did any temporal patterns, order or new understandings emerge as they narrated the story of their relationship with their loved one? Where will they place their sensory portal?

CASE ILLUSTRATION

The following case illustration is drawn from a group workshop for suicide-bereaved adults. The comments were made in the period immediately after participants created their sensory portals.

Pablo, a young man grieving the loss of Luis, his brother, assembled a 3D collage featuring his brother's worn wallet, an intricately carved flute and a battered leather travel journal. Finishing, he reflected that the process left him feeling different, less heavy, and he felt that his brother had been helping him:

> In the beginning I felt quite frozen . . . and now I'm smiling, and I feel like I've opened up. I feel different, so the process was good—and I was pretty skeptical about the whole thing. I'm pleased. It feels less heavy—it felt very heavy, definitely. But once I started, it just kind of happened, and I felt I was getting some assistance from Luis.

Pablo talked further about the process and his reservations:

> I was almost not going to come, to be honest. . . . But when I sat down here to do it, I was looking at Luis's stuff and kind of ignoring it for a while, not knowing. And then I started to get into the flow a bit, and I felt like it just happened on its own. . . . I didn't really think about it . . . like he was guiding it.

Petra, who was grieving the loss of James, her husband, drew nourishment from the evidence of James's love for her and their children, which could be seen in his work-worn glove.

> It was very emotional for me, doing it and when I gathered his things to bring here. But as I started laying everything out, I felt calm. I had a pretty good sense of what it was I wanted. I look at this and all the happy times. It doesn't matter that it isn't going to happen again because we've done it, and it was full. James lived a full life; he didn't waste a moment. [Indicating the glove, with tears in her eyes] He really worked hard for us, to look after us; he really did look after us.

Julie, who was grieving the loss of David, her son, was surprised to note how the items, which included her son's guitar pick, an old T-shirt he loved and a leather thong with protective amulet, seemed to arrange themselves. Julie surmised that David had helped her:

> It didn't work out the way I kind of visualized. I took everything out, laid them out and took a photo and thought that would be it. But it's turned out how David was . . . and I took comfort in it being disorganized, in a semi-organized way, like he was. It felt like David was helping me.

Carol, who was grieving the loss of Mark, her brother, was visibly moved throughout the process, shedding tears that in other places she held in check. Despite initial reservations, Carol enthused:

> I love it—it's us together. Before I was thinking this is a stupid thing to do. . . . I'm not arty and could hear Mark laughing. I was a bit half-hearted, but I absolutely love it—it's us together, me and my brother [crying]. We were really close. . . . I will put some more things in later. I'm really glad I did it, and I completely love it. It was a worthwhile thing to do, spending the time with Mark.

Further insights were offered when participants talked about where they would place their work. Petra wanted to display her sensory portal in the hub of the household to encourage family conversations.

> *I would like to have this in the center of the table so we can sit and talk about these good times, about any of this. Where the grandkids could look and say, "What's this?" So they can ask, and we can talk about James. I want to be able to do that, to tell the stories. Each time, it will get easier, and I'll get to look and feel it and maybe not feel the sadness anymore.*

Julie explained her thoughts.

> *I did think in David's bedroom on the wall. I'm one of those people—I haven't cleaned out his room. I can't. People say do it when you're ready, but I don't think I'll ever be ready. But I think I might put this out in the main area where people come in, where they visit, put it on the wall there. Yes, that's what I'll do.*

CONCLUDING THOUGHTS

The richness of creating a sensory portal is that it brings into relationship that for which there is no words, weaving together the different ways people find symbolic language for love, loss, and hope. Constructing a sensory portal moves mourners into their bodies, their hearts and their imaginations to create an enduring bond with their loved ones. Held in the frame and in their homes, the resulting memories can reach beyond death and provide support for living and a re-evaluated appreciation of life and relationship.

References

Gabaldon, D. (1997). *The drums of autumn*. London: Arrow.

Klass, D., & Steffen, E. (Eds.). (2017). *Continuing bonds in bereavement*. New York: Routledge.

Ogden, P., Minton, K., & Pain, C. (2006). *Trauma and the body: A sensorimotor approach to psychotherapy*. New York: Norton.

Sands, D. C. (2014). Restoring the heartbeat of hope following suicide. In B. Thompson & R. A. Neimeyer (Eds.), *Grief and the expressive arts: Practices for the creation of meaning*. New York: Routledge.

Sands, D. C., Jordan, J. R., & Neimeyer, R. A. (2011). The meanings of suicide: A narrative approach to healing. In J. R. Jordan & J. L. McIntosh (Eds.), *Grief after suicide*. New York: Routledge.

42

Working With Blocks

An Hooghe and Peter Rober

CLIENTS FOR WHOM THE TECHNIQUE IS APPROPRIATE

This technique is often helpful at the beginning of family therapy for many issues, but certainly for loss and grief. In a playful way, the therapists create a space for a multitude of themes in the family, particularly for the place the deceased holds for each family member. Family dynamics around and after the death are given a space in the many differences in how the blocks are placed and how families work together in this. However, it is less suitable for adolescents who might feel that "child's play" threatens their sense of growing maturity.

DESCRIPTION

In using blocks as one of many expressive arts media in grief therapy (Thompson & Neimeyer, 2014), therapists offer a wooden board slightly larger than a piece of printer paper and a bag with various wooden cubes,[1] which vaguely resemble human figures. They offer this bag with the words, "*I would like to meet your family. Can you show me, making use of these cubes and this board, what your family looks like?*" The instruction is given to the family, not to one specific person.

Therapists then sit back and observe what happens. Children are often very curious and want to see what is in the bag. They often get started very enthusiastically. Some parents are more hesitant. Most important is that the therapists observe what happens and try to notice what is important in the here-and-now interactions of the family, with the goal of talking about important themes later in the session.

Specifically in working with grief, this technique gives the opportunity to examine how a family relates to the deceased. Sometimes the deceased gets a special place. Sometimes he or she gets no place. Sometimes there is discussion about the place the deceased occupies. It is then up to the therapists to make room for a conversation about the place of the deceased in the family, through the medium of the cubes.

CASE ILLUSTRATION

Stefan contacted the clinic because he was worried about his older daughter Laura, age ten. He told us that his wife had died of breast cancer a year and a half ago. Since her death, Laura had cried a lot and had difficulty falling asleep. His younger daughter Brit, who was eight years old,

DOI: 10.4324/9781351069120-52

seemed to cope more easily with the loss of her mother. Stefan wanted to make an appointment together with Laura. Laura indicated that she preferred to come without her little sister. After Stefan and Laura arrived in the therapy room and everyone had chosen a chair, the therapist immediately proposed, "I would like to start to get to know you, and I would like to do that with a practical exercise. I would like you to show me, together, here, what your family looks like." The therapist took out a bag with cubes and a board and put them in the middle of the table. "Here are all the cubes you can use to represent people. Let me see what your family looks like."

Stefan and Laura smiled at each other and immediately opened the bag together. Dad said to Laura, "Let's have a look first at what is inside." He got the cubes out and put them on the table in front of Laura. He then went on, "Do you see one for you? Which one would be you?" Laura took one from the pile, and laughingly said, "Look what a weird head!" Stefan chuckled and asked, "Will we grab one for Brit as well?" Laura said yes and indicated the block that she had just taken out. "Oh, okay," Dad said. "And which one are you then?" Laura took a block that was a bit bigger and put it next to the first block. "Oh, is that you?" he asked, and Laura replied, "I don't know." She smiled and looked at the cube very closely. "And who am I?" her father asked. Laura picked up a cube that was even larger that was already on the table. "This one," she said and laughed out loud when looking at the three cubes.

"Okay," Stefan said. "Put it on the table. Where are you going to put them?" Laura took the cubes and put them on the board. She went and knelt on the floor at a low table with the board and the cubes on it. She put the three cubes close together on the board and looked at Dad. "Like this?" Dad asked. "Yes? Very good." They both then looked at the therapist.

The therapist came closer to the table and looked at the board with the blocks.

He asked, "Can you explain what your family looks like?" Laura immediately started explaining, touching a cube and saying, "Uh, that's Brit, my sister. She's eight years old. And that is my dad." She touched another cube that fell by accident, and her dad added laughingly, "And you just fell!" Laura smiled and continued, "And this is me."

The therapist looked to the board in silence. Then he continued. "Okay. Are we missing something or someone?" Laura looked at her father and suddenly became very quiet. "Yes," her father said, and they look at each other. The therapist continued, "Most children have a mommy, right? Where is Mom?" Laura started to cry, and her father stroked her hair in silence. "Do we need to put her in the picture or is that too sad if we put her in it, Laura?" the therapist asked gently. Laura looked to the floor and cried. "Maybe you need have a look in the bag if there is a cube that can represent Mom." Stefan looked to his daughter in a caring way and said, "Are we going to do that?" He took the bag and laid some of the cubes out one by one on the table. Immediately Laura started to help as her father asked if she saw one that was suitable. Laura did not say anything as her father slowly continued to empty the bag. When all the blocks were on the table, the therapist asked, "Is there a cube that could represent your mommy?" Laura stared in front of her at the blocks. Her father asked her, "Which one are we going to take?" Laura hesitantly selected a large cube. "This one," she said quietly. "This one? asked her father, "And where are we going to put it?" Laura put the cube close to the others as her father asked her, "Close to us?" Laura nodded, and they both looked again to the therapist.

The therapist looked at the cubes and said, "Your mommy is standing close to you. Is that the place of Mommy, close to you?" Laura nodded yes. "Closer than the others?" he asked. Laura looked confused. "Maybe," the therapist suggested, "you can think about it together? What is the place of Mommy at this moment? Is this the way it was before? Or is this as it is now?" Stefan looked lovingly at Laura and waited, eventually asking her, "Do you think this is a difficult question?" Laura nodded yes, and Father offered to help and stroked her hair. The therapist added. "That's good. I think it is very good that daddies help their children with such difficult things." He added, "I have heard from An (the co-therapist) that Mommy passed away recently, and that is something that is so sad. And that you come here to talk about that and to find out how to

Figure 42.1 Positioning the Blocks Representing Family Members on the Board

Figure 42.2 The Final Position, with the Block Representing Mother Still Near the Family

deal with that. I would like to see, Laura, and maybe you can help me with that, how your family looked before Mommy passed away. Can you show me that?" After they searched together through the blocks for a while, the therapist added, "Some of the kids who have been here and who had lost their mommies, too, say, 'Yes, a lot has changed, but Mom is still there, but she is just a little bit farther away. But she is still here, and she is still very important.' And then they put Mommy sometimes farther away—for example, here [indicates edge of the board]—or they put her at this place [indicating a place just beyond the edge], and then they say, 'Look, this is our family with everyone who is alive, and that is our mommy, who is very important, and we put her next to us. She is still there, but we put her in another place.'" Stefan and Laura continued to search, using the cubes, for the place of Mommy now and the place of Mommy when she was still alive. At the request of the therapist, they also considered how the sister would place the cubes. Stefan said that he thought Brit would put Mommy next to the board and showed it with the cubes.

All parties took a moment to look at the family configuration depicted on the board. The therapist asked, "How does that feel for you, Laura? Is this how you think about it, too, or would you do it differently?" Laura immediately said no, while Daddy asked if Mother's placement was too far away for her. Laura tearfully replied that it was too far as Mommy was still in her memories. The therapist took the box with the tissues and put it on the table. For the remainder of the session, the therapist left the cubes on the table and talked about memories of Mom and the ways that Laura could still be close to her.

CONCLUDING THOUGHTS

As the case of Stefan and Laura illustrates, the work with cubes in family therapy is not so much a diagnostic tool as a way to make space for a dialogue about the family, the deceased and the grieving process of all family members. What happened in this session could be divided into three parts. In the first part, the cubes were used so that the family could represent themselves in a playful way. In this way, young children immediately are given a role in the family conversation. In the second part, the therapist quickly created space to talk about the deceased, asking "Are we missing somebody?" This question was an emotionally evocative one for both for the therapist and the family members as it emphasized that the sadness, however big it might be, was to be acknowledged and given a place without fear of talking about it. In this, the therapist has to be brave enough to talk about the loss and the sadness and also sensitive to the hesitation of the members of the family to speak about them. The therapist can express this sensitivity through reflecting, in a empathic way, how difficult or painful it is to speak about. In the third part, the blocks are used as a pretext to talk about a multitude of things, such as any differences between family members in their way of grieving or maintaining a connection with the deceased. Woven into the therapeutic interaction in a fluid way that encourages interactions between family members, block work can set the stage for exploring and restoring family bonds that have been stressed or severed by death.

Note

1. Different kinds of blocks can be used for this. We bought these blocks at Praxis-Konkret in Germany (www.pk-ch.de/).

Reference

Thompson, B. E., & Neimeyer, R. A. (Eds.). (2014). Grief and the expressive arts: Practices for creating meaning. New York: Routledge.

43

The Secure Base Map

*Jakob van Wielink, Leo Wilhelm
and Denise van Geelen-Merks*

CLIENTS FOR WHOM THE TECHNIQUE IS APPROPRIATE

This technique is appropriate for practically all clients, though clients should possess the conceptual skills to grasp the deeper meaning of secure bases when compared to general sources of support and comfort.

DESCRIPTION

Attachment behavior is any form of behavior that results in a person attaining or maintaining proximity to some other clearly identified individual, who is conceived as better able to cope with the world. . . . . For a person to know that an attachment figure is available and responsive gives him a strong and pervasive feeling of security, and so encourages him to value and continue the relationship.

(Bowlby, 1988, pp. 29–30)

In the 1950s, British psychiatrist John Bowlby developed his attachment theory, which became the basis for our modern-day insights regarding how the attachments between children and their parents and (later on) other attachment figures are formed. Attachment provides the child with a sense of security and with care and enables the child to discover the larger world one step at a time. Attachment provides a safe departure point for exploring the world, to investigate things and to take risks. The attachment figure functions as a secure base that the child can always return to safely to then venture back out into the world to explore it further.

In other words, a secure base is a person, place, objective or object that provides a sense of protection, security and being cared for (*caring*). At the same time, it provides a source of inspiration and energy to challenge, explore, take risks and look for new challenges (*daring*) (Kohlrieser, Goldsworthy, & Coombe, 2012, p. 8).

Secure bases are attachment figures when they are people, but they can also be transitional objects: (physical or virtual) objects from the outside world that hold specific symbolic meaning in our inner world and are beneficial for us when taking on challenges, such as stuffed animals during childhood. Examples include:

DOI: 10.4324/9781351069120-53

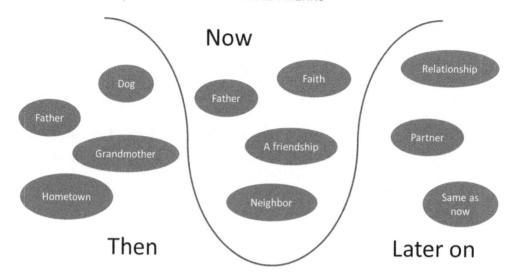

Figure 43.1 Example of a Secure Base Map

- *People*: parents, grandparents, partners, friends, mentors etc. (Note: Young children cannot function as secure bases for their parent(s) so long as it is the parent('s)/(s') job to care for the children.)
- *Places*: a country, a house, nature, a specific city or village etc.
- *Others*: pets, religious figures, personal values, ideologies, symbols etc.

Secure bases may vary from one stage of life to the next. Obtaining insight into secure bases and their meaning can help clients draw on these resources in the event of loss. Likewise, continuing bonds with a deceased loved one can offer a secure base in spite of the loss. While the physical form of the relationship may come to an end, the security-enhancing connection may persist, even if in a different form.

When exploring underlying themes dealing with loss and grief, explain to your client the concepts of secure bases (psychoeducation). Have your client then create an inventory of their various secure bases at three separate periods in time: then (the past), now (the present) and later (the future). A brief list as inventory is perfectly fine, but feel free to encourage your client to be more artistic about it by drawing people, places and other secure bases or symbolizing them in other ways. This often deepens the emotional value of the exercise.

Then explore the continuing bonds between the various time periods with the client to determine which inspiring aspects of the secure bases can be integrated into the client's own life and personality. This enables the client to internalize secure bases and potentially to be a secure base for others in turn.

CASE STUDY

Alex had been with Jody for 30 years. It felt like a lifetime. They were both students when they first began dating. He remembered how they used to spend nights talking and making love in his rickety single bed. They then moved in together, bought a house and had kids—so many memories. Jody had known his parents, who died many years ago; she had known his childhood home. He had met her grandparents once. In losing her, he lost not only his wife, his buddy, but also his past; that was what it felt like to him.

Two years ago, a sudden shadow was cast on their comfortable life together. They were on holiday in Mexico when Jody began experiencing stomach cramps. Initially, they figured it must be something she ate, but it persisted, and when she could barely stand up straight because of the pain several days later, they went to a Mexican doctor. He prescribed some painkillers and recommended that she have someone examine the issue as soon as possible once they went home to Canada.

Once they got back home, things progressed quickly. Jody went to see her physician, got X-rays taken at the hospital and was then referred to an oncologist. Initially, things seemed under control, but appearances can be deceiving. The cancer turned out to be an aggressive type that is hard to treat. Jody died exactly six months after her first doctor's visit.

"It's like my foundation in life has been wiped away," said Alex, his face stricken. Jody was Alex's secure base. The thing he misses the most is her ability to always look on the bright side, to put things into perspective. Now that she's gone, he misses the safe sense of belonging and the trust she had in him and in the good in life.

"What did she teach you?" This question helped the therapist direct the client's focus to himself. Instead of focusing on the person who was no longer with him, Alex now focused on the parts of her that were still present within him (in his memories, his convictions and his behavior). "She taught me to trust in the good. Every night before we went to sleep, we would name one thing that we were grateful for. I still do that. It's not easy, but it helps. And she was big on healthy eating for the both of us, which helps me make the effort to cook for myself every night." He smiled faintly. "Before she died, she told me that she would come visit me every once in a while, in the shape of a butterfly, to say hello. I never used to believe in such things, but I was visited by a butterfly in the middle of winter once while I was out for a walk." Jody was no longer physically available as a secure base. This was hard on Alex, but the relationship he had with her could give rise to new secure bases. Butterflies now made him feel safe and encouraged, enabling him to take steps, such as finding new or other secure bases.

For Alex, creating a secure base map was a very emotional process. Many of his former secure bases had passed away. Alex realised that he kept them alive by talking to Jody about them but that he never truly said goodbye to them. He was profoundly affected by the pain of the loss. At the same time, he recognized his neighbors as important new secure bases. They frequently stopped by unannounced or invited him over for dinner or just to have a beer. This realization encouraged him to accept their invitation to take part in a tennis competition. He used to play tennis all the time, but Jody had never gotten into it. He rediscovered his old passion and even participated in the tennis club's championships. His neighbors and also the tennis club, which he frequents several times a week, became his new secure bases. Although he continued to miss Jody terribly, he began regaining his lust for life slowly but surely and even began to open to the idea of a new love.

CONCLUDING THOUGHTS

Creating a secure base map is a fairly easy exercise in some ways; all that's needed is a sheet of paper, preferably a large one, and a selection of multi-colored markers or oil pastel artist crayons. The therapist is able to give clients free rein in terms of what they want their map to look like. Sometimes clients turn it into a work of art, full of drawings and colors; sometimes, it consists only of a bunch of words. The objectives of the exercise are manifold. It helps the client become aware of who and what they draw strength from or could draw strength from and helps them examine how they deal with that strength. Mapping things out may help them realize that they never took the time to process the loss of past secure bases and never considered the impact they still have on them in the present day. Moreover, it teaches them to reach out to their secure bases in the present day in order to cope with those past losses properly.

The internal form of continuing bonds is essentially about the internalization of secure bases (Wielink, Wilhelm, & van Geelen-Merks, 2020). This puts continuing bonds in a larger framework as more than just a lasting connection with a loved one who has passed away, as secure bases can take many forms. For example, people may draw strength from a continuing bond with their home country, which they have left; with an organization they used to be involved with; or a relationship that has since been ended. This internalized strength has a positive effect on the client's capacity to cope with loss and enter into new bonds and even their potential to be a secure base for others in turn.

In addition to the different types of secure bases covered in this chapter, certain experiences or life goals can present themselves as sources of pride and self-esteem, enhancing a sense of security and belonging. Especially when clients can connect with them on a deeper level and draw inspiration from them, clients could consider adding such elements of support to their secure base maps.

References

Bowlby, J. (1988). *A secure base: Parent-child attachment and healthy human development. Tavistock professional book*. London: Routledge.

Kohlrieser, G., Goldsworthy, S., & Coombe, D. (2012). *Care to dare: Unleashing astonishing potential through secure base leadership*. San Francisco: Jossey-Bass.

Wielink, J. P. J. van, Wilhelm, L., & van Geelen-Merks, D. (2020). *Loss, grief and attachment in life transitions: A clinician's guide to secure base counselling*. London and New York: Routledge.

44

Player of Life

Carolyn Ng and Joanne Ng

CLIENTS FOR WHOM THE TECHNIQUE IS APPROPRIATE

The technique is applicable for group settings with bereaved children and adolescents, aged seven and above, who lost their main caregiver, such as a parent or grandparent. While this was originally designed for those whose main caregiver died of cancer, it may be suitable for other causes of death as well. However, it may not be appropriate for children who are in the first three months of bereavement because they are likely in the midst of acute post-loss adjustment. Furthermore, it may not be suitable for those who had a difficult relationship with their late caregiver (e.g., abuse history) or those who show signs of complications in grief, unless screening assessment is done. As for children with special needs, like autism, modifications would likely be needed in order to cater to their unique conditions.

DESCRIPTION

The death of a primary caregiver is never a natural and anticipated incident from a child's point of view, even though it may be perceived as "natural" and "anticipated" from adults' perspectives or in a medical assessment. As a result, losing a caregiver can be highly stressful and have devastating effects on the child's life. While young children are generally perceived as more vulnerable to such stressors, adolescents are not exempt from the distress and struggles resulting from the loss of their main caregiver. At the same time, there is no child who is too young to grieve for such a significant loss because "grief does not focus on one's ability to 'understand' but instead upon one's ability to 'feel.' Therefore, any child mature enough to love is mature enough to grieve" (Wolfelt, 1983, p. 20).

Though there is no way to take the threat away and protect children from death, it is essential to render them appropriate psychosocial support in order to help ease their post-loss grief and adjustment. Unlike adults, however, bereaved children may not be able to thoroughly explore their thoughts and feelings rationally or to articulate these thoughts and feelings fully in words. Rather, they often immerse themselves in activities and games in an attempt to work out their feelings and anxieties (Howarth, 2011) because play is children's natural language and medium of self-expression. Therefore, while we provide a safe space for bereaved children to process their grief and learn to adjust to their post-loss lives, it is important to incorporate play into therapeutic interventions.

DOI: 10.4324/9781351069120-54

The *LIFE* Series is a program for bereaved children who lost their main caregiver to cancer in a community-based psychosocial service for children impacted by cancer. Using play and various experiential activities, it aims at enabling bereaved children to *Leap* over the adversities of loss, *Illuminate* their inner resilience in grief, *Foster* a safety net for their growth and *Envision* their lives ahead with hope despite having lost their main caregiver during their growing-up years. In each session, different activities are crafted to help bereaved children discover their inner tenacity and master different coping strategies while processing their grief and addressing different stressors resulting from the loss and its aftermath. Such activities incorporate theoretical concepts from Worden's (2009) tasks of mourning, as well as Stroebe and Schut's (1999) dual process model (DPM). In addition, activities facilitating continuing bonds with their late caregiver are also crafted (Klass, Silverman, & Nickman, 1996), because death cannot end these children's relationship with their main caregiver, though it has robbed them of the caregiver's physical presence.

The Player of Life is one of the sessions held under the *LIFE* Series. In this session, bereaved children are invited to be "players" in an indoor soccer game. They are grouped into teams of four to six players (depending on the total number of children registered) with mixed genders and ages. Before the start of the matches, they are each given a bib, which they personally decorate. They are also asked to choose a special number representing themselves on one side and another special number representing their late caregiver on the other side. They subsequently enter into the game displaying the bib with their chosen number in front and their late caregiver's number on their backs. After getting warmed up within their teams and playing two or three rounds of ten-minute matches against one another, they take a resting break during which they get to nominate a teammate to be their team's most valuable player (MVP). Shortly after their cheers and celebration, they receive the sudden news that their respective MVPs will be removed from their teams, and the remaining team members have to finish the game on their own.

Group processing of their "post-loss" reactions is done with those who remain on their teams by their respective *LIFE* coaches. Meanwhile, all the elected MVPs are grouped together for separate processing by another *LIFE* coach as their experiences will be different from the rest. Through coloring their feelings, as well as using a Post-it pad to stick their thoughts or questions on different parts of a huge gingerbread man drawn on the floor, children become attuned to their personal reactions to the bad news and its wave-like impacts. In addition, through the group sharing, they also get to empathize and identify with each other as they realize the commonalities among their reactions. Such processing is important for bereaved children to take in the reality of loss and learn to manage the emotional distress resulting from it, as illustrated in the tasks of mourning (Worden, 2009) and DPM (Stroebe & Schut, 1999).

Afterward, the remaining teams discuss and strategize how they will continue the game without their MVPs. This corresponds to the task of adjusting to life without the loved one, as suggested by Worden (2009), and the need to cope with restoration-oriented stressors, as highlighted in DPM (Stroebe & Schut, 1999). Their *LIFE* coaches subsequently help them draw parallels to how they can do likewise as they continue their life journey and when they encounter any difficult moments in future. Such experiential learning is important to bereaved children as it helps promote their process of redefining and reintegrating themselves into a life without their late caregiver's physical presence (Howarth, 2011).

Meanwhile, as the MVPs can no longer participate in the game directly but can only stay at the edge of the field to watch the remaining matches, they are invited to discuss what they wish for their teams and how they can continue to support them, be it to cheerlead or to strategize with them. In the process, their *LIFE* coach helps them connect with the idea of continuing the bond (Klass et al., 1996) with their late caregiver, whose departure resembles their experience of being removed from their teams. Remembering how their late caregiver used to play a part in their lives and knowing that they can remain connected with each other in various forms of continuing bonds are important to these bereaved children. This experiential process not only brings them solace, but also facilitates their mastery of Worden's (2009) last task of mourning, in terms of finding an enduring connection with their loved one while moving forward with life.

Upon completing the remaining two or three matches, the LIFE coaches invite sharing from both the MVPs and the left-behind teammates in a big group. As they negotiate the ups and downs together, the LIFE coaches remind them that they are not alone in this journey of grief and loss. A supportive network is important to bereaved children as their grief and loss experiences can be validated and empathized. Moreover, they can also learn from one another and grow together regardless of the challenges encountered in the aftermath of their caregiver's death. On the contrary, the lack of such a safety net is found to hinder their post-loss adjustment and eventually lead to poorer outcomes (Howarth, 2011).

At the end of the session, they design their own jersey with their chosen number in front and their late caregiver's number on the back. They are also invited to write a love message or decorate it in a way to honor their late caregiver. This jersey then serves as a linking object (Klass et al., 1996), symbolizing the continuing bond between them and their late caregiver. Such an object is important to bereaved children as they gradually learn to reconstruct their bond with their late caregiver into a mental representation that is less reliant on physical proximity.

CASE ILLUSTRATION

Following the death of a parent or grandparent to cancer, we recruited 16 bereaved children and adolescents, ages 7 to 14, into the LIFE program, and conducted the Player of Life activity with them as a part of the larger support service. When we first invited them to take turns to introduce themselves and the loved one they had lost, many of the children were surprised to find so many others who shared losses similar to theirs because the death of a primary caregiver was hardly a social norm at their age. As illustrated in the wide-eyed response of 7-year-old Joshua to 9-year-old Emma, "You mean your mom is also dead? Me too!" The discovery of bereaved companions soon broke the ice and bonded the bereaved children together as they could not readily find such peers in their natural settings. Instead of being the odd ones in their social circles, their identity as bereaved children was immediately normalized and validated in this community.

Subsequently, when the children decorated their bibs and selected their special numbers, their LIFE coaches invited them to share what these numbers meant for them. For the late caregiver's number, many chose their caregiver's favorite number or birthday month or date while others further shared their associated fond memories with their late caregiver. When they later knew that they would wear this bib for the soccer game, they were also reminded that their late caregiver would always "have their backs" in spite of their physical absence from their lives. In response to this idea, nine-year-old Shane told his twin sister and his LIFE coach, "I like it. Our dad is always behind us because the bib has our dad's name!"

At the point when the teams were told that their MVPs would be removed from their teams while the game still needed to go on, understandably, a spectrum of feelings including shock, sadness, a sense of loss and even anger arose. Many of them were also confused, asking "Why?" while others tried to bargain with their LIFE coaches. For instance, as a left-behind teammate, Daniel (age 11) exclaimed, "Oh no! How are we going to play the next match?" while Megan (age 8) mumbled, "What will we do now?" In the process, it was interesting to see how these children intuitively drew parallels between their game experiences and their loss experiences. "That time when my daddy died, it's also like that. Very sudden," was shared by 12-year-old Nina while she recalled the incident. On the other hand, 14-year-old Irfan disagreed, saying, "I knew it was coming because my mother and aunts kept talking secretly when we were in hospital. Just now I also saw you two [the LIFE coaches] whispering, so I knew there must be something happening."

At the same time, a removed MVP, Collin (age 13) also grumbled, "I don't like it because it didn't go in order. It's not fair!" while Selina (age 11) bargained with her LIFE coach, asking if she could join her team again later after skipping one match. It was fascinating to see how they instantly had a taste of what it might have been like for their late caregivers, having to leave them behind though it was not their wish. Just as they tried to appeal their removal from their team, they realized that their late caregiver had made similar attempts in the process of illness. They also recognized that such attempts were made out of their caregiver's love and concern for them because their caregiver valued them, similar to how they wanted to be there for their teammates simply because they cared for their teams.

In the subsequent matches, it was heartening to see how adaptable the remaining teammates were as they adjusted their ways of playing and even stretched themselves beyond their original positions in order to fill in the gaps and juggle additional roles (e.g., goalkeeper-cum-defender). It was also amazing to see how resourceful they were as they sought support from other teams, and vice versa, in times when the matches became more intense and challenging. At the edge of the field, it was equally heartwarming to see how the removed MVPs held their banners, specially decorated for their teams with encouraging messages, while shouting cheers for their teams. In the process, they actually experienced a continuing bond with their late caregiver, believing that their caregiver has been equally wishing the best for them, watching over them, and cheering for them from afar, just as Ashley (age ten) expressed: "It felt like my mom was cheering me on too!"

At the end of the day, not only did these bereaved children get to unload and process their grief reactions as a result of their loss experiences, both in the soccer game and in their real-life situations, but they also realized that they shared many feelings and thoughts in common that, in turn, validated their felt experiences. Furthermore, they recognized that their late caregiver had "had their backs," as represented on their bibs throughout the matches and on their personal jerseys that they brought home after the game. In addition, they also experienced strong social support from their peers and LIFE coaches in this special peer community.

CONCLUDING THOUGHTS

Bereaved children experience different forms of turbulence in the aftermath of losing a primary caregiver and hence are at risk for adverse psychosocial consequences. So it is essential to provide them with a safe space in which they can benefit from developmentally appropriate interventions facilitated by helping professionals to learn to leap over these adversities and illuminate their inner resilience in the midst of grief and loss. In addition, gathering bereaved children into group settings also fosters a safety net in which they gain support from peers who share similar grief and loss experiences. All in all, bereaved children deserve our creative companionship as they move through the seasons of grief so that they can envision life with hope despite the loss of a primary caregiver at a young age.

References

Howarth, R. A. (2011). Promoting the adjustment of parentally bereaved children. *Journal of Mental Health Counselling, 33*(1), 21–32.

Klass, D., Silverman, P. R., & Nickman, S. L. (1996). *Continuing bond: New understanding of grief.* New York: Routledge.

Stroebe, M. S., & Schut, H. (1999). The dual process model of coping with bereavement: Rationale and description. *Death Studies, 23,* 197–224.

Wolfelt, A. (1983). Children's understanding and response to death (with caregiver behaviors). In *Helping children cope with grief* (pp. 19–50). New York: Routledge.

Worden, J. W. (2009). *Grief counselling and grief therapy: A handbook for the mental health practitioner* (4th ed.). New York: Springer.

45

Habits of the Heart

Joshua Magariel

CLIENTS FOR WHOM THE TECHNIQUE IS APPROPRIATE

This technique can be used as an individual and relational intervention, particularly in the context of bereavement. This technique may not be effective for bereaved persons who are experiencing acute grief in the immediate period following the death of a loved one. While *Habits of the Heart* was created in the context of grief therapy, this reframe could perhaps be used in different therapy settings.

DESCRIPTION

Habits of the Heart is merely one example, yet a comprehensive example, of attachment-oriented, narrative reframing. Attachment reframing is an essential strategy in emotionally focused therapy (EFT) that interprets cognitions, emotions, behaviors and relational dynamics through an attachment perspective (Johnson, 2004). The goal of EFT in general and the use of attachment reframing in particular is to create connections or bonds between people who have attachment injuries or are in need of deepening bonds. When a therapist begins looking for attachment-related themes in bereavement, certain statements begin to stand out among the rest. One familiar statement we hear from the bereaved is a version of "I reached toward my phone to call him when I realized halfway that he wouldn't answer the phone because he is no longer here," or "I started to set a second place at the table for her before I caught myself." When asking a bereaved client to describe the meaning of statements like these, we hear many responses, ranging from identifying the emotional pain, confusion about forgetfulness or shame connected to being triggered. In the grief therapist's toolbox are many possible explanations as well. Here, attachment reframing can be used as a powerful intervention in grief therapy. Referring to this moment as a "habit of the heart" can address multiple meanings simultaneously as well as begin to provide language and a framework to facilitate continuing bonds, heal attachment injuries and foster overall attachment-related adjustment.

    Habits of the Heart is a term to describe how our lives are emotionally, psychologically and behaviorally organized by our relationships and their heart-related habits (see Panksepp, 2009; Porges, 2009; Shear, 2016). *Habits of the Heart* is best understood as a visceral experience that is rooted in the ways we've learned to connect with people we love. We have these moments because these are the ways we shared our lives with people. We've learned to expect

DOI: 10.4324/9781351069120-55

our loved one's presence in a predictable and real way. These habits are connected to themes of love and attachment, and in loss, they are deeply affected. When working with bereaved clients, we frequently notice the following *Habits of the Heart* themes:

- Reminders of love
- Habits to reach toward
- Habits of receiving love
- Habits of belonging
- Habits of safety and security
- Habits of caregiving and care receiving
- Habits of their presence
- Habits of influence

The use of the *Habits of the Heart* reframe is to encourage bereaved clients to see these experiences as reminders of love instead of something to be overcome. For some, this perspective will help dissipate some of the shame and anxiety connected to grief. And, ideally, *Habits of the Heart* can help provide language that will ultimately facilitate continuing bonds or attachment adjustment.

Inherent in adjusting to life-changing loss, the narratives related to attachment dynamics require examination and adjustment (Magariel, 2016). Connecting the possible meanings of *Habits of the Heart* with the relational dynamics of attachment theory can be a powerful reframe for the bereaved and a helpful tool for the therapist. Furthermore, *Habits of the Heart* can assist the bereaved and the therapist in navigating three essential loss-related narrative categories: (1) the stories of the client's relationship to the loved one before death; (2) the stories of illness, death and loss; and (3) the stories of how a connection is still possible and can be maintained after a death (Magariel, 2016). The goal here is to provide affirming language that helps the bereaved in adjusting to the changing attachment dynamics of a relationship that are impacted by loss as well as establishing an integrated narrative of one's relationship that is adaptive and meaningful.

CASE ILLUSTRATION

Barbara was a 74-year-old woman, self-referred for bereavement counseling 12 months after the death of James, her husband of 50 years. James had died shortly after being diagnosed with stage 4 cancer. In the first 12 months of her bereavement, Barbara was diagnosed with and treated for cancer herself. Once on the other side of her treatment, Barbara was overwhelmed with her longing for James and entered counseling looking for support.

Over an 18-month period, the primary intervention of our work was relationship review (Magariel, 2016). In other words, Barbara's narratives related to attachment dynamics, or her story of love, required adjustment, and the focus of her treatment was to examine the three loss-related narrative categories mentioned earlier (i.e., stories of love, loss and possible ongoing connection). As is common in the beginning of grief therapy, Barbara shared the story of her husband's illness and how he died. Then our conversations started to shift, and Barbara would tell me stories about their relationship before his death—their travels, listening to music, what shows they would watch on TV and how they would laugh together. Barbara shared that they never had children, and to her, this elevated the meaning and feeling of connectedness that they shared. We talked often about how she "put all her eggs in one basket" in the relationship department, highlighting her feeling of great loss and the significant loneliness that she then felt. I would also hear story after story of specific difficult moments of grief since James died.

One story in particular stood out to me in our time together. It was late spring, and Barbara was grocery shopping in the produce section and noticed that the black plums were in season. Then it hit her that black plums were her husband's favorite, and since Barbara did the grocery shopping, she would bring home and surprise James with black plums every spring. This was an act of love from her toward James. As this settled in, in the middle of the produce section, Barbara began to cry uncontrollably, and she left the store in a hurry. This was the first time in our work that I offered this particular attachment reframe, and I labeled this moment a "habit of the heart." Barbara was profoundly moved by this phrase and very quickly on her own began referring to this moment and many others the same way. Habits of the Heart became the language that Barbara would use as part of her coping with James's death, softening these nostalgic moments of recalling her love and her loss and hinting that their continuation in some form could enhance her sense of connection with James. Significantly, she began buying black plums again in his honor.

CONCLUDING THOUGHTS

A final thought is related to the potential for creativity in clinical practice, which is maximized by a therapist's (1) *empathy* and genuine caring; (2) developing knowledge and expertise in *theory and interventions*; and 3) acceptance of the power of his or her role in a helping relationship, fostering respectful and ethical *therapeutic leadership*. My formulation of *Habits of the Heart* seemed to arise from such a spontaneous moment of therapeutic creativity, and I encourage other therapists to be similarly open to theirs.

References

Johnson, S. (2004). *The Practice of emotionally focused couple therapy: Creating connection* (2nd ed.). New York: Routledge.

Magariel, J. (2016). Relationship review. In R. A. Neimeyer (Ed.), *Techniques of grief therapy: Assessment and intervention*. New York: Routledge.

Panksepp, J. (2009). Brain emotional systems and qualities of mental life: From animal models of affect to implications for psychotherapeutics. In D. Fosha, D. Siegel, & M. Solomon (Eds.), *The healing power of emotion: Affective neuroscience, development, and clinical practice* (pp. 27–54). New York: Norton.

Porges, S. (2009). Reciprocal influences between body and brain in the perception and expression of affect: A polyvagal perspective. In D. Fosha, D. Siegel, & M. Solomon (Eds.), *The healing power of emotion: Affective neuroscience, development, and clinical practice* (pp. 27–54). New York: Norton.

Shear, M. K. (2016). Grief is a form of love. In R. A. Neimeyer (Ed.), *Techniques of grief therapy: Assessment and intervention*. New York: Routledge.

Part XI
Dialoguing With the Deceased

46

Consulting the Deceased

Wendy G. Lichtenthal, Aliza A. Panjwani
and Melissa Masterson

CLIENTS FOR WHOM THE TECHNIQUE IS APPROPRIATE

Adults struggling to maintain a connection with the deceased and those seeking greater self-compassion could benefit from this technique. It may also help bereaved individuals experiencing difficulty connecting with valued activities, roles and relationships as a result of having lost a loved one. The technique may be less effective if the deceased was not a provider of emotional support or was overly critical of the bereaved.

DESCRIPTION

Therapeutic writing has a long tradition in grief therapy, with several variations described in prior volumes of *Techniques of Grief Therapy* (Neimeyer, 2012, 2016). Directed, theoretically driven writing may have particular value in reducing more severe grief symptoms (Lichtenthal & Cruess, 2010; Lichtenthal & Neimeyer, 2012). With this in mind, *Consulting the Deceased* directs the client to write a letter to the deceased describing how she would like to keep the deceased as an active part of her story. This can encourage the bereaved to consider future meaningful goals while maintaining a connection to the deceased. The client is then asked to respond as the deceased to share what the deceased wants for the griever and to affirm the griever's plans to re-engage in life while coexisting with her grief. Invoking the deceased's encouraging perspective in this way can foster self-compassion in the griever.

Consulting the Deceased is suggested in the fourth session of meaning-centered grief therapy (MCGT), a 16-session intervention designed to enhance meaning and purpose in bereaved individuals experiencing intense, protracted grief reactions. The exercise applies two core principles of MCGT. The first principle is that the griever has the ability to author her story and choose her life narrative (Neimeyer, 2012, 2016). The other is that the connection to the deceased can continue as a source of meaning to the griever (Lichtenthal, Lacey, Roberts, Sweeney, & Slivjak, 2017). After writing the letter—ideally outside the session, but possibly during the session if the patient was unable to outside therapy—the griever is asked to read the letter addressed to the deceased aloud, followed by the deceased's response letter. Creating a warm, compassionate atmosphere, the therapist can then assist the griever with sharing and processing the contents of the letters.

Of note, this exercise can be conceptualized as a gentle opportunity to help the griever build distress tolerance. To cope with their intense grief and manage fears of feeling overwhelmed,

DOI: 10.4324/9781351069120-57

bereaved individuals may naturally engage in experiential avoidance. However, while providing relief from pain in the short term, chronic avoidance can inhibit the processing of grief-related emotions, potentially contributing to prolonged grief reactions (Eisma et al., 2013). Consequently, the therapist is encouraged to observe and highlight the griever's ability to tolerate intense emotions as grief emerges during the writing, sharing or processing of the Consulting the Deceased letter.

CASE ILLUSTRATION

Mark, a married 67-year-old retired man, lost his 37-year-old daughter, Chrissy, with whom he was very close, to a battle with stomach cancer approximately a year and a half ago. After a second recurrence, treatment was no longer working. Doctors predicted that Chrissy had one week to live and recommended hospice. After Chrissy transitioned to home hospice at her parents' house, Mark became her primary caregiver. Chrissy ended up living an additional four months, during which time the bond between father and daughter grew even stronger as they engaged in meaningful conversations and activities, such as taking long walks together. Mark described how in awe he was about the way Chrissy chose to spend her final days and, really, how she had lived her entire life.

When Mark began MCGT, he was not particularly avoidant of his grief, describing several rituals he engaged in to maintain his connection to Chrissy since her death. Mark was, however, despondent, reporting a strong lack of motivation to engage in life. While his relationship with Chrissy remained meaningful, he felt disconnected from other sources of meaning, describing life as "colorless." He and his therapist worked closely to understand factors contributing to his sense of emptiness. Mark struggled in part because he and his wife coped very differently with Chrissy's illness and the loss, leading to a sense of disconnection from her and, consequently, from their shared activities. Although he had close friendships, he observed himself withdrawing more and more, and as this occurred, he became more self-critical. He was able to articulate that Chrissy would want him to be happy, but it was more of an intellectual statement than emotionally connected.

In the fourth session of MCGT, he was asked to write a letter to Chrissy. He shared the letter with his therapist, becoming very emotional and engaged. Here is an excerpt from this letter:
    Good morning my beautiful daughter,

I hope you had a good night. You know I think about you every day. I know that you are not in pain anymore. I love the fact that you send me signs that you're always with me. When I am out with my friends, I talk about you. Things you have said, things you've done. Things you don't like, things you like. I love keeping you in my daily routine. It makes me feel close to you even though I know you are far away from me. . . . It is the hardest thing to lose a child. I don't have the energy or the will to do things that make me happy. I am trying my best to live my life with you in my heart like the way you want me to.
    Love,
    Dad

He then shared Chrissy's response letter. Here is an excerpt of her response:

Hi Dad,

I do feel your pain up in heaven. I see the tears roll off your face. I told you many times, "Dad, don't cry." I am fine here and have no pain. It was the best thing for me to leave the Earth and be with God. I want you to be happy and live your life to the fullest. I want you to travel and see the world. Do it now before it is too late, Dad. . . . I am right here next to you, keeping you safe and sound. Please, Dad, don't spend any more time crying for me. I am fine and I need you to be fine too. Play with [my] little cute dog and take long walks in the park like we used to do. He loves them and so did I. Dad, it is time for you to live your life to the fullest. And when God calls you home, I'll be waiting for you with open arms. Thanks, Dad, for all you have done for me. I love you, Dad. Talk to you soon. Remember, I am always right next to you. Keep looking for my signs.

    Love,

    Chrissy

After he read these letters, Mark expressed that this was one of the most challenging things he had done since her passing but that he felt better after "letting out" his emotions. Doing so also helped him feel more emotionally connected to Chrissy's message to re-engage in life and live it more fully. Mark described how Chrissy had modeled this with her seize-the-day spirit, often traveling and creating new adventures. Engaging his daughter's voice also helped affirm the legacy she left behind and the way he wanted to tell her story and, consequently, his own.

The themes in Chrissy's letter were carried forward through the course of therapy, making discussions about reconnecting with sources of meaning all the more powerful. The therapist gently invoked Chrissy's voice from the letter to remind John of the mantra to which she herself subscribed till the very end of her days: live your life to the fullest. Mark reached out to his best friend, who he noted could always make him laugh, and began taking trips with his beloved son just as they used to. One of the most powerful outcomes of the work was the growing sense of reconnection with his wife; in an effort to strengthen their relationship, he began planning a vacation with her. In this way, he was honoring Chrissy's wish that he live his life fully and meaningfully.

CONCLUDING THOUGHTS

Consulting the Deceased capitalizes on the power of the "symbolic bond" with the deceased as well as the widely accepted benefits of letter writing (Neimeyer, 2012). It can facilitate meaning making, helping bereaved individuals construct a coherent narrative that incorporates the significance of the deceased's life into their own life story (Lichtenthal & Breitbart, 2015). In guiding the patient through this exercise, the therapist should highlight the choice the griever has in how she tells the story and in how she keeps the deceased a part of her story. Gently referring back to the contents of the letter and the specific language used (i.e., "*Do it now before it is too late*"; "*it is time for you to live your life to the fullest.*") in subsequent sessions engaged the deceased's voice in supporting the griever's plans for the future. Though bereaved individuals may be reluctant to think about living a meaningful life without the deceased physically present, incorporating the deceased's voice can encourage the bereaved in making this transition with self-compassion and a powerful continued connection.

ACKNOWLEDGEMENTS

Support for research on meaning-centered grief therapy was provided by National Cancer Institute (NCI) grants R03 CA13994 (Lichtenthal) and K07 CA172216 (Lichtenthal).

References

Eisma, M. C., Stroebe, M. S., Schut, H. A. W., Stroebe, W., Boelen, P. A., & van den Bout, J. (2013). Avoidance processes mediate the relationship between rumination and symptoms of complicated grief and depression following loss. *Journal of Abnormal Psychology, 122*(4), 961–970. doi:10.1037/a0034051

Lichtenthal, W. G., & Breitbart, W. (2015). The central role of meaning in adjustment to the loss of a child to cancer: Implications for the development of meaning-centered grief therapy. *Current Opinion in Supportive and Palliative Care, 9*, 46. doi:10.1097/SPC.0000000000000117

Lichtenthal, W. G., & Cruess, D. G. (2010). Effects of directed written disclosure on grief and distress symptoms among bereaved individuals. *Death Studies, 34*(6), 475–499. doi:10.1080/07481187.20 10.483332

Lichtenthal, W. G., Lacey, S., Roberts, K., Sweeney, C., & Slivjak, E. (2017). Meaning-centered grief therapy. In W. Breitbart (Ed.), *Meaning-centered psychotherapy* (pp. 88–99). New York: Oxford University Press.

Lichtenthal, W. G., & Neimeyer, R. A. (2012). Directed writing to facilitate meaning making. In R. A. Neimeyer (Eds.), *Techniques in grief therapy: Creative practices for counseling the bereaved* (pp. 165–168). New York: Routledge.

Neimeyer, R. A. (Ed.). (2012). *Techniques in grief therapy: Creative practices for counseling the bereaved.* New York: Routledge.

Neimeyer, R. A. (Ed.). (2016). *Techniques in grief therapy: Assessment and intervention.* New York: Routledge.

47

Interviewing the Internalized Other

Nancy J. Moules and Kenneth J. Doka

CLIENTS FOR WHOM THE TECHNIQUE IS APPROPRIATE

Interviewing the internalized other is particularly useful with bereaved individuals who struggle with guilt or anger or have unfinished business with the deceased that demands answers. It can allow the bereaved to express resentment or regret, say goodbye, forgive or offer an apology—all while reaffirming an unbroken bond. Since the intervention implies that a significant relationship existed between the deceased and bereaved using the method, it would not work well in cases where there really was not a relationship (e.g., a sibling or parent who died before a significant relationship existed). Likewise, it also might be inappropriate in highly negative, abusive or hostile relationships from which the bereaved person needs more to disengage than to internalize the deceased person.

DESCRIPTION

The technique of interviewing an internalized other has been described and applied to bereavement work by Moules (2010) and draws on a variety of sources including gestalt therapy, narrative therapy and continuing bonds (Klass & Steffen, 2018). The naming of this technique is attributed to Karl Tomm, a Canadian marriage and family therapist (Tomm, Hoyt, & Madigan, 1998). Basically, the approach asks clients to engage in a conversation with the therapist while voicing the perspective of someone now deceased. Once a clinician has made the decision that interviewing the internalized other would be an appropriate and timely therapeutic intervention, he or she generally asks permission to interview the deceased by simply stating, "I would like to ask if I could interview (Name), with you speaking (Name's) part. Would you permit me to do that?" Clients can be somewhat confused and surprised by the question, yet, if simply out of curiosity, they generally agree. Once they have agreed, the clinician informs the client that he or she will be addressing the internalized other by name and asks that the respondent reply in the other's voice in the first person, using "I" language.

Typically, the interview begins with gentler, more benign questions, often taking the internalized other to an earlier time in the relationship. For example, in the case of a bereaved wife, Sandy, grieving over the death her husband, Jim, questions might begin like this: "*Jim, when did you first meet Sandy? What was she like then?*" The interview then would gradually shift into more therapeutic topics. For example, if there were issues of guilt

DOI: 10.4324/9781351069120-58

or apology, the clinician eventually might ask, *"Jim, Sandy feels guilty that, in the last months of your life, she had to seek assistance with nursing aides. What do you think about that?"* Other lines of inquiry might be *"Jim, if there were anything you wished to say to Sandy now, what would that be?"* The conversation might take many turns, guided by the therapist's discernment about what might provide therapeutic leverage. The clinician generally concludes the interview by asking the internalized other if there are any other questions that it would be important to ask. Throughout the interview, the clinician should continue to use the internalized other's name as this not only keeps the focus on the voice of the internalized other but also serves as a reminder to the clinician. There could be questions that the internalized other is unable to answer at the time, and these can be the focus of subsequent sessions and interventions.

When the interview is completed, the clinician again addresses the client by his or her name and begins to process the conversation just completed. Clients often express surprise at some of the responses and frequently feel reassured that they could reach so deeply into the essence of the deceased. They often express both recognition of and comfort in the continuing bond that they hold with the deceased. In the context of family or group therapy, the clinician can invite others who are present into the conversation at this point for their own observations, reflections and insights. It is not unusual for other family members to want to offer their own internalized versions of responses to the questions, such as *"I think Dad was relieved that you brought in nursing aides. He often expressed fears early in his illness that he was a burden and that you were doing so much."* The power in such conversations lies in their ability to generate healing dialogue that can ease further suffering.

CASE ILLUSTRATION

Jason was an eight-year-old boy and the eldest child when his father, George, was diagnosed with lung cancer. At the time, he lived with both parents and a younger sister. George's illness created a number of issues for the family—primarily financial, as his father worked for a contracting company. As George's health deteriorated, the family finances deteriorated as well. Jason's mother then had to go to work in a local store to assist with the bills—leaving Jason with increased responsibility for his younger sibling. Jason understood the implications of his father's illness, but he did harbor unexpressed resentment over the added responsibilities and limited finances that forced him to give up cherished activities such as sports. He was particularly troubled that the family had to move in order to be closer to his mother's job and other family members who lived in that community.

When Jason was ten years old, his father's condition became terminal, and he was hospitalized. By this time, as his body was wracked by cancer, George's appearance was skeletal. Jason and his family regularly visited his Dad. On one particular occasion, Jason declined to hug his father before he left. His dad died that night.

Jason came into therapy at 12 years old—two years after his dad died. His mother thought Jason would benefit as he had begun to have constant nightmares about his dad's death. Jason was reluctant but not really resistant as he hoped that the nightmares would cease.

After initially establishing trust and developing rapport with the therapist, Jason shared his regret that he did not hug his father that last night. A mature child for his age, Jason was able to express his resentment at his dad's illness, the impact it had on the family and on himself and his discomfort at his dad's appearance. Yet he was still deeply troubled at his failure to give his father what would have been a final hug.

The therapist than asked Jason if he could speak to his father—explaining that it would be through Jason. Jason was both skeptical and curious, but he agreed. Here, the therapist combined a traditional "empty chair" approach with interviewing the internalized other. Jason first imagined his dad sitting in an empty chair beside him. He spoke to his father, offering a tearful apology about the fact that he had failed to hug him that fateful last night.

He then sat in his dad's chair. The therapist asked "George" a few questions to calm Jason down—questions about their relationship and activities they shared together when George was in good health. He then asked how he was now. "George" (through Jason) said that he was well and preparing their home in heaven but not to hurry there as it would take time to finish. He then asked George about Jason's heartfelt apology. George's response was "Is that what was bothering you, Champ? Do you even think I did not know you loved me?" At that moment, Jason laughed and stated, "That was exactly what my father would say." He noted that his Dad often joked about remodeling the house in heaven when he arrived there—telling the family it would take a while to get ready, so they did not have to hurry.

The session offered a strong sense of relief to Jason. As Jason and his therapist processed the conversation with his dad, Jason was able to acknowledge his father's forgiveness as well as his continued connection with him. Soon, Jason was able to terminate therapy, and his nightmares became increasingly rare.

CONCLUDING THOUGHTS

The vignette illustrates the versatility of the approach. In Jason's case, it was combined with another familiar gestalt technique—the use of an empty chair. In other circumstances, it can be used with a variety of therapeutic interventions, such as therapeutic ritual (see Doka & Martin, 2010). One also can see the flexibility of the approach. Jason essentially terminated the interview once he felt that his father would have forgiven him easily.

It is little wonder that this can be a successful intervention as it draws from and is compatible with a number of theoretical sources—most notably gestalt therapy but also systems therapy, narrative therapy, the theory of mind and social constructionism (see Moules, 2010). In addition, there is evidence of its successful use in a number of other circumstances (see Moules, 2010). Most importantly, it affirms one of the most significant understandings of continuing bonds theory—that love and connection never end.

References

Doka, K. J., & Martin, T. (2010). *Grieving beyond gender: Understanding the ways men and women grieve* (rev. ed.). New York: Routledge.

Klass, D., & Steffen, E. M. (2018). *Continuing bonds in bereavement: New directions for research and practice*. New York: Routledge.

Moules, N. J. (2010). Internal connections and conversations: The internalized other interview in bereavement work. *Omega: Journal of Death and Dying, 62,* 187–199.

Tomm, K., Hoyt, M., & Madigan, S. (1998). Honoring our internalized others and the ethos of caring: A conversation with Karl Tomm. In M. Hoyt (Ed.), *The handbook of constructive therapies* (pp. 198–218). Philadelphia: Brunner-Routledge.

48

Induced After-Death Communication

César Valdez, John R. Jordan and Allan Botkin

CLIENTS FOR WHOM THE TECHNIQUE IS APPROPRIATE

IADC is potentially appropriate for anyone who is experiencing an intense and debilitating grief response to the death of a loved one. All potential clients for IADC therapy should be thoroughly screened. IADC therapy is generally not recommended for the first six months following the loss, as the earliest stages of grief are characterized by shock, disbelief and emotional numbing. For IADC to be effective, clients must be able and willing to access their sadness during the sessions. For nearly all people, it takes some time for the sadness to become fully assimilated.

DESCRIPTION

This chapter describes a new and cutting edge brain-based treatment for grief that is called induced after-death communication, or IADC (Botkin, 2014). After-death communications (ADCs) occur in random and spontaneous fashion in about 20% of the general population (Guggenheim & Guggenheim, 1995) and are recognized as greatly accelerating the grieving process. In an ADC, the grieving person has an experience of perceived contact with and/or communication from a deceased loved one. IADC seems to be a technique that may both reduce the deep sadness that can accompany important losses and significantly increase the chances that a person will experience an ADC.

We recognize that some readers may find this technique to be too "unconventional" to be used as a part of standard mental health treatment for complicated grief. And it does raise intriguing metaphysical questions about whether there is some kind of life after death and whether that needs to be a focus of the grief therapy. Interesting or controversial as these questions may be, however, our interest in the technique and our report on it in this chapter are motivated by our clinical experience that use of the IADC procedure seems to be exceptionally helpful to many of our clients—regardless of whatever meaning they (or we) choose to make of the larger implications of the experience. We encourage readers to consider use of the technique from this same "agnostic" position about the existential issues it raises. In terms of research on IADC, Holden and her colleagues at the University of North Texas have recently completed a control group design study of IADC that has not yet been published (Holden, personal communication).

DOI: 10.4324/9781351069120-59

The IADC Method

Training in IADC is offered only to licensed mental health practitioners and requires a full day of training. Therefore, only general principles of IADC therapy can be offered here.

Although the symptoms of grief and depression overlap considerably, IADC therapists view each as having different causes. Grief is a psychological response to a loss, and people therefore feel sad when they are thinking about their loss. During brief moments when not thinking about their loss, they are able to experience positive emotions. In depression, however, people feel sad and hopeless without moments of positive emotions. This suggests that the basis of depression is biochemical. While grief responds very well to IADC, depression does not. Therefore, if the potential client is experiencing depression in addition to grief, it is important that the depression be treated prior to IADC. In our clinical experience, in nearly all cases, an effective anti-depressant is all that is needed.

Also, because of the underlying mechanisms of IADC, clients need to be able and willing to address their most distressing issue first. IADC strictly follows the principle of "worst first." Although this may seem counterintuitive, it allows the brain to process grief without unwanted complications and intrusions.

IADC is derived from eye movement desensitization and reprocessing therapy (EMDR), which is now recognized as an established and evidence-based treatment for PTSD (Shapiro & Forrest, 2004). In the original EMDR protocol, client are first taught self-soothing skills. Then they are asked to recall a traumatic experience (usually through visualization of it) while receiving rhythmic "bilateral stimulation" of the brain—either through following a moving object (e.g., the therapist's fingers) with the eyes or through tactile stimulation of the left and right palms of the hands. The prevailing theory of EMDR is that the eye movements induced during treatment put the brain into a higher processing mode, similar to dream or REM sleep, which allows the traumatic memories to be reprocessed and integrated into regular memory functioning.

One major difference between IADC and standard EMDR should be noted. Unlike EMDR, which asks the client to recall a traumatic memory or image, IADC directly asks the client to focus on the core emotional issue in grief—namely sadness—while receiving the bilateral stimulation. In our clinical experience, we have found that when we address and successfully process this core sadness with accelerated brain processing, other attendant issues, such as anger, guilt and irrational cognitions, typically are also greatly diminished. In IADC therapy, once the sadness is processed and greatly reduced, additional eye movements allow an ADC experience to naturally unfold in about 75% of all cases (Botkin & Hannah, 2013; Hannah, Botkin, Marrone, & Streit-Horn, 2013). Since ADCs are naturally occurring experiences, no suggestion is offered. In fact, any suggestion offered by the therapist will likely prevent the ADC experience. Therefore, the instruction to clients is simply to "just be open to anything that happens." It should be pointed out, however, that research analyses indicate that from a statistical point of view, the processing of the core sadness accounts for most of the positive therapeutic changes (Hannah et al., 2013). A successful ADC induction near the end of treatment offers an additional therapeutic benefit.

CASE ILLUSTRATION

Sixty-four-year-old Miguel worked as a high-level administrator in a university hospital setting. He presented for IADC therapy hoping to address his profound sadness related to the death of his wife of 36 years. Rose had died of pancreatic cancer one year prior to Miguel's treatment. Upon intake, Miguel reported a high degree of anger, guilt and sadness and that he was experiencing distressing thoughts and images related to her death. Miguel felt heartbroken, cheated and lost without Rose.

Miguel and Rose had been eagerly anticipating the arrival of their first grandchild when Rose was diagnosed with cancer and given a grim prognosis. Additionally, the couple was looking forward to Miguel's upcoming retirement and to extended travel in various parts of the world, something of which they had long dreamed. Rose died seven months after being diagnosed and just weeks prior to the arrival of their granddaughter.

Anger and guilt featured prominently in Miguel's grieving process. He felt angry that Rose didn't get to meet their granddaughter and about their dreams for retirement being cut short. He also questioned whether or not he had taken adequate care of her during her illness and felt guilty for feeling relieved of the burden of caring for her after she died. During his IADC treatment, Miguel required only minimal help in redirecting his focus away from anger and guilt and toward his sadness. He identified several pieces of sadness, the strongest of which was the fact that his granddaughter would never know her grandmother. This was identified as his first target for processing with eye movements (EMs). Through many tears, Miguel productively processed this and other pieces of sadness, including the cancellation of a long-planned-for trip to Italy and watching Rose physically deteriorate as her illness progressed.

As processing of all pieces of sadness reached completion, Miguel arrived at a state of peace, which was reinforced by an additional set of EMs. Miguel was then given the instruction to remain open and receptive to anything that arose, and another set of EMs was given. Upon closing his eyes at the end of the set, Miguel became tearful again. After a brief period, he opened his eyes and reported that he had felt Rose kiss his cheek and heard her say, "I love you, baby." He was given another set of EMs followed by closing his eyes, and with eyes closed, Miguel exclaimed, "I can see her! It's like she's right here!" After some time, he opened his eyes and, smiling, reported having seen Rose holding and rocking their baby granddaughter. Another set of EMs was administered with the same instruction to remain open to anything that arose. This process was repeated several times as Miguel continued to perceive seeing Rose and sensing impressions of loving and reassuring messages about her ongoing presence in his life. Among these impressions was that he should renew plans to travel to Italy and that she would accompany him on this trip. At one point during his ADC, Miguel also saw his father standing behind Rose. He and his father had been estranged when his father died in Miguel's 20s, and he perceived a feeling of mutual love and forgiveness between them. Toward the end of his ADC experience, Miguel reported that he saw Rose and his father wave goodbye.

During a follow-up phone call nine months after Miguel's IADC treatment, Miguel reported no anger, no guilt and only minimal sadness. He stated, "Of course, I miss her, and I'm still sad that my granddaughter will never meet her, but I don't feel tortured by grief like I used to." Miguel reported that when he thought of Rose, it was now with a sense of love and gratitude for their many years together and that he no longer experienced intrusive images of her dying process. He also reported on his recent trip to Italy.

CONCLUDING THOUGHTS

IADC seems to offer a powerful and rapid method for helping an individual access and integrate intense (and often debilitating) sadness. It also, on many occasions, seems to increase the chances that the client will experience an ADC, which in its own right can be a powerful healing experience. Most of the "messages" that people receive seem to indicate that (a) their loved one continues to exist and is "okay," (b) that their loved one is journeying with the client as they go forward with their own life, (c) that all residual issues of guilt, anger and blame have been "forgiven" and replaced by unconditional love, and (d) that the deceased wishes for the survivor to be happy and to go forward with their own life. Whatever the source of these messages, they seem to be uniformly healing for those clients who have a "successful" course of IADC therapy.

Of course, what we have presented is based almost exclusively on clinical experience (although EMDR as a technique is well established in randomized controlled trials). We strongly encourage careful research investigation of this new "discovery" and look forward to actively exploring further for whom, and how, IADC can be helpful for bereaved individuals in clinical practice.

References

Botkin, A. L. (2014). *Induced after death communications: A miraculous therapy for grief and loss.* Charlottesville, VA: Hampton Roads Publishing.

Botkin, A. L., & Hannah, M. T. (2013). Psychotherapeutic outcomes reported by therapists trained in induced after death communication. *Journal of Near Death Studies, 31*(4), 221–224.

Guggenheim, W., & Guggenheim, J. (1995). *Hello from heaven! A new field of research confirms that life and love are eternal.* New York: Bantam.

Hannah, M. T., Botkin, A. L., Marrone, J. G., & Streit-Horn, J. (2013). Induced after death communication: An update. *Journal of Near Death Studies, 31*(4), 213–220.

Holden, J. (2017). Personal communication, Allan Botkin.

Shapiro, F., & Forrest, M. S. (2004). *EMDR: The breakthrough therapy for overcoming anxiety, stress, and trauma.* New York: Basic.

Part XII
Validating Lives

49

Dignity Therapy

Harvey Max Chochinov and Lori Montross

CLIENTS FOR WHOM THE TECHNIQUE IS APPROPRIATE

Dignity therapy requires participants who are cognitively able to engage in this legacy-making approach and have a degree of *existential readiness* that encourages personal reflection and life review. It may be inappropriate for very young patients or those whose cognitive impairments preclude self-reflection, as well as those whose lives have been filled with conflict and alienated relationships, who could find the *Lessons Learned* approach described elsewhere in this volume more fitting and useful.

DESCRIPTION

Dignity therapy is an individualized brief psychotherapy, based on an empirical model of dignity in the terminally ill (Chochinov, 2002), designed for patients who are facing life-threatening or life-limiting conditions. Researchers and clinicians are beginning to examine its application in other populations, such as the frail elderly and those with neurodegenerative disorders and in the earlier stages of malignant illness.

The most detailed description of this approach can be found in *Dignity Therapy: Final Words for Final Days* (Chochinov, 2011). Dignity therapy consists of a trained therapist using a framework of open-ended questions to guide patients through an audio-recorded discussion that identifies matters that are most important to them and that they would most want others to know or remember. These questions include the following:

- "Tell me a little about your life history, particularly the parts that you either remember most or think are the most important. When did you feel most alive?"
- "Are there specific things that you would want your family to know about you, and are there particular things you would want them to remember?"
- "What are the most important roles you have played in life (family roles, vocational roles, community service roles etc.)? Why were they so important to you, and what do you think you accomplished in those roles?"
- "What are your most important accomplishments, and what do you feel most proud of?"
- "Are there particular things that you feel still need to be said to your loved ones or things that you would want to take the time to say once again?"

DOI: 10.4324/9781351069120-61

- "What are your hopes and dreams for your loved ones?"
- "What have you learned about life that you would want to pass along to others? What advice or words of guidance would you wish to pass along to your (son, daughter, husband, wife, parents, others)?"
- "Are there words or perhaps even instructions you would like to offer your family to help prepare them for the future?"
- "In creating this permanent record, are there other things that you would like included?"

These questions are not designed to be a structured interview guide, but rather a highly flexible framework meant to elicit memories of important moments or events, relationships, accomplishments, roles and lessons learned, as well as the patient's hopes, dreams, advice and guidance for loved ones. Some of these questions may be salient, while others may not be, or patients may have other issues they wish to address. Exquisite communication skills will enable therapists to follow the patient's cues, always being mindful of using language that respects their degree of insight and acceptance (Chochinov, 2007; Chochinov et al., 2013). Patient responses are recorded, transcribed and edited, resulting in a *generativity document* for them to bequeath to individuals of their choosing.

Dignity therapy consists of three or four meetings between the therapist and patient, ideally over the course of seven to ten days. In the first brief meeting, the therapist meets the patient to describe the process, answer questions and provide a copy of the question framework. During this initial consultation, patients are asked who the generativity document is intended for and what they hope to achieve by taking part in dignity therapy. In the second meeting, the therapist uses the question framework to guide the patient in a 30- to 60-minute discussion about their life and the things that matter most to them. Therapists also need to be vigilant regarding the effect disclosures may have on the recipient(s) of the generativity document and help patients navigate any that could be harmful.

The audio-recorded discussion is transcribed, and the therapist edits the transcript to transform the conversation into a carefully constructed, highly readable generativity document. The therapist then meets with the patient a third time to review the document and read it to them in its entirety. The patient may ask the therapist to make revisions (e.g., to correct errors, omit passages the patient does not want included or add additional content). Once the patient is satisfied with the result, they are provided with the finalized copy for them to bequeath to individuals of their choosing.

CASE ILLUSTRATION

Melinda was a 42-year-old single mother who had been diagnosed with breast cancer three years prior to completing dignity therapy. As the disease progressed, she had found her definition of "hope" as well as her life goals slowly shifting. Now, having entered hospice care with a prognosis of six months or less to live, she was focused on preserving a legacy for her two sons, Chad (age 14) and Todd (age 18).

During the dignity therapy interview, Melinda beamed proudly about having raised "amazing young men who are very respectful and mannerly." Notably, not all Melinda's memories were positive as she candidly described a life that included family adversity, divorce and a series of difficult sacrifices. Such a mixture is common as people often share a wide range of experiences during the interview. In fact, dignity therapy is not intended to solely record times of happiness but aims to provide an open, nonjudgmental environment in which people can reflect on the authentic highs and lows of their lives. For example, after sharing some of her challenges, Melinda also smiled as she recalled spontaneous trips to amusement parks, attending her sons' football games ("no matter what") and her relief knowing that both Chad and Todd understood the value of hard work.

In the final editing of her legacy document, Melinda titled her story, "A Mother and Her Cubs." She also thought carefully about the last page of her story, which conveyed her simple yet important hope for her sons to "live comfortably and stay close to God." When seeing the finished document, Melinda tearfully shared an increased sense of comfort. She felt relieved knowing her document tangibly conveyed how much she cared for her sons and explicitly said, "I think the boys will always be able to feel my presence, but this story allows them to read it whenever they want."

Although not part of the formal dignity therapy process, this case did allow for follow-up. Chad and Todd spoke at Melinda's funeral four months later, where they read part of her dignity therapy document. Both said they were "kind of skeptical" of the process at first but were now grateful for their mother's final words. Demonstrating the very grace and poise that Melinda was so proud of, the boys concluded their eulogy by saying, "I hope that wherever she is now, she is in peace and knows that she gave us the best. We promise to become men that are a reflection of her."

CONCLUDING THOUGHTS

There have been over 100 peer-reviewed papers published on dignity therapy, including at least 30 that report the results of primary data analyses (Martínez et al., 2017). Findings from six randomized controlled trials (RCTs) have been published, and at least three additional RCTs are in progress. While not all trials have shown positive outcomes on primary measures, most trials have found overwhelmingly positive self-reported patient satisfaction, including perceived heightened sense of dignity, increased sense of purpose, increased will to live and greater increases in generativity and ego-integrity scores compared to life review and control groups, and those patients who reported higher levels of baseline distress demonstrated significant improvements in depression, anxiety and demoralization (Julião, Oliveira, Nunes, Carneiro, &, Barbosa, 2017).

A sample of patients' family members interviewed 9 to 12 months after the patients' deaths reported that dignity therapy had helped the patients (95%), increased patients' sense of dignity (78%) and purpose (72%) and helped patients prepare for death (65%) and that it was as important as any other aspect of the patient's care (65%). Most family members also reported the generativity document was helpful during their time of grief (78%) and would continue to be a source of future comfort (77%). Almost all bereft family members reported they would recommend dignity therapy to other patients or family members confronting a terminal illness (McClement et al., 2007).

Dignity therapy allows patients to narrate their own stories and, through a supported process of legacy making, preserve those stories in a form that will outlive them, hence affirming their sense of meaning, purpose and dignity. While only a few studies have examined its effect on bereft family members, the current available data suggest that dignity therapy has benefits for recipients of the generativity document. Further research on this important facet of dignity therapy will help establish its role as a bereavement intervention.

References

Chochinov, H. M. (2002). Dignity conserving care: A new model for palliative care. *Journal of the American Medical Association, 287,* 2253–2260.

Chochinov, H. M. (2011). *Dignity therapy: Final words for final days.* New York: Oxford University Press.

Chochinov, H. M. (2007). Dignity and the essence of medicine: The A, B, C and D of dignity conserving care. *British Medical Journal, 335*(7612), 184–187.

Chochinov, H. M., McClement, S. E., Hack, T. F., McKeen, N. A., Rach, A. M., Gagnon, P., . . . Taylor-Brown, J. (2013). Health care provider communication: An empirical model of therapeutic effectiveness. *Cancer, 119,* 1706–1713.

Julião, M., Oliveira, F., Nunes, B., Carneiro, A. V., & Barbosa, A. (2017). Effect of dignity therapy on end-of-life psychological distress in terminally ill Portuguese patients: A randomized controlled trial. *Palliative and Supportive Care, 7,* 1–10.

Martínez, M., Arantzamendi, M., Belar, A., Carrasco, J. M., Carvajal, A., Rullán, M., & Centeno, C. (2017). Dignity therapy, promising intervention in palliative care: A comprehensive systematic literature review. *Palliative Medicine, 31,* 492–509.

McClement, S., Hack, T., Chochinov, H. M., Hassard, T., Kristjanson, L., & Harlos, M. (2007). Dignity therapy: Family member perspectives. *Journal of Palliative Medicine, 10*(5), 1076–1082.

50

A Hike to Remember

Erica D. Huber and Laurie A. Burke

CLIENTS FOR WHOM THE TECHNIQUE IS APPROPRIATE

Grievers who have experienced a variety of types of losses (i.e., both violent and natural death) and who enjoy the outdoors, hiking and the potential benefits of participating in a group activity with other grievers are likely to benefit from this activity. However, it may be contraindicated for individuals with medical conditions that preclude them from hiking, as well for those who do not participate in holiday tree decorating, unless the activity is suitably modified.

DESCRIPTION

When loved ones die, celebrating important holidays without them can become increasingly difficult for the griever (Burke, Neimeyer, Young, Piazza Bonin, & Davis, 2014). Finding ways to be able to continue to celebrate and find joy following loss can be a daunting task, especially because grief intensity tends to rise prior to important events/activities such anniversaries or celebrations (Robinaugh, Marques, Bui, & Simon, 2012). For instance, when the deceased is no longer present at family parties and unable to take part in holiday traditions, it means, at a bare minimum, that the griever is robbed of the joy of watching their loved one open the perfect gift or card or enjoying their presence around the Christmas tree or holiday table.

To address these struggles, we invited current and former clients to participate in what we called the Hike to Remember. The group activity entailed hiking in the Columbia River Gorge, east of Portland, Oregon, eight miles round trip from the Multnomah Falls Lodge to a little-known, discrete side trail called the Ornament Trail that is lined with ornaments hung from tree limbs over the years by hikers. Hiking the Ornament Trail with a group of fellow grievers and hanging their carefully selected ornament provided a novel way for mourners in our group to celebrate the holidays, remember and honor the person who died and, in an very personal way, maintain a continuing bond with the person who died (Klass, 2006). Additionally, for those who chose to, the hours on the trail created space for sharing stories about their deceased loved one's life and death, as well as affording opportunities to formulate new friendships.

DOI: 10.4324/9781351069120-62

Guidelines for preparing a Hike to Remember:

1. Plan to hike to a destination where you can hang ornaments as a group or, if possible, develop a new place if one does not exist.
2. Create a flier advertising your hiking event to give to potential participants. Include a brief description of the hike, its purpose, contact information, date, time, length of hike, estimated duration, elevation gain and what to bring (e.g., water, food, extra clothing, trekking poles, ornament).
3. Require all participants to sign a detailed informed consent form that outlines the boundaries of responsibility prior to embarking on the hike.
4. Include at least two people who are familiar with the trail and two mental health professionals who are knowledgeable about grief and who are also experienced hikers. For example, our hike included two licensed clinical psychologists who provide targeted grief therapy, one of whom had previously completed this hike several times. Additionally, one of the grievers knew the trail well and served as our primary hike leader.
5. Ensure that leaders are ample in terms of number (e.g., our ratio of grievers to leaders was 3:1).
6. Provide each participant with a detailed, written description of the trail. Where applicable, place these directions in plastic sheaths to protect them from rain damage.

CASE STUDY

Erica's story: "*In 2014, my healthy, happy, newly college-graduated son went for a late-evening run on the track of a nearby community college and didn't come home. Griffin was found early the next morning by an early morning walker. He had died from an undetected heart defect. In that moment, my life was turned upside down. It took me a year and a half to finally receive bereavement counseling and only then at the strong encouragement of my sister, who is a physician. Up to that point, I used hiking as the sole means of coping with my grief. Initially, I hiked to force myself to breathe deeply. The intense calm and beauty of the trail, as well as the ability to connect with Griffin, kept me coming back. I talked to Griffin on the trail, lit candles, took pictures and posted my grief journey on social media. However, like many bereaved individuals, as the holidays approached, I began to dread the sense of loss even more. Griffin wouldn't be there at the family celebrations, so what did it matter?*

"In my search for new places to hike, I found notes about a secret unmarked trail in the Columbia River Gorge, called "The Ornament Trail." I decided to search for this magical place, and, if I found it, I would hang an ornament for Griffin. The first time I mastered it, the snowy trail provided me with some much-needed joy during the holidays. Making this hike a new tradition helped me to cope with the loss of all the traditions Griffin would no longer be attending. In 2016, I shared my experience of the Ornament Trail with my grief psychologist. By this point in my bereavement, I realized how helpful it was to connect with others who had experienced significant loss. I suggested that I would like to lead a hike to the Ornament Trail for others who were in deep grief. She was extremely supportive and offered to accompany us on the hike as well as make her other clients aware of this opportunity. We took six grievers and two therapists up the trail. The grievers picked out ornaments that held significance to them and their loved ones. We enjoyed the incredible beauty of the trail, passing multiple waterfalls in a Pacific Northwest rainforest. People were given the freedom to talk and share as little or as much as they wished. It was incredibly meaningful to meet other grievers and hear stories about the lives and loss of their dear loved ones. It has always been helpful to me to be able to share stories about Griffin. Upon arrival to the Ornament Trail, we spread out and hung our sacred ornaments. I brought a griffin toy and hung it near a dinosaur that I had hung for Griffin on an earlier trek. On the

bottom of the ornament, I wrote "Griffin Huber, 1992–2014." One person hung a pocketknife with her dad's name on it. She mentioned her dad had collected pocketknives for years, so this was her way of keeping his memory alive. Another person hung a glittery red ball. She said the red was for her dad's favorite color and the sparkle was to tease him. A mother and daughter hung a beautiful red cardinal in honor of their husband and dad. They said he would love to know there was a red cardinal hanging in a Pacific Northwest rainforest. One person had lost two family members in a matter of weeks. His ornament honored them both with their names. Given that I spend so much time alone on the trail, I especially liked the fact that we did this hike as a group, as it was helpful to connect with others in such a special way. Now, when I return to the trail, I will remember my fellow grievers/hikers and each of their loved ones. Hopefully, in the days ahead, they will feel inspired to return to the trail themselves or with a future group."

CONCLUDING THOUGHTS

Facilitating a Hike to Remember can be an effective technique in the treatment of grief, especially for mourners who find sharing nature with others to be a therapeutic way to connect with their deceased loved one. Modifications to this therapeutic activity might include using a group hike to memorialize clients' deceased loved ones in ways other than hanging an ornament in the forest. For instance, such modifications could include scheduling a hike with a particularly breathtaking view or to an area with particular meaning for local inhabitants or the inclusion of a picnic meal together halfway through the hike, where grievers share and remember their loved one along with his/her favorite food. Additionally, if you choose to hang ornaments, it is important to note that the hike need not take place in the winter or near the holidays in order to be meaningful for grievers. Inclement winter weather in our area meant that our hike was rescheduled multiple times, and, even then, our mid-June hike included unprecedented rainfall, which seemingly only served to bond drenched, cold participants together as we sought shelter in a conveniently located and warmly welcomed alpine club's lodge. Even when things do not go as planned, grievers seemingly still can benefit from a group hiking experience, especially when they choose to view it as a personal challenge to push themselves physically and emotionally as a way of remembering and keeping their loved ones close.

References

Burke, L. A., Neimeyer, R. A., Young, M. J., Piazza Bonin, B., & Davis, N. L. (2014). Complicated spiritual grief II: A deductive inquiry following the loss of a loved one. *Death Studies, 38*, 268–281. doi:10.1080/07481187.2013.829373

Klass, D. (2006). Continuing conversation about continuing bonds. *Death Studies, 30*(9), 843–858.

Robinaugh, D. J., Marques, L., Bui, E., & Simon, N. M. (2012). Recognizing and treating complicated grief. *Current Psychiatry, 11*(8), 30.

51
The Sharing Plate

Cynthia Louise Harrison

CLIENTS FOR WHOM THE TECHNIQUE IS APPROPRIATE

Grieving and bereaved individuals of all ages as well as families searching for meaning and purpose at a time of loss and transition can benefit from this legacy project. As a shared ritual and symbol of the life of a loved one, this technique allows space for a reflective process that is strength based and person centered yet honors the losses, values and influences of the deceased. However, it could be inappropriate if the relationship with the deceased had been marked by oppression, abuse or deep ambivalence, which would call for therapeutic procedures facilitating healing rather than celebration.

DESCRIPTION

No art or creative experience is necessary to benefit from this technique. The value is in the creating and sharing of what is meaningful and the experience of designing a remembrance plate/platter that can offer the bereaved a creative approach to a challenging situation while supporting feelings of empowerment, continuing bonds and capacity for hope amidst loss. "Reconstructing rather than relinquishing the bond can restore the attachment security challenged by death" (Neimeyer, 2012). Further, Thompson and Neimeyer (2014) argue that the expressive arts, used historically to acknowledge and explore grief and loss, are equally relevant today in assisting the bereaved to recreate meaning from the experience.

The remembrance plate activity utilizes creative art, the written word and color while incorporating key interventions of reconstruction of meaning, reworking continuing bonds, life review, legacy work, self-awareness and emotional regulation, mindfulness, connection with others and behavioral activation. This person-centered technique can be beneficial to stimulate the expression of emotions otherwise repressed during the grief process. The remembrance plate activity can be a refreshing alternative to celebrate the lives of the deceased through commemoration of the gifts of their memories, values, skills and knowledges. A tangible legacy project is created that honors individual grief and the memory of the deceased by giving significance to their lives and journeys in a way that allows for their integration into a new way of being after loss. The bereaved may want to include the deceased on special occasions with this decorative serving plate that can be used at family reunions and

 DOI: 10.4324/9781351069120-63

times of celebration. Re-membering practices such as this allow the deceased to continue being a valuable presence in our lives moving forward. Michael White (2005), an innovative social worker, family therapist and co-founder of narrative therapy, characterized remembering conversations as "purposive engagements with the significant figures of one's history." Through exploring these relationships, many realizations, preferences, accounts of identity, values and ways of being are richly described and can then contribute to the person's sense of being knowledged, empowered, reconnected and hopeful about how to move forward in their lives.

I was blessed to recently complete my master of social work program with a focus in grief and bereavement support. My learning goals included the exploration of expressive arts for grief, loss and trauma. After extensive research and valuable insights, I found myself deeply inspired by the works of Alan D. Wolfelt (2004), Robert Neimeyer (2012) and Michael White (2005), which motivated me to create a legacy project called the *Sharing Plate*, which I was able to implement in a group format. This workshop proved beneficial for attendees by facilitating the sharing of emotions and memories of their deceased while allowing for support and celebration in the present and in the form of a legacy ritual to be shared with others for years to come. I found this project to be an appropriate fit for a stand-alone workshop as well as integration into a longer support group program in conjunction with hospice-, hospital- or community-based services for the bereaved. The format described here is especially suitable for the final celebratory session of these programs.

CASE ILLUSTRATION

The two-hour workshop began with a warm welcome to the eight attendees and a brief around-the-circle introduction. We followed the opening with a grounding exercise to become more present in the moment and to set the intention for our session in the honoring of each other's stories, creating a safe, respectful communal space for creative expression of grief and loss and remembrance of the deceased. Check-in consisted of having the group members share one word to describe their loved one. The remembrance plate technique specifically allocated approximately an hour for reflection and creativity and then followed up with discussion and acknowledgement of the importance of celebrating the legacy of the deceased as a beneficial aspect of grief work and grief reconciliation.

The energy in the room was a kaleidoscope of anticipation, hesitation, grief, tears, bittersweet joy and even some laughter in the mix. Grief work is hard, yet the communal spirit is strong. Attendees were seated around a table with a white plate or platter at each setting, an abundance of Sharpie markers in every color imaginable scattered around for easy access and sharing and a list of the following contemplations, which I read verbatim, allowing for time to reflect on each.

- *Name of person (or preferred name)*
- *How you want to remember this person—what you want to celebrate*
- *Person's favorite quote/recipe/hobby/song/place etc.*
- *What you appreciate about this person (e.g., values, skills, life lessons)*
- *Any memory of this person that has contributed to your being the person you are right now*
- *What this person might say they appreciate about you*
- *Legacies you learned from this person that you want to pass on to others (values, skills, life lessons)*
- *What you want to say to this person now*

- *What this person might say to you now*
- *Any memories that are important in honoring this person*

Participants then enthusiastically began decorating their plates with memories of their loved ones; recollecting their favorite song lyrics, quotes, poems, memorable trips, accomplishments and foods; and sharing all that they appreciated about them and the times they experienced together. One older widow embellished her plate with a French flag and a rendition of the Eiffel Tower, a memento of a special 30th anniversary trip with her husband. A bereaved daughter depicted a flower garden to honor her mother's lifelong passion for cultivating roses and gardenias, while another drew a box of recipe cards to commemorate a grandmother's cooking. One man encircled his plate with musical notes to invoke his father's career as a jazz musician, and many added names, birth and death dates, nicknames, hearts, butterflies and expressions of love and remembrance. This is where the tremulous smiles and tears joined with laughter filled the room, amidst the collective sound of verbal sharing of happier times and hopes and dreams for the future. The room became industriously alive with the hum of brainstorming around legacy work and the carrying forward of values and preferences for future generations. Conversation turned to the joy that children and grandchildren brought to their lives and the wonderment around how cathartic this creative reflection activity turned out to be. Once the creative buzz of activity started, it was hard to stop as participants added one more color, one more word or design or a new idea that was generated by the creative flow and release of emotion.

Upon completion of their remembrance plates, participants went around the table sharing their works of art, what they were taking away from the group today and how they planned to incorporate the legacy plate as a memorial and celebration ritual. Closing included taking time to celebrate the time shared together as a collective grief support and how members would cope moving forward. We also acknowledged their courage in attending and creatively expressing and sharing the intense thoughts and emotions experienced along the grief journey. Many expressed feelings of sadness that the session was drawing to a close but were thankful to have had the opportunity to explore their grief in this way, especially in the creation of a tangible legacy piece to take home and share with others.

Finally, as homework, attendees were asked to take time throughout the week to honor and celebrate their memories, the moments shared and the imprints left behind. In doing so, they also acknowledged the impacts they made on the lives of the deceased and recognized how they could continue the legacy within their lives and family context. Homework also included curing the plates. To set the ink, the plate needed to be placed on a cookie sheet and baked in a 150-degree Fahrenheit, 55-degree Celsius oven for 30 minutes. The plates are safe to use once cured at home at the attendee's convenience. Plates will be extremely hot after being baked in the oven, so if you are doing this with children, please make sure they will have parental supervision or arrange in the session time to allow for appropriate cool down.

CONCLUDING THOUGHTS

In summary, the *Sharing Plate* activity supports space for remembrance and celebration, grief support, movement away from limiting emotions, embracing of memories and awareness of a new understanding of the relationship with the deceased, meaning making and hope building. The experiential nature of this activity typically has a profound and cathartic effect on both the attendees and facilitators. Remarkably, even in the midst of grief, attendees speak of having gained a sense of direction and power that offers a renewal of energy. This energy resonates around the room as stories are shared, and the atmosphere transforms into celebration, restoration and positive hope for the future.

References

Neimeyer, R. A. (Ed.). (2012). *Techniques of grief therapy: Creative practices for counseling the bereaved.* New York: Routledge.

Thompson, B. E., & Neimeyer, R. A. (Eds.). (2014). *Grief and the expressive arts: Practices for creating meaning.* New York: Routledge.

White, M. (2005). *Workshop Notes.* Retrieved from http://dulwichcentre.com.au/wp-content/uploads/2014/01/michael-white-workshop-notes.pdf

Wolfelt, A. (2004). *The understanding your grief support group guide.* Fort Collins, CO: Companion Press.

52

Life Lessons Learned

Kenneth J. Doka

CLIENTS FOR WHOM THE TECHNIQUE IS APPROPRIATE

People facing their mortality with a history of conflictual or alienated relationships with others can benefit from this specialized form of life review to reflect on, formulate and perhaps share some of the important life lessons learned in looking back on their lives. However, this procedure could be inappropriate for people who are incapable of self-reflection, who are highly narcissistic or who tend to project total blame on others for their own actions and limitations.

DESCRIPTION

It has been long recognized that one of the spiritual needs of individuals who are dying or aging is to find some sense of meaning in life (Erikson, 1963; Doka, 1988). This recognition led Butler (1963) to suggest that life review is an integral part of the aging process. While that is certainly true, it is perhaps less an aspect of aging than of the awareness that one is facing finitude—either through aging or life-limiting illness. In my work in the early 1980s, even the foster parents of HIV-infected children—most of whom died prior to three years of age—often sought to find some value in the short, often painful years of the child's life. As a result, reminiscence and life review therapies have long been tools for individuals facing death (see Magee, 2011). In fact, the process of life review is now at the heart of such well-known approaches such as dignity therapy (Chochinov, 2012), living eulogies and moral/ethical wills (Baines, 2002).

However, persons who led highly self-destructive lives full of troubles and alienated relationships may find little meaning as they review their lives. In fact, the process may be painful—reminding them of both the chaos of their own lives and the havoc they may have created in the lives of others. The technique of *Life Lessons Learned* can be a useful alternative here as it allows persons to positively reflect on what their experiences—however negative—taught them. In addition, it allows such individuals to leave a legacy that may positively affect those around them.

Life Lessons Learned should begin with an assessment of the client that indicates that traditional life review strategies including living eulogies or dignity therapy are not appropriate as the client has had life experiences characterized by a predominance of conflicted and alienated relationships. This assessment should also affirm that the client is capable of

DOI: 10.4324/9781351069120-64

self-reflection and does accept at least some responsibility for the choices that he or she has made in life. In the assessment it is useful, although not necessary, to identify an individual or individuals who might benefit from hearing what the client learned. In some cases, it may be a child or family member from whom they are now alienated. When no one is identified, the recipient can be phrased as "individuals like the client" or "younger people who seem to be traveling the same path."

Once an assessment is made, the counselor can suggest that the client's life, however destructive, might have taught the client a great deal. The client then could be asked if he or she could offer advice to a younger person based on what the client learned from his or her experiences. This younger person may or may not have—or even ever had—a relationship with the client. This can be done as a letter or as a video or audio recording—any format that allows the client to preserve his or her advice. The counselor then listens reflectively—occasionally commenting on the client's life lessons—either clarifying or affirming the lessons learned. At the conclusion, the client and counselor should discuss who may be granted access to the document and how it might be shared. The counselor should then thank the client for participating and affirm the importance of what was shared—specifically calling it a critical and important legacy that has the potential to really help others.

CASE ILLUSTRATION

Doug is a 35-year-old man dying of acute liver failure—the result of a lifelong pattern of both alcohol and drug abuse, complicated by chronic hepatitis and HIV infection. In Doug's words, he "never caught a break." He was raised in a white family with Appalachian roots, growing up with a single mother, herself struggling with chronic alcoholism, in one of the worst slums in Detroit. Learning disabled, he was often teased and bullied at school. His older brother introduced him to marijuana when he was 10 years old—beginning a pattern of drug and alcohol abuse that would continue throughout his life.

Doug dropped out of school as soon as he could at 16 years old and basically hustled—engaging in petty theft, selling of drugs and, occasionally, homosexual prostitution, as well as a history of small unskilled and "off the books" jobs. Despite his sporadic prostitution, Doug defined himself as straight and did have relationships with a number of women—one of whom he believed infected him with HIV. In fact, Doug found out he had been infected when this woman, also an IV drug user, informed him that she had tested positive. He also had a child with another woman—who broke off any relationship with him after she found he had, despite a promise and an attempt at rehabilitation, relapsed. Doug had never seen his child and did not where the child and mother resided. In fact, he didn't even know the child's gender. At the time of his hospitalization, the child would have been 14 years old.

I was called to advise a chaplain who was counseling Doug since he was despondent. Doug had noted that he "never should have been born," that "he was a total failure," and that he "never accomplished a damn thing—except to ruin a lot of lives." The chaplain had attempted using dignity therapy—a modality in which he was trained—but Doug was resistant. The chaplain's attempts at life review and even reminiscence approaches were equally unsuccessful. As Doug said, "I ain't got anything worth remembering."

After our consultation, the chaplain remarked to Doug that although his life must have been very hard, he probably had learned a great deal from his mistakes. Doug agreed—indicating that he wished there were "do-overs in life." The chaplain then noted that would be great but that maybe by sharing what he had learned, he could help others. Doug was intrigued by the possibility and explored it further with the chaplain—deciding that he wished to record his observations.

Because Doug became easily exhausted at this point in his illness and because the subject matter was troubling, taping took a number of days. Doug recounted a series of lessons. Some were obvious, such as the importance of staying in school and avoiding drug and alcohol abuse. But other lessons showed far more insight as Doug spoke about the need to find positive role models (and how he recalled rejected attempts by teachers, school counselors, and the Big Brother program to offer such opportunities) as well as how he might have mastered some of the challenges he faced—such as learning disabilities—in more positive ways. When the process was completed, Doug seemed much more at ease. He indicated that he wished the tape shared with a nephew with whom he had limited contact and with his child, should the chaplain be able to locate the child. He also gave the chaplain freedom to use the tape and share it wherever he found it useful. Doug was very satisfied with the tape as he listened to it—describing it as "almost as good as a do-over" and pressed the chaplain to make use of it with others "on a bad path." Within two weeks of making the tape, Doug became comatose and died few days later. He was buried in a potter's field.

The chaplain was able to locate his brother and nephew—both of whom expressed appreciation for the legacy. No one seemed to know whatever happened to his girlfriend and child.

CONCLUDING COMMENTS

The *Life Lessons Learned* technique, even if rarely used, offers an alternative to dignity therapy and other approaches to life review and reminiscence that assume at least some positive life experiences as a reference point. Since a segment of the population may have had few such experiences, it adds another useful tool to find value and meaning in a more difficult life experience. The technique certainly could be modified to assist bereaved persons in finding meaning for deceased persons who were self-destructive or victims of negative life experiences.

References

Baines, B. K. (2002). *Ethical wills: Putting your values on paper.* Cambridge, MA: Perseus Books.
Butler, R. (1963). The life review: An interpretation of reminiscence in the aged. *Psychiatry, 26,* 65–76.
Chochinov, H. M. (2012). *Dignity therapy: Final words for final days.* New York: Oxford University Press.
Doka, K. (1988). The awareness of mortality in mid-life: Implications for later life. *Gerontology Review, 1,* 19–28.
Erikson, E. (1963). *Childhood and society.* New York: MacMillan.
Magee, J. (2011). *Paradox for life review: A guide for enhancing older adults' self-esteem.* Plymouth, UK: Jason Aronson.

Part XIII
Re-storying Loss

53

Grief Dialogues

Elizabeth Coplan

CLIENTS FOR WHOM THE TECHNIQUE IS APPROPRIATE

Adults who suffer from grief and connect with an empathic and compassionate listener can benefit from watching live theatrical productions or short films on themes of grief and loss. This approach to grief therapy can be held one on one or in a group setting or classroom. It may be less appropriate for individuals who are not assured of caring and skilled listeners or whose experience of traumatic or fresh loss requires highly tailored individual or family-centered intervention.

DESCRIPTION

Using theater as a means to start a conversation regarding experiences of loss serves as an effective practice for clients in mourning and students. It invites them to experience a major emotional, cognitive and physical shift regarding death and grief and demonstrates that contact with a live experience, such as observing a play, can foster sensations, movements, emotions and images known as affective embodied experience (Stanley, 2016, pp. 1–3). This practice can evoke subtle feelings and offers an opportunity to confront the terror so often associated with death.

Watching a ten-minute play, a short film, or an excerpt of a longer film, supplemented with follow-up questions and discussion, can awaken the opportunity for mourners and students to be in and move through their fears. Often, in conjunction with a specific scene from a play, clients recall certain emotions, stories and personal meanings connected to their grief. By watching the performance with clients and students, facilitators create a safe environment that affirms their experience with openness and empathy.

Plays from the *Grief Dialogues*, our unique experiential technique, allow the audience to move proactively through their fears by witnessing actors create characters in a particular situation. Through the actors' gestures, tone of voice and expressions, clients generally associate with particular characters' experiences. Actors often employ "method acting" in an "as if" approach to the role. Lee Strasberg, often considered the "father of 'Method acting' in America" (Gussow, 1982), wanted actors to make use of experiences from their own lives to bring them closer to the experiences of their characters. In turn, our approach also brings the audience closer to the experience of the characters. Additionally, the questions associated with this practice allow clients and students to express their own answers through both

DOI: 10.4324/9781351069120-66

gut response and reflection. With these new insights into the feelings of death and grief, clients and students can orient themselves and begin to move through the healing process. With awareness of emotions, we can guide our internal unresolved experience into knowing through images and reflection (Stanley, 2016, p. 193).

For this technique, we prefer live theater over film, though some of the work in the *Grief Dialogues* project described in this chapter can be presented in either medium. One of the key attributes of theater is its liveliness. In an article titled "How Can Watching Theatre Benefit the Mind," Dr. Glenn D. Wilson explains, "There's a bond that forms between the performers and the audience, and research demonstrates how brief, magical moments can only happen when spectators and performers share a physical space" (Butler et al., 2014). This idea was further supported when the University of Arkansas Department of Education studied the effects on students after observing a live performance. Emotional benefits that surfaced included an increased ability to comprehend and empathize with other people's feelings and reactions. Those results were less apparent with the control group that only read the play or watched a movie adaptation.

For two years, *Grief Dialogues* invited submissions by contemporary playwrights to curate a variety of death, dying and grief stories. All plays were reviewed by an advisory council, a panel of 15 professionals from a variety of disciplines including medicine, psychology, end of life, theater, marketing, visual arts, music, pop culture, education and social work, as well those

Table 53.1 Sample of Plays in the *Grief Dialogues* Library

Play	Cast	Actors	Theme	Notes
Dead Giveaway	1 M / 1 F	Any age	End of life planning	Humorous play about planning for the future. Husband buys a funeral plot to surprise wife for V-day. But if he dies before her, she's getting remarried.
Dog Dreams	2 M or 1 M / 1 F	Any age, Straight or gay	Avoidance of reminders	A couple. One can't sleep. One dead, asking, "Take the dog to the park where my body was found."
Full Circle	2 M / 1 F	Young & old	Letting Dad die	Cruel father is visited by son for first time in 25 years—who just visits to watch his father die.
Hospice: A Love Story	2 F	Any age	Our faulty memories and childhood transgressions	A darkly comic look at two sisters the day after their mother's death who remember alarmingly different accounts of their mother's care and her final days.
LA 8AM [also available as short film]	1 M / 1 F 2 any	Young	Death is coming	A young couple has a petty fight without knowing that she will soon die. A pair of future beings countdown their life.
Life Lines	2 M / 1 F	1 young / 2 old	Yearning, ambivalence	A mom struggles with reading her dead son's diary.
The Last Night	2 F	Young & old	Jewish/ghost	An expectant mother is visited by her dead mother and both discuss the importance of Hanukkah gifts.
The Number	1 M / 1 F	Young	Jewish/ Holocaust	A brother and sister prepare to say goodbye to their grandmother, who was a survivor of the Holocaust.

suffering recent loss. The panel of 12 women and three men chose the plays listed in Table 53.1 from the 118 semifinalist submissions, ultimately selecting them based on their specific topic, originality, character development, dialogue, minimal reliance on props or set and adherence to the *Grief Dialogues* vision: to create a compassionate environment where sharing our stories about death and grief can help us and help others. The result was a library of 12 ten-minute plays (like vignettes) for performance in a therapeutic, educational or other group setting. This list is updated on a semi-annual basis as new work is submitted and accepted. Readers interested in a fuller introduction to the project are encouraged to visit www.griefdialogues.com.

The easiest and most economical way to produce one or more of these plays is to contact a local college or university theater department and request actors and a director. Experience shows that students love the opportunity to perform. We recommend that producers pay actors a small stipend to compensate for their time (at least one rehearsal and the performance).

As an illustration of plays in *Grief Dialogues*, here is an excerpt from *Life Lines*, a play by Donna Hoke. *Life Lines* focuses on the anguish of a bereaved mother sorting through the belongings of her deceased young adult son. When she discovers her dead son's journal, she fights her conscience over her right to read it. The action takes place in a living room with a fireplace. The characters include Andrew, the deceased son who is college age; Lily, Andrew's mother; and Mac, Andrew's father and Lily's husband. At the beginning of the play, Lily takes each item out of the box. She unpacks some CDs, a handheld game, a sports cap, some books and several blank notebooks that she flips through idly. She holds each item, tears coming closer. When Mac enters, Lily looks at him helplessly. Andrew's girlfriend has sent the items left in her apartment, and Lily has just found his journal. She wants to read it, but Mac takes the journal from her hands and places it on a table across the room. Mac exits. Lily retrieves the journal and starts leafing through it when her deceased son starts to talk to her.

Excerpt

LILY: Your last phone message. Do you remember what it said?

ANDREW: "My last final was a piece of cake! Heading home now. Don't go get the tree without me!"

LILY: Miss you guys!

ANDREW: Miss you guys!

LILY: We never got a tree. Because you never—

ANDREW: You should get one this year.

LILY: I don't know. This is the year I won't send cards. Last year was too soon to count, I think.

ANDREW: But you love a tree. And besides, it always covers the

PUKE STAIN.

LILY: It doesn't bother me.

ANDREW: Remember how when I was little, you always hid a special present in the tree for me to find?

LILY: Santa Claus did that.

ANDREW: I stopped believing in Santa Claus when I was four.

LILY: Four! That's impossible!

ANDREW: I got up to pee and I saw Dad putting together my bicycle and you eating the cookies.

LILY: You never told me that! All these years.

ANDREW: At first, I was afraid I wouldn't get presents. (beat) Later, I knew it made you happy. I wanted to keep the illusion alive for you.

LILY: I want more. I ache for more.

ANDREW: That journal isn't going to give it to you, Mom. College kids are stupid.

LILY: Your voice. I'll hear your voice in my head as I read the lines. It will be more.
ANDREW: But you don't get to choose what you get.
LILY: What could you possibly say in here that would matter?!
ANDREW IS SILENT.

Processing Prompts

Once a play is performed, or the film viewed, ask the following questions of the audience. These questions work well in both individual and group or class settings. In a group or class setting, break the participants into small groups. After they talk through their answers in the small group, allow the participants to share their thoughts and ideas with the larger group. You know your clients and students best; feel free to add some of your own questions.

1. How did this play speak to your own experience of loss?
2. What thoughts occupy the characters' minds? Do they question themselves? Do you question their motives?
3. What kind of support do you believe the characters need in processing their unresolved experiences?
4. Did the play end in a healthy way? If not, how do you imagine a different ending?
5. How do you process loss similarly or differently from these characters?

These are general questions, designed to be used with any *Grief Dialogues* play. Each play also comes with its own specific questions. For example, in another play, *Dead Giveaway*, questions designed for the play include "Do you feel the couple's relationship will grow because of this experience? Why or why not?" "Do you think the play brings awareness to the topic of death, or is it just a silly idea to begin with?" and "Do you have your own plan for disposal of your body after death or specific end-of-life wishes?"

If the actors are open to discussion after their performances, consider asking them a few of the following questions in an interactive session with the audience:

1. Have you personally experienced grief?
2. Did your personal experience influence how you played your character? If yes, how?
3. What feelings came up for you as you rehearsed and performed these pieces?
4. If you could improvise on this plot or rewrite the script in a way that felt interesting to you, how might you do so?

Finally, in more academic settings, instructors might also pose broader attitudinal, sociological or historical questions for learner reflection and discussion, such as "Do you believe that the culture of silence around death should be broken through discussion, gatherings, innovation and scholarship? Why or why not?" or "Do you feel there are shifts in the perception of death from generation to generation?" Also, "In what ways do you believe the human perspective on death varies?" and "Are there cultural or socioeconomic differences?" Such questions can help bridge more personal relevance with critical analytic thinking if this is a goal of the educational setting in which the plays are used.

CASE ILLUSTRATION

After her mother died, Monica, age ten, was told by her father never to speak of her mother again. Despite the fact that her mother died of cancer, in her father's eyes, the death represented failure: a failure of the medical community and a failure of himself to keep his wife safe. Monica lived in a beautiful home with her father for several years, but the two of them rarely ventured outside, except for school and work. They lived as if paralyzed with fear. Monica stopped growing and maturing physically.

Three years later, Monica's father, no longer able to deal with his grief, ended his life. Monica was devastated, but her 13-year-old self knew not to cry or show emotion, other than an extreme fear of death. When she came to live with her guardian aunt, she also started therapy. Traditional talk therapy worked to calm Monica, but it was only when Monica saw Life Lines at a Day of the Dead celebration that she began to express her true grief.

Triggered by the play, Monica experienced perceptual, cognitive and emotional sensations toward the character of the mother. Monica first reacted emotionally, then, with her therapist, was able to reflect and problem solve. Finally, she was able to demonstrate empathy toward the mother's character. Life Lines allowed Monica to step outside herself and gain perspective on her own circumstances. Her mood began to shift as a door opened for her that allowed her to talk in more detail about both her parents' deaths, as well as grief's physical effects.

CONCLUDING THOUGHTS

Creating empathy is a relatively new concept in Western culture. In fact, the word "empathy"—from the German word "Einfühlung"—is only a century old. However, people have demonstrated interest in the moral implications of feeling our way into the lives of others for a long time. Paul Bloom wrote in *The New Yorker* that Adam Smith, in "*The Theory of Moral Sentiments*" (1759), observed that what made us moral beings was the imaginative capacity to "place ourselves in [the] situation [of another] . . . and become in some measure the same person with him, and thence form some idea of his sensations" (Bloom, 2013).

When it comes to dying, death and grief, Bloom suggests that "some spark of fellow-feeling is needed to convert intelligence into action" (Bloom, 2013). By integrating the viewing of the *Grief Dialogues* into their practice, clinicians help create an empathic space in which clients and students not only see and hear aspects of dying, death and grief in the plays but also can feel it and identify with it. This empathetic approach begins in the intrapersonal world of the practitioner and then enables this helpful practitioner to truly know and accompany others in their shifting yet healing, moment-to-moment experience of loss, anguish, sorrow, pain, yearning and joy (Stanley, 2016, p. 193).

In some cases, it may be too early to explore these images, or the memory of the loss may be too vivid. Many times, clients are immobilized or stuck. However, using theater to explore death and grief can provide opportunities to draw out clients and students in a nonthreatening way.

Barbara Thompson and Robert Neimeyer, in *Grief and the Expressive Arts* (2014), address the need for this safe environment in prompting emotionally resonant reflection and integration of loss experiences. Using the *Grief Dialogues* to help clients distance somewhat from their own perception of loss can help them acknowledge the inevitability and pain of loss, revise their own assumptions about dying and death through the eyes of a fictional character, reconstruct a relationship that may have been lost and reinvent themselves by trying on new roles and identities as they acknowledge their fears, loss, connections to others and will to live.

While the safe environment created by these live theatrical performances is crucial, the therapist does not need prior experience in the performing arts. The plays were chosen for their simplicity. Facilitators should attend the rehearsal(s) to be certain they are comfortable with this art form (Rogers, 2007). It's also important to understand the sense of interconnection and community when working with clients and students, for it is through this sense that we form a respect for the individual in context, which is at the heart of constructive therapy

(Stanley, 2016). Grief Dialogues now offers works written and produced for health care professionals. For more information about Grief Dialogues Health Care Education, visit education.griefdialogues.com.

References

Bloom, P. (2013, May 20). Baby in the well. *The New Yorker.* Retrieved from www.newyorker.com/magazine/2013/05/20/the-baby-in-the-well

Butler, R. A. et al. (2014). How can watching theatre benefit the mind. *Erickson Living.* Retrieved from www.ericksonliving.com/articles/2014/12/how-can-watching-theater-benefit-mind

Gussow, M. (1982, February 18). Lee Strasberg of Actors Studio dead. *The New York Times.* Retrieved from www.nytimes.com/1982/02/18/obituaries/lee-strasberg-of-actors-studio-dead.html

Rogers, J. E. (Ed.). (2007). *The art of grief: The use of expressive arts in a grief support group.* New York and London: Routledge.

Stanley, S. (2016). *Relational and body-centered practices for healing trauma: Lifting the burdens of the past.* New York: Routledge.

Thompson, B. E., & Neimeyer, R. A. (Eds.). (2014). *Grief and the expressive arts: Practices for creating meaning.* New York: Routledge.

54

Response Writing Dialogues

Katarzyna Małecka and Janie Taylor

CLIENTS FOR WHOM THE TECHNIQUE IS APPROPRIATE

This technique of engaging in written reflection on published grief memoirs is most appropriate for grieving clients who would typically find meaning in literature and writing in other domains of their life, beyond their loss, per se. It is also applicable as an educational aid in psychology courses and for individuals who are not actively grieving yet who are willing to prepare for approaching or future losses. However, it could be inappropriate as a stand-alone intervention for highly traumatized mourners, who could find reading about and reflecting upon mortality and the losses of others to be potentially triggering or overwhelming.

DESCRIPTION

Texts talk with each other in a wide context of academic and literary traditions. By coining the term "intertextuality" in the 1960s (Kristeva, 1969/1980, pp. 64–69), the field of literary studies admitted explicitly that no text is an autonomous entity created by a single author. In the literary world, T. S. Eliot's *The Love Song of J. Alfred Prufrock* and *The Waste Land* exemplify how alluding to pre-existing texts can result in unique expressive and (self-) reflective works. In the context of this volume, the lists of in-text citations speak volumes about how preceding ideas can inspire, reinforce and deepen the grief research and therapeutic practices of others.

The technique of entering into a dialogue with other texts is a significant literary device used in the *grief memoir*, a literary genre that has been solidifying its position for the last two decades. In general terms, a grief memoir is a self-reflective and, to a large extent, self-therapeutic narrative, documenting the grief process and enabling the author to make meaning of a loss and integrate it into a larger life story. Like an individual grief experience, each grief memoir is different, yet patterns emerge, one of them being the technique of referencing other writers to set one's emotions in a broader informative and empathic context. For instance, Joan Didion seeks solace and understanding of her own grief in poems, prose and clinical literature (Didion, 2006, pp. 44–52), as do many others.

The discourse with other texts practiced by grief memoirists inspired the response writing technique presented here. This type of discursive response writing can be used as part of bibliotherapy with grieving clients and as an educational aid in psychology courses. The dialogue between the student and mentor that exemplifies the technique morphed out of

DOI: 10.4324/9781351069120-67

presentations on grief memoirs and follow-up homework assignments prepared for university students in classes on the psychology of loss and grief. The focus of this exercise was to use texts other than psychological textbooks in order to shift perspectives as well as broaden and deepen reflections on loss and grief for the many students who were grieving at that time as well as for those who were not or had never actively grieved. For grief memoirists, the dialogue with other writers performs three main functions: (1) it helps the authors find words to express the often inexpressible emotions after a loss; (2) it provides an unconditional source of support and understanding (unlike even the most caring family members, texts never get impatient or tired); and (3) it facilitates self-reflection which, in turn, helps process grief and practice the awareness of mortality as part of a life after loss. All these functions are applicable in the case of grieving clients as well as in the case of those readers who are willing to draw on memoirs to prepare for future losses.

The actual method of stimulating a reflective dialogue is simple but requires thoughtful preparation on the part of the teacher or clinician. It consists of framing a few questions that prompt engagement with one or more grief memoirs, read in their entirety or in excerpts provided by the mentor. Students or clients then respond in writing to each, thus beginning an exchange of careful reflections between the two parties. The content of initial questions can be general, as when offered to a group of people, or tailored to a particular person's experience, in the case of individual therapy or independent study. The case example that follows illustrates the process of response writing in a university classroom context.

CASE ILLUSTRATION

At roughly the midpoint of the semester, the first author/instructor (KM) offered a three-hour presentation to an undergraduate class of university students on the therapeutic potential of grief memoirs, both for their writers and their readers. Among the ten responses to the optional assignment that accompanied this unit, the reflections of the second author (JT) stood out for two reasons: (1) She was a nursing assistant whose tasks included hygiene, nutrition and caring for the body after death, as well as an applicant to graduate programs in clinical psychology with a focus on gerontology, and (2) Janie's carefully worded, in-depth thoughts easily elicited additional responses from the instructor, which, in turn, inspired an organic, meaningful dialogue via emails. The excerpts of the dialogue presented here show how grief narratives can be an accessible and apt inspirational source for reflection on mortality and grief validation for the student or client and mentor alike. Before the presentation on grief memoirs, the class had explored several artistic creations (film, poetry, memoirs) discussing grief. The following dialogue references some of these works. The questions were part of the aforementioned homework assignment.

> QUESTION 1: *In The Year of Magical Thinking, Joan Didion researches literary sources, music and clinical texts on bereavement to understand her feelings after the loss of her husband. "There were days when I relied on W. H. Auden, the 'Funeral Blues'," Didion remembers. In Four Weddings and a Funeral (1994), at Gareth's funeral, his partner Matthew also turns to Auden's "Funeral Blues" to express his grief because, as he states, he ran out of words. Can you think of a song, poem or quote that you have found helpful in your life when faced with grief or other challenging emotions or events? Did it help you express your emotions? Did it help you put things in perspective? If so, how?*
>
> JANIE TAYLOR (JT): *A quote that has helped me is "In life there is death; in death there is life." I am unaware of the source, but I have held this quote close to me for a long time. I haven't had much personal experience with grief over the death of anyone close to me, yet this utterance is consoling. Even though the nature of death has many variables—time,*

place, how it happens—we know that it will occur. Death is imminent: in living there is dying; in life there is death. Keeping this in mind, I don't fear my death or the deaths of those close to me. I know their deaths will bring me sadness and grief, but I'm not hiding myself from the fact that they will die. This is the very matter-of-fact part of the quote that helps the logical thinking aspect of my reactions to death. The other half of this phrase, I think, helps more with the emotional aspect and the meaning-making aspect. In death, there is life. Contrary to how it might feel after a death, not everything dies with the deceased. Their memories are alive; their habits, likes and dislikes are all alive in the people who are still living. In a way, they are living in the connections we all have to them and to each other. To realize this, it is necessary to reconstruct our meaning and understanding of those deceased loved ones. I sometimes like to extend this quote to mean a reconfiguration of energy. Energy is never created or destroyed—it is shifted around. We can still find the dead's energy in other forms, so as to mean they are not entirely dead. Thinking this way helps me to emotionally prepare for and cope with deaths of loved ones.

KATARZYNA MAŁECKA (KM): Life and death are interdependent; they exist simultaneously, not consecutively. There is no single source of the quote you mention. Over the years, I have seen its versions in various writings (Whitman, Rilke, Beckett) as well as on many tombstones. In his essay "On Death," Francis Bacon, the father of empiricism, says: "I have often thought upon death, and I find it the least of all evils. So much of our life as we have discovered is already dead; and all those hours which we share, even from the breasts of our mother, until we return to our grandmother the earth, are part of our dying days.... All sorrow, anguish, disease, calamity, or whatsoever can fall in the life of man . . . are familiar unto us, and we suffer them every hour; therefore we die daily, and I am older since I affirmed it" (Bacon, 1625/1850, p. 334). Your words on the awareness of mortality echo and continue this philosophical discourse, which proves that certain ideas are innate in us and can be expressed in many ways in order to fully comprehend, as you put it, the very matter-of-factness of mortality with less anxiety. I think how you choose to see death in life is often accepted with great difficulty. Once we taste life, especially when it is good and peaceful, it is hard to let it go. Practicing the awareness of mortality, at least from time to time, is one of the ways to prepare us for grief. I practice mine by reading and analyzing literature on mortality and grief, which is not only an academic choice but has become a necessity to cope with losses in my life. Texts on grief let me test, often daily, my belief in the notion that we need death in our life so that we can see life in a different light. Death has never failed me in this respect. Hard as it was to process the deaths of my loved ones, some very prolific transformations took place in my life just because of them.

"Energy is never created or destroyed—it is shifted around. We can still find the dead's energy in other forms, so as to mean they are not entirely dead." A similar thought is expressed in "Do Not Stand at My Grave and Weep" by Mary Elizabeth Frye, a consoling elegy that sees the dead as part of winds that blow, "the diamond glints on snow," "the sun on ripened grain," "the gentle autumn rain" (Frye, 1932, lines 3–6). I can relate to the idea that even if our loved ones are gone physically before we go, they still live as part of our journey. Modern grief approaches have been using this concept extensively in recent years to make grievers aware that it is normal to continue the bonds with the deceased. Much more significantly for me, writers such as Shakespeare, Whitman, Wordsworth or Dickinson created their own versions of the continuing bonds theory long before psychology sanctioned this particular approach.

JT: "We need death in our life so that we can see life in a different light. Death has never failed me in this respect." What I gather from your statement is that death can be a learning experience, preparing us for facing our own imminent death. Since I have yet to experience a significant loss, I base my assumption that it can be beneficial on the idea that most anything can be viewed as a learning experience in some way. By truly confronting our mortality—melting away the layers of sugar-coating, the idioms and euphemisms and really, really understanding that we will die, I think we can better live our lives. Knowing that every consecutive breath brings us closer to our last can help us enjoy each sweet inhale and all that comes with it. Not only do I think facing our mortality can help us live our own lives better, but I think it can help us make better connections with others and be more considerate, respectful and empathetic. It is a humbling admission to face mortality, and if we all did it a bit more often, I think it would have a far-reaching impact. This is not to say we must idle over thinking about death, and it doesn't mean we should fixate and ruminate. As with anything, moderation is key, and over- or under-consumption hardly constitutes a healthy lifestyle.

KM: *The British literary theorist Terry Eagleton shares your point of view: "To accept death would be to live more abundantly. By acknowledging that our lives are provisional, we can slacken our neurotic grip on them and thus come to relish them all the more. Embracing death is in this sense the opposite of taking a morbid fancy to it. If we lived permanently at the point of death, it would presumably be easier to forgive our enemies, repair our relationships . . . . It is partly the illusion that we will live forever which prevents us from doing these things. Immortality and immorality are closely allied" (Eagleton, 2004, pp. 210–211). Lord Voldemort in J. K. Rowling's books is the embodiment of the last sentence.*

QUESTION 2: *What would the title of your grief memoir be at this point in your life?*

JT: *As I stated above, I haven't had much experience with grief or death, yet. As I age, my family members are also aging, and for some, I know their deaths are a lot closer than I'd care for them to be. If I were to title my grief memoir, I would maybe call it "The Silver Spoon is Starting to Rust." While I have not been "fed from a silver spoon" in most ways throughout my life, I have not yet experienced a significant loss, but I know they will be coming. Soon I will experience great losses and will grieve.*

KM: *Janie, your title is significant on so many levels—there is even this beautiful "hissing" quality to it with all the "s" sounds that gives it ominous undertones. Very sophisticated, insightful and sincere, to load up more hissing sounds. The correspondence between the metaphorical title and your life makes it easy to relate to for someone who may be in a similar situation. The title also has this beautiful rhythm to it—I read it out loud a couple of times—have you tried it? The seeming simplicity of the diction hides so much. If I were you, I would use this title to write a poem or song! Amazing metaphorical thinking. Thank you.*

QUESTION 3: *Think about two benefits of writing a grief memoir. What is a grief memoir?*

JT: *I think a grief memoir can be highly beneficial in many ways. In one way, it is a more structured form of journaling, in that it follows a journey in which the arc of grief is traced through its progression. I tend to think of a journal as writing down thoughts and feelings as we think of them, but a memoir is an organized and directional reflection on how we have experienced grief and how it has shaped or changed us, sometimes without our knowledge of it. This more structured, self-reflective way of writing might bring us to a new understanding of our grief and can help us make sense of it. I think a grief memoir is also beneficial in that it takes something so personal, and often times painful, and shares that experience with others. It is a platform for the writer and the reader to find solace in a shared reaction to very different experiences. A grief memoir opens the world up to an experience that society has deemed a highly individual experience. But it shouldn't be just an experience we have to deal with on our own and alone. A grief memoir says it is okay to grieve and to be open about sharing those raw moments of emotion publicly.*

*****

The exchange of ideas continued for a few more paragraphs, prompted by more questions and answers, in each of which both student and mentor were moved to further personal disclosures, insights and reflections. In the course of this, Janie aptly summarized:

> Writing gives us the freedom to express how we are feeling and it is free of judgment. It also helps us process and discover aspects of our pain that we might not have found if we didn't explore it through writing. Furthermore, reading allows us to grieve at a distance with the knowledge that there are others out there who are also grieving, sometimes in the same way. I think it helps to destigmatize dying and grief when we are open with ourselves and when we open up to others.

Janie also reflected on her own experience as a nursing assistant, commending one memoirist's decision to prepare the body of her husband before the funeral:

> It is the real concreteness of facing the body of the deceased that can sometimes be the hardest part, initially. As a nursing assistant, it is my role to clean the body soon after death. I welcome this role because, although it is just a body, it is my patient's body, and I care for my patients—it is as simple as that. I believe these experiences have lent themselves to my awareness and frankness with death and my own mortality. In a society where death is hidden underneath a thick sheet, it is important for us to sometimes pull that back and confront death head on, before it's too late.

CONCLUDING THOUGHTS

The denial of death on various levels is what, for many, makes their grief particularly hurtful. In Western cultures, where death "is hidden underneath a thick sheet," the growing number of grief memoirs is not a mere coincidence or new trend. The awareness of mortality needs to resurface somehow both in private and social life because it is an integral part of life. For many people, their closest contact with death takes place when someone they care about dies, leaving many with thoughts and feelings for which they are often unprepared. Like happiness and love, grief is an experience that becomes most meaningful when shared with others, yet many Western cultures ostracize mourners, reinforcing the denial of life's tentativeness.

Many people exercise regularly to feel better and cushion their bodies from the aging process. Exercising the awareness of mortality and of the body's limitations should be equally important to us. Engaging in written dialogues similar to those described in this chapter can be a relatively safe way to look at life's finality. The use of published writings on the subject helps people express what may be initially unutterable. By responding to literary takes on mortality and then responding to those responses, we engage in a more focused, self-reflective and, thus, more effective kind of talking/writing as a learning and, when grief strikes, also healing process. For helping professionals, especially those still in training, discussions inspired by literature other than course textbooks written in psychological jargon may be valid sources of developing more creative counseling techniques that will enable them to connect with their clients on deeper levels.

References

Bacon, F. (1625/1850). An essay on death. In *The works of Lord Bacon* (Vol. 1). London: Henry G. Bohn.
Didion, J. (2006). *The year of magical thinking*. New York: Vintage.

Eagleton, T. (2003). *After theory*. New York: Basic Books.

Frye, M. F. (1932). Do not stand at my grave and weep. In *Family Friend Poems*. Retrieved January 14, 2018, from https://www.familyfriendpoems.com/poem/do-not-stand-by-my-grave-and-weep-by-mary-elizabeth-frye

Kristeva, J. (1969/1980). *Desire in language: A semiotic approach to literature and art* (Thomas Gora, Alice Jardine, & Leon S. Roudiez, Trans.) New York: Columbia University Press.

55

Writing to Heal

Rhonda Davis

CLIENTS FOR WHOM THE TECHNIQUE IS APPROPRIATE

Adults who are open to writing about their grief process and are able to be self-reflective can benefit from this flexible technique. Implementing a *Writing to Heal* group is especially beneficial to bereaved participants who tend to shy away from traditional grief support groups but would like to participate in a healing practice within a supportive community. One of the many benefits of the group is that it attracts introverted personality types in addition to extraverts because there is no pressure to read what the participant has written, and there is adequate space to reflect on one's own grief process. It may be inappropriate for traumatized mourners in the early aftermath of a violent death loss, who require crisis stabilization prior to reflective processing.

DESCRIPTION

Carol Henderson, author of *Farther Along: The Writing Journey of Thirteen Bereaved Mothers* (2012), writes:

> My experience has taught me this: a person dies; the relationship does not. . . . Creating a healing space helps ground people, gives them a private haven of their own words that they can always return to. It reminds them that they have a self and a center, even if they sometimes lose track of these inner resources.
>
> (Henderson, 2012, pp. 54–55)

The inspiration for the *Writing to Heal* group began with an encounter with Carol Henderson's work with bereaved mothers and her book, *Farther Along*. In a *Writing to Heal* group, the facilitator and participants create sacred, healing space for personal and collective healing through creative writing exercises. The facilitator uses writing prompts from literature, poetry, song and art to invite self-reflection and self-care as bereaved clients engage in a deeply healing creative writing process. The facilitator also invites group members to read what they have written in response to creative prompts, and participants practice respectful listening and honoring of the written word. *Writing to Heal* is a carefully constructed, supportive writing group that is quite different from a traditional grief therapy group.

DOI: 10.4324/9781351069120-68

The *Writing to Heal* group leader must facilitate the group by creating a safe environment for bereaved participants to spend time reflecting on their inner voice of wisdom as they seek the intersection of their grief process with the poems or creative writing prompts. Group members may choose to read aloud what they have written, which creates a rich bond between the participants. The guidelines for the group help set the intention of creating the safe space for reflection through writing, reading aloud and sacred listening without judgment or critique. If participants want to share their writing but are too emotional to do so, they can ask another group member to read the piece they want to share. The person can also pass and just listen. Group member Linda Miller chose never to read aloud due to the nature of her grief process. She said,

> It was impossible for me to share what I wrote. I was grateful for those that did and impressed with some of their writings. I appreciate the leader's making it clear it was okay to share or not and I chose not to share. I also appreciated the flexibility the leader gave with each writing assignment. We could reflect on a particular sentence or another. It was a defined activity which was 'no pressure.'

Julie Lloyd, another group member, said, "Sometimes I found it hard to share my writing by reading it aloud, but I was always glad afterward that I did."

CASE ILLUSTRATION

The <u>Writing to Heal</u> *group begins with a set of group expectations that provide the foundation of confidentiality and respectful listening when members read. The guidelines state clearly that this is a writing group, not a therapy group. The writing is for each person, so participants can tell the truth and not focus too much on spelling/grammar issues. There is also a clear expectation that group members read only what's written on the paper and not speak extemporaneously about their grief process. Additionally, there is a strong focus on listening devoutly, to self and others, and being conscious to check internal judgments or critique about the writing/listening process. The group facilitator models respectful response in a very limited way after someone reads; this is not a time to discuss anything about the grief process or the individual's shared words. This is only a time to honor the creative offering shared and express gratitude and compassion for the courage to read aloud. Finally, the facilitator gives permission for the writers to use the creative prompts in several different ways, or, if they have no interest in the prompt, they can use another poem/quote or idea to write from. Ultimately, the* <u>Writing to Heal</u> *experience is individualized to facilitate healing in each person, regardless of the specific writing prompts used in the moment. We write with several prompts before stopping to read aloud and listen devoutly to each other.*

In the first session, even prior to introductions (which are also written and read aloud), we write about our special place, a safe place we visit in our minds. The leader can use guided visualization techniques to help participants envision the safe place and then write about this place so the bereaved can return to this peaceful place if emotions are intense or grief feels raw during the writing/reading process. Next, we have introductions, which are written and include name/age/birthday of deceased as well as when/how the person died. After introductions are read aloud, there is time for written reflection about what participants heard. Following introductions, we start with warm-up activities using sentence stems or lists. An example is inviting participants to list "three things I learned from my loved one," "what I have lost," "what I have found" and "three things for which I am grateful at this moment." After listing, participants can then choose one item from the list and write a paragraph about it. The facilitator uses a printed collection of poetry and inspirational quotes as writing prompts. One may also choose to use art activities as a writing prompt as well. The following is my poem, which was inspired by the original anonymous poem, "I Will."

I Will *(author unknown)*

> As long as I can I will look at this world for the both of us.
> As long as I can I will sing with the birds,
> I will laugh with the flowers,
> I will pray to the stars for both of us.

I Will *(Rhonda Davis)*

> As long as I can I will carry your heart in my heart.
> As long as I can I will look for signs of you;
> Reminders of your beautiful soul that passed my way and held my soul.
> I will open myself to the great mysteries of this life
> And life beyond death.
> I will pray to the stars, the sea, the flowers—
> Knowing that as God created them, so too
> God is holding you, holding me, in forever.

Another favorite activity is "It Belonged to My Loved One." Participants bring an object that belonged to their loved one, and the facilitator guides them in the writing process about this special object. Writers will use descriptive words about what the object looks like and meaning or feelings attached to the object. They may use similes and metaphors to write about the special item. They may even write from the point of view of the object and the impact the object has on their grief process. Group member Sheila Ayers describes this writing process:

> One activity that was very compelling for me was when we were asked to bring in an object that belonged to our loved one. Looking at this object right in front of me, pondering it, holding it, really helped me to unblock and release in a new and different way. It really helped my creative process.

The following is an example of Julie Lloyd's reflection on her mother's hair.

My Mother's Hair

> Angled toward the sun they glisten
> Those beautiful red strands caught in a blue hairbrush
> A piece of you still here on Earth. . . .

The dream was the most surreal thing I have ever experienced. I was touching my mother's hair. We were lying on our L-shaped sofa in my childhood home. I think I knew she was dying or had already died but come back to me. I asked her if I could cut some of her hair. She said, "yes," and "I'm okay." You see, when she died, I found myself wishing I had cut a lock of her hair to keep. I loved her hair! It was so thick and fiery red . . . curly and a little bit wild!

When I woke from the dream, I felt a sense of urgency to drive to my mother's house and look for her hairbrush. When I opened the first drawer in her bedroom chest, there it lay with those beautiful red strands caught in it. If I hold it just right in the light, they glisten. I carefully placed the brush in a plastic bag so they wouldn't get away.

For some reason, I opened a second drawer in the chest and there lay another hairbrush in a plastic bag. A note was with it in my mother's handwriting that simply said, "My mother's hair." I took this one with me also.

Kindred spirits, my mother and I—finding a way to keep a little bit of our mamas here with us.

CONCLUDING THOUGHTS

Writing to Heal is a sacred and powerful experience with bereaved clients who are interested in introspective reflection and creative writing. The experience of both writing and sharing with creative prompts from poetry, art, and everyday life is quite healing for participants, who harness the courage to participate and write from their innermost core. I believe that we are all experiential learners and that much of our deepest healing comes from meaningful experiences with our grief memories and feelings shared in the context of safe community. The *Writing to Heal* group offers such deeply healing opportunity for those who dare to participate through writing, reading and devout listening to self and to others. Yvonne Stewart, a group member, offers these words of wisdom about *Writing to Heal* group experiences after participating in all six groups offered over the past three years. Yvonne says,

> The group experience has been a challenge as well as a very important part of my moving forward with my grief experience. It takes me a while to involve people in my inner thoughts and takes time to gain their trust. All involved are going through the same thing. Even though different people handle their grief in their own way, we are still like a family, sharing thoughts and emotions that cannot be shared elsewhere. For a short time, we can all relate to each other and learn from one another. Although challenging at times, I learned through other participants that the more you bring to the surface, the easier the journey. My grief journey has really been an easier walk thanks to this class and the people who have entered my life through this class.

In summary, *Writing to Heal* groups have the potential to offer participants a creative way to transform their grief in powerfully healing ways. The healing that evolves through writing, reading aloud, and sacred listening to the creative process is a gift to all who engage in the *Writing to Heal* group process.

Reference

Henderson, C. (2012). *Farther along: The writing journey of thirteen bereaved mothers.* Chapel Hill, NC: Willowdell.

56
Karuna Cards

Claudia Coenen

CLIENTS FOR WHOM THE TECHNIQUE IS APPROPRIATE

The Karuna Cards are appropriate for adolescents and adults who are able to write and use their imagination to help themselves process grief. Some of the cards may be used with children in a counseling setting with guidance from a competent therapist or grief counselor. The cards are not indicated for use immediately following a death when the raw pain of loss is most prevalent.

DESCRIPTION

The Karuna Cards were developed through grief counseling in a hospice environment and with clients in private practice. I frequently recommend journal writing but found that people needed assistance in getting started. Those interested in writing welcome the guidance, and the cards are currently used in grief therapy and support groups and are also being utilized by therapists for anxiety, PTSD, trauma and other mental health issues where loss is felt.

Karuna is a Sanskrit word which means "compassion for all." Its root, *kara*, means action, indicating that Karuna is an active compassion. Karuna is both empathic and responsive, stimulating a desire to relieve suffering (Yogapedia, 2017). Grievers often long for action to help them through their pain but don't know what to do. The Karuna Cards recommend grounding, ideas to release anxiety and stimulate inquiry into how one feels about death and its impact on one's life. In addition, the cards advocate compassion towards one's grieving self, which is an often forgotten but equally important activity. Writing through grief allows clients to explore their inner world, alleviate difficult emotions and clarify thoughts by placing them within the container of the journal. Journaling helps grievers discover meaning and insights within their experience. Specific prompts encourage exploration of grief, release emotions and reframe the grief story since different views of the narrative can lead to a transformation of how one feels.

The prompts are simple and can be responded to with writing, talking or by engaging with art modalities. For example, collage is a powerful metaphor for the reparative work of grief, as art therapist Sharon Strouse discovered while grieving the suicide of her daughter (Strouse, 2013). The act of making new images out of torn paper was a way Strouse navigated the "labyrinth of unspeakable grief" since she found that talk therapy was not helpful in the first year of grief. Other cards suggest using color as sketching or scribbling the energy of inner

DOI: 10.4324/9781351069120-69

feelings allows the griever to engage different parts of the brain and body, leading toward reintegration after the shattering feeling of death.

Bereavement work is process work, and the cards guide users through various types of process. For an intuitive griever, they prompt contemplation and mindfulness while encouraging emotional expression. For an instrumental griever, activities such as connecting with nature or gathering images to work with encourage "doing" something with one's grief (MacWilliam, 2017). The compelling need to tell the grief story is prompted in several cards so that the narrative can be shifted, even transformed.

How to Use the Karuna Cards

Shuffle the cards and choose one. Reflect and respond. If the card suggests an activity, the invitation is to try it, notice how it makes you feel, then reflect in the journal if you wish. The cards are effective as a personal grief-processing tool or can be shared with a family member or friend. In relation to grief therapy, if the cards are being used at home, the client might bring the journal in to share what has been written, drawn or collaged, then talk about the experience. A Karuna Card may also be used within a therapy session, or a card might be chosen at the end of a session and used as "homework" until the next time, when the response will be processed.

If a card does not resonate at the time it is chosen, simply shuffle and choose another. As an alternative, this resistance could be explored, and the client might use the card they did not like. This approach would be useful if the same card is drawn several times. The Karuna Cards can be used many times as grief changes.

Examples of Karuna Cards

One card asks, "What do you miss the most? What do you not miss at all?" One prompts you to write a letter, saying something you wish you could have said. Another suggests a slow walk outdoors, as if taking a bath in nature. Another card invites you to "Make a list of people who have loved you, including those who love you now. Reflect on each one, writing a little about them."

CASE ILLUSTRATION

Anna is a 63-year-old businesswoman, the younger of two sisters. I met Anna when her 93-year-old mother entered hospice and began working with her shortly before the death of her mom. Anna's sister, Ellen, married young and stayed home to raise her two daughters, now grown. Anna enjoyed being the aunt who gave them experiences, such as the theater and ballet. One of the nieces is gay and married to her partner. While the sisters were not close, they celebrated holidays together. Anna had no children of her own and was expected to attend every event at Ellen's house. Anna had lived with her boyfriend for many years and wanted to host some holidays, but Ellen always resisted.

Both sisters were close with their mother; their father had died some 20 years before. The mother was a vivacious woman who avoided confrontation. She had a lifelong habit of talking with one daughter about the other. This pattern played out in her daughters: Anna would speak to her mother about her sister, or Ellen would speak to her daughter about Anna, but the sisters were disinclined to speak directly to each other.

Before she died, the mother exhorted Anna to stay close to her sister, and Anna promised to try. While Anna was sad that her mother had died, most of our counseling sessions revolved around her relationship with her sister.

One reason for the lack of closeness had occurred a few years before. When Anna finally married at age 60, Ellen did not seem very interested. Unbeknownst to Anna, Ellen told her gay daughter that Anna was not comfortable with this daughter's partner. This was patently untrue, but Anna's niece believed it and did not attend the wedding. Anna was hurt and felt her sister had deliberately kept her niece from coming with false information. Anna spoke to Ellen about this but did not call her niece directly to explain how she felt. Anna was upset that her small family did not seem to celebrate her happiness.

Keeping her promise to her mother, Anna invited her sister to spend a weekend with her, hoping that they could rekindle a connection. Ellen made excuses but finally consented to come, bringing her husband along. Anna did not get along with Ellen's husband, feeling that he often interfered with direct communication between them. Still, they went to the city together. The weekend was disappointing to Anna and very awkward.

Anna was asked to identify the shape of the relationship between her mother, herself and her sister. She answered that it was a triangle, confirming what this counselor saw as classic triangulation. Anna began to notice how her family was indirect. She wished that she could speak openly to her sister and wanted her sister to be more supportive.

Anna shuffled the Karuna Cards and responded to this one:

> Is there someone in your life who does not act the way you wish they would?
> Write a fairy tale in which they are everything you wish they would be.
> Then write the story of how they really are. Compare these two stories.
> What story can you truly live with? Write that new story.

Anna liked this card and decided to make this her homework between counseling sessions. Anna wrote three brief stories. The first was a fairy tale in which she had a perfect supportive sister who wanted the best for her, and Anna returned the same feelings. In this fantasy story, she and her sister worked together to help their mother, Ellen rejoiced when Anna got married, and all family members celebrated.

Anna's second story expressed the reality of her relationship with her sister, which was not very honest. The story recounted the many times she had tried to collaborate with her sister on decisions regarding their mother's placement in a nursing home or on planning Anna's wedding, only to find her sister unwilling to participate. This "reality" story was filled with hurt as Anna wondered, "How do you get past the history and the baggage?"

Writing the fairy tale had come easily since it was fantasy, but writing the reality brought her face to face with certain patterns in her own behavior. In her third story, Anna wrote that she did not want either the fantasy or the reality but wanted to develop a more honest relationship with her sister.

Anna read all three stories aloud in session. We processed her feelings, and she explored how to develop better communication with her sister. She recognized how she continued the patterns set up by her mother and that this no longer worked. We discussed how Anna might change, but there was no guarantee that her sister would follow suit. Still, Anna could release her own resentment and give up the habit of being indirect and even undermining.

Anna's response to writing these stories was positive. The exercise allowed her to look deeply at the relationship and notice her own part in the dynamic. Recognizing how her mother had instilled triangulation was difficult for Anna but allowed her to see her mother as human. Anna took steps to change her own reactions and hoped that a shift in herself might create a closer relationship with Ellen.

Anna contacted me nearly three years after the death of her mother to share that she now has a better relationship with her sister and her nieces. She felt that this was a result of working with this Karuna Card and writing these stories. Anna also called her niece directly to let her know *how much she loves her, is happy that her niece is in a loving relationship and does not care whether it is a same sex one or not. Anna gently told her niece how it hurt that she had missed her wedding and apologized for not calling her then to tell her. Now, Anna finds that she can be more honest with her sister, and they have taken several weekend trips together.*

This Karuna Card helped Anna examine her relationship with her sister as well as the recurring pattern set up by their mother. By approaching her story as if it were a fairy tale, she was able to release some of the unfulfilled longings and see them as not only unattainable, but unnecessary. Rewriting her narrative allowed Anna to create a new way of relating to her sister and other members of her family.

CONCLUDING THOUGHTS

Writing your way through grief can be very helpful. In the 1980s, James Pennebaker studied college students, asking them to write about a traumatic experience daily for several days, contrasted with students who simply wrote about daily events. He noted a reduction of stress and a boost to the immune system in those who expressed disturbing experiences in journals (Pennebaker, 1997). Nearly 300 studies have been conducted since then that validate the benefits of expressing feelings through journaling and through art. Pennebaker's most recent book identifies specific areas that positively respond to emotional writing (Pennebaker, 2014). In addition to the physiological affects listed here, Pennebaker notes that one's mood might be initially depressed following writing, but the long-term benefits are clearly positive.

> Emotional writing . . . can positively affect people's sleeping habits, work efficiency and their connections to others. Indeed, when we put traumatic experiences into words, we tend to be less concerned with the emotional events that have been weighing us down.
>
> (Pennebaker, 2014, pp. 3–4)

The Karuna Cards help bereaved persons process grief through journaling and expressive modalities, either in a therapeutic setting or on their own. The cards are a concrete tool to help with the emotional, nonlinear aspects of grieving as well as supporting spiritual connection, cognitive understanding and meaning making.

References

MacWilliam, B. (2017). Concepts in treatment. In B. MacWilliam (Ed.), *Complicated grief, attachment and art therapy* (p. 89). London and Philadelphia: Jessica Kingsley.
Pennebaker, J. (1997). *Opening up: The healing power of expressing emotions.* New York: Guilford Press.
Pennebaker, J. (2014). *Expressive writing: Words that heal.* Eunenclaw, WA: Idyll Arbor.
Strouse, S. (2013). *Artful grief.* Bloomington, IN: Balboa Press.
Yogapedia. (2017, May 18). Retrieved from www.yogapedia.com/definition/5305/karuna

Part XIV
Facilitating Support

57

Envisioning Transitions

Robert A. Neimeyer and Doris Chambers Vaughans

CLIENTS FOR WHOM THE TECHNIQUE IS APPROPRIATE

Adults (children or other relations) who are faced with transitioning senior loved ones from their homes to alternative residences or care facilities can benefit from this compassionate and empathic technique. Implementing *Envisioning Transitions* in a group setting is especially beneficial as it allows opportunities for participants to share insights and engage in creative brainstorming. It may be less appropriate for family caregivers of patients with advanced dementia, as well as those being transitioned to skilled nursing care following a medical trauma such as sudden and severe stroke or injury, especially one that leaves the patient cognitively impaired.

DESCRIPTION

The term "proactive coping" is used to describe the process of anticipating future events or stressors and preparing for them in advance (Pope & Kang, 2010). *Envisioning Transitions* is an effective technique for adult children to engage in proactive coping on behalf of their senior loved ones. It can help them better address the loss needs of their seniors that are likely to accompany the major transition of moving, especially from the senior's own home to a care facility. This major transition of changing residences during the final season of one's life can invoke subtle and ambiguous feelings common to nonfinite losses and disenfranchised grief. According to Harris and Gorman (2011), such nonfinite and ambiguous losses often go unrecognized and unaddressed and can lead to chronic sorrow.

Harris (2020) describes nonfinite losses as internal in nature and as encompassing a sense of ongoing uncertainty, vulnerability and helplessness. The empathic engagement of "envisioning transitions" allows the adult child to achieve experiential insights into how his or her parent or other senior loved one may be enduring this major transition at this point in their lifespan. The *Envisioning Transitions* technique also provides support for having hard yet meaningful and healing, collaborative conversations with loved ones that potentially can lower resistance to moving, provide meaningful and compassionate support and help them feel more empowered to adapt and adjust to their new residence. Detailed instructions are embedded in the case study that follows.

DOI: 10.4324/9781351069120-71

CASE ILLUSTRATION

I (DCV) was invited to present at a senior living residence facility to a group of adult children who were contemplating relocating their senior parents from their homes to this facility. The stated objective was to present information that would be beneficial to adult children having "hard conversations" with their parents, as an alternative to, "Mom/Dad, I'm moving you to a facility." Being convinced that this process of transition is lined with losses that must be addressed or, at minimum, included in whatever conversations are embarked upon, I consulted with Dr. Robert Neimeyer. In addition to words of advice and encouragement, he created Envisioning Transitions, *a technique that proved dramatic in its effect on the attendees and the staff of the facility. Following a few introductory remarks about the theme, the technique comprises a 30-minute group exercise of guided meditation, role-play and discussion.*

The evening of the presentation, the room was filled with approximately 30 adult children and other family caregivers (grandchildren, siblings), including several couples. Most looked anxious and uncertain, and I sensed that all of them experienced anxiety, sometimes coupled with frustration, about the pending discussion with their senior family members. The presentation began with a slide presentation that provided information about reasons for transitions (e.g., diminished physical ability, diminished health status, change in family constellation such as widowhood, decreased socialization/increased isolation and downsizing, to name a few). To provide context, we also touched on types of losses, grieving, shattered assumptions, meaning making and re-storying losses (e.g., Neimeyer, 2015) before introducing the topic of having hard conversations. On Dr. Neimeyer's suggestion, I shifted from a psychoeducational focus on "how-to" instructions for the conversation to a more tangible way of helping families cope more compassionately with this hard transition.

At this point, I invited the attendees to participate in the Envisioning Transitions *exercise, introducing it by reading the following paragraph verbatim:*

> *Though we rarely stop to think of it, life is fraught with loss. Little by little or suddenly and tragically, we will lose everyone and everything we love, at least in an earthly sense, from the point of our birth to the point of our death. Though these losses are sometimes obvious and profound—the death of a spouse, the development of a life-limiting illness—they are often subtle and ambiguous, as in the gradual loss of strength, freedom, and independence that comes with age. Moving residences, even under hopeful or necessary conditions, entails countless such losses, uprooting us heart and soul from the home, neighbors, possessions and routines we once cherished, and that gave our life story context and meaning. When these losses are involuntary or reluctant, we are denied even the basic sense of choice and voice over our future, as much that constituted our valued past is scattered or stripped away. Grief is the common response to such losses, whether named or unnamed, and we can only hope that those who love us will broach these unwelcome changes with compassion and understanding.*

Inviting audience members to close their eyes, I then led them in an exercise, slowly and evocatively reading the following script, pausing frequently between instructions to allow participants to visualize and feel the impact of each scenario:

> *It can be helpful for us to really try putting ourselves in our parents' shoes prior to opening this conversation.*
>
> *First, imagine that we are unemployed, with no children living in our home. . . . Then take in the daily reality of their health, imagining that we live with the same limitations and uncertainties they do. Take a few minutes with your eyes closed to make these*

imaginings vivid and real: I have no work, and no marketable skills. My children are grown and into their own lives. I can't do many of the things I once did, and don't know how much quality time I have left, because of this medical problem with. . . . You get the picture. Say the words in your own mind repeatedly until they seem real, and see what feelings rise up as you do.

Now add the next piece: My spouse has died, and I am alone. Sit with this, repeating the words. Continue the meditation and attend to the resulting feelings.

Then, add the next piece: Now my children want me to move out of my home, my neighborhood, and leave behind most of my possessions and most of my spouse's. Sit with that a few minutes and track the feelings.

Finally, "channeling" your parent in this empathic state, take out a sheet of paper, and title it, "What I will lose," listing at least ten things that [would] matter to you if you were in this position that will be lost with this move into a facility. These can be physical things (my bed, my mother's tableware, my garden, my workshop), people (my visits with my neighbors) or valued dimensions of living (my ability to control my life, my sense of safety).

After you have finished this, you might consider role playing a conversation with another person acting the part of your child engaging you in this hard conversation for ten minutes. Then process with each other how the conversation went, and reverse roles, with you now playing the part of their child raising the same issue. If you do this as part of a larger group, then process this a bit more together.

Following along with the instructions, many participants looked visibly uncomfortable, shifting in their seats or sighing audibly. Several others wept silently, and one or two opened their eyes and began taking notes early. Moving to dyadic and group processing, discussion deepened and became more compassionate as they jointly imagined and shared ideas for having hard but necessary conversations with their loved ones about the pending transition. As the presentation ended, more than a few people approached me to express gratitude for the experience and to further brainstorm about their unique situations.

CONCLUDING THOUGHTS

Envisioning Transitions can be a powerful and effective exercise to enhance accurate empathic understanding and empowerment of adult children and other family caregivers for seniors facing a difficult residential transition. Members of the facility staff likewise benefit from participation, even if they are uninvolved in decision making about the transition, as they report understanding the hidden losses of residents with greater clarity after taking part. While deepening empathy for the senior stands at the heart of the exercise, open-ended questions following the visualization and role play can help underscore both the emotional and the practical learning of participants: *What feelings did you notice in yourself as you walked through the exercise in your imagination? What was the hardest loss for you to envision? What questions or approaches on the part of your role-play partner felt most helpful to you? What is one practical thing you learned about what to do, or not to do, in having this conversation with your loved one?* As different participants voice their responses in the group, summarizing responses to each question visibly on a large-format writing tablet and affixing these to the wall can help participants harvest the lessons learned. Likewise, reviewing the losses they encountered during the visualization can generate numerous common thematic concerns, including leaving behind cherished people and possessions, a loss of familiarity and safety at a time of life when these are treasured and the potential loss of financial security for the future, due to the substantial cost of assisted living or residences with still higher levels of care. As these and many other losses are acknowledged, participants tend to feel less alone at a pivotal moment in their family life cycle and more appreciative of how difficult such transitions can be for all concerned. In summary, *Envisioning Transitions* can empower participants to engage in hard conversations from a more compassionate and empathetic stance that reinforces the care and concern at the heart of their relationships with those they love.

References

Harris, D. L. (Ed.). (2020). *Non-death loss and grief*. New York: Routledge.

Harris, D. L., & Gorman, E. (2011). Grief from a broader perspective: Nonfinite loss, ambiguous loss, and chronic sorrow. In D. L. Harris (Ed.), *Counting our losses* (pp. 1–14). New York: Routledge.

Neimeyer, R. A. (2015). Treating complicated bereavement: The development of grief therapy. In J. Stillion & T. Attig (Eds.), *Death, dying and bereavement: Contemporary perspectives, institutions and practices* (pp. 307–320). New York: Springer.

Pope, N. D., & Kang, B. (2010). Residential relocation in later life: A comparison of proactive and reactive moves. *Journal of Housing for the Elderly, 24*, 193–207.

58

The Meaningful Conversation

Wendy G. Lichtenthal, Melissa Masterson
and Aliza A. Panjwani

CLIENTS FOR WHOM THE TECHNIQUE IS APPROPRIATE

Adults who are struggling to connect or communicate with important others in their lives or who could benefit from an opportunity to share more about their needs with close relations can benefit from this approach. The grievers may cite challenges connecting with others but not be so isolated that they cannot identify a significant other who could join them in the exercise. The technique may be less effective for relationships that are high in conflict or in circumstances where significant others are critical, provide negative social support or exhibit personality traits that hinder adaptive communication.

DESCRIPTION

Low social support has been associated with prolonged grief in numerous studies (Bellet, Holland, & Neimeyer, 2018; Lobb et al., 2010; Villacieros, Serrano, Bermejo, & Magaña, 2014). Disconnection from others can leave a griever feeling as if her life does not matter. Therefore, identifying ways to enhance support and to foster meaningful relationships is crucial to adaptation. Supportive relationships offer opportunities to process emotions and make meaning of the loss; they are often a source of meaning in and of themselves.

The Meaningful Conversation is intended to help bereaved individuals by facilitating communication between the bereaved adult and someone important in her life. This technique is used in the ninth session of meaning-centered grief therapy (MCGT), a 16-session manualized intervention designed to enhance a sense of meaning and purpose for bereaved individuals struggling with more prolonged, intense grief symptoms (Lichtenthal & Breitbart, 2015; Lichtenthal, Lacey, Roberts, Sweeney, & Slivjak, 2017). The ninth session focuses on strengthening meaningful connections in the griever's life and, to this end, asks the patient to invite a significant other to reinforce the major ideas of MCGT outside therapy, help brainstorm how the griever can more strongly connect to others in her life and strengthen the bond to the significant other through the Meaningful Conversation.

The technique involves the therapist facilitating a brief, structured conversation about the griever's and significant other's respective needs and concludes with expressions of appreciation. To prepare for this, the therapist should help the griever identify someone who has been a source of support but with whom additional communication about the patient's needs may be helpful. The therapist should mention that the session is not an invitation for family or

DOI: 10.4324/9781351069120-72

couples counseling, but rather an opportunity to help the significant other learn about the patient's therapy and for them to engage in conversation about what they need from—and appreciate about—one another.

During the session with the dyad, some time should be spent describing the importance of connection in adapting to loss. It is important to note that the significant other may also be grieving the deceased. While special care should be taken to acknowledge the difficulty of providing care in the midst of grief, the therapist should also be mindful that this exercise is not intended to be a family or couples therapy intervention.

To facilitate communication and the opportunity to feel heard and supported, this technique employs the speaker-listener technique (Gottman, Notarius, Gonso, & Markman, 1976; Stanley, Markman, & Blumberg, 1997). The speaker-listener technique is an approach to communication in which each person takes a turn speaking while his or her partner listens and paraphrases what the speaker said before sharing a response. The Meaningful Conversation begins with the therapist inviting the patient to share with the significant other what she needs and what would help her feel most connected to this person. The therapist asks the significant other to summarize what the patient said and then invites the significant other to express his needs and desire for connection. An important role the therapist plays during this exercise is facilitating each person's paraphrasing of the other's needs, allowing ample time for clarification and strategizing how to meet them. As these conversations are often emotionally charged, the role of the therapist is to encourage constructive communication through the use of the speaker-listener technique as well as to hold a safe space for both parties to share and to be heard. The exercise concludes with the patient and significant other sharing what they appreciate about one another, which allows the interaction to end on a positive note.

Following the structured conversation, the therapist can invite the patient and significant other to process the interaction. Throughout the exercise, the therapist should ensure that the patient is speaking directly to her significant other (and vice versa), that each person is provided ample time to share without interruption or rebuttal and that mutual respect and a desire for understanding are maintained throughout. Finally, the therapist should highlight both the patient's and the significant other's individual strengths and their strengths as a pair before bringing the session to a close.

Meaningful Conversation Instructions

Begin by reading or spontaneously paraphrasing the following instructions to both participants.

This conversation will use what has been referred to as the speaker-listener technique. This involves each of you taking turns speaking while the other person listens and then paraphrases what the speaker said without responding or rebutting. The goal is to express yourself and feel heard without making efforts to "problem solve" at this time. When you are in the speaker role, you have the floor. The speaker can hold an object, like a pen, to indicate who is in the speaking role. Please use "I" statements to express your feelings and thoughts when you are speaking. The listener then will paraphrase what the speaker expressed, not rebutting or responding, but rather stating what he/she heard in his/her own words. Then, that person becomes the speaker and has the opportunity to express his/her own needs and thoughts.

Using these ground rules, speak to your support provider and share what you need and would like from him/her and what would help you feel most connected. Once you have finished speaking, your support provider should respond using the listener ground rules. Your support provider should then share what he/she needs and would like from you and what would help him/her feel most connected to you. You and your support provider should continue the exchange using the speaker-listener approach for about five to ten minutes, allowing each of you to express your wishes about how to enhance your connection to one another. Conclude by indicating what you appreciate about your support provider and allow your support provider to indicate what he/ she appreciates about you.

A handout with the speaker-listener "ground rules" (Gottman et al., 1976; Stanley et al., 1997) is provided to the dyad for reference.

CASE EXAMPLE

Katherine is a 61-year-old, Caucasian, married mother of four children and retired nurse. Nearly five years ago, Katherine lost her oldest son, 31-year-old Brian, to colon cancer. At the start of therapy, Katherine was experiencing frequent, intense yearning to be with her son and persistent anger related to his death. She spoke about the unfairness of losing a son who she envisioned would take care of their family when she and her husband were no longer able. Specifically, Katherine feared for the future of her youngest daughter, Amelia, who had neuro-cognitive and physical disabilities and was dependent on Katherine and her husband. Katherine related that Brian was an incredibly responsible and loyal son who had clearly expressed his commitment to taking care of his sister in the future. His commitment to his sister had been a tremendous source of comfort to Katherine; thus, losing Brian not only left her yearning for her beloved son but also left her in a state of chronic anxiety about Amelia's future.

Katherine frequently expressed her wish to discuss this concern with her two surviving children as well as her discomfort about burdening them. Katherine's therapist encouraged her to invite one of her children to join her in session as an opportunity to foster their connection and express needs. Katherine invited her oldest daughter, 34-year-old Nicole, to attend the session with her. The therapist began the session by thanking Nicole for her willingness to support her mother, inviting Katherine to share with her daughter the main goals of the therapy and how the experience has been for her. As part of MCGT, the session then focused on barriers Katherine has faced in connecting with others. Nicole supported her mother in problem-solving strategies to overcome those barriers.

The therapist then introduced the Meaningful Conversation exercise. After reviewing the speaker-listener ground rules, the therapist asked Katherine and Nicole to face one another and invited Katherine to share with her daughter what she needed from her. Katherine began, "I need her to—" The therapist gently interrupted Katherine to direct her to speak directly to her daughter, rather than speaking through the therapist. Katherine began again, "I need a commitment from you about Amelia. I'm sorry. It's what I really need. I'm so worried about her," Katherine said. Without hesitation, Nicole replied, "Obviously, I'm going to take care of her and take responsibility for her." This was an example of the common push to respond or rebut that so commonly occurs in such interactions. In these instances, the therapist ideally asks that the significant other pause before responding and paraphrase the patient's stated needs.

When it was Nicole's turn to speak, she expressed her fear that she would not be able to fill her brother's shoes. In response to this, the therapist invited Katherine to share what she heard her daughter say. Katherine reiterated that Nicole did not think that she would do a good job but added, "That's not true; she'll do a better job." Given the power of this statement, again the thera-pist instructed Katherine to speak directly to her daughter. As the structured dialogue continued, Katherine shared her admiration for her daughter's unique qualities and, most importantly, her belief in her abilities. Nicole remained quiet as she processed what her mother had just shared and then affirmed her commitment to caring for her sister in the future. During this exchange, the therapist aided Katherine and Nicole in expressing what they needed from one another, and, subsequently, each left the session with their needs heard. Katherine had explicitly asked for commitment while Nicole had implicitly asked for validation that she was smart and capable and could fill the enormous shoes of her beloved brother.

The therapist then invited Katherine to share with her daughter what she appreciated about her. Katherine tearfully replied, "That you call me every day, and you still depend on me and take me out. It means that you think about me and make sure I'm okay. You're my best friend." The therapist allowed for a pause during which Nicole could absorb her mother's words and formulate her own words of appreciation. Nicole ultimately shared her appreciation of her mother's demonstration of unconditional love. Both Katherine and Nicole thanked the therapist for the opportunity to connect and express their needs and appreciation to one another.

After the Meaningful Conversation, Katherine and the therapist met for another seven sessions. Over the course of these sessions, the therapist and Katherine explored the self-reflection that the exercise had catalyzed. Katherine reflected on the intensity of her anger in the past and realized how hard it must have been for others to support her at that time. Given this newfound insight, coupled with the closeness that the exercise helped bring to her relationship with Nicole, Katherine decided to engage in a meaningful conversation with her surviving son outside therapy. She shared how she apologized to her son for allowing her anger and grief to fracture their relationship and demonstrated her commitment to fostering their connection in the future. The therapist highlighted the courage in Katherine's choice to confront her painful past in service of repairing and fostering important relationships in her life.

The Meaningful Conversation provided Katherine with an opportunity to share her needs with her daughter, addressing a major source of anxiety, as well as the chance for she and her daughter to express their love and appreciation for one another. During Katherine's final session of MCGT, she reflected on the significant positive impact of the therapy, expressing tearfully, "That session with Nicole, that was the best thing that has happened to me in years."

CONCLUDING THOUGHTS

In its ideal form, the Meaningful Conversation creates an opportunity to clearly articulate those needs and wishes that often go unspoken. In well-functioning relationships, for example, this might be an expressed need to have the significant other speak more about the deceased. In relationships that have become tense or distanced, positive feelings commonly emerge with the concluding expressions of appreciation. The structuring helps what might be emotionally charged exchanges to remain focused and, hopefully, productive. Ultimately, it can help strengthen the relationship, which may be connected to meaningful roles and/or a source of love, friendship or companionship. The strengthened relationship, in turn, can contribute to existential well-being, reduce feelings of isolation and provide a reason for continuing to engage in life despite enduring grief.

ACKNOWLEDGEMENTS

Support for research on meaning-centered grief therapy was provided by National Cancer Institute (NCI) grants R03 CA13994 (Lichtenthal), K07 CA172216 (Lichtenthal), and P30 CA008748 (Thompson).

References

Bellet, B. W., Holland, J. M., & Neimeyer, R. A. (2018). The social meaning in life events scale (SMILES): A preliminary psychometric evaluation in a bereaved sample. *Death Studies, 43*, 103–112. doi:10.1080/07481187.2018.1456008

Gottman, J., Notarius, C., Gonso, J., & Markman, H. (1976). *A couple's guide to communication.* Champaign, IL: Research Press.

Lichtenthal, W. G., & Breitbart, W. (2015). The central role of meaning in adjustment to the loss of a child to cancer: Implications for the development of meaning-centered grief therapy. *Current Opinion in Supportive and Palliative Care, 9*(1), 46–51.

Lichtenthal, W. G., Lacey, S., Roberts, K., Sweeney, C., & Slivjak, E. (2017). Meaning-centered grief therapy. In W. Breitbart (Ed.), *Meaning-centered psychotherapy* (pp. 88–99). New York: Oxford University Press.

Lobb, E. A., Kristjanson, L. J., Aoun, S. M., Monterosso, L., Halkett, G. K., & Davies, A. (2010). Predictors of complicated grief: A systematic review of empirical studies. *Death Studies, 34*(8), 673–698.

Stanley, S. M., Markman, H. J., & Blumberg, S. L. (1997). The speaker/listener technique. *The Family Journal, 5*(1), 82–83.

Villacieros, M., Serrano, I., Bermejo, J. C., & Magaña, M. (2014). Social support and psychological well-being as possible predictors of complicated grief in a cross-section of people in mourning. *Anales de Psicología, 30*(3), 944–951.

59
Dyadic Eye Gazing

Rickie Simpson and Kerry-Lyn Stanton-Downes

CLIENTS FOR WHOM THE TECHNIQUE IS APPROPRIATE

Dyadic eye gazing provides an opportunity for us to be known in our grief, whether it arises from death, divorce, deployment or any other transition that brings about loss. It is appropriate for adults of any age as well as late adolescents who have the capacity for a depth of intimacy and demonstrated self-regulation. However, in the absence of relational safety, a sustained level of eye gazing can cause cognitive overload and a high level of helplessness. Therefore, highly reactive couples, young children or those with major neurocognitive disorders are poor candidates for this intervention. This work is not appropriate if you are short of time or with some cultures in which there is a strong bias against eye contact.

DESCRIPTION

> *It's such a secret place, the land of tears.*
> —Antoine de Saint- Exupéry (1943), *The Little Prince*

So much of grief is deeper than the spoken word. When walled off, grief penetrates every aspect of our being, leaving us painfully alone yet longing to be known. The intimacy of dyadic eye gazing is a way to bridge to this secret place where two people in family or couples therapy context can silently witness, and be witnessed, in their experience of grief.

Some of the most powerful healing occurs in silence. Just as the loss of connection brought us grief, restoration of connection is the very thing that will begin to bring about healing. It can be arduous to heal our grief alone because separation is such a painful condition for human beings (Lieberman, 2013). In the silent intimacy of eye gazing, often blinking becomes synchronized and is thought to bind people into a "singular connected system" (Koike, T. et al., 2016). Therefore, when bound together in this way, we are seen and known in our disconnection, making eye gazing a powerful antidote to aloneness (van der Kolk, 2014).

Dyadic eye gazing is a therapist-led intervention carried out during a course of treatment at the point when there is an appropriate level of relational safety. This is evidenced by the clients' capacity to sustain loving eye contact, self-regulate and be present before moving to the intimacy of eye gazing. If unsure, ways to evaluate relational safety in a

DOI: 10.4324/9781351069120-73

couples-therapy context are to look for the following: soft eyes, leaning in, quietness in their bodies and reaching for each other if they aren't already touching (Simpson & Stanton-Downes, 2017).

Within any given session, the act of eye contact will occur, be it brief or sustained. What is important is to stay connected to whether is appropriate to deepen the eye contact into an eye-gazing intervention. In the case illustration that follows, the eye-gazing process took close to an hour within a two-hour session.

CASE ILLUSTRATION

Sarah and Jack came to therapy five years after the sudden death of their only daughter, Elizabeth. Dangerously close to separating, they decided to engage in therapy as a way to help them decide whether or not to divorce. At their initial consultation, it became clear that there was very little relational safety to talk about death, grief or loss. This was visible in the positioning of their chairs in relation to each other and their avoidance of eye contact. They spoke about how little time they spent together and how infrequently they spoke to each other. The disconnection between Sarah and Jack was palpable.

By the third session, the couple were able to face each other, maintain eye contact for a minute or two, use gentle tones when speaking to each other, sit with their tears, lean in toward each other and display a quietness in their bodies (Simpson & Stanton-Downes, 2017). Therapeutically, this relational change was achieved by slowly titrating eye gazing in each session up to this point.

Given the shift, it felt appropriate to ask the question "What is sitting in the space between you right now?" Sarah responded, "The death of our daughter," and Jack nodded. This was a clear indicator that they felt safe enough to turn to one another in their grief. I (KLSD) asked their permission to facilitate the eye-gazing process by asking them, "Would you be willing to share with your partner exactly how you feel about this right now by just using your eyes?" Asking permission allowed them to take ownership of their experience at a time when so much agency had been lost in Elizabeth's death.

Having received a resounding yes from both parties, I invited them to take some deep breaths with eyes shut, noticing the air entering and exiting their nose while extending the exhale. Next, I asked them to become aware of their thoughts and emotions and how their bodies were holding or experiencing their loss and grief. Through closed eyes, tears began to gently trickle down their cheeks.

While maintaining warm, positive regard for Sarah and Jack in their suffering, I invited them to slowly open their eyes and let their partner see into their world through their eyes—noticing moment by moment their experience. As they sat in silence, the air weighed down with sadness and pain. There was little space for words other than my soft voice saying, "Breathe."

While they continued to look deep into each other's eyes, I gently encouraged them to "Show your partner what it is like to live in that place of grief and loss." At this moment, Sarah reached up and held Jack's forearms while his thumbs gently caressed her arms. His chin began to quiver, and her hand moved up to wipe away his tears. We sat together in the vulnerable, open silence for nearly five minutes.

While having an embodied experience, it became clear that it was important for the couple to begin to verbalize and integrate this experience together right now (Lee, 1997). After a minute of reflection, both acknowledged they had something to share. Sarah decided to speak first, and I invited her to check that Jack was available to listen. He said yes. This process of checking in gives agency to both parties to continue the process or not. Therapeutically a "no" from either person is a marker that more relational safety is needed before proceeding to the next level of intimacy.

After I invited both Sarah and Jack to take a few breaths, she said, "I am so sorry. I never knew you were in so much pain. I never get to see it this way. I see you busy, so I never feel it like I see it now. I can see that you keep busy as a way to stay away from the pain." When an experience is so profoundly limbic, language becomes simple, honest and direct. As she shared her experience, he began to sob, and she leaned in and hugged him until his body became still.

Knowing it was important for Jack to also have the opportunity for integration, I asked, "Is there anything you would like to share with Sarah right now?" Jack said, "I am in so much pain I cannot be with myself, let alone you. But I love you more than life itself." It was as if the flood gates had opened, and they held on to each other and sobbed—that kind of whole-body sobbing that comes from the depths of one's being. I sat silent and completely present.

Holding both the process and their moment-by-moment experience and only once the sobbing had stopped, I checked in with the couple to see if there was anything more to say. Jack said yes, so once again, I supported him to check in with Sarah as to whether she was still available to listen to him. She said yes.

After I guided them through a short breathing exercise with an extended exhale, Jack shared, "When I looked into your eyes, everything was blank. I couldn't find you. It feels like you died with Elizabeth." As tears softly fell, he continued, "Can you ever come back to me? I love you." Almost spontaneously, Sarah said, "I do feel numb and dead inside. I don't know how to come back to you, but please stay with me." Jack's response was instantaneous: "I will never leave you; I am right here." This was a very sacred moment as they connected deeply with each other and in their need of each other in their grief.

After some time, I took a breath and asked each of them to share what this experience had been like for them. Jack's reflection was that it had been "surprising and very emotional. I am glad we have done this." Sarah's response was, "I never knew we were both suffering so much. I didn't know how to reach him or show him me."

CONCLUSION

When a couple is dealing with death, each brings with them their graveyard of regret (Leriche, 1951). This was certainly true as Sarah and Jack grappled with the death of Elizabeth. While the experience of Elizabeth's death was shared, their regrets about the experience were not. As their regrets contained different images, words, emotions and sensations, dyadic eye gazing allowed them to be seen in their difference. By pooling their resources (Lieberman, 2013), Sarah and Jack were able to begin the process of moving from disconnection to connection in this devastating experience.

References

Koike, T., Tanabe, H. C., Okazaki, S., Nakagawa, E., Sasaki, A. T., Shimada, D., . . . Sadato, N. (2016, January 15). Neural substrates of shared attention as social memory: A hyperscanning functional magnetic resonance imaging study. *Neuroimage, 125*, 401–412. Retrieved September 4, 2016, from www.ncbi.nlm.nih.gov/pubmed/26514295

Lee, M. (1997). *Phoenix rising therapy: A bridge from body to soul.* Jacksonville, FL: HCI.

Leriche, R. (1951). La philosophie de la chirurgie. In H. March (Ed.), *No harm done.* New York: Picador.

Lieberman, M. D. (2013). *Social: Why our brains are wired to connect.* New York: Crown.

Saint-Exupéry, A. (1943). *The little prince.* New York: Harcourt, Brace & World.

Simpson, R. T., & Stanton-Downes, K. L. (2017). From me to we: The transformative nature of couples' yoga therapy. *Yoga Therapy Today, 13*(2), 26–30.

van der Kolk, B. A. (2014). *The body keeps the score: Brain, mind, and body in the healing of trauma.* New York: Viking.

Name Index

Subject Index

Made in the USA
Las Vegas, NV
03 November 2022

58681158R00208